THE STEPHEN S. WEINSTEIN SERIES
in Post-Holocaust Studies

The Stephen S. Weinstein Series in Post-Holocaust Studies carries on the work and publications of the Pastora Goldner Series (2004–2007), exploring questions that continue to haunt humanity in the aftermath of Nazi Germany's attempt to destroy Jewish life and culture. Books in this series address the most current and pressing issues of our post-Holocaust world. They are grounded in scholarship undertaken by the Stephen S. Weinstein Holocaust Symposium, whose membership—international, interdisciplinary, interfaith, and intergenerational—is committed to dialogue as a fundamental form of inquiry and understanding. The symposium and the series are generously supported by Stephen S. Weinstein, who, with his wife, Nancy, is dedicated to the work of *tikkun olam*, the healing of the world, and whose commitment to combating present-day evils in our world has inspired the participants in the symposium who contribute to this series.

THE STEPHEN S. WEINSTEIN SERIES
in Post-Holocaust Studies

Different Horrors / Same Hell

Gender and the Holocaust

Edited and Introduced by

MYRNA GOLDENBERG and AMY H. SHAPIRO

UNIVERSITY OF WASHINGTON PRESS
Seattle and London

© 2013 by the University of Washington Press
Printed and bound in the United States of America
Composed in Minion Pro, typeface designed by Robert Slimbach
17 16 15 14 13   5 4 3 2 1

UNIVERSITY OF WASHINGTON PRESS
PO Box 50096, Seattle, WA 98145, USA
www.washington.edu/uwpress

LIBRARY OF CONGRESS CATALOGING-IN-PUBLICATION DATA
Different horrors, same hell : gender and the Holocaust / edited and introduced
by Myrna Goldenberg and Amy H. Shapiro. — 1st.
pages ; cm. — (The Stephen S. Weinstein series in post-Holocaust studies)
Includes bibliographical references and index.
ISBN 978-0-295-99242-6 (cloth : alk. paper)
ISBN 978-0-295-99243-3 (pbk. : alk. paper)
1. Holocaust, Jewish (1939–1945)—Influence. 2. Holocaust, Jewish (1939–1945)—
Psychological aspects. 3. Holocaust, Jewish (1939–1945)—Moral and ethical
aspects. 4. Jewish women in the Holocaust—Psychological aspects. 5. Jewish
Women—Violence against—Europe—History—20th century. 6. World War,
1939–1945—Atrocities—Moral and ethical aspects. 7. Feminist theory.
8. Psychic trauma in literature. I. Goldenberg, Myrna, editor.
II. Shapiro, Amy H., 1954–editor.
D804.47.D54 2012   940.53'18081—dc23   2012034418

Jacket and part illustrations: First Station: Auschwitz-Birkenau, by Arie Galles
(1998, 47 1/2 x 75 in., charcoal and white Conté on Arches with barbed wire-
impressed wrought-iron frame), from the suite of fifteen drawings Fourteen
Stations/Hey Yud Dalet (Hashem Yinkom Damon), the latter phrase meaning
"May God avenge their blood." The title of the suite refers both to the Stations
of the Cross and to the fact that the Nazi concentration camps and killing
centers were near railroad stations. Galles's drawings are based on Luftwaffe
and Allied aerial photographs of those sites. Within this drawing and all
the others are invisibly embedded, hand-lettered phrases from the
Kaddish, the ancient Jewish prayer for the dead.

AMY: Dedicated to Michael, dear one, and to my mother, Enid Shapiro

MYRNA: Dedicated to Neal, as always, and to the memory of my parents, Fay and Harry Gallant

CONTENTS

Foreword

ELIZABETH MINNICH

Different Horrors/Same Hell: Gender and the Holocaust is a book that matters. Speaking responsibly to scholars and movingly also to a wider audience, it is informative in ways that turn out also to be transformative. It is a work of retrieval, of recognition, of reinterpretation, of memory individual and collective. It goes into the small as well as large arenas to be with its subjects. The authors speak in their differing voices, approach their subjects from various fields, draw on differing methods, and together reach toward no single resounding conclusion even as sharable meaning and memories are corrected, deepened, extended.

It is courageous, such work. With each of these studies, and with all together, editors and authors step forward to take up a purpose that ought to be common but assuredly still is not. Writing as scholars of the Holocaust, an interdisciplinary field in which racializations overwhelm other forms of categorization of humans by "kind" for the most obvious of reasons, these authors draw also, and richly, on sex/gender as an illuminating lens—or, simply, look as clearly as they can at females both actual and signified, leaving gender theorization to others while providing materials to ground and test it. Readers will find no one feminist method, theory, or consciousness in play here.

Whether or not they use analytic categories of *gender* or *gendering,* of *race, racializing,* or *racial formations,* the authors of the papers here enable us, as scholars, as citizens, as moral individuals, to relearn what we thought we knew best insofar as it may turn out to have been, in fact, partial.

The information gathered, interpreted, formalized into knowledge by scholars that informs us always more than we may realize is not and never will be complete, but that does not release us from commitments to seek better, truer, fuller facts, observation, data. Nor does it release us from obligation to move past old ordering concepts, paradigms, theories when a richness of sound scholarship challenges us to see the whole anew, and differently. This is how we keep learning, continue coming to know ourselves, each other, our shared and divided worlds.

Some knowledge is not just additive. The recognition that the meaningful existence of half of humankind (defined, even across other essentialized categories of "kind," as naturally alike in being female and so non-normatively "man") cannot be set aside as if it were a distraction without limiting—skewing—meanings of *human*. And when *human* is a partial term, knowledge of those defined out of and down a scale of worth from it can by no means just be tacked on later. Consider again, for instance, how differently war looks when we remember and fully include women, real women who serve and oppose and suffer from and are used daily with and without their agreement to serve male warriors, as well as women as symbols and those gendered prescriptions of masculinity that are so glaringly obvious in talk of war. How long has it taken to realize, as finally we have, that rape can be, has been, is a genocidal act? That sexual violence against women is endemic to war? Tell the full story, fully honoring the realities of women, and a remarkable number of conventions, clichés, assumptions transfigures. We begin afresh to think, and so also to judge more aptly, to act more truly.

This book thus honors the simple albeit still too often avoided truth that, in scholarship as in all areas of human concern, the invisibility, the silence of the female half of humankind is the very opposite of trivial. Indeed, the silence and invisibility of women can violate professional, personal, moral, and political values of the first order. Overlooking women, paying no attention to girls, pretending that gendering systems that reach into every aspect of our shared and private lives do not have significance for scholarship: of course such massive failures of attentiveness have serious consequences for, and far beyond, scholarly circles. Decades of research across virtually all fields have now variously demonstrated that such exclusions have deformed both our precious store of shared knowledge and our far more widespread opinions, beliefs, behavior—right along with all our social systems. Failure to be attentive to hierarchical systems of human differentiation is neither correct, nor, judged by searing realities, safe.

Holocaust scholars of course know that we must not ignore the "othering" of groups of people, and still this book is needed. Prejudices—prejudgments: I already know *this* about *that "kind"*: about females, despite all their differences; about racialized groups, despite all their differences—are failures of mind as much as they are failures of heart. They have infected epistemologies as well as practices of justice because what we think and think we know has everything to do with the ways we make judgments and choices, the ways we act, and the systems we establish, or submit to, or resist. Who speaks and who is not heard; what is studied and what is neglected; who is supported and who is devalued as a result of such decisions and practices affect us in all aspects of our lives.[1]

There is, then, nothing "merely academic" about how we think and what we think we know. We are creatures and creators of meaning. Among the many meanings that interweave our varied worlds, the meanings of *human being* are central. They can sustain us in peaceful, caring, just relations with others and with the earth we share. They can divide and rank us within systems of dominance. They can open us to love, friendship, respect, justice, nurture. They can enable us to enslave, exploit, rape, kill those who have been defined as less than fully human. We are called by inspiring and by disturbing meanings of *human being* to keep thinking, to hold horizons open. We, who are conscious creatures and creators of meaning, remain responsible.[2]

The work of memory, essential to comprehension, cannot remain partial and still suffice.

NOTES

1 Elizabeth Kamarck Minnich, "Liberal Learning and the Arts of Connection for the New Academy" (Washington, DC: Association of American Colleges and Universities, 1995), 37.

2 Elizabeth Kamarck Minnich, *Transforming Knowledge*. 2nd ed. (Philadelphia: Temple University Press, 2005), 1.

DIFFERENT HORRORS / SAME HELL

Introduction

Different Horrors / Same Hell

MYRNA GOLDENBERG AND AMY H. SHAPIRO

In *Notes from the Warsaw Ghetto,* Emmanuel Ringelblum singled out the women in the Warsaw ghetto for praise: "The story of the Jewish woman will be a glorious page in the history of Jewry during the present war. And the Chajkes and Frumkes will be the leading figures in this story."[1] Despite this call for recognition of Jewish women, Holocaust historians and scholars, while nodding agreement with Ringelblum, did little or nothing about the subject for decades. Over time, however, and after considerable controversy[2] and the persistence of Joan Ringelheim, the first among feminist scholars to pursue this research, and others who followed her, women and the Holocaust has grown into a serious, complex subset of Holocaust studies.

In 1984, *When Biology Became Destiny: Women in Weimar and Nazi Germany,* edited by Renate Bridenthal, Atina Grossman, and Marion Kaplan, daughters of German-Jewish women survivors, legitimated historical study of German Jewish and non-Jewish women and the Third Reich and soon became an acknowledged standard in the field of European women's studies.[3] In 1986, Marlene Heinemann focused on literary memoirs of women survivors in *Gender and Destiny: Women Writers and the Holocaust.*[4] Both of these groundbreaking volumes attracted little attention except among feminist academics. John Roth and Carol Rittner's *Different Voices: Women and the Holocaust* (1993) broadened the subject and appealed to academics in both women's studies and Holocaust studies.[5] *Different Voices* addressed the absence of women's voices and corrected that omission by excerpting women survivors' testimonies and included historical and philosophical analyses of women's experiences; this book also featured the first woman-centered chronology of the Third Reich. Dalia Ofer and Lenore Weitzman, editors of *Women in the Holocaust* (1998) organized their anthology chronologically and limited their content to Jewish women under the Nazis.[6] Elizabeth R. Baer and Myrna Goldenberg's *Experience and Expression: Women, the Nazis, and the Holocaust* (2003) added to the field by including the experiences of non-Jewish women.[7] *Experience and Expression*'s interdisciplinary perspectives drew attention to the visual arts as well as to the role of German nurses in the euthanasia program. Esther Hertzog, editor of *Life, Death and Sacrifice: Women and Family in the Holocaust* (2008) introduced the next generation of Holocaust scholars and acknowledged the debt to early feminist work on the Holocaust.[8] Hertzog extended gender analyses to family life, sexual violence, narrativization, and altruism. Individually authored books contributed both descriptive and interpretative full-length studies to the knowledge base, e.g., Nechama Tec's *Resilience and Courage,* Nathan Stoltzfus's *Resistance of the Heart*, and Marianne Hirsch, *Family Frames: Photography, Narrative, and Postmemory.*[9]

Thus, scholars of the last twenty-five years have done much to answer the fundamental question that informed early women's studies programs: where are the women? Study of the Holocaust that does not acknowledge the experiences of women as victims, perpetrators, rescuers, and bystanders is limited and limiting. Yet despite its interdisciplinarity, not until recently has Holocaust Studies generally enlisted feminist or gender theory in its analyses, nor have academics shown much, if any, awareness of their own gender assumptions.

One of the insights gender theory brings about is a deepening and expansion of our knowledge of historical events, including the Holocaust, because it focuses on the relationships between humans, specifically in terms of issues of power and control. Indeed, it is instructive to consider Joan Wallach Scott's assertion that gender refers to the relationships between men and women, one of which is "the connection between authoritarian regimes and the control of women [which] has been noted but not thoroughly studied."[10] Gender theory is not only an indispensable tool for analysis, but it also stimulates research that yields information about women's and men's lives. Expanding the field of women's studies to include gender studies not only helps preserve a place for a separate examination of the experiences of women but also contextualizes those experiences by exploring their significance and meaning in social and political relationships. For example, in her discussion of Art Spiegelman's *Maus,* Sara Horowitz demonstrates the significance of Vladek's destruction of Anja's diary:

> In the absence of her words, Anja's story is reversible only through the reconstruction of Vladek's and Art's memories, bearing their interpretation; anything she experienced while apart from them is utterly lost. Similarly, in many male Holocaust narratives, women figure as peripheral and helpless victims. These skewed depictions of women impel us to ask not only what is hidden but also what is transacted through the construction of gendered Holocaust narratives. . . . Anja's absent journals can serve to exemplify the marginality of women's experience in constructing a master narrative of the Nazi genocide.

Horowitz shows the importance of gender analysis through her discussion of a male-authored book, proving that such analysis is appropriate in the "teaching of any Holocaust representation, not only those by or about women."[11] Her consideration of the marginal position of women's experience that has led to the "constructing [of] a master narrative of the Nazi genocide" should influence all aspects of Holocaust scholarship and lead scholars to consider the implications feminist and gender theory might have for their own work. But feminist scholars are still more likely to be cited by their feminist colleagues than by others in the field. Gender analyses have remained on the margins; despite the excellent work that feminists have contributed, their work has still not reshaped nor significantly influenced the approach or nature of most of the scholarly research on the subject.[12]

As editors and as members of a Symposium dedicated to the examination of the Holocaust from a variety of disciplines and with a depth that may border on our own discomfort, we felt a profound need to raise and extend the sorts of questions that academic feminists have been asking for forty years—questions that have usually been avoided, neglected, or only occasionally considered. In what ways can Holocaust Studies benefit from women and gender analysis? is a central question of this volume. How might our approach extend and expand and transform our knowledge of the history, literature, philosophy, psychology, sociology of the Holocaust?

How might gender-focused analyses help us better understand the lives and experiences of its victims, the experiences of the next generations, the world of children, the role of the arts, and, most challenging, our own responses? In other words, until we have addressed the question "How has work on women and the Holocaust influenced our particular disciplines?" we will not have challenged our assumptions sufficiently. Nor will we have laid the groundwork for deeper analyses and interpretations.

Different Horrors / Same Hell: Gender and the Holocaust does much to lay that groundwork. An eclectic volume, its eleven chapters represent diverse fields of study, wide-ranging approaches to issues of gender and the Holocaust, and a variety of essays from strictly academic writings such as Doris Bergen's incisive historical overview of the feminist contributions in Holocaust Studies to the closing essay of Britta Frede-Wenger's imagined conversation with Ruth Klüger. The contributors are as diverse as their essays, representing multi-layered international voices from Canada, Germany, the United States, Poland, and England. Their perspectives defy any attempt to locate their voices in any single discipline or nationality while throughout the volume their writings raise issues of language, communication, ethics, and politics.

The wide range and varied nature of the essays acknowledge the breadth of voices and variety of approaches that feminist theory and gender analysis can bring and have brought to the study of the Holocaust. In her 1991 essay "Under Western Eyes," Chandra Talpade Mohanty states that

> feminist scholarship, like most other kinds of scholarship, is not the mere production of knowledge about a certain subject. It is a directly political and discursive *practice* in that it is purposeful and ideological. It is best seen as a mode of intervention into particular hegemonic discourses (for example, traditional anthropology, sociology, literary criticism, etc.); it is a political praxis which counters and resists the totalizing imperative of age-old "legitimate" and "scientific" bodies of knowledge.[13]

This collection of essays is meant to introduce new discourses, to upset traditional ways of knowing and telling, to stimulate the creation of new knowledges that reflect a diversity of experiences and ways of knowing, and to offer sophisticated interpretations of the relationships between men and women and the experiences of women in regard to the Holocaust. But, as Mohanty implies, it is also meant to inspire scholars and theorists to rethink their understanding of the Holocaust in light of this gendered study and examination of what European Jewish and non-Jewish women did and had done to them between 1933 and 1945. We hope these chapters will disrupt or at least create some discomfort around traditionally accepted assumptions, interpretations, and perspectives on the Holocaust so that theorists will ask, "How does the introduction of a gender analysis change or inform what I know?" As Bergen states in the opening of this book, learning about women and the Holocaust "shifts the terms of analysis from individual motivations to social relations. It complicates familiar and outworn categories, and it humanizes the past in powerful ways. In the process, studies of women, gender, and sexuality help to answer some persistent questions about the perpetrators, witnesses, and victims of the Shoah." Mohanty and Bergen demonstrate how applying feminist analysis provides new approaches to the study of the Holocaust and, consequently, will result in new questions and new understandings.

We have divided the book into two major parts, "History of Feminist Theory and Gender Analysis of the Holocaust" and "Practice of Feminist Theory and Gender Analysis of the Holocaust." Part I contextualizes the issues of women's experiences. It begins with Bergen's trenchant discussion of the problems and inevitable distortions raised by excluding, consciously or otherwise, the matter of women's lives during the Holocaust. This chapter is followed by analyses that begin to rectify such exclusions. These groundbreaking studies in literary analysis, religious contradictions, film narrative, and sexual violence challenge us to reconsider or, at the least, begin to re-think our assumptions from a gendered perspective. Part II demonstrates the power of gender analysis of specific historical events that have not been subjected to such scrutiny: the attack on the idea of Jewish motherhood specifically and on the Jewish family generally, and the impact of survival on the second generation, both children of survivors and children of the perpetrator generation.

The editors of this volume have been among the initial thirty-six participants in the Pastora Goldner Symposium on the Shoah that began in 1996 and which has now become the Stephen S. Weinstein Symposium on the Shoah. Organized by Professors Henry Knight and Leonard Grob, the biennial Symposium is administered by Fairleigh Dickinson University and held at their British campus of Wroxton College. Until now, a significant absence from this collaboration has been writings and conversations regarding women, gender, and the Holocaust. As this volume shows, the Symposium and the Stephen S. Weinstein Symposium Book Series offer opportunities to raise significant questions and bring them into public view.

With the exception of Karen Baldner, with whom Björn Krondorfer wrote chapter 6, all of the contributors to this volume are or have been members of the Stephen S. Weinstein Symposium and have been involved in the biennial meetings, some as original members and some as newer ones. As Holocaust scholars, we are acutely aware of the valiant efforts of those who study, write about, and work with issues of the Holocaust. Such an endeavor is never merely an academic one and can certainly take its toll on the emotional life of any of us who are engaged in Holocaust-related pursuits. For many, the addition of issues related to women and gender seems an add-on that can only serve to confuse the issues. In fact, however, the absence of frameworks related to women and gender has helped obscure and undermine Holocaust study. As Myrna Goldenberg shows in her chapter on sexual violence and the Holocaust, there is a great deal to understand about Nazi attitudes toward Jewish and non-Jewish women. She points out that ignoring or minimizing sexual violence against women suggests that "violence against women is less consequential than violence against men." This prevents us from fully recognizing women's circumstances in the Holocaust and seeing the connections with and distinctions from the use of rape in other genocides. Amy Shapiro uses her analysis of two films and their place in the Holocaust film lexicon to consider the traditional means that have been used to disconnect women from the conversation and the resulting sexism and underlying misogyny. She concludes, "to disengage antisemitism and racism from sexism is itself an act of sexism that contributes to a status quo that fails to understand how all three— antisemitism, racism, and sexism—play a role in the very structures of our ways of knowing."

We expect that readers will find, through the breadth and scope of this collection of essays, multiple approaches and ways of thinking about the significance of gender as a crucial construct for study of and encounter with the Holocaust. As Mohanty says toward the end of her essay, "It is not the center that determines the periphery, but the periphery that, in its boundedness, determines the center."[14]

NOTES

1   Emmanuel Ringelblum, *Notes from the Warsaw Ghetto: The Journal of Emmanuel Ringelblum,* ed. and trans. Jacob Sloan (New York: Schocken Books, 1958), 274. Referring to Jewish women who repeatedly put themselves in danger by smuggling contraband and other goods, Ringelblum writes that "they are a theme that calls for the pen of a great writer." Note that Ringelblum also points out the heroism of nurses, "the only ones who save people from deportation without [asking for] money" (311).

2   Elizabeth R. Baer and Myrna Goldenberg, eds. *Experience and Expression: Women, the Nazis, and the Holocaust* (Detroit: Wayne State University Press, 2003), xxxiii, n. 43, 5–22.

3   Renate Bridenthal, Atina Grossman, and Marion Kaplan, eds., *When Biology Became Destiny: Women in Weimar and Nazi Germany* (New York: Monthly Review Press, 1984).

4   Marlene E. Heinemann, *Gender and Destiny: Women Writers of the Holocaust* (New York: Greenwood Press, 1986).

5   Carol Rittner and John Roth, eds., *Different Voices: Women and the Holocaust* (St. Paul, MN: Paragon House, 1993).

6   Dalia Ofer and Lenore J. Weitzman, eds., *Women in the Holocaust* (New Haven: Yale University Press, 1998).

7   Baer and Goldenberg, eds., *Experience and Expression.*

8   Esther Hertzog, ed., *Life, Death, and Sacrifice: Women and Family in the Holocaust* (Jerusalem: Gefen Publishing House, Ltd., 2008).

9   Nehama Tec, *Resilience and Courage: Women, Men, and the Holocaust* (New Haven: Yale University Press, 2003). Nathan Stoltzfus, *Resistance of the Heart: Intermarriage and the Rosenstrasse Protest in Nazi Germany* (New York: W. W. Norton and Company, 1996). Marianne Hirsch, *Family Frames: Photography, Narrative, and Postmemory* (Cambridge, MA: Harvard University Press, 1997).

10 Joan Wallach Scott, "Gender: A Useful Category of Analysis," in *Feminism and History,* ed. Joan Wallach Scott (New York: Oxford University Press, 1996), 172.

11 Sara Horowitz, "Gender in Holocaust Representation," in *Teaching the Representation of the Holocaust,* ed. Marianne Hirsch and Irene Kacandes (New York: MLA, 2004), 111–12.

12 Doris Bergen, *War and Genocide: A Concise History of the Holocaust* (Lanham, MD: Rowman and Littlefield Publishers, Inc., 2003). *War and Genocide* is an exception; it is a general history that incorporates research on women.

13 Chandra Talpade Mohanty, "Under Western Eyes: Feminist Scholarship and Colonial Discourses," in *Third World Women and the Politics of Feminism,* ed. C. T. Mohanty, A. Russo, and L. Torres (Bloomington: Indiana University Press, 1991), 53.

14 Mohanty, "Under Western Eyes."

HISTORY OF FEMINIST THEORY AND GENDER ANALYSIS OF THE HOLOCAUST

Holocaust research has generated a vast body of work that honors the loss and destruction of two-thirds of European Jewry. To compose a master narrative of the catastrophe that excludes any group or individual would be to amplify the loss and destruction of the victims, as well as to do a disservice to the field. Doris Bergen's historical assessment of the contributions of feminist theory to Holocaust Studies, "What Do Studies of Women, Gender, and Sexuality Contribute to Understanding the Holocaust?" demonstrates that, to be true to its subject, any historical study of the Holocaust cannot and should not result in a master narrative of the Holocaust. Perhaps one of the most significant contributions of feminist theory has been to emphasize attention and focus on individual lives and experiences. Researchers often universalize experience and understanding at the expense of theories and perspectives, and it is often easier to draw broad conclusions than to attend to the singularity of experiences that lead to complications of theory and variations in understanding. The essays in this section demonstrate how a focus on particularity through the lenses of feminist theory and gender analysis expands knowledge and produces new questions and prompts.

Once asked, the question "How can gender be ignored in a culture that hinged on labels such as blood and race?" seems obvious. Bergen states: "Gender analysis is indispensable in any effort to understand Nazi constructions of 'race' and 'blood' because systems of gender are so central to how people organize and give meaning to their world. The line dividing insiders and outsiders, life and death, in German-occupied Europe ran directly through the bodies of women."

Yet, in fact, the role of gender has largely been ignored in the examination of Nazi ideology, race, and power. Despite early cutting-edge work by Bridenthal et al., Koonz, Heinemann, and Martin, to mention only a few, examinations of power and perpetrators have rarely considered the significance of gender.[1] John Roth has pointed out that the exploration of gender honors the particularities of difference, including the particularity of gender, among perpetrators, victims, rescuers, resisters, and bystanders and thereby adds to our knowledge[2]; even when scholars debunk the importance of gender, he says, they are considering the matter of gender. In fact, gender identity is fundamental not only in our perceptions of ourselves and others but also in the investigations that occupy us as scholars of the Holocaust.

It is too easy, however, to include women or gender and anticipate applause. Gender analysis is complicated and requires that historians rethink their narratives. How does our understanding of the history of the Holocaust change when we approach it through gender-informed frameworks? Does the history of the Holocaust change when it is written from a feminist perspective and, if so, how? What becomes important? What is left out? Whose stories are told? By what criteria is history examined and told and re-told?

Each of the essays in Part I proves that gender influences just about every aspect of Holocaust Studies. Bergen provides excellent and comprehensive examples of the application of feminist theory to Holocaust history, a history which demonstrates the influence of women on the everyday life of victims, perpetrators, and rescuers. Without inclusivity, there is little need to pay attention to the full impact of Nazi policy and practice on women *and* on men. Where would be the need to study, for example, the issues of rape and motherhood during the Holocaust? Until feminist historians challenged the status quo, these topics were not explored. When historians integrate, rather than merely add, women and gender into their analyses, the history of the Holocaust is both broadened and deepened.[3]

History is only one of many disciplines that benefits from the integration of women and gender. One cannot neglect the influence of gender analysis on the arts, literature, philosophy, theology, the social sciences, medicine, and ethics—all of which are based on a sound historical underpinning. In addition to their focus on women philosophers, the authors of chapters 2 and 3 share an approach to the study of three philosophers that is highly influenced by not only the gender of the philosophers but by the gender of the writers. They reveal how attention to the role of gender in our relationships to our subjects can unearth a great deal about the subjects and their infianacialuence on our understanding of the Holocaust.

In chapter 2, "Philosophy in the Feminine and the Holocaust Witness: Hannah Arendt and Sarah Kofman," Dorota Glowacka offers the reader a luminous examination of the philosophies of Hannah Arendt and Sarah Kofman in their struggles to be recognized within their respective philosophical communities given their relationships to the Holocaust and their Jewish identities. Through her examination of how both Arendt's and Kofman's biographies link with their philosophies, Glowacka arrives at a significant supposition: "These interventions by two female philosophers of Jewish origin not only reveal philosophy's inability to confront the Holocaust, but also show a correlation between that inexcusable silence and philosophy's millennial exclusion of woman. In both cases, this philosophical failure hinges on the erasure of biography, that is, of the particularities of embodied, gendered human agents." She reaches the stunning conclusions that "a reading of Arendt's work alongside Kofman's reveals that, despite their 'complicity,' the writings of both successfully break through philosophy's multiple erasures—of woman, of the Jew, and of the Holocaust."

In "Simone Weil: A French-Jewish Intellectual Journey in the 1930s and 1940s," Rochelle Millen engages a theological approach to another female philosopher of Jewish origin, Simone Weil. Starting from her first introduction to Weil's work while in graduate school, she examines the significance of Weil's relationship to her Jewish origins and femaleness to elucidate the theological underpinnings of her relationship to Christianity in order to make sense of Weil's response or lack of response to the plight of Jews in the Holocaust. What made Weil anti-Jewish and anti-women given that she was born Jewish and female? Sorting through her theology, Millen attempts to answer this question; in doing so, she offers a vivid examination of Weil's philosophy.

We can see from both Glowacka's and Millen's reflections how profoundly they have been affected by their engagement with philosophers and the Holocaust, while enlisting a particularly gendered-informed approach.

Amy Shapiro's analysis in "Patriarchy, Objectification, and Violence against Women in *Schindler's List* and *Angry Harvest*" demonstrates how texts reveal and shape perspectives. Her essay illustrates the success of particularity in reaching a better understanding of the epistemologies that govern and influence how we know and interpret the Holocaust especially but not only in popular culture. Shapiro assumes the presence of a Holocaust canon, especially in film. She analyzes *Schindler's List* to reveal the constructed narrative that has become significant to the popularization of the Holocaust; the fact that the film is often used to teach the Holocaust in high school and college classrooms speaks to the way it is valued not only in mass culture but also by teachers of the Holocaust. By juxtaposing Spielberg's film with *Angry Harvest*, Shapiro brings to light both the explicit and implicit sexism of *Schindler's List*. In doing so, she demonstrates how attention to these films in their particularity presents startlingly different narrative views of the experiences of women in the Holocaust and in Holocaust narrative. Her ultimate goal is not only analysis of the two films but the uncovering of implicit assumptions regarding the value of women and their experience. To echo Bergen, Shapiro shows how "systems of gender are so central to how people organize and give meaning to their world" and to their interpretations of the Holocaust. Shapiro's conclusions raise central questions about how individuals develop moral identity.

And what are some of the most lethal consequences of patriarchy? Interestingly enough, one of the most disturbing consequences is the role of rape in an androcentric world. The fact that there has been so much silence about the rape of women in the Holocaust is one of the most glaring examples of the androcentrism at work in Holocaust Studies. Myrna Goldenberg's chapter, "Sex-Based Violence and the Politics and Ethics of Survival," which concludes Part I, is a stunning and comprehensive examination of sexual violence and what it reveals about Nazism, racism, and sexism: "It behooves us to acknowledge, at the outset, that the Holocaust was not about gender or sex. However, because Jewish women were vulnerable in different ways than men were, gender and sex cannot be dismissed by responsible scholars. Moreover, acknowledging women as victims of violence simultaneously asserts that women's lives are as valuable as men's. To ignore or neglect the abuse and murder of women is to assert that the murder of women is less consequential than the abuse and murder of men." While considering the role of rape and its connection to *Rassenschande* in the Nazi legal code and national mentality, she is willing to also consider the rape of Jewish women by Jewish men, a subject that has been taboo for many reasons. Here we can see quite vividly how lack of gender analysis and, in turn, failure to attend to particularity of experience have conspired to maintain a master narrative of the victims of the Holocaust.

While scholars are able to discuss the experiences of Jews of different nationalities, classes, and religious affiliations, differences in experiences as a result of gender have not been viewed as a legitimate and valuable category of analysis. Each chapter in this section demonstrates that it is. Each explores the significance of feminist theory to study of the Holocaust and reflects the thorny and challenging practice of gender analysis.

NOTES

1   Renate Bridenthal, Atina Grossmann, and Marion Kaplan, *When Biology Became Destiny: Women in Weimar and Nazi Germany* (New York: Monthly Review Press, 1984); Claudia Koonz, *Mothers in the Fatherland: Women, the Family, and Nazi Politics* (New York: St. Martins, 1987); Marlene E. Heinemann, *Gender and Destiny: Women Writers and the Holocaust* (Westport, CT: Greenwood, 1986); Elaine Martin, ed. *Gender, Patriarchy, and Fascism in the Third Reich: The Response of Women Writers* (Detroit: Wayne State University Press, 1993).

2   John K. Roth, "Equality, Neutrality, Particularity: Perspectives on Women and the Holocaust," in *Experience and Expression: Women, the Nazis, and the Holocaust,* ed. Elizabeth R. Baer and Myrna Goldenberg (Detroit: Wayne State University Press, 2003), 5-22.

3   Consider *Maus I* and *II* and the way Art Spiegelman subtly valorized his mother's life and death by countering his father's dismissive negative description of Anja. Spiegelman's inclusion of his mother's biography illuminates Vladek's motivations and selective memory. We learn more about the Holocaust because Spiegelman used *his* memory of his mother to correct his father's depiction of her. Thus, the history and biography of this survivor family is made accurate by the author/artist's empathy and refusal to neglect his mother's presence in the family's history, painful and tortuous as it was for him. See *Maus I* and *Maus II* (New York: Pantheon Books, Inc., 1986 and 1991, respectively).

1

What Do Studies of Women, Gender, and Sexuality Contribute to Understanding the Holocaust?

DORIS L. BERGEN

What do studies of women, gender, and sexuality contribute to an under-standing of the Holocaust? The short answer is "a lot." A focus on women, gender, and sexuality shifts the terms of analysis from individual motiva-tions to social relations. It complicates familiar and outworn categories and humanizes the past in powerful ways. It can also help to answer some persistent questions about the perpetrators, witnesses, and victims of the Shoah. What drove the perpetrators to act as they did? What was the rela-tionship between Jews and their gentile neighbors? How does the integra-tion of Jewish sources challenge master narratives of the Holocaust? The answers to these questions are both obvious and elusive. Like much every-day history in general, studies of women, gender, and sexuality frequently generate insights that at first glance might appear small or even insignifi-cant. Sometimes the most profound insights evoke the response, "I knew that all along."

About nine hours into Claude Lanzmann's film *Shoah*, two women are shown singing a song. Identified in a caption only as "Gertrude Schnei-der and her mother, New York, survivors of the ghetto," they appear for barely a minute. They sing, in Germanized Yiddish, *Azoi muss sein*: "That's the way it has to be." Neither a translation nor subtitles are provided. The younger woman does most of the singing, her face composed, her hands busy knitting or perhaps crocheting, her body inclined toward her mother, seated next to her on a sofa. The older woman weeps and shakes her head, her hands covering her face.[1]

In a moving and insightful essay, Marianne Hirsch and Leo Spitzer point to this scene as a demonstration of "the double speechlessness of women" in Lanzmann's *Shoah*.[2] Present, but only in the background, women provide "emotional texture" and serve as the "shadowy intermediary voices between language and silence" in the film's exploration of the machinery of death and "the hell created by the encounter between past and present."[3] Hirsch and Spitzer's observation and the voices and faces of Gertrude Schneider and her mother hint at how much can be learned about the Holocaust by studying women.

Women's histories of the Holocaust have proliferated since the first path-breaking studies appeared in the 1980s.[4] Three decades later, dissertations, articles, and monographs have appeared in a range of disciplines, and numerous volumes of essays, college courses, panels, and entire conferences have been devoted to issues of gender and sexuality in the Shoah.[5] Yet to a remarkable extent this work remains outside the mainstream of Holocaust studies. It is true that we rarely hear anymore the kinds of objections that Dalia Ofer and Leonore Weitzman describe in the introduction to their 1998 volume *Women in the Holocaust*, that focusing on women draws attention away from the assault on all Jews, or that feminist scholars instrumentalize the Holocaust for their own ends.[6] Instead, studies of gender and sexuality are accepted, but as "different voices," to borrow the title of Carol Rittner and John Roth's influential anthology,[7] voices that speak from and for the most part to a "separate sphere," removed from what count as the big questions in the field. And yet, as this chapter contends, the study of women, gender, and sexuality is no mere sideshow. Instead, consideration of these often sidelined issues sheds light on at least three major debates in Holocaust historiography: How did the killers carry out their task? Who collaborated and why? And do we need victims' voices to understand genocide?

THE PERPETRATORS:
ORDINARY PEOPLE, FAMILY MEMBERS

Attention to women's experience shows that perpetrators of the Holocaust were embedded in social and familial contexts. Family and intimate relationships facilitated the murderers' actions by providing emotional and material support and easing troubled consciences after the fact. To borrow a cliché, it takes a village to commit genocide. Women, both as individuals and through relationships with men, played essential roles in the complex, collaborative effort of destruction we now call the Holocaust.

Many studies of Holocaust perpetrators focus on issues of motivation and ideology at the individual level or among groups of men. But a focus on women's roles reveals that killers found legitimation, approval, and a means of rationalization through intimate and familial relations, an insight only touched on in the accounts of Christopher Browning and Daniel Goldhagen.[8] Claudia Koonz's *Mothers in the Fatherland* was the first study to redefine the notion of "perpetrators" by considering German "Aryan" women as accomplices, enablers, beneficiaries, and partners in crime.[9] Koonz's insight transformed thinking about women—at least non-Jewish women—and the Holocaust, but its relevance to male perpetrators has only begun to be addressed. Gudrun Schwarz's important study of SS wives has not been translated into English,[10] and only a sample of Karin Orth's important research on the "concentration camp SS" is available in translation.[11] Nor have Sybille Steinbacher's examination of the "model town" of Auschwitz and her analysis of the ways its domestic comforts normalized life for the killers been adequately recognized.[12] In Auschwitz, Steinbacher writes, "mass murder and respectability were closely interwoven."[13]

Photographs taken at sites of killing provide one illustration of the way men's relations with women affected the dynamics of extreme violence. Many such pictures exist: close-ups of mass graves in Yugoslavia and Ukraine filled with the bodies of Jews and other victims; shots of smiling, uniformed Germans posing with the dead and still living targets of humiliation and destruction.[14] Members of the Einsatzgruppen, Order Police, and Wehrmacht took countless such photographs, and in many cases sent them home to loved ones: wives, girlfriends, family members. Many of the men behind the camera believed they were participating in deeds of world historical significance; some felt pride and excitement in conquest and domination.[15] But why share those graphic images with people back home?

One factor is an urge to spread the burden of guilt. In legal terms, very little separates a passive witness of murder from an accessory to the crime. In daily life, the connection is even closer. By sharing a photograph of the atrocities with someone close to him, a man drew those at home into his shame and, in the process, unloaded and dispersed some of his bad feeling. A related impulse stems from a need to be loved and accepted, even or especially after committing terrible violence against innocent people. If an intimate partner—a wife or girlfriend—saw such pictures, she would know at least something of what her man had seen, done, and become in the war. If she still accepted him, loved him, and remained close to him, she allowed him to see himself as still lovable, decent, and human. For her to see and know yet never speak of his crimes enabled him in turn to normalize abnormal experiences and monstrous acts.[16]

In other words, German men sent photographs of atrocities home not simply because they were proud of what they had done but because, on some level, they were ashamed. Men appear to have been more likely to share such images with their girlfriends, wives, and sisters than with their mothers. Because the image of "mother" as the guardian of traditional, Christian virtue thrived among sentimental Nazis,[17] this hesitation is another indication that the braggadocio captured in the photos coexisted with a sense of wrong. To explain how "ordinary men" became killers in the first place, the factors Browning identifies in his analysis of Order Police Battalion 101—peer pressure, disorientation, careerism—may suffice. But to understand how those men continued killing for weeks, months, and years, and to comprehend how they returned to their homes, lives, and families after the war ended and how they lived with themselves and their memories, we need to see them in relation to the people they loved.

Of course, women were not only accomplices and enablers in the Holocaust; at least some were hands-on perpetrators. A few scholars, notably Susannah Heschel and Wendy Lower,[18] have pointed out the continuing dearth of analyses that address the issue of women as practitioners of extreme violence. In Nazi Germany, women did not serve as soldiers or police, but an estimated 4,000 women worked as guards at concentration camps and killing centers. These women played active roles and, though under male supervision, they exercised considerable power. Women prisoners, like their male counterparts, also served as *kapos* and heads of blocks and barracks. Study of these women, who were part of the machinery of destruction, sheds important light on the social dynamics of extreme violence.

Because most women operated at the lower levels of the Nazi hierarchy, they provide ways to analyze perpetrators beyond the usual suspects. Consider an individual case, taken from the memoir of Liana Millu, an Italian Jewish prisoner in Auschwitz in 1944.[19] One of the six chapters in Millu's book—a collection of short stories narrated by an eyewitness, presumably the author herself—depicts a female *kapo*, a German inmate whom Millu calls Mia.[20] Enraged when her Polish *kapo* lover shows affection toward a beautiful Hungarian Jewish woman, Lili, Mia beats her rival half to death, then hands her over to Mengele to be sent to the gas: " 'This one, *Herr Doctor.*' She pointed to Lili. 'Always *kaputt.* She can't do the work.' "[21] Here the woman perpetrator, herself a prisoner, embodies at once the absolute brutality of the camp and the ongoing potency of desire, pleasure, and intimacy within its extreme conditions. Judging from the evidence that Millu provides, it is neither an ideology of racial supremacy nor a form of antisemitism, eliminationist or otherwise, that motivates Mia to destroy Lili. Instead, Mia's ability to inflict death on a Jew is a by-product of the Nazi German war of annihilation. This dynamic, which harnesses every-day routines and feelings—insecurity, jealousy—to the cause of mass mur-der, helps us understand how genocide functioned as a network of atrocity perpetrated by people who did not need to subscribe to Nazi ideas or even to be on the winning side of the genocidal equation to be agents of destruc-tion. In the context of a program of annihilation, normal, or at least famil-iar, human drives became vehicles of atrocity.

Studying women also points to Holocaust perpetrators' quests to pre-serve or restore normalcy in the most extreme circumstances. If "degen-dering" was a means of dehumanizing victims, as Marianne Hirsch and Leo Spitzer have argued,[22] then insistence on gender boundaries was a way that perpetrators sought to maintain a sense of their own human decency. One long sequence in Lanzmann's *Shoah* features Franz Suchomel, a high-ranking SS man at Treblinka. Prodded by Lanzmann to describe how trains full of Jews were "processed" from arrival at Treblinka to their death, Suchomel says that Ukrainian and Latvian auxiliaries beat the men as they drove them into the gas chambers. What about the women, Lan-zmann wants to know. Were they beaten, too? No, Suchomel responds, not the women. Lanzmann seizes on this bizarre lapse into chivalry. "Why not?" he demands, "Why this humaneness? They were already dead anyway." Lanzmann ends the exchange with Suchomel's lugubri-ous concession: "No doubt the women, too." Here Suchomel's words and Lanzmann's editing point to the assumption that masculine chivalry and feminine privilege are markers of normalcy and their absence, in turn, signifiers of monstrous aberration.[23] He may have been a mass murderer,

Suchomel implies, but in contrast to the Latvian and Ukrainian "hell-hounds," he never beat a woman nor even saw such a thing happen.

BYSTANDERS, WITNESSES, BENEFICIARIES: GENTILES AND JEWS ENMESHED

Study of women, gender, and sexuality gives content to the vague and often vacuous category of the bystander. "Bystanders," along with subgroups including witnesses, facilitators, and beneficiaries, are marked by indirect participation or non-participation. Such amorphous roles leave few traces in most historical sources. Women's historians are trained to deal with this kind of category, and the related challenges involving sources, by reading between the lines, uncovering what is invisible or obscured, and identifying forms of agency among people outside centers of power. These skills are essential for study of non-perpetrators and non-victims in the Holocaust in order to move beyond dichotomies of power and powerlessness and toward a more nuanced view of agency and complex power (inter)relations. Study of women deepens our understanding of central questions, from the role of antisemitism in the Holocaust to the significance of greed and the fate of property, including household items. For example, Marion Kaplan's study of German Jewish women and their families leads to a key insight about "social death" and how it connected to the physical and communal death of Jews under Nazi rule.[24]

Witnessing, we are reminded if we contemplate women's less visible roles in the Holocaust, is not passive. A person who sees terrible things is also involved in and changed by the experience. Women, like men and children, lived at and near sites of killing. Their encounters with killing and destruction affected them, perhaps teaching them to blame the victims rather than confront the horror of their world. At least in some cases, their gaze also added to the torment of the victims. In his memoir *Survival in Auschwitz*, more aptly titled in its Italian original *Se questo è un uomo* (If this is a man), Primo Levi describes the women who worked in the laboratory where he performed his labor duties.[25] They were not prisoners but German and Polish employees of the camp. Indifferent, contemptuous, and disgusted, to Levi they were unbearable witnesses to his social and physical destruction. The regard of male witnesses was excruciating, too: Levi records his humiliation when a German official in the laboratory wiped his dirty hand on his body as if it were a rag. Yet Levi dwells on the women witnesses in a different way because they made him think of home, he says, and because, unrealistically but not surprisingly, he expected more from them. To him, their failure reflected his betrayal by all of humanity.

Women and families were central to Nazi processes of categorization and to the violence of the German conquerors' new European order. Since the early 1990s, the *Volksdeutschen* (ethnic Germans) of Eastern Europe have been the subject of innovative work that points to links between resettlement schemes and genocide[26] and draws attention to processes of ethnic delineation and their arbitrary nature.[27] Some work has been done to consider gender in this context.[28] At least some historians have begun systematically to question Nazi categories that too often are accepted at face value. Studies of people who defied the obvious polarity of "Aryan" and "Jew" encourage this tendency.[29] Gender analysis is indispensable in any effort to understand Nazi constructions of "race" and "blood" because systems of gender are so central to how people organize and give meaning to their world. The line dividing insiders and outsiders, life and death, in German-occupied Europe ran directly through the bodies of women.

Consideration of women also challenges dominant views of rescuers, a group Raul Hilberg considers under the heading "bystanders."[30] Usually presented as dramatic stories of heroism, popular accounts of rescue feature individuals, "great men": Oskar Schindler, Raoul Wallenberg, Chiune Sugihara, Nicholas Winton. Accounts by, of, and about women show another side of rescue: small acts of solidarity, unavoidable personal compromise, even humor. In her memoir *Under a Cruel Star*, Heda Kovály describes how she and a few fellow Czech Jews escaped from a death march.[31] Hungry, filthy, and completely disoriented, the young women hesitated outside the barn where the rest of the prisoners and their guards lay sleeping. Where were they? Where should they go? Help came in an unlikely form: a little Czech girl with bread and her mother's permission to lead them to the road to Prague. And it was not the arrival of Allied soldiers that told Kovály she was liberated but the sound of her own laughter.

Numerous other accounts depict rescue in similar ways. Women, keepers of the home, usually took the lead in offering shelter. Some, like the young Polish woman Irene Gut (later Opdyke), bought silence from powerful men with sexual favors.[32] Not a grand gesture but a simple "come in" marked Magda Trocmé's willingness to give refuge to desperate Jews in southern France.[33] Family ties moved the women who assembled in Berlin's

Rosenstrasse to protest for the release of their German Jewish husbands in 1943. Beauty, charm, and immense charisma enabled Robert Melson's Polish Jewish mother to procure false papers for her husband, her son, and herself to "pass" as Catholics.[34]

Rescue, it is easy to forget, occurred amidst moral and communal devastation. In *Neighbors*, Jan Gross provides testimony from a Polish nanny who saved the lives of two Jewish children only by pretending she had taken them from her home and drowned them.[35] Studying rescue through the lens of the everyday life in war and genocide shows the hopeless entanglement of loyalty and betrayal analyzed by Omer Bartov in his work on the Eastern Galician town of Buczacz.[36] With the help of methods from women's history, the amorphous category of the bystander becomes a window onto the myriad connections between Jews and gentiles, women and men, children and adults in Europe during the Holocaust. Viewed in the context of ubiquitous violence, these connections speak most often not of heroism or solidarity but of desperation and poisonous misery.

Perpetrators, witnesses, and victims occupied overlapping spaces, and their fates were intertwined. Elem Klimov's astounding 1985 film *Come and See* shows the German destruction of a Belorussian village in 1943.[37] With the help of collaborators, the Germans force the inhabitants into a wooden building and set it on fire. When a search turns up a Jew, the man's identity ascertained by pulling down his pants, the attackers toss him in with the rest. Then, to select unattached people for forced labor, a German announces through a window that people without children can come out. A woman emerges clutching a baby. One of the collaborators grabs the child and throws him into the already burning building. He seizes the woman by the hair, lights a cigarette, and drags her for a few steps until he is stopped by an officer. "Later," the German instructs him; first finish the job, then the reward. In this unbearable scene, every detail of which can be found confirmed in eyewitness accounts of the hundreds of such anti-partisan actions in Belorussia alone, severed family ties and sexual violence reveal the absolute and inescapable brutality of the war and the Holocaust. Here there is no option of non-involvement, no possibility of a measured moral decision, only a force field of violence fueled by the aggression of the perpetrators and feeding on the desperation of their targets.

Investigation of the Holocaust and its bystanders, collaborators, enablers, witnesses, and rescuers shows the porous boundary between past and present. Scholars, too, are embedded in social, political, and professional relations. Attention to women, gender, and sexuality illuminates the many ways that forces outside the academy shape history, memory, and scholarly interpretation. Massive expansion of Holocaust studies in the 1980s and 1990s coincided with the growth of interest in women's history. The 1990s also saw genocide and massive human rights violations in Rwanda and the wars associated with the break-up of Yugoslavia. Rape and sexual violence were widely publicized features of those extremely violent situations. Observing and reflecting on those cases helped scholars develop tools to approach and unravel issues around sexual violence in the Holocaust and led interviewers to ask questions that had long been taboo. Some women survivors who had been silent about sexual violation spoke in public about their experiences. It is no coincidence that key studies of sexual forced labor, rape, and sexuality in the camps emerged in subsequent years.[38] In turn, recognition of the presence—indeed, ubiquity—of sex and sexual violence in the Holocaust has enabled productive comparison with other cases of war and genocide in ways that highlight similar dynamics and particular qualities

Paying attention to women, gender, and sexuality also raises our awareness of the ethical, methodological, and professional challenges of working on the Holocaust. The heated debates that have emerged around issues of German women as partners in genocide and the strong defenses raised in some quarters against Joan Ringelheim's critiques of feminist approaches to the study of Jewish women in the Holocaust confirm this observation.[39] As with women's studies, scholars of the Holocaust must confront issues of credibility, risk-taking, identity, and exposure, and scholarship in women's history and the history of sexuality helps to shed light on the ways scholars themselves can be implicated in their subjects. Charges of collaboration and opportunism, so central to analyses of the Holocaust, are also uncomfortably close to accusations that critics of the "Holocaust industry" have leveled at its practitioners.[40] The old feminist slogan "the personal is political" applies in extended form to study of the Holocaust: the personal is also professional and historical.

VICTIMS' VOICES, VICTIMS' BODIES: TOWARD AN INTEGRATED HISTORY

The Holocaust, like every genocide, was enmeshed with everyday life, and study of women, gender, and sexuality is essential in order to fully grasp this terrifying fact. Saul Friedländer's concept of an "integrated and integrative history" can be seen as a means of confronting the reality of the Holocaust, not as rationalized by its perpetrators but as experienced by its victims.[41] Historians of women, accustomed to listening to silences and reading traces left by erasure, might be equipped to analyze a key moment in Lanzmann's *Shoah*, the interview with Abraham Bomba, a Jewish barber from Częstochowa who cut victims' hair in the gas chambers at Treblinka. As a member of the *Sonderkommando*, Bomba was one of a small number of men the Germans kept alive to serve their needs. With very few exceptions, Jewish women who arrived at the killing center had no such possibility of survival—they were in effect already dead.

Filmed in a barber shop in Israel, Bomba appears in a completely male space. Because Lanzmann and Bomba speak in English, not even the female voice of the translator intervenes. Only the beautiful face, delicate shoulder adorned with black brassiere strap, and bare bosom of a calendar girl hover like an apparition over them when the camera approaches from certain angles.[42] Yet Lanzmann and Bomba talk almost exclusively about women. What was it like, Lanzmann wants to know, to see all those naked women coming into the gas chambers and to cut off their hair, knowing they were about to be killed? What did Bomba feel? "To have a feeling in that place," Bomba replies, "was impossible. You were dead with your feelings." And yet he reveals a range of emotion as he snips away at a man's hair, alternating between answering Lanzmann's questions, saying nothing, and wiping his eyes.

He saw women he knew, Bomba tells Lanzmann, women from his town. What could he tell them? A friend of his, he says, his voice breaking after a painfully long silence, saw his own wife and sister come in, and he cut their hair. All he could do was to "try to hug them just a bit longer, to hold them, because he knew they would never come out of there alive again."[43] Here the horror of the Holocaust—viewed from inside the belly of the beast—coexists with the most everyday matters: a meeting of people from the same town, barbers cutting hair, an embrace between a woman and her husband. Lanzmann's film conveys the reality of genocide—of the perpetrators and their victims as human beings—by simultaneously evoking the unimaginable and the familiar. Women—present, absent, alive, and dead—embody and evoke both those qualities. There is no actual woman in Lanzmann's film who can speak for those Jewish women suffocated in the gas chambers of Treblinka, nor does Lanzmann comment on that fact.

Women gain a presence in this scene through the men's words, and as seen through men's eyes. Nevertheless, their lives and deaths assert themselves here as central, individual, and distinctly female parts of the total, and totally human, agony of the Shoah.

Study of gender and perhaps particularly of sex and sexuality contributes to an integrated history by providing access to the horror via things intimate. Here postwar accounts sometimes find ways to open topics— and wounds—that sources produced at the time or closer to it might not have been able to bear. Henry Friedman's 1999 memoir offers a poignant example. In 1943, the fifteen-year-old Friedman was hiding in a barn in eastern Poland with his mother, his younger brother, and their teacher. Friedman's mother was pregnant, and before she gave birth, the members of the group discussed what to do. They took a vote, Friedman recalls, and decided three to one (his mother dissented) that the teacher would deliver the baby and then drown it. The Ukrainian woman who was sheltering them agreed to bury the body.[44] Could there be any more vivid illustration of the price of hiding, the "choiceless choices" produced by the pressures of genocide on family ties, and the endless suffering of the Shoah?[45]

Contrary to the promises made on book jackets, study of the Holocaust is not often uplifting. Paying attention to sex, to bodies, brings out the pain in immediate ways that one can feel within one's own body. Such familiarity can tip toward banality or can block analysis by eliciting the desire to close one's eyes—or the book. But when pursued with courage and rigor, emotional identification can also cut through abstraction to open up insights.

Study of the Holocaust stumbles against many taboos, subjects that are unspeakable and invisible yet also explosive. Historians of sexuality are practiced at negotiating such waters, and it is no coincidence that Klaus Theweleit, Günter Grau, Elizabeth Heineman, Dagmar Herzog, Geoffrey Giles, and others have contributed so much to Holocaust scholarship.[46] Issues of shame and stigma abound in accounts of all kinds. Survivor Bernard Gotfryd writes in his memoir of an encounter with a Jewish woman he calls Ilka, who served in the brothel at Majdanek.[47] Gotfryd recalls meeting her in the camp, where he was dazzled by her beauty and good health. Years later, when he saw her at a gathering of survivors of the Shoah, he recognized her immediately but said nothing about her past. Gotfryd's sketch conceals as much as it reveals, as it gestures toward the rare but not infrequently reported presence of a Jewish woman in the so-called Puffhouse. At the same time, Gotfryd's vignette points to the immense challenge of writing a history of the Holocaust that integrates sources from the victims, not only their wartime letters and diaries but their unspoken assumptions, second-hand accounts, and faulty memories, all evidence of destruction that extended far beyond the geographic and chronological borders of the Shoah.

Attention to sex and the victims of the Holocaust may help illuminate patterns of popular representation. Instructive in this regard is Liliana Cavani's 1974 movie *The Night Porter*.[48] Charlotte Rampling stars as Lucia, a Jewish survivor of Auschwitz who travels to Vienna after the war, where she re-encounters Max (Dirk Bogarde), the SS man whose sex slave she had been in the camp, now a night porter at a hotel. Max has a flashback that forms the core of the movie. He recounts a night of debauchery that culminated in Lucia, clad only in SS trousers, suspenders, and cap, dancing for him and his friends. In a gesture he self-consciously links to the story of Salomé and John the Baptist in the Christian Bible, he rewards her for her beauty with the head of a fellow prisoner on a platter. Compromised by this "gift" and sexually and emotionally tied to Max, Lucia does not turn him in but resumes their love affair until both are killed by Max's old SS cronies. Primo Levi called the film "beautiful and false,"[49] a characterization that fits its aesthetically compelling but historically unsupportable vision of Nazism as sado-masochistic perversion. The feminist author Joan Smith is equally scathing in her dismissal of what she calls pop culture's "Holocaust girls."[50]

Still, something can perhaps be learned even from Cavani's unreal and unrealistic representation. It raises the question: what is the relationship between sex and violence, or, more accurately, between sex and popular representations of extreme violence? What does the appeal of such depictions suggest about the perpetrators and, more to the point, about those of us who buy, watch, and respond? Jonathan Littell's sensational 975-page bestseller *The Kindly Ones* raises an updated version of these questions.[51] The answer has several interlocking parts. One explanation for the draw of sexualized portrayals of the Holocaust is the contradictory yet coexisting desires to normalize killers and at the same time to stigmatize them as freaks; such representations also serve to reflect women's vulnerability. Also at play is a drive to see victims as somehow complicit in their own destruction, an interpretation that offers some comfort to observers: if their suffering was somehow their own fault, others need not worry that the same could happen to them. Study of sex, in other words, is both a window to the past and a mirror of our present, although neither window nor mirror offers an unimpeded view.

Attention to women provides insight into a basic aspect of the Holocaust: its assault on Jewish solidarity. In this regard, the mother-daughter relationship is of particular significance. Undertheorized in marked contrast to relationships between fathers and sons,[52] bonds between mothers and daughters function in the accounts of Holocaust victims and survivors as symbols of life, hope, tradition, and continuity, as well as containing a measure of rupture and devastation. In a wrenching account of her experiences as a Jewish child in France during the Holocaust, Sarah Kofman gives voice to this emotional complexity when she describes how she rejected her mother in favor of the gentile woman who sheltered them both:

> My mother suffered in silence: no news from my father; no means of visiting my brothers and sisters; no power to prevent Mémé from transforming me, detaching me from herself and from Judaism. I had, it seemed, buried the entire past: I started loving rare steak cooked in butter and parsley. I didn't think at all any more about my father, and I couldn't pronounce a single word in Yiddish despite the fact that I could still understand the language of my childhood perfectly. Now I even dreaded the end of the war![53]

Elsewhere we read that when the mother-daughter bond was broken, it meant the end of human life in a community, the end of faith. In her memoir of Auschwitz-Birkenau, Sara Nomberg-Przytyk presents Cyla, a young Czech Jewish woman who became a dreaded *kapo*. How she could be so cruel, Nomberg once asked Cyla? It is easy, came the response. I saw my own mother go to the gas, and since then there is nothing in the world too terrible for me to bear.[54] Judith Magyar Isaacson, a Hungarian Jewish survivor of Auschwitz, gives voice to the inverse of this equation: her mother, present with her in the camp, embodied decency and belonging.[55] Ties of loyalty and the intense pain of parting characterize the mother-daughter relationship described by Sara Ginaite, a partisan fighter from Kovno.[56] Spectacularly successful in protecting her son, Robert Melson's mother was crushed by her inability to save her own parents, who died in the Warsaw Ghetto.[57]

In their fleeting appearance in *Shoah*, Gertrude Schneider and her mother speak to issues of despair, meaning, and survival. Almost voiceless, they, like the women present and absent in the rest of Lanzmann's film, nevertheless assert their presence. The song they sing—*Azoi muss sein*—gives words to the mixture of resilience and fatalism at the heart of the movie, a message they express—and Lanzmann presents—in unmistakably female voices.

From the film's outtakes, it is clear that Lanzmann interviewed Gertrude Schneider at length and that the film's label for her—"survivor of the ghetto"—omits some significant information. A trained historian with a PhD from the City University of New York, Schneider has published several books about the Holocaust in Latvia.[58] The ghetto that she, her mother Charlotte Hirschhorn, and her younger sister Rita survived was not in Warsaw, as the sequence of scenes in *Shoah* implies, but in Riga. In the course of their two-hour conversation, Schneider responds to Lanzmann's questions about a wide range of subjects including relations between Latvian, German, and Austrian Jews; suicides; and the German prohibition against sex in the ghetto and its repercussions for Jewish women. At Lanzmann's request, Schneider and her sister Rita Wassermann, who is present throughout and participates in the conversation but rarely appears in the frame, sing a variety of songs—folksongs, songs from the ghetto, and partisan songs—in Polish, Russian, Yiddish, and German. Lanzmann and Schneider both also try to draw Hirschhorn into the interview, but she speaks little and seems confused about details. Near the end of the meeting, Lanzmann asks Schneider whether children ever despised parents made powerless by the Germans. "It only made us love them more," Schneider insists.[59]

Muted in Lanzmann's film but not silenced, Gertrude Schneider, her mother, and her sister embody and express a view of history that integrates past and present and encompasses victims, witnesses, and scholars of the Holocaust. Together, these women convey the reality of bottomless trauma at the same time that they offer a glimpse at the astonishing human capacity to survive, live, and connect. Their song—the only part of their interview to survive into the film—strikes a note of resignation that is also somehow hopeful and maybe even defiant: "These words I've written to you not with ink but with tears," they sing. "It's hard to repair what's been destroyed / And it's hard to bind our love. / Oh, look at your tears, / But it's not my fault, / Because that's the way it has to be."[60]

NOTES

Many thanks to my colleague Jennifer Jenkins at the University of Toronto for feedback on an early draft and to Pamela Klassen, Ruth Marshall, Andrea Most, and the other members of the Religion, Culture, Politics working group at the Jackman Humanities Institute for their suggestions.

1   *Shoah*, directed by Claude Lanzmann (1985; New York: New Yorker Video, 2003), DVD. See also Lanzmann, *Shoah: An Oral History of the Holocaust* (New York: Pantheon, 1985); and the French text of the film, *Shoah* (Paris: Fayard, 1985), 212. The title of the song is rendered elsewhere as "*Asoi muss seyn*" and "*Azoy mis es zayn*." Gertrude Schneider was born in Vienna and deported to Riga in 1942. She survived the ghetto there with her sister Rita Hirschhorn, later Wassermann, and their mother, Charlotte Hirschhorn, née LeWinter, who was born in 1898 and died in 1982 in New York.

2   Marianne Hirsch and Leo Spitzer, "Gendered Translations: Claude Lanzmann's *Shoah*," in *Claude Lanzmann's Shoah: Key Essays*, ed. Stuart Liebman (New York: Oxford University Press, 2007), 180. Originally published in *Gendering War Talk*, ed. Miriam Cooke and Angela Woolacott (Princeton, NJ: Princeton University Press, 1993), 3–19.

3   Hirsch and Spitzer, "Gendered Translations," 180, 186, 187.

4   Key works include Vera Laska, *Women in the Resistance and in the Holocaust: The Voices of Eyewitnesses* (Westport, CT: Greenwood, 1983); Esther Katz and Joan Ringelheim, eds., *Proceedings of the Conference, Women Surviving: The Holocaust* (New York: Institute for Research in History, 1983); Sybil Milton, "Women and the Holocaust: The Case of German and German-Jewish Women," in *When Biology Became Destiny: Women in Weimar and Nazi Germany*, ed. Renate Bridenthal, Atina Grossmann, and Marion Kaplan (New York: Monthly Review, 1984), 297–333; Joan Ringelheim, "The Unethical and the Unspeakable: Women and the Holocaust," *Simon Wiesenthal Center Annual* 1 (1984): 69–87; Joan Ringelheim, "Women and the Holocaust: A Reconsideration of Research," *Signs* 10, no. 4 (1985), 741–61; Marlene Heineman, *Gender and Destiny: Women Writers on the Holocaust* (New York: Greenwood, 1986); Gisela Bock, *Zwangssterilisation im Nationalsozialismus. Studien zur Rassenpolitik und Frauenpolitik* (Opladen: Westdeutscher Verlag, 1986); Claudia Koonz, *Mothers in the Fatherland: Women, the Family, and Nazi Politics* (New York: St. Martin's, 1987); Ruth Schwertfeger, *Women of Theresienstadt: Voices from a Concentration Camp* (New York: Berg, 1989); Myrna Goldenberg, "Different Horrors, Same Hell: Women Remembering the Holocaust," in *Thinking the Unthinkable: Meanings of the Holocaust,* ed. Roger Gottlieb (New York: Paulist Press, 1990), 150–66.

5   The following list of important works is necessarily incomplete but suggests the widening range of scholarship: Myrna Goldenberg, "Lessons Learned from Gentle Heroism: Women's Holocaust Narratives," *Annals of the American Academy of*

Political and Social Science 548, no. 1 (1996): 78–93; Myrna Goldenberg, "'From a World Beyond': Women in the Holocaust," *Feminist Studies* 22, no. 3 (Fall 1996): 667–87; Rachel Feldhay Brenner, *Writing as Resistance: Four Women Confronting the Holocaust* (University Park: Pennsylvania State University Press, 1997); Ann Taylor Allen, "The Holocaust and the Modernization of Gender: A Historiographical Essay," *Central European History* 30, no. 3 (1997): 349–64; Judith Baumel Tydor, *Double Jeopardy: Gender and the Holocaust* (London: Vallentine-Mitchell, 1998); Brana Gurewitsch, ed., *Mothers, Sisters, Resisters* (Tuscaloosa: University of Alabama Press, 1998); S. Lillian Kremer, *Women's Holocaust Writing: Memory and Imagination* (Lincoln: University of Nebraska Press, 1999); Marion A. Kaplan, *Between Dignity and Despair: Jewish Life in Nazi Germany* (New York: Oxford University Press, 1999); Jack G. Morrison, *Ravensbrück: Everyday Life in a Women's Concentration Camp, 1939–45* (Princeton, NJ: Markus Wiener, 2000); Barbara Distel, ed., *Frauen im Holocaust* (Gerlingen: Bleicher, 2001); Marianne Hirsch, "Nazi Photographs in Post-Holocaust Art: Gender as an Idiom of Memorialization," in *Crimes of War: Guilt and Denial in the Twentieth Century*, ed. Omer Bartov, Atina Grossmann, and Mary Nolan (New York: The New Press, 2002); Insa Eschebach, Sigrid Jacobeit, Silke Wenk, eds., *Gedächtnis und Geschlecht. Deutungsmuster in Darstellungen des nationalsozialistischen Genozids* (Frankfurt/M: Campus, 2002); Nechama Tec, *Resilience and Courage: Women, Men, and the Holocaust* (New Haven: Yale University Press, 2003); Elizabeth R. Baer and Myrna Goldenberg, eds., *Experience and Expression: Women, the Nazis, and the Holocaust* (Detroit, MI: Wayne State University Press, 2003); Pascale Bos, "Women and the Holocaust: Analyzing Gender Difference," in Baer and Goldenberg, *Experience and Expression*, 23–52; Sara R. Horowitz, "The Gender of Good and Evil: Women and Holocaust Memory," in *Gray Zones: Ambiguity and Compromise in the Holocaust and Its Aftermath*, ed. Jonathan Petropoulos and John K. Roth (New York: Berghahn, 2005), 165–78; Gisela Bock, ed., *Genozid und Geschlecht. Jüdische Frauen im nationalsozialistischen Lagersystem* (Frankfurt and New York: Campus, 2005); Zoë Vania Waxman, *Writing the Holocaust: Identity, Testimony, Representation* (Oxford, UK: Oxford University Press, 2006), esp. 122–51 on "Writing Ignored: Reading Women's Holocaust Testimonies"; Nancy Wingfield and Maria Bucur, eds., *Gender and War in Twentieth-Century Europe* (Bloomington: Indiana University Press, 2006); Esther Hertzog, ed., *Life, Death and Sacrifice: Women and Family in the Holocaust* (Jerusalem and New York: Gefen, 2008); Margarete Myers Feinstein, *Holocaust Survivors in Postwar Germany, 1945–57* (New York: Cambridge University Press, 2010).

6 Dalia Ofer and Lenore J. Weitzman, eds., *Women in the Holocaust* (New Haven, CT: Yale University Press, 1998), 12–16. Some criticism appears in Ofer and Weitzman's volume itself; see Lawrence Langer, "Gendered Suffering? Women in Holocaust Testimonies," including Langer's assertion that "gendered behavior" played a "severely diminished role" during the Holocaust (351). A biting attack on Ofer and Weitzman, other feminist scholars, and on Holocaust Studies in general comes from Gabriel Schoenfeld, a senior editor of *Commentary*. Referring to Ofer and

Weitzman's volume, Schoenfeld claims that "feminist scholarship on the Holocaust is intended explicitly to serve the purposes of consciousness-raising—i.e.: propaganda." Gabriel Schoenfeld, "Auschwitz and the Professors," *Commentary* (June 1998): 42–46. Schoenfeld's accusations provoked a flood of letters, mostly defending the validity of addressing gender in the Holocaust; twenty-one of them appeared in the August 1998 issue of *Commentary*. In response to a subsequent rejoinder by Sara Horowitz, Schoenfeld maintained he had been misunderstood. He had "no objections to inquiry into the way women experienced the Holocaust," he wrote, "only the misuse of such inquiry to advance the contemporary ideological agenda of feminism, and also to promulgate sheer nonsense." Gabriel Schoenfeld, "Controversy: Feminist Approaches to the Holocaust," *Prooftexts: A Journal of Jewish Literary History* 21, no. 2 (Spring 2001): 277–79. See also Sara R. Horowitz, "Gender, Genocide, and Jewish Memory," *Prooftexts* 20, nos. 1 and 2 (Winter/Spring 2000): 158–90.

7   Carol Rittner and John K. Roth, eds., *Different Voices: Women and the Holocaust* (St. Paul, MN: Paragon House, 1993).

8   Christopher Browning, *Ordinary Men: Reserve Police Battalion 101 and the Final Solution in Poland* (New York: HarperCollins, 1992); Daniel Jonah Goldhagen, *Hitler's Willing Executioners* (New York: Knopf, 1996).

9   Claudia Koonz, *Mothers in the Fatherland: Women, the Family, and Nazi Politics* (New York: St. Martins, 1987). See also Claudia Koonz, "A Tributary and a Mainstream: Gender, Public Memory, and the Historiography of Nazi Germany," in *Gendering Modern German History*, ed. Karen. Hagemann and Jean H. Quataert (New York: Berghahn, 2007), 147–68, esp. 159–61. Very important, too, although the scope is broader, is *Brutality and Desire: War and Sexuality in Europe's Twentieth Century*, ed. Dagmar Herzog (Houndmills, Basingstoke: Palgrave Macmillan, 2009).

10   Gudrun Schwarz, *Eine Frau an seiner Seite. Die Ehefrauen in der 'SS-Sippengemeinschaft'* (Berlin: Aufbau, 2000).

11   See Karin Orth, "The Concentration Camp SS as a Functional Elite," in *National Socialist Extermination Policies: Contemporary German Perspectives and Controversies*, ed. Ulrich Herbert (New York: Berghahn, 2000), 306–34.

12   Sybille Steinbacher, *'Musterstadt' Auschwitz. Germanisierungspolitik und Judenmord in Ostoberschlesien* (Munich: K. G. Saur, 2000).

13   Sybille Steinbacher, *Auschwitz: A History*, trans. Shaun Whiteside (London: Penguin, 2005), 43.

14   Ernst Klee, Willi Dressen, and Volker Reiss, eds., *The Good Old Days: The Holocaust as Seen by Its Perpetrators and Bystanders*, trans. Deborah Burnstone (New York: Simon and Schuster, 1991).

15   See, for example, Walter Manoschek, "Es gibt nur eines für das Judentum: Vernichtung," in *Das Judenbild in deutschen Soldatenbriefen, 1939–1941* (Hamburg: HIS Verlag, 1995).

16   This dynamic is evident in Gitta Sereny, *Into That Darkness: An Examination of Conscience* (New York: Vintage, 1984), esp. 361 with Sereny's account of her

exchange with Franz Stangl's wife, Teresa Stangl.

17 For discussion of the role of mother as conscience and guardian of virtue, see Doris L. Bergen, *Twisted Cross: The German Christian Movement in the Third Reich* (Chapel Hill: University of North Carolina Press, 1996), esp. 121–32 and 192–98.

18 Susannah Heschel, "Does Atrocity Have a Gender? Feminist Interpretations of Women in the SS," in *Lessons and Legacies VI: New Currents in Holocaust Research,* ed. Jeffry M. Diefendorf (Evanson, IL: Northwestern University Press, 2004), 300–321. For a fascinating discussion of the popular demonization of a woman perpetrator, see Alexandra Przyrembel, "Transfixed by an Image: Ilse Koch, the 'Kommandeuse' of Buchenwald," trans. Pamela Selwyn, *German History* 19, no. 3 (2001): 369–99; also important is Wendy Lower, "Male and Female Holocaust Perpetrators and the East German Approach to Justice, 1949–1963," *Holocaust and Genocide Studies* 24, no. 1 (2010): 56–84.

19 Liana Millu, *Smoke over Birkenau,* trans. Lynne Sharon Schwartz (Evanston, IL: Northwestern University Press, 1991).

20 For insightful discussion of Millu's memoir and its format, see Elizabeth R. Baer, "Rereading Women's Holocaust Memoirs: Liana Millu's *Smoke Over Birkenau,*" in *Lessons and Legacies VIII: From Generation to Generation,* ed. Doris L. Bergen (Evanston, IL: Northwestern University Press, 2008).

21 Millu, "Lili Marlene," in *Smoke over Birkenau,* 47.

22 See Hirsch and Spitzer, "Gendered Translations"; also Marianne Hirsch, "Marked by Memory: Feminist Reflections on Trauma and Transmission," in *Extremities: Trauma, Testimony, Community,* ed. Nancy K. Miller and Jason Tougaw (Urbana: University of Illinois Press, 2002), 71–91.

23 The words are somewhat different in the revised English version of the published text of the film. See Claude Lanzmann, *Shoah: The Complete Text of the Acclaimed Holocaust Film* (New York: Da Capo, 1995), 101.

24 Kaplan, *Between Dignity and Despair,* esp. 5–9.

25 Primo Levi, *Survival in Auschwitz,* trans. Stuart Woolf (New York: Touchstone, 1996), 129–30. Originally published as *Se questo è un uomo* (1958).

26 Götz Aly, *"Final Solution": Nazi Population Policy and the Murder of the European Jews,* trans. Belinda Cooper and Allison Brown (London: Arnold, 1999).

27 Isabel Heinemann, "Rasse, Siedlung, deutsches Blut," in *Das Rasse- und Siedlungshauptamt der SS und die rassenpolitische Neuordnung Europas* (Göttingen: Wallstein, 2003); Chad Bryant, *Prague in Black: Nazi Rule and Czech Nationalism* (Cambridge, MA: Harvard University Press, 2007); Tara Zahra, *Kidnapped Souls: National Indifference and the Battle for Children in the Bohemian Lands, 1900–1948* (Ithaca, NY: Cornell University Press, 2008).

28 Doris L. Bergen, "Sex, Blood, and Vulnerability: Women Outsiders in German-Occupied Europe," in *Social Outsiders in Nazi Germany,* ed. Robert Gellately and Nathan Stoltzfus (Princeton, NJ: Princeton University Press, 2001), 273–93; Elizabeth Harvey, *Women and the Nazi East* (New Haven, CT: Yale University Press, 2003); Nancy R. Reagin, *Sweeping the German Nation: Domesticity and National Identity in Germany, 1870–1945* (New York: Cambridge University Press, 2007).

29 Beate Meyer, *Jüdische Mischlinge: Rassenpolitik und Verfolgungserfahrung* (Hamburg: Dölling and Galitz, 1999); Aleksandar-Saša Vuletić, *Christen jüdischer Herkunft im Dritten Reich: Verfolgung und Selbsthilfe 1933-1939* (Mainz: P. von Zabern, 1999); Cynthia Crane, *Divided Lives: The Untold Stories of Jewish Christian Women in Nazi Germany* (New York: Palgrave Macmillan, 2000); Bryan Mark Rigg, *Hitler's Jewish Soldiers* (Lawrence: University Press of Kansas, 2002); Thomas Pegelow Kaplan, *The Language of Nazi Genocide: Linguistic Violence and the Struggle of Germans of Jewish Ancestry* (New York: Cambridge University Press, 2009).

30 Raul Hilberg, *Perpetrators, Victims, Bystanders: The Jewish Catastrophe, 1933-1945* (New York: HarperCollins, 1992), esp. 212-14: "Helpers, Gainers, and Onlookers"; 217-24: "Messengers"; and 225-48: "The Jewish Rescuers."

31 Heda Margolius Kovály, *Under a Cruel Star: A Life in Prague, 1941-1968*, trans. Helen Epstein and Franci Epstein (New York: Holmes & Meier, 1997), 18.

32 Carol Rittner and Sondra Myers, eds., *The Courage to Care: Rescuers of Jews During the Holocaust* (New York: New York University Press, 1986).

33 Philip Hallie, *Lest Innocent Blood Be Shed: The Story of the Village of Le Cambon and How Goodness Happened There* (New York: Harper Colophon Books, 1980), 119-28; "Magda Trocme," in *The Courage to Care*, ed. Carol Rittner and Sondra Myers (New York: New York University Press, 1986), 100-107.

34 Nathan Stoltzfus, *Resistance of the Heart: Intermarriage and the Rosenstrasse Protest in Nazi Germany* (New York: W. W. Norton, 1996); Robert Melson, *False Papers: Deception and Survival in the Holocaust* (Urbana: University of Illinois Press, 2000).

35 Jan Gross, *Neighbors: The Destruction of the Jewish Community in Jedwabne, Poland* (Princeton, NJ: Princeton University Press, 2001), 108.

36 Omer Bartov, "Interethnic Relations in the Holocaust as Seen Through Postwar Testimonies: Buczacz, East Galicia, 1941-1944," in Bergen, ed., *Lessons and Legacies VIII.*

37 *Come and See,* directed by Elem Klimov, 1986; Russian with English subtitles. Original title *Idi i smotri*, 1985.

38 See Christa Schulz, "Weibliche Häftlinge aus Ravensbrück in Bordellen der Männerkonzentrationslager," in *Frauen in Konzentrationslagern Bergen-Belsen, Ravensbrück,* ed. Claus Füllberg-Stolberg et al. (Bremen: Edition Temmen, 1994); Christa Paul, *Zwangsprostitution: Staatlich errichtete Bordelle im Nationalsozialismus* (Berlin: Edition Hentrich, 1994); Wendy Jo Gertjejanssen, "Victims, Heroes, Survivors: Sexual Violence on the Eastern Front During World War II" (PhD diss., University of Minnesota, 2004); Christa Schulz, "Forced Prostitution in the Nazi Concentration Camps," in *Lessons and Legacies VII: The Holocaust in International Perspective,* ed. Dagmar Herzog (Chicago: Northwestern University Press, 2006), 169-78; Doris L. Bergen, "Sexual Violence in the Holocaust: Unique and Typical?" in Herzog, ed., *Lessons and Legacies VIII,* 179-200; Regina Mühlhäuser, "Rasse, Blut und Männlichkeit: Politiken sexueller Regulierung in die besetzten Gebieten der Sowjetunion (1941-1945)," *Feministische Studien—Zeitschrift für*

Interdisziplinäre Frauen- und Geschlechterforschung 25, no. 1 (2007): 55–69; Na'ama Shik, "Infinite Loneliness: Some Aspects of the Lives of Jewish Women in the Auschwitz Camps According to Testimonies and Autobiographies from 1945–1948," in Herzog ed., *Lessons and Legacies VIII*, 125–56; Gaby Zipfel with Regina Mühlhäuser et al., "'*Meine Not ist nicht einzig.' Sexuelle Gewalt in kriegerischen Konflikten — Ein Werkstattgespräch,*" *Mittelweg* 38, no. 18 (2009): 3–25; Rochelle G. Saidel and Sonja M. Hedgepeth, eds., *Sexual Violence against Jewish Women during the Holocaust* (Lebanon, NH: University Press of New England, 2010).

39 Joan Ringelheim, "Women and the Holocaust: A Reconsideration of Research," in Rittner and Roth, eds., *Different Voices*, 373–418. I have used this version of Ringelheim's piece many times with students, and in every class, there are people who insist they prefer the first half, where Ringelheim assembles the position that she later "undoes" as a cultural feminist distortion of the Holocaust.

40 Norman G. Finkelstein, *The Holocaust Industry: Reflections on the Exploitation of Jewish Suffering* (London: Verso, 2000).

41 See Saul Friedländer, *Nazi Germany and the Jews*, vol. 1, *The Years of Persecution, 1933–1939* (New York: HarperCollins, 1997); vol. 2, *The Years of Extermination* (New York: HarperCollins, 2007).

42 I am grateful to Noah Shenker for drawing this picture of a woman in the barber shop scenes to my attention. I had watched this sequence scores of times without ever noticing that image, but once I saw it, it was unmistakable. Dr. Shenker told me he in turn owed the insight to Stuart Liebman.

43 Lanzmann, *Shoah: The Complete Text* (1995), 101–8.

44 Henry Friedman, *I'm No Hero: Journeys of a Holocaust Survivor* (Seattle: University of Washington Press, 1999), 25–26.

45 The phrase "choiceless choices" comes from Lawrence Langer, who used it in an article, "The Dilemma of Choice in the Death Camps," later expanded into a book by Lawrence Langer, *Versions of Survival: The Holocaust and the Human Spirit* (Albany: State University of New York Press, 1982).

46 Klaus Theweleit, *Male Fantasies*, 2 vols., trans Stephen Conway (Minneapolis: University of Minnesota Press, 1987); Günter Grau, ed. *Hidden Holocaust? Gay and Lesbian Persecution in Germany, 1933–1945*, trans. Patrick Camiller (London: Cassell, 1995); Elizabeth Heineman, "Sexuality and Nazism: The Doubly Unspeakable," *Journal of the History of Sexuality* 11, nos. 1/2 (January–April 2002): 22–66; Dagmar Herzog, *Sex After Fascism: Memory and Morality in Twentieth-Century Germany* (Princeton, N.J.: Princeton University Press, 2005); Geoffrey J. Giles, "The Denial of Homosexuality and Same-Sex Incidents in Himmler's SS and Police," in *Sexuality and German Fascism*, ed. Dagmar Herzog (New York: Berghahn, 2005), 256–90, originally published in *Journal of the History of Sexuality* (2002). See also the personal account of Josef Kohout in Heinz Heger, *The Men with the Pink Triangle*, trans. David Fernbach (Boston: Alyson Publications, 1980). Also of interest in this regard is Omer Bartov, "Kitsch and Sadism in Ka-Tzetnik's Other Planet: Israeli Youth Imagine the Holocaust," *Jewish Social Studies* 3, no. 2 (1997): 42–76.

47 Bernard Gotfryd, *Anton the Dove Fancier and Other Tales of the Holocaust* (New

York: Washington Square Press, 1990), 139–42. For a Polish gentile's account of the prevalence of sex in Auschwitz, see Tadeusz Borowski, *This Way to the Gas, Ladies and Gentlemen,* trans. Barbara Vedder (originally published 1947; New York: Penguin, 1967), 86–93; also relevant here is Anna Hájková, "Sexual Barter in the Time of Genocide: Sexual Economy of the Theresienstadt Ghetto," manuscript.

48 *The Night Porter (Il portiere di notte)*, directed by Liliana Cavani, 1974.

49 Primo Levi, *The Drowned and the Saved,* trans. Raymond Rosenthal (New York: Summit, 1988), 48.

50 Joan Smith, "Holocaust Girls," in *Misogynies: Reflections on Myth and Malice* (New York: Fawcett Columbine, 1991), 125–38.

51 Jonathan Littell, *The Kindly Ones,* trans. from French by Charlotte Mandell (New York: Harper, 2008), originally published as *Les Bienveillantes* (2006).

52 An important exception is Marianne Hirsch, who examined mother-daughter relationships in literature in *The Mother/Daughter Plot: Narrative, Psychoanalysis, Feminism* (Bloomington: Indiana University Press, 1989) and foregrounds daughters and the mother-daughter connection as a crucial site of memory and postmemory transmission. See Hirsch, *Family Frames: Photography, Narrative, and Postmemory* (Cambridge, MA: Harvard University Press, 1997); and Hirsch, "The Generation of Postmemory," *Poetics Today* 29, no. 1 (2008): 103–128.

53 Sarah Kofman, *Rue Ordener, Rue Labat,* trans. Ann Smock (Lincoln: University of Nebraska Press, 1996), 57.

54 Sara Nomberg-Przytyk, *Auschwitz: True Tales from a Grotesque Land,* trans. Roslyn Hirsch (Chapel Hill: University of North Carolina Press, 1985), 57.

55 Judith Magyar Isaacson, *Seed of Sarah: Memoirs of a Survivor* (Urbana: University of Illinois Press, 1990), esp. 83–86, "Stay Together."

56 Sara Ginaite-Rubinson, *Resistance and Survival: The Jewish Community in Kaunas, 1941–1944* (Oakville, ON: Mosaic Press and the Holocaust Centre of Toronto, 2005).

57 Melson, *False Papers,* 185–86.

58 Gertrude Schneider describes her publications on the Holocaust in Latvia as a trilogy: *Journey Into Terror: Story of the Riga Ghetto* (New York: Ark House, 1979; new and expanded edition, Westport, CT: Praeger, 2001); *Muted Voices: Jewish Survivors of Latvia Remember* (New York: Philosophical Library, 1987); and Schneider, ed., *The Unfinished Road: Jewish Survivors of Latvia Look Back* (Westport, CT: Praeger, 1991), in which she makes a reference to this as "the last book in a trilogy" on page v. Schneider's subsequent publications include *Exile and Destruction: The Fate of Austrian Jews, 1938–1945* (Westport, CT: Praeger, 1995) and, evidence of her expertise in songs, *Mordechai Gebirtig: His Poetic and Musical Legacy* (Westport, CT: Praeger, 2000).

59 Outtakes from *Shoah* are available in the Steven Spielberg Film and Video Archive at the United States Holocaust Memorial Museum; excerpts can be accessed through the museum's website (www.ushmm.org). Interview with Gertrude Schneider is RG-60, 5015, Tape 3221-3225, 2 hours 18 minutes. Note the contrast in

the defense of their parents offered by Gertrude Schneider and Rita Wassermann and the position of Ruth Klüger in *Still Alive: A Holocaust Girlhood Remembered* (New York: Feminist Press, 2001).

60 My translation of the lyrics as sung in *Shoah*.

2

Philosophy in the Feminine and the Holocaust Witness

Hannah Arendt and Sarah Kofman

DOROTA GLOWACKA

Shoah! this word full of tenderness,
    Now terrible
    Compels us to silence:
Scha, still,
    One says in Yiddish
Shh! Shh! One says in French.
Shoah makes all voices stop speaking.
Open mouth screaming in anguish,
Shoah, brief as lightening,
Is this mute cry that no word
Could soothe,
that bears witness, while suffocating,
To the unnameable, to the ignoble immensity
Of this event without precedent, Auschwitz.
    This happened: *ist geschehen*
    It *must* be said.
                  —Sarah Kofman, "Shoah (or Dis-grace)"

At the time of the rise of National Socialism, during the Final Solution, and immediately after the war, attempts to come to terms with the Holocaust on philosophical grounds were rare. The philosophers who did respond to the menace of Hitlerism during these years were all Jewish (Hannah Arendt, Walter Benjamin, Emmanuel Levinas, Martin Buber, and Theodor Adorno), with the exception of Karl Jaspers, who, however, spent the war saving the life of his Jewish wife. In the decades following the war, as Alan Rosenberg and Paul Marcus put it succinctly, "philosophy . . . has been written as if the Holocaust had never occurred."[1] Seeking an explanation, Hegelian scholar and Holocaust survivor Emil Fackenheim argues that the Holocaust was too context and race specific and historically determined to be considered within the framework of traditional philosophy, whose mandate had always been to deal with universal and timeless ideas.[2] Drawing on that insight, French philosopher Jacques Derrida relates traditional philosophy's silence on the Holocaust to its erasure of biography and the life stories of embodied human beings, citing as an example Heidegger's comment that insofar as it is relevant to his philosophy, Aristotle's life can be summed up as "Aristotle was born, worked, and died."[3] Empirically determined and not linked to their philosophical systems by any necessity, philosophers' lives are considered accidental to the essential part of who they are: their thinking.

Yet "after Auschwitz," philosophy's gesture of separating thinking from biography necessitates closer scrutiny. This chapter examines the writings of two thinkers, Hannah Arendt (1906–1975) and Sarah Kofman (1934–1994), whose lives and work were significantly touched by this particular and particularly horrifying chapter in Jewish history, by events that, as Fackenheim argues, refuse to be explained away as Hegelian sacrifices on the slaughter bench of history.[4] The problem of "biography" is central in both thinkers' works, and it forms a pivot for their interventions into traditional philosophical narratives. These interventions by two female philosophers of Jewish origin not only reveal philosophy's inability to confront the Holocaust, but also show a correlation between that inexcusable silence and philosophy's millennial exclusion of woman. In both cases, this philosophical failure hinges on the erasure of biography, that is, of the particularities of embodied, gendered human agents.

The writings of Hannah Arendt and Sarah Kofman differ significantly in terms of genre, subject matter, and commitment to feminism. The two women never met in person or commented on each other's work.[5] Their biographies, however, converge since they both were raised in Jewish households (though Arendt in an assimilated one) and both escaped the Nazi Final Solution; as a result, the writings of both reflect a complicated relation to Judaism and Jewishness. Arendt's and Kofman's intellectual paths intersect in their encounters with great (male) figures of Western metaphysics—both wrote on Plato, Aristotle, Kant, Rousseau, Nietzsche, and Heidegger—and in the hardships both experienced as women within the masculine philosophical milieu.

Both Arendt and Kofman strongly asserted their positions as women in a traditionally male domain and were among a handful of contemporary women philosophers who were recognized and respected by their male counterparts (together with Simone de Beauvoir and Simone Weil). Still, they were never granted full status as philosophers. As Arendt—arguably the most influential political thinker of the twentieth century—once revealed in an interview, she never felt accepted into the circles of philosophers and could only hope that "a woman will one day be a philosopher."[6] Kofman wrote over a dozen books on the subjects of philosophy and psychoanalysis, yet she was seen mainly as a "commentator" on the works of Plato, Rousseau, Kant, Nietzsche, and Freud. For decades she was marginalized within the academic field and denied a permanent teaching post at the Sorbonne.

The writings of both women, nevertheless, were largely a product of their training in philosophy, and they were indebted to their philosophical forefathers and male mentors. Neither engaged with feminist thought or focused on female thinkers. Referring to Arendt especially, feminist scholars have written ruefully of "the tragedy of a female mind nourished on male ideologies,"[7] pointing out her failure to reflect on the gender assumptions that underlie the categories she uses in her work, in *The Human Condition*, in particular.[8] The only sustained text by Arendt on the question of women is a short review entitled "On the Emancipation of Women," written in 1933.[9] Kofman, for her part, was strongly critical of traditional feminism, and she also refused any association with the so-called New French Feminists (Irigaray, Cixous, Kristeva, and others).

Although they were ensconced in the masculine language and the conceptual framework of the Western tradition, Arendt and Kofman, albeit in very different ways, sought to break ranks with the philosophy that had formed them as thinkers. Arendt's positive valuation of natality as the font of the political, for instance, is remarkably different from philosophy's privileging of death as the ultimate horizon of human action, and her articulation of human plurality as the foundation of our being in the world undermines philosophical narratives of totality and unity.[10] Kofman is known for her interventions into seminal works of philosophy and psychoanalysis, through which she seeks to recover the woman in patriarchal texts, insisting that philosophy's emphasis on the universal occurs at the expense of the feminine, of the body and matter. Even though their writings are dissimilar, they resonate in their knotting together of biography and philosophy, against the grain of the tradition.

HANNAH ARENDT: "LIFE IS A STORY"

Arendt grew up in a non-religious milieu, and she rarely makes reference to Jewish culture and history. Some of her most passionate writing, however, is on Jewish authors such as Franz Kafka or Walter Benjamin whose relation to Jewishness is as complex as her own. She always expressed comfort with both her gender and her Jewishness, and to the escalating persecutions of Jews in Nazi Germany in the 1930s, Arendt responded as a Jew: she participated in the resistance and she worked for Jewish Zionist organizations in Berlin and Paris. She was interned by the French as an enemy alien, yet managed to escape to America in 1941, where she continued to work for Jewish organizations and supported the cause of the Jewish homeland in Palestine.[11]

The Holocaust was undoubtedly a transformative event in Arendt's intellectual development. The majority of her work immediately after the war, including her groundbreaking study *The Origins of Totalitarianism*,[12] was, in her own words, a shocked, passionate, and indignant response to the disaster.[13] Arendt's contributions to Holocaust scholarship, such as her analyses of the history of European political antisemitism, her examination of the mechanisms that led to the creation of Nazi death camps, and her reflections on fascism and on postwar German responsibility are crucial. Her thesis that the Holocaust, as the most gruesome face of totalitarianism, was a novum in the history of humankind that cannot be understood in terms of previously accepted categories, predates similar reflections by Emil Fackenheim by almost two decades. Her analysis of the collapse of moral categories grounded in the ideal of freedom (the ability to choose between good and evil) anticipates Primo Levi's famous reflection on the "grey zone" and Zygmunt Bauman's argument about the exclu-

sion of ethics in post-Enlightenment thinking.[14] Her description of the
Nazi concentration camps as an attempt to "destroy the essence of man,"[15]
calling into question the very conception of the human, inspired Giorgio
Agamben's analysis of the *muselmänner* in *Remnants of Auschwitz*. With
the exception of a passing reference in Agamben, none of these thinkers
acknowledge Arendt's contributions. Her multifaceted reflection on the
Holocaust and on the history of European Jewry was overshadowed by the
scandal accompanying the publication of *Eichmann in Jerusalem*, which
condemns the role of the Jewish Councils and makes vituperative comments about Jewish passivity during the Holocaust.[16]

While Arendt scholars comment on the impact of the Holocaust on
Arendt's life and work, and occasionally consider her writings in feminist
contexts, the relation between her responses to the fate of the Jews during
the Holocaust and her guarded reflection on the "woman question" has
not been directly addressed.[17] This juncture is explored in this chapter by
bringing together the motifs of Arendt's own biography and her passionate interest in the biographies of others, expressed in her thesis that "life is
a story."[18]

In *The Human Condition*, Arendt writes, "The chief characteristic of
this specifically human life, whose appearance and disappearance constitute worldly events, is that it is itself always full of events which ultimately can be told as a story, establish a biography."[19] She distinguishes
between three spheres of human life: labor, the activities that pertain to
the maintenance of the body and the necessities of life; work, the produc-
tion of artifacts fashioned by human hands; and action, which consists
of events enacted by individuals in the world. Arendt values action most
highly since, although it yields no tangible products, it situates us, as political animals, within the fabric of human relationships. In this context,
Arendt's assertion that "life is a story" means that for action to be real and
to survive impermanence, it must be repeated in the form of a narrative.
The book's chapter on "action" is prefaced by a motto from Isak Dinesen:
"All sorrows can be borne if you put them into a story or tell a story about
them."[20] Arendt's thesis thus has two distinct yet interrelated dimensions:
it entails the presence of another, of a witness and storyteller who will craft
the events of a life into a story, but it also suggests that for these events
to be immortalized in retelling, the actor must, in her lifetime, have the
courage to insert herself into the world of human affairs and initiate the
story that will be told. It is because of this double narrative imperative that

individual biographies become part of a collective story, embedded in the realm of human interaction; without it, as Arendt says, historical phenomena would remain inchoate, "an unbearable sequence of sheer events."[21]

Thus Arendt's philosophical reflection on the relation between action—the essence of what makes us human—and storytelling is related directly to her interest in the genre of biography, that is, in the life stories of individual men and women. A significant subset of her work consists of biographical sketches. Of special interest here are the monograph *Rahel Varnhagen: The Life of a Jewess*[22] and a chapter on Rosa Luxemburg in *Men in Dark Times* since it is in these two works that Arendt combines her reflections on "Jewishness" and on "the woman question." Excepting her thesis on St. Augustine, the book on Varnhagen is Arendt's first sustained piece of writing, and the fact that Arendt's entire oeuvre is clasped between *The Life of the Jewess* and her unfinished last work *The Life of the Mind* imbues her own writing life with a certain narrative consistency of a well-conceived beginning and end.[23]

Arendt started writing *Rahel Varnhagen* in 1933, "with an awareness of the doom of German Judaism,"[24] although the book was not published until more than two decades later in the United States. Varnhagen was a nineteenth-century German-Jewish hostess of a literary salon, and her life reflected the difficult situation of Jews in Germany during her time. As Arendt later argues in *The Origins of Totalitarianism*, the problem lay in the attempts by the educated, well-to-do Jewry to escape their Jewishness through assimilation. For Arendt, the fact that German Jews considered Jewishness their "private misfortune," rather than understanding it in political terms, was symptomatic of their increasing alienation in the public sphere. Relegated to pariah status, Jews were excluded from the political realm. At the beginning of the twentieth century, Jews' increasing loss of political efficacy worsened and then deteriorated in the 1930s into statelessness, depriving them of legal rights and later of human status altogether. This progressive exclusion was the precondition for extermination.[25]

In Varnhagen's biography, Arendt shows that at the inception of this process, in the nineteenth century, the lack of political participation among German Jews, combined with ever-present antisemitism, resulted in a sense of interiorized "Jewish shame." As documented in her diaries and in her correspondence, for most of her life Varnhagen considered Jewishness a disgrace: "as it is I do not forget this shame for a *single* second. I drink it in water, I drink it with air; in every breath."[26] In addition to her self-hatred as a Jew, Varnhagen also grappled with the *Frauenproblem*. "Not rich, not cultivated and not beautiful,"[27] she was forced to seek marriage as the only way out of poverty and social abandonment.[28] Facing social ostracism, Varnhagen was soon to find out that she was fettered to Jewishness as inescapably as she was to being a woman. Toward the end of her life, however, she came to embrace her Jewishness, which she had always considered the source of her unhappiness. In fact, Arendt begins the monograph with the words that Varnhagen reportedly uttered on her deathbed: "The thing that all my life seemed to me the greatest shame, which was the misery and misfortune of my life—having been born a Jewess—this I should on no account now wish to have missed."[29] By "clinging to both conditions,"[30] of womanhood and Jewishness, and eventually embracing her identity in positive terms, Varnhagen manages to transform her pariah status into a strength, to transform herself into an acting being, and to endow her life with significance. In Arendt's account, despite her inability to grasp her double misfortune in political terms, Varnhagen's death-bed confession is an act of completion, a *sui generis* self-creating moment. This dénouement allows her to gather her life together into a story to be told and to become a participant in the shared life of remembrance.

The book on Varnhagen—whom Arendt calls "a friend even if she died a long time ago"—has been interpreted as Arendt's projection of her own struggle as an emancipated Jewish woman in a male-dominated milieu.[31] Another such "friend" whose life Arendt recounts in a biographical vignette is Rosa Luxemburg, a revolutionary manquée, who, in a spiritual affinity with Varhnagen, was an outsider not only as a Jew (worse yet, a Jew from Eastern Europe) but also because she "was so self-consciously a woman." Unlike Varnhagen, Luxemburg, for her entire life, "remained passionately engaged in public life and civil affairs, in the destinies of the world."[32] Like Varnhagen, however, she was cast into oblivion by history, which has remembered her in clichés as scary Red Rosa, as a misguided romantic, or as a "quarrelsome female."[33] Arendt seems to be lending her own voice to Luxemburg when she describes Luxemburg's defiant rejection of a woman-specific agenda in favor of *Vive la petite difference!* : the undeniable fact of sexual difference that must be considered within a larger matrix of differences between humans.[34] According to Arendt, it is this multiplicity that constitutes and continuously shapes us as agents within human plurality. Through this analysis, "the Jewish question" and "the woman question" are again intertwined. Arendt's refusal to lend her voice to an essentialist feminist agenda parallels her rejection of the Jewish destiny as religion or race-specific: for her, these terms point to interrelated political issues. For Arendt, an individual life can only become meaningful among the plurality of humankind, and it is revealed as meaningful thanks to the storytelling ability of a witness. We can draw the conclusion that, through the narrative refashioning of the lives of Varnhagen and Luxemburg against the forces of oblivion, and by crafting her own biography as a mirror of these women's lives, Arendt inscribes the woman and the Jew into the space of collective memory and history.[35]

"Action reveals itself fully only to the storyteller, that is, to the backward glance of the historian," writes Arendt.[36] Likewise, it is as a storyteller and biographer that Arendt assumes her responsibility as a philosophical witness. As a thinker, she pays her debt to humankind when she gives testimony to the lives of others and thus allows them to take up their place in history. This is a unique responsibility: to be a philosopher, concludes Arendt in her homage to Karl Jaspers, is "to take it upon oneself to answer before mankind for every thought."[37] Arendt's emphasis on the post-Auschwitz philosopher's responsibility must be noted, since this view is usually credited to such (male) philosophers as Adorno, Bauman, Levinas, and Fackenheim. Thus despite the lack of direct references to the Holocaust in her later work, Arendt's entire oeuvre is animated by a deep concern for the future of thinking "after Auschwitz." As she explains in the introduction to *The Life of the Mind*, it was the spectacle of utter "thoughtlessness" that she witnessed during the Eichmann trial that made her feel obligated to pursue that inquiry.[38] For Arendt, however, such philosophical witness is inseparable from the life narratives of particular men and women who live and act in the world.

SARAH KOFMAN:
"I ALWAYS WANTED TO TELL THE STORY OF MY LIFE"

Arendt's and Kofman's writings are significantly different. Kofman takes no interest in the political, which is the main focus of Arendt's oeuvre, while Arendt rejects, even scorns, psychoanalysis, which is one of Kofman's primary terrains of exploration. However, the two thinkers share a passionate interest in biography. Kofman's life work could be said to consist in excavating and reconstructing life stories from the philosophical texts of Western metaphysics—a tradition built, she repeatedly argues, upon the erasure of the biographical. As Derrida describes it in a posthumous tribute to Kofman, her analyses perform a "scratching" or clawing of the biographical (*autobiogriffure*: auto-bio-claw-graphy) out of the philosopher's "pure" system, apparently uncontaminated by the mundane demands of life.[39] Unlike Arendt, however, Kofman is distrustful of narrative as a vehicle for the memory of another's life.

She expresses this view in her book *Smothered Words*,[40] which combines a commentary on a short récit by French writer Maurice Blanchot with the story of the murder of Kofman's father in Auschwitz and a reading of Robert Antelme's *L'Espèce humaine*.[41] Drawing on Blanchot's discussion of narrative in *The Writing of the Disaster*, Kofman argues that, *pace* Arendt, narratives are always attempts to appropriate the life of another and as such can be complicit in totalizing structures of power and knowledge.[42] Yet in a short piece entitled " 'My Life' and Psychoanalysis," written a few years earlier, Kofman confesses that "I always wanted to tell the story of my life."[43] As her scattered autobiographical fragments show, Kofman struggled to gather the events of her life into a narrative.[44] It was not until 1994, shortly before her suicide, that Kofman penned a short autobiographical account entitled *Rue Ordener, Rue Labat*, in which she discloses for the first time the details of her survival as a hidden child and her subsequent path to a vocation as a woman philosopher. This contradiction between a philosophical repudiation of narrative and the desire to tell her own story points to other deep-seated disjunctions in her life and work.

Kofman's Holocaust experience was shattering. In July 1942, her father, Rabbi Berek Kofman, was deported to Drancy and then to Auschwitz where, according to an eyewitness, he was beaten by a "Jewish butcher-turned-kapo" for saying prayers on Sabbath, and then buried alive.[45] Kofman's mother, Fineza Konig (Kofman never mentions her mother's name in her autobiography), managed to save her six children by placing them in different hiding spots. Kofman herself, for the most part, stayed in hiding with her mother, with whom she refused to part, hidden by a Christian woman she refers to as Mémé. In the Christian household, Kofman, an observant Jewish girl who had obstinately refused to eat non-kosher even in the times of greatest scarcity, assimilated to Christian customs and diet, and eventually emotionally abandoned her Jewish mother for Mémé. As her Orthodox upbringing and her identification with Jewishness unraveled, the conflict of religious and filial loyalties manifested violently in the form of an eating disorder.[46]

In the opening paragraph of *Rue Ordener, Rue Labat*, Kofman suggests that the trauma of her childhood experiences represents the unavowed origin of all of her writings, the "detours required to bring me to write about 'that.'"[47] In *Smothered Words*, Kofman wrote: "Because he was a Jew, my father died in Auschwitz: How can it not be said? And how can it be said? How can one speak of *that* before which all possibility of speech ceases? Of this event, my absolute."[48] What she implies in the opening of her autobiographical account, therefore, is that her entire work so far—her interpretations of Nietzsche, Kant, and other philosophical figures—has been a displaced form of autobiography. She was also writing by proxy an inscription of her father's "smothered" story. In the same opening paragraph, Kofman recalls her father's broken pen. Lying on her desk and useless as a writing tool, a symbol of the destruction of her father's voice, it nevertheless makes her "write, write."[49] In this final work, Kofman's deconstructive imitations of philosophers (she refers to her rereadings as acts of mimicry) are replaced by imitation of her father's actions: just as Berek Kofman bore witness to the untestifiable infinity of God, on pain of death by suffocation, so Kofman testifies to the unspeakable event of his death at Auschwitz, choking on the wounded words of her testimony.[50] Kofman's interpretations of texts by her philosophical forefathers are often rebellious and irreverent, signaling her disagreement with the philosophical tradition that shaped her. Yet there is no laughter or rebellion in her autobiographical texts: both *Smothered Words* and *Rue Ordener, Rue Labat* are a solemn testimony to her father's suffering and death.

In contrast to the sanctification of her father's memory, Kofman expresses hostility and distaste for the two women who saved her life, her biological mother and the Christian woman Mémé. Kofman portrays her mother in dark, unforgiving colors: she is a smothering "Jewish mother," a caricature of loud, unenlightened Jewishness, of whom the writer is "ashamed" and whom she finds repugnant. In one episode she is shown hitting her daughter in a blind rage and screaming, in Yiddish, "I am your mother! I am your mother!"[51] *Rue Ordener, Rue Labat* ends with an abrupt mention of Mémé's death: "I was unable to attend her funeral. But I know that at her grave the priest recalled how she had saved a little Jewish girl during the war."[52] The only reference to the death of Kofman's biological mother in the book comes in the context of the loss of the father: "When my mother died, it wasn't possible to find that card [the last communication which the father had sent to the family from Drancy]. It was as if I had lost my father a second time."[53] Kofman thus erases her mother from the narrative of her life, as if forbidding herself to mourn her.

This silencing of the mother's voice in favor of the voice of the father in Kofman's Holocaust narrative stands in contrast to her efforts to recover the mother in the texts of thinkers such as Kant, Rousseau, and Freud. Perhaps the two best-known examples of this work are her rereadings of Rousseau and Kant in *Le respect des femmes*. Writing of Rousseau, Kofman shows that the philosopher's references to nature serve to rationalize the subordination of women by confining them to motherhood as their "natural destiny." Yet, as she argues, Rousseau's appeal to mother nature (in *Emile, La Nouvelle Heloise*, and "On Women") is in actuality a reflection of his own obsession with dominant, maternal women. The voice of nature then functions as a displacement of the voice of Rousseau's own nature, tormented with paranoiac obsessions. Kofman concludes that the female figures in Rousseau's texts—whether put on a pedestal (mothers, wives, sisters) or debased (prostitutes)—function as substitutes for the mother who died bringing him into the world, while he nearly suffocated in her womb. Kofman suggests that these displaced tropes of the feminine in Rousseau have an apotropaic function, warding off the danger of being smothered by the mother.[54]

In her reading of Kant, Kofman examines the philosopher's account of mutual respect between the sexes. Kant argues that women's modesty and reserve save men from the moral defilement that stems from unrestrained fulfillment of the sexual drive. Men are thus prevented from descending to the level of beasts and they can remain human, acting according to the dictates of their moral faculty. The repugnance, shame, and horror that man naturally feels for his animal side (the same sentiments Kofman reports she harbored toward her biological mother) are the obverse of his fascination with woman, the mother substitute. Kant concludes that the sentiment of respect that the sexes have for each other must be subordinated to a higher system of morals, and ultimately must become respect for the moral law. Drawing on Freud, Kofman conjectures that, since the female figures in a man's life are always substitutes for the first woman—his mother—Kant's categorical imperative is a sublimation of his disavowed attachment to the mother. Thus she argues that the purity of Kant's moral law is always already contaminated by the empirical "given" of sexual difference, and the biographical is always interwoven with the philosophical text rather than opposed to it. More fundamentally, perhaps, biography is philosophy's unacknowledged condition of possibility, although it has been expunged from it like an indigestible morsel.[55]

If the focus of Kofman's astute inquiries is the recovery of the mother in the philosopher's text, why, then, the repudiation of her own mother in her autobiographical narrative? It seems that the narrative disarticulation of both women who saved her life allowed Kofman to found her genealogy as a writer and philosopher in her father's act of witness, at the moment of his death in Auschwitz. Yet if Kofman is substituting her own witness for that of her murdered father, the story of her mother continues to be inscribed in her text as a negative trace.

Both Oliver and Chanter, in their commentaries on *Rue Ordener, Rue Labat*, have linked the ambiguity of Kofman's self-presentation as a daughter caught between the paternal law and the maternal imperative to Kofman's position as a female philosopher ensconced in the masculine tradition.[56] Kofman's struggle between Jewish identification and assimilation can also be read as a symptom of the conflict between Jewish tradition, which Kofman's mother defended with a strap, and the Graeco-Christian philosophical thought to which Kofman would dedicate her life. The silhouette of this vacillation is sketched subtly throughout the text: for instance, Kofman describes her father's sacrifice—he went willingly to the transport so that his family would not be taken away—in terms of the biblical sacrifice of Isaac, a central event in Jewish history. Yet she ends this chapter with a reference to Greek tragedy: "When I first encountered in a Greek tragedy the lament 'O, popoi, popoi, popoi,' I couldn't keep myself from thinking of that scene from my childhood where six children, their father gone, could only sob breathlessly, knowing they would never see him again, 'oh, papa, papa, papa.'"[57]

The symbolic eating of gentile food, for which she developed a preference (although she continued to vomit rare meat sautéed in butter), corresponds to Kofman's ingestion of gentile philosophy. Additionally, she writes that she first heard some of the names associated with this philosophical tradition from Mémé, in the context of antisemitic remarks, which, as she writes, she and her mother had to "swallow."[58] It is then possible to relate the narrative silencing of the mother to Kofman's aspiration to become a philosopher, which is tantamount to dissociating herself from Jewish heritage and history, although this is by no means a straightforward correlation. The Jewish mother nevertheless continues to haunt Kofman's philosophical writings as a powerful absence, the absence that she diagnoses in her commentaries on philosophical father-substitutes. Perhaps, then, unbeknownst to Kofman herself, all of her writings, while ostensibly a veiled tribute to her father, are also always about "that." The contradictions regarding the figure of the mother in Kofman's philosophical and autobiographical texts reveal a conflict between (but also the intertwining of) her self-understanding as a philosopher and her attempt to work through her own biography, marked by the traumatic loss of her father but also the disavowed loss of her mother.

If the entire body of Kofman's psychoanalytic inquiries into the history of philosophy constitute (by her own admission in *Rue Ordener, Rue Labat*) a thickly veiled work of mourning, while her autobiographical texts resituate her philosophical corpus as a deferred, highly mediated testimonial, whose life story is she thus "clawing out" in her Holocaust-related texts? In their posthumous tributes to their friend, both Derrida and Nancy describe Kofman as "the laughing, mocking little girl," both in her interactions with her male colleagues and in her relations with the philosophers she writes about.[59] Yet what is the function of this laughter? Kofman repeatedly speaks of the apotropaic function of the feminine figures in the philosophical texts she analyzes. Possibly this repeated performance as the laughing little girl of philosophy is her own apotropaic defense against the memory of the sad little girl of her childhood, who cried and refused to eat when separated from her mother. Perhaps it is this unhappy girl Kofman is grieving for while ostensibly mourning her father. At the same time, her demeanor as a "laughing girl" continues to serve as an apotropaic device, allowing her to pursue the study of the Graeco-Christian, patriarchal thought that she thus continues to "swallow."[60] This displaced labor of mourning, performed through the writing of an autobiographical narrative, is necessary so that the adult Sarah Kofman can begin to bear witness to herself. In that sense, Kofman's gesture of penning her autobiography shortly before her death is not unlike Arendt's *porte parole* Rahel Varnhagen's statement on her deathbed—an act of completion through which she initiates her own life story—as a Jewish woman and a woman philosopher.

ARENDT AND KOFMAN: AN INFINITE BEGINNING

In her sketch on Isak Dinesen, Arendt writes that "without repeating life in imagination you can never be fully alive."[61] Imagination and passion are crucial elements in forging the life story through which one's self is revealed in the world. Thinking must remain "passionate" because, as Arendt writes in the preface to *Men in Dark Times*, it is not abstract theories and concepts but individual lives and works that can "kindle, under almost all circumstances, an uncertain, flickering and often weak light" from which illumination can come, even in the darkest of times.[62] Imagination and passion are thus inextricably linked with "action," that which brings us into the human plurality and defines us as human. Imagination is the power of the new through which human beings continuously reinvent themselves and insert themselves into the world, "like a second birth."[63] It is an essential faculty that enables human beings to act spontaneously and to envision a future. Imagination is also what makes it possible to fashion a life into a story and thus bring an individual into the life of the community and into remembrance. Yet as Arendt bemoans in *The Life of the Mind*, philosophy has been unable to engage imagination in this way and thus to remain open to the power of creating "the new." She states, "Bergson was quite right when he writes: 'Most philosophers . . . are unable to conceive of radical novelty and unpredictability.' "[64] What Arendt sees as philosophy's failure to engage imagination is its inability to accommodate the lives of individual men and women, those who act in the world and create infinitely new beginnings.

Earlier, in *The Origins of Totalitarianism*, Arendt writes that spontaneity—that is, the ability to imagine beyond the constraints of immediate circumstances—is annihilated under the conditions of total domination. It was the destruction of the faculty of imagination in concentration camps that resulted in the reduction of human beings to *muselmänner*, automatons passively responding to stimuli, neither dead nor alive. This is why Arendt concludes that imagination, "with its incalculability, is the greatest of all obstacles to total domination"[65] and must continue to be opposed to totalizing forces. For Arendt, the intellectual "after Auschwitz" has an obligation to exercise this faculty to its full potential because "the fearful imagination of those who have been aroused by the events but have not themselves been smitten in the flesh" makes it possible to think about the horrors in such a way that we will "dread the concentration camp as a possibility for the future."[66] Imagination also makes it possible to move beyond those horrors and create new narratives that affirm life.

For Kofman, imagination labors to transform "the unimaginable" of Auschwitz into a story to be told, though always at the price of betraying what "really" happened. Resigning oneself to "the unimaginable" is to foreclose new beginnings. Kofman writes of "Knotted words, demanded and yet forbidden . . . which stick in your throat and cause you to suffocate, to lose your breath, which asphyxiate you, *taking away the possibility of even beginning.*"[67] Bearing witness requires that we continue to imagine, to transform memory into a story. Writing the story of a life, a biography, is testimony to an individual's having acted in the world. This is also the case in Kofman's autobiography *Rue Ordener, Rue Labat,* in which she "claws out" her own life. In a way, that narrative has a happy ending: Sarah Kofman is accepted to the faculty of philosophy at the Sorbonne. Yet the tensions and contradictions that pervade the text, the struggle to write it, and the pain concealed behind the matter-of-fact tone of the account betray the difficulty, impossibility perhaps, of reconciling the success of becoming a philosopher and the necessity of telling and affirming her life story. Perhaps, then, Arendt's thesis that "life is a story" and that it must be told as a story helps explain what seems to be a contradiction between Kofman's rejection of the narrative and her desire to create a narrative of her life. On the other hand, Kofman's distrust of the narrative and the conflicted performance of her own narrative, with its erasures and traumatic gaps, draw attention to the necessary incompleteness of any narrative. It is because of that lack of dénouement, however, that the life stories must be constantly re-imagined and told always anew. Thus it is crucial to consider Arendt's insistence on the importance of the story as that in which the life of the individual and the life of the collective are gathered together into meaningful wholes, but also to heed Kofman's deep suspicion of the narrative form. It allows us to both embrace the Arendtian vision of the promise of the new beginning yet remain distrustful of any story's claim to narrative closure and to be mindful of the traumatic remainder that will always continue to haunt and lacerate every narrative.

The subjects of Arendt's and Kofman's biographical excavations hail from very different philosophical and literary realms, and only once do they come into relative proximity: Arendt's analysis of the Nazi concentration camps is prompted by her reading of the concentration camp narrative *L'Univers concentrationnaire* by David Rousset, a former inmate of the

Buchenwald concentration camp, while Kofman's reflections in *Smothered Words* are enabled by the life story of Robert Antelme, who was an inmate of the same camp (and both were French political prisoners).[68] It is striking that neither Arendt nor Kofman draws on testimony from Jewish survivors of the Holocaust.[69] Kofman's recollection in particular was written at the time when she could have availed herself of an abundance of such testimonies. Neither does she mention the name of Jewish philosopher Emmanuel Lévinas, to whom Blanchot was strongly indebted in his articulation of the ethics of alterity, especially in the works that Kofman evokes in *Smothered Words* (*The Infinite Conversation* and *The Writing of the Disaster*), which is perhaps another subtle gesture of her preference for the gentile "food for thought" for which she developed a taste under Mémé's tutelage.[70] Kofman's only sustained, and largely indirect, philosophical reflection on "the Jewish condition" is her book on Nietzsche, written late in her life, entitled *Le mépris des Juifs: Nietzsche, les Juifs, l'antisémitism*, in which she passionately defends Nietzsche against the charge of antisemitism and seeks to rescue the German philosopher from "a dangerous, scandalous misinterpretation and appropriation" of his thought by National Socialism.[71]

Arendt's and Kofman's works reveal the tension between their position as Jewish women and the philosophical heritage that shaped them. In different ways (and to a much greater degree in Arendt) the writings of both, insofar as they remained "faithful" to their philosophical mentors, were complicit in the philosophical exclusion of the feminine, even if Kofman ostensibly sought to overcome it. Both, at different moments in their lives, reflected on Jewishness and Jewish history (and, in Kofman's case, on the tragic impact of that history on her own family), yet remained entrenched in Western philosophy's "Graeco-philia." Their complicated relation to the politics of gender on one hand and to Jewishness and the legacy of the Holocaust on the other is a reflection of that conflict. For both, however, the Holocaust, "the opening of the abyss," to use Arendt's phrase, not only deeply affected their sense of self-identity as Jewish women, but also influenced their subsequent intellectual trajectories so that their grappling with the legacy of the Holocaust cannot be separated from their self-identity as women philosophers. A reading of Arendt's work alongside Kofman's reveals that, despite their "complicity," the writings of both successfully break through philosophy's multiple erasures—of woman, of the Jew, and of the Holocaust—thus undermining "received narratives about the history of philosophy."[72]

At this complex juncture of their reflections on the Holocaust, on the Jewish condition in general, and on the woman question, as they all hinge on the question of biography and autobiography, the works of Hannah Arendt and Sarah Kofman can be fruitfully reconsidered as acts of philosophical witness to the Holocaust in the feminine. Not least, their interventions into philosophy raise the question of whether there may exist an uncanny collusion between philosophy's inability to confront the Holocaust and its longstanding erasure of women's voices. The re-articulation of the task of the philosopher in terms of "post-Auschwitz" witness, which hinges on the question of biography, must be inseparable from that question.

NOTES

The chapter epigraph is from Sarah Kofman, *Selected Writings* (Stanford, CA: Stanford University Press, 2007), 245.

1   Alan Rosenberg and Paul Marcus, "The Holocaust as a Test of Philosophy," in *Echoes from the Holocaust: Philosophical Reflections on a Dark Time*, ed. Alan Rosenberg and Gerald E. Myers (Philadelphia: Temple University Press, 1988), 204. See also Alan Milchman and Alan Rosenberg, "The Need for Philosophy to Confront the Holocaust as a Transformational Event," *Dialogue and Universalism*, nos. 3–4 (2003): 65–80.

2   See Emil Fackenheim, "The Holocaust and Philosophy," *The Journal of Philosophy* 82, no. 10 (October 1985), 505–14.

3   *Derrida: The Movie*, directed by Amy Kofman and Kirby Dick (New York: Zeitgeist Films, 2002).

4   See Emil L. Fackenheim, *Jewish Return Into History* (New York: Schocken Books, 1978).

5   Only once does Kofman make a reference to Arendt when she says, in an interview, that "there weren't any great women philosophers who had a corpus you could study sustainedly, except perhaps Hannah Arendt." Quoted in Penelope Deutscher, "'Imperfect Discretion': Interventions into the History of Philosophy by Twentieth-Century French Women Philosophers," *Hypatia* 15, no. 2 (2000): 163.

6   Hannah Arendt, *Essays in Understanding, 1930–1954: Formation, Exile, Totalitarianism*, ed. Jerome Kohn (New York: Harcourt Brace and Company 1994), 2.

7   Adrienne Rich, quoted in Mary G. Dietz, "Hannah Arendt and Feminist Politics," in *Hannah Arendt: Critical Essays*, ed. Lewis P. Hinchamn and Sandra K. Hinchamn (Albany, NY: SUNY Press, 1995), 231.

8   See Hannah Arendt, *The Human Condition* (Chicago: University of Chicago Press, 1998). See also Seyla Benhabib, *The Reluctant Modernism of Hannah Arendt* (New York: Rowman and Littlefield, 2003). As both Dietz and Benhabib point out, the

book contains no discussion of women's exclusion from the public realm or of the sexual division of labor in the family.

9   In Arendt, *Essays in Understanding*, 66–69.

10   In the late 1980s, feminist theorists began to reevaluate Arendt's reflection on the human condition with a view to recovering it for the feminist project. See, for instance, Elisabeth Young-Bruehl, *Hannah Arendt: For Love of the World* (New Haven, CT: Yale University Press, 1982).

11   See Perrine Simon-Nahum, "Hannah Arendt: Repères chronologiques," in *Le Magazine Littéraire*, no. 445 (September 2005): 36–38.

12   Hannah Arendt, *The Origins of Totalitarianism* (New York: Meridian Books, Inc., 1958).

13   Arendt scholars Elizabeth Young-Bruehl and Mary Dietz both argue that, despite the lack of direct references, even Arendt's later works were inspired by the Holocaust. Dietz proposes, for instance, that Arendt's innovative conception of the political in *The Human Condition* is offered as "a way back out of the abyss" for humankind after Auschwitz. See Mary Dietz, *Turning Operations: Feminism, Arendt, and Politics* (New York: Routledge, 2002), 188.

14   See Primo Levi, *The Drowned and the Saved*, trans. Raymond Rosenthal (New York: Vintage Books, 1988), and Zygmunt Bauman, *Modernity and the Holocaust* (Ithaca, NY: Cornell University Press, 2000).

15   Arendt, *Origins of Totalitarianism*, viii.

16   Until recently, Arendt's work was virtually banned from academic curricula in Israel, and Holocaust scholars were also reluctant to engage with her work. Wolin and Steinberg go so far as to claim that, having escaped Germany, Arendt remained loyal to and in fact became a proponent of the philosophical tradition that made the Holocaust possible. See Richard Wolin, *Heidegger's Children* (Princeton, NJ: Princeton University Press, 2001) and Jules Steinberg, *Hannah Arendt on the Holocaust: A Study of Suppression of Truth* (Lewiston, NY: The Edwin Mellen Press, 2000).

17   *Turning Operations*, Mary Dietz's account of Arendt's political theory in the context of feminism, for instance, ends with a chapter on the Holocaust, but the two agendas are not brought together. The author provides an insightful analysis of the Holocaust as a problem of historiography for Arendt (how to write about events that one does not wish to preserve), yet at the point when she turns to the impact of the Holocaust on Arendt's work, she seems to abandon the feminist inquiry that has guided her analysis up to that point.

18   Arendt uses the term "story" rather than "narrative," although "narrative" appears in the translation of Kristeva's book on Arendt, entitled *Hannah Arendt: Life is a Narrative*, trans. Frank Collins (Toronto: University of Toronto Press, 2001). The title of the French original was *Le génie féminin: La vie, la folie, les mots : Hannah Arendt, Melanie Klein, Colette*. I draw on Kristeva's reading of Arendt when I refer to Arendt's conception of life as a narrative.

19   Arendt, *The Human Condition*, 97.

20   Ibid., 175.

21 Hannah Arendt, *Men in Dark Times* (San Diego, CA: Harcourt Brace Jovanovich Publishers, 1968), 104.

22 Hannah Arendt, *Rahel Varnhagen: The Life of a Jewess*, trans. Richard and Clara Winston (Baltimore, MD: Johns Hopkins University Press, 1997).

23 Hannah Arendt, *The Life of the Mind* (New York: Harcourt Brace Jovanovich, 1978).

24 Arendt, *Rahel Varnhagen*, 4.

25 See Arendt, *The Origins of Totalitarianism*, chapter 3, "The Jews and Society," 54–88, and chapter 9, "The Decline of the Nation-State and the End of the Rights of Men," 269–302.

26 Arendt, *Rahel Varnhagen*, 97.

27 Ibid., 87.

28 Varnhagen achieved her goal relatively late in her life (in her forties) by marrying August Varnhagen, receiving baptism, and changing her name to Antonie Friedrike, the name that was to help her "become one human being among others."

29 Arendt, *Rahel Varnhagen*, 85.

30 Ibid., 258.

31 See, for instance, Seyla Benhabib, "Hannah Arendt and the Redemptive Power of the Narrative," in *Hannah Arendt: Critical Essays*, ed. Lewis P. Hinchman and Sandra K. Hinchman (Albany, NY: SUNY Press, 1994), 111–37.

32 Arendt, *Men in Dark Times*, 51.

33 Ibid., 41.

34 Ibid., 44.

35 In her unflattering portrayal of Jewish behavior during the Holocaust, Arendt is admiring of only one Jewish individual, and it is a woman: Zivia Lubetkin Zuckerman, one of the founding members of the Jewish Fighting Organization and a survivor of the Jewish Ghetto Uprising, whose testimony at the Eichmann trial "was completely free of sentimentality or self-indulgence, her facts well organized." See Hannah Arendt, *Eichmann in Jerusalem* (New York: Viking, 1963), 121.

36 Arendt, *The Human Condition*, 192.

37 Arendt, *Men in Dark Times*, 76.

38 Arendt, *The Life of the Mind*, 4.

39 Jacques Derrida, "Sarah Kofman (1934–1994)" in *The Work of Mourning* (Chicago: The University of Chicago Press, 2003), 165–88. Derrida borrows the neologism *autobiogriffure* from Kofman's book entitled *Autobiogriffure: Du Chat Murr d'Hoffmann* (Paris: Galilée, 1984).

40 Sarah Kofman, *Smothered Words*, trans. Madelaine Dobie (Evanston, IL: Northwestern University Press, 1998).

41 Robert Antelme *L'Espèce humaine* (Paris: Gallimard, 1947). Translated into English as *The Human Race*, trans. Jeffrey Haight and Anne Mahler (Chicago: Northwestern University Press, 2003).

42 See Maurice Blanchot, *The Writing of the Disaster*, trans. Ann Smock (Lincoln: University of Nebraska Press, 1995).

43 Kofman, *Selected Writings,* 250.

44 For Kofman's autobiographical fragments, see *Selected Writings,* 247–51.

45 Sarah Kofman, *Rue Ordener, Rue Labat,* trans. Ann Smock (Lincoln: University of Nebraska Press, 1996), 10.

46 In the autobiographical fragment entitled "Damned Food," Kofman writes, "Put in a real double bind, I could no longer swallow anything and vomited after each meal" (*Smothered Words,* 248). For an excellent discussion of this double bind, see Kelly Oliver, "Sarah Kofman's Queasy Stomach and the Riddle of the Paternal Law," in *Enigmas: Essays on Sarah Kofman,* ed. Penelope Deutscher and Kelly Oliver (Ithaca, NY: Cornell University Press, 1999), 174–88.

47 Kofman, *Rue Ordener, Rue Labat,* 3.

48 Kofman, *Smothered Words,* 9; emphasis mine.

49 Kofman, *Rue Ordener, Rue Labat,* 3.

50 In *Rue Ordener, Rue Labat,* Kofman recalls, in a telling detail, how, in the first years of the war, her father used to draw the outlines of his children's hands as signatures on letters to relatives (53). Throughout the war, Kofman kept drawing the outline of her hand; thus, her first act of "writing" consisted in substituting her own signature for that of her father.

51 Kofman, *Rue Ordener, Rue Labat,* 61.

52 Ibid., 85.

53 Ibid., 9.

54 See Sarah Kofman, "Rousseau's Phallocratic Ends," excerpt from *Le respect des femmes,* trans. Mara Dukats, *Hypatia* 3, no. 3 (Fall 1988): 123–36.

55 See Kofman, "The Economy of Respect: Kant and Respect for Women, in *Selected Writings,* 187–202.

56 See Tina Chanter, "Eating Words: Antigone as Kofman's Proper Name," in *Enigmas,* 189–202, and Oliver, in *Enigmas,* 174–88.

57 Kofman, *Smothered Words,* 7.

58 Ibid., 47.

59 As Ann Smocks summarizes in the introduction to *Rue Ordener, Rue Labat,* Kofman "liked to play the role of mocking girl whose laughter interrupts the philosopher at his desk, scatters his grave truths" (x). See also Jean-Luc Nancy, "Forward: Run, Sarah, Run!" in *Enigmas,* viii–xvi.

60 I would like to thank Myrna Goldenberg for suggesting this analogy.

61 Arendt, *Men in Dark Times,* 97. What draws Arendt to Isak Dinesen is her girlish laughter; hence Danish writer Karen Blixen's choice of the male pseudonym "Isak," the one who laughs. This laughter, comments Arendt, serves to "take care of several problems," such as the fact that it was unbecoming for a woman to be an author, "hence a public figure" (95).

62 Arendt, *Men in Dark Times,* ix.

63 Arendt, *The Human Condition,* 176. Arendt argues that this human potential of infinite beginning is grounded in natality, that is, in the actual appearance in the world of the new individuals who harbor the power of unforeseeably new action.

64 Arendt, *The Life of the Mind,* 32.

65 Arendt, *Origins of Totalitarianism*, 456.

66 Ibid., 441.

67 Kofman, *Smothered Words,* 39; emphasis mine.

68 For a commentary on Antelme, see Kofman, *Smothered Words,* 70–73. David Rousset's *L'Univers concentrationnaire* was translated into English as *A World Apart* (London: Secker and Warburg, 1951).

69 A notable exception is Arendt's essay "On Responsibility for Evil," in which she quotes several passages from testimonies by Jewish survivors and offers them as "rare moments of truth" against the grand lie of the post-Holocaust trials of the Nazi criminals. In *Crimes of War,* ed. Richard A. Falk et al. (New York: Random House, 1971), 500.

70 Maurice Blanchot, *The Infinite Conversation*, trans. Susan Hanson (Minneapolis: University of Minnesota Press, 1992).

71 Sarah Kofman, *Le Mépris des Juifs: Nietzsche, les Juifs, l'antisémitism* (Paris: Galilée, 1994). Citation from *Selected Writings,* 124.

72 Deutscher, "'Imperfect Discretion,'" 165.

3

Simone Weil

A French Jewish Intellectual Journey
in the 1930s and 1940s

ROCHELLE L. MILLEN

The year I took a graduate seminar with the noted Canadian professor George Grant, his subject was the writings of a Frenchwoman whose name was then new to me: Simone Weil (1909–1943). Weil's writings offered new perspectives on religion and spirituality and on social and political issues in a prose that was incisive and elegant, even in translation.

Aspects of Weil's thinking also shocked me. For the essays and jottings of this brilliant, if eccentric, woman, written during the years of Nazism, articulate a vehement anti-Judaism more characteristic of the language and theology of the early Church fathers and the Marcionites than of an assimilated French Jew with a prestigious graduate degree in philosophy from the École Normale Supériere. Of her militant left-wing political positions—her friendships with Simone Petrement, Simone de Beauvoir, Alain, and Raymond Aron and her often deep and immediate identification with those who suffered—none indicated the eventual development of the strong anti-Judaic elements scattered throughout her writings.

Here, I explore Weil's essays and comments on Judaism and use these writings to assess her identity as a French Jewish female intellectual during the rise of fascism, the Nazi occupation of France, and the genocidal destruction of European Jewry. Although Weil vehemently denies her

Jewishness and develops an extreme devotion to a Gnostic, Platonic formulation of Christianity, her self-hatred manifests a deep resonance with and connection to her Jewish roots. The notion of what constitutes Jewish identity is complex and the contortions of Weil's religious journey, entangled with the thinking of Nazism, increase that complexity. At the same time, Weil's often abstract excursus into mysticism, religion, and political philosophy emanate from a particular person, from an unusual mind and sensitive soul embedded in the body of a woman living in the male-dominated world of French, indeed European, intellectual life. As Adrienne Rich writes,

> Her life and thought will only become clear to us when we begin to ask what it meant to be a woman of her genius and disposition. Her stunning insights into domination and oppression, her self-derogation, her asceticism, her attempts at self-creation, her final self-destruction—all have to be examined in this light.[1]

Thus, in Weil, Jewishness, gender, and the Holocaust coalesce in an unusual and complicated manner.

Weil's writings reflect a stubborn, fierce independence of mind and heart. Perhaps this is one way to understand her practice of peeling away layers of herself, regarding them as false or defective, and calling attention to the inner, brightly burning flames of high abstraction, focused suffering, and pure spirituality. How else to understand Weil's belief that regarded both her Jewishness and her femaleness as defects? Such pejorative designations seem to me an internalization of societal norms. In regarding both "women" and "Jews" as Other, Weil's thinking reflected Nazi ideology. But Weil was foremost determined—always—to be pure subject. In another place and time, her self-abhorrence—the attempt to vilify her cultural and religious roots and to become a noncorporeal spirit—would not have mattered the way it did in the context of the Holocaust.

One might also inquire how it is that this self-hating Jew, who refused to be baptized but regarded herself as Catholic, dealt with the silence of the Church and of most of her fellow Christians during the months of Nazi preparation and collaboration in France for the eventual murder of French Jews. Should not the "love of affliction" and the "Jesus of the cross"—both of which she explores with deep feeling—have led to greater Christian compassion for Jewish victims of Nazi round-ups? She had come to Christianity out of deep philosophical conviction and spiritual compatibility and thus was no "ordinary" Christian. Having grown up without the anti-semitism embedded in Church teachings, and with her powerful emphasis upon compassion, her capacity for empathy with the victims of Nazism might be assumed to have been greater than that of the usual bystander. But this was not the case: Weil repudiates her Jewishness but does not question the "God of love" of Christianity, even in relation to the Holo-caust's many Jewish victims. It is ironic that the choices one truly has—to be ethical and to empathize with and try to diminish suffering—were not choices upon which Weil acted in relation to Jews. Rather, she desired to alter that which could not be altered: her gender and, in the context of Nazism, her Jewish identity.

Although she eschews both her Jewishness and her femaleness, Weil nonetheless is important in an examination of the broad theme of women and the Holocaust. Her relationship to women's issues is complex. Some characterize her as "maternal" in her ethics, even quoting Sara Ruddick in support. Ruddick understood "maternal thinking" as characterized by world preservation, protection, and repair. But in the words of Richard H. Bell, "Weil's views about chastity and her own body would have limited the range of her 'maternal' thinking," although "her moral instincts have the quality Ruddick calls 'holding.'"[2] While Weil emphasizes love, trust, reciprocity, and compassion in her ethical formulations, these qualities emanate from a complex conceptual matrix that clearly excludes a feminist perspective. It is this very ambiguity regarding Weil's sense of identity that brings her to our consideration in this volume. There is a gap between her professions of love, especially religious love, and the choice of actions that might demonstrate such love.

"THE THREE SONS OF NOAH"

Taken together, Weil's references to Judaism offer a consistent perspec-tive that denigrates Judaism, both theology and practice. She demonstrates this perspective when she writes on the Hebrew Bible, on the three sons of Noah, on Jewish and Christian spirituality, and on the love of affliction (clearly much more a Christian than a Jewish concept) as fundamental to a religious world view. The religious framework she works to articulate is one in which self-sacrifice is lauded and Jews are portrayed as materialistic and nonspiritual. The former concept signifies anti-feminism (i.e., females are supposed to suffer and to sacrifice for the benefit of the male), while the latter is a staple of anti-Judaism from the time of the early Church Fathers. How did Weil develop this viewpoint, and how was it affected by the anti-semitic propaganda of the 1930s and 1940s? Did she internalize the racism and sexism that categorized her as a subhuman, causing her to separate herself in order to maintain her dignity? Her upbringing in an assimilated home with little Jewish identification is one avenue of insight into the puzzle of Weil's consistently pejorative statements about historical Judaism during the years of Nazi rule. It was not until Weil was ten years old that she and her older brother, Andre, already a brilliant mathematics student, were told by their parents that they were Jewish.[3] Even given this biography, how does one respond to her criticisms and devaluations of Judaism?

Weil's essay "The Three Sons of Noah and the History of Mediterranean Civilization" (1950) offers insight into these questions. In several of her writings, she expresses negative views about the Hebrew Bible, but her remarks are usually incidental and not well-developed.[4] The essay on the sons of Noah, in contrast, is a direct explanation of Weil's rejection of the Hebrew Bible, while, at the same time, it constitutes a positive statement of her own beliefs. The essay offers her interpretation of the incident in Genesis chapter 9 in which Noah becomes drunk; when his son Ham mocks his drunken nakedness, Noah curses Ham's descendants, the Canaanites. In telling the story of Noah, Weil asserts, the Israelites added to and distorted the original text of the Hebrew Bible "out of hatred," when they ascribed "a fault to Ham and [made] a curse fall upon one of his sons named Canaan."[5] This interpretation on the part of the Hebrews or Israelites, she continues, "does not agree with the tradition." "The tradition" reflects her understanding of the history of biblical and Mediterranean civilization. At the same time, she sees the conquest of Canaan in the book of Joshua as the retrospective reason for the depiction of Noah's curse on the destiny of Ham and his descendants. "Give a dog a bad name," Weil goes on, "and you can hang him."[6]

"The Three Sons of Noah" contains three elements. It is historical, drawing upon Weil's immense knowledge of ancient history and literature; it is exegetical, purporting to interpret specific passages of the Hebrew Bible; and it is, on its most fundamental level, theological. Particularly in comparison to other commentators, this essay demonstrates Weil's rejection of Judaism as a workable theology and helps to show how her complex attitude toward her own Judaism informs her theological thinking and the tenets of her religious philosophy. Weil's desire to be genderless and to erase her Jewish roots during the years of Nazi hegemony seems to motivate her to disparage the Hebrew Bible and its traditions and undermines the possibility of straightforward textual elucidation. Her explication of biblical verses does not attempt to understand the verses within their original context, i.e., the ancient Near East, or in relation to the Hebrew Bible as a whole. Furthermore, her writing reflects no familiarity with the centuries-long literature of biblical commentary in the rabbinic tradition.

Various biblical critics share her view that this story can be seen as an etiology, a later formulation designed to explain why Israel was able to overtake the Canaanites.[7] The text also seems to be an adumbration of an earlier tale found among the Canaanites as well as in similar legends among the Greeks and others. But in coming to her conclusion, Weil does not examine the many possible interpretations of Noah's curse of Ham and the Canaanites. Did the act of Ham consist of seeing and deriding his father's nakedness, or castrating him, or raping him? The twentieth-century Italian Jewish biblical scholar Umberto Cassuto goes through the various options and their sources, insisting that "we must not read into the Pentateuchal narrative more than it actually states, taking the words at their face value."[8] Cassuto's conclusion is that the blatant viewing of Noah's nakedness constitutes a transgression of sexual morality according to the Israelites. This interpretation is reflected in the listing of forbidden relations in Leviticus 28, which begins by warning the Israelites to emulate neither the morality of Egypt nor that of Canaan. Some interpreters attribute the offense to Canaan, an explanation found in both ancient Jewish as well as modern Christian sources. It seems, however, that this is not a case of a son being punished for his father's offense. Rather, Ham is seen to represent the Canaanites, as they were known to the Hebrews, "and his actions merely symbolize the practices of the children of Canaan."[9] The extensive rabbinic commentary on this biblical passage, which spans hundreds of years, comes neither to a consensus nor to a conclusion. There is no way to know to what the allusions in these verses refer and in what sense, if any, the punishment meted out to Canaan might be justified.

Weil's positive reevaluation of Ham's lineage is based on the idea that the Phoenicians, the Egyptians, and the Pelagians[10] are descended from Ham, a claim borne out by both classical and contemporary biblical commentators[11] (although ethnologists disagree about the Philistines and the Hittites). In contrast to the general accuracy of her historical formulations, however, Weil's exegesis leaves much to be desired. On the one hand, she does cite various similarities between the biblical text and the myths of other traditions that could be illuminating.[12] As she notes, there is an interesting parallel between the planting of Noah's vineyard after he is saved from the waters of the flood and the Greek legend of Deucalion, the hero of the deluge, who is connected with the myth of Dionysus and beginnings of wine making. This parallel is also pointed out by Cassuto.

Weil continues to emphasize this theme of wine, implying that Abraham does homage to Melchisedec because the wine of Melchisedec indicates a unique spirituality, although the biblical text accords no special meaning to the wine. In contrast, the Babylonian Talmud, Nedarim 32b, gives a different reason for Abraham's public acknowledgment of Melchisedec when it identifies him as Shem, a son of Noah, thus linking Melchisedec to the Israelites, said to be Shem's descendants. Weil, however, may be alluding to the book of Hebrews in the Greek Bible, in which Jesus is viewed as a priest of the order of Melchisedec, a supersessionist interpretation of the significance of Jesus. That is, according to Christian theology, in offering Abraham bread and wine, Melchisedec foreshadows Jesus as Christ. Thus the intent of the Hebrew Bible is to explain the later flowering of the true religion, Christianity. Weil's implied supersessionist position helps to explain her inability to engage her Christianity as a tool of compassion for Europe's Jews.

A second example of Weil's inconsistent approach to biblical exegesis is found in the addendum to "The Three Sons of Noah." There, Weil claims as additional proof that Noah's drunken nakedness should be considered a revelation of the earlier pact or covenant that God made with Noah. If Weil accepts this part of the Hebrew Bible, even to the extent of considering Noah's sacrifice as an adumbration of that of Jesus, why is she unable to accept other covenants in the text, such as that of Abraham or Sinai? She offers no criteria, evaluation, or validation. But her underlying supersessionist perspective offers an explanation: her reading of the Hebrew Bible attempts to create a spiritual lineage leading to her unique view of Christianity. This lineage depends on biblical verses referring to Noah (Genesis 9:21), Melchisedec (Genesis 14:18), and Jesus indicating that each drank wine while wine was forbidden to the priests of Israel in the Temple. Weil compares the nakedness resulting from Noah's drunken stupor to that of Adam and Eve before the fall. Physical uncovering becomes spiritual purity, the stripping of "carnal and social thoughts."[13] To be naked in this world is to be "perfect," contends Weil, and only a few select persons merit such during their earthly existence, among them St. Francis and St. John of the Cross. The only remedy for sinful men and women is the wine of the altar, causing spiritual nakedness or mystical ecstasy. But note: spiritual nakedness can only be borne in drunkenness.

Weil, the genderless woman who seeks spiritual denuding and ultimate sacrifice, whose ethical principles express more compassion for the French Resistance than for Jews under Nazism, thus finds a basis for her theology in the Noah incident. Weil uses the paradigm of spiritual nakedness as the basis of the ultimate necessary condition upon which genuine religion and spirituality must be based. In this formulation, the historical aspect is of great importance; from one perspective, Weil's essay on Noah may be construed as an attempted proof of her statement that "a current of perfectly pure spirituality would have flowed across Antiquity from pre-historic Egypt to Christianity."[14] Her unusual interpretation of the Noah story indicates the influence of Gnostic commentators on the Hebrew Bible. They, like Weil, generally disparaged the Hebrew Bible and rejected its traditions.

Weil also may have found such deep meaning in the Noah story because, as she notes in the essay, "The Christian liturgy compares the ark of Noah with the cross."[15] This connection is especially prominent in the liturgy for Good Friday, Holy Saturday, and Palm Sunday. Weil's theology is obsessed with the cross and the Passion which took place on the cross: "And if the Gospel omitted all mention of Christ's resurrection, faith would be easier for me. The Cross by itself suffices me."[16] Thus, it may have been the liturgical comparison, as well as the historical elements involved, that led Weil to examine the biblical text of Noah and to arrive at her unusual interpretation. The sacrifice signified by the cross—sacrifice of self as a sign of God's intense and ultimate love—remained for Weil a well of spiritual meaning. Eventually, it led to her immolation of self through starvation—her way of emulating Jesus' suffering and affliction. The cross sufficed for her own salvation, yet Weil's understanding of its meaning prevented her from responding to the suffering of Jews.

Most importantly for the attempt to understand Weil's lack of response to suffering, Weil's explication of the Noah incident articulates and elucidates her theology. The theological points may be enumerated positively, through her doctrines and formulations, and negatively, in contrast with the Hebrew Bible. To summarize: first, Noah's drunkenness is compared

to an overabundance of wine, "which flows daily on the altar"; its consequence is not the physical drunkenness of Noah, but rather "nakedness of
spirit," a stripping away of "carnal and social thoughts."[17] As a corollary, true
compassion for humanity comes about only by "participation in the compassion of God."[18] By this I take Weil to mean that one must have a mystical
experience akin to Noah's, or her own, in order for the capacity for compassion to be realized. Both Noah and Jesus manifest the spiritual nakedness that is a precondition of true love of God. One must suffer deeply to
understand God's love; one must be stripped down to the barest framework
of human identity.

Second, Weil claims that the Egyptians knew "that it is only given to
man to see God in the sacrificial lamb."[19] Hence the idea of a God who creates by self-sacrifice and who mediates this notion to humanity through the
Passion of Jesus. But it seems insufficient to Weil that Christianity arrived
at a concept of God as the sacrificial lamb; it must also be that the earlier
descendants of Ham had the same notion. This connection is analogous to
Weil's statement in "The Pythagorean Doctrine": "It is marvelous, it is inex-
pressibly intoxicating, to think that it is love, and the desire of the Christ,
which caused the invention of demonstration to spring up in Greece."[20] This
ecstatic reading back into history serves to validate Weil's theology. And
again, as a corollary, "what the nations had found beneath the branches of
the marvelous tree of Ham's daughter-nation," that is, the Egyptians, was
the knowledge and love of a second divine person, a mediator whose suffering and incarnation united human nature with God. This mediator, according to Weil, appears in many traditions, becoming known in diverse ways.

This leads to Weil's third point, that Israel rejected the God of Noah's
mystical, private revelation. Rather, they accepted "a God who made his
presence known to the nation as a whole."[21] Certainly the biblical covenant
at Sinai is public, communal, and historical, in contrast with that of Abraham, which is private and individual. But, according to Weil, the Israelites
desired "power and prosperity." As she writes, "Israel rejected the supernatural revelation, for they did not want a God who spoke to the soul in secret,
but a God who made his [*sic*] presence known to the nation as a whole and
protected them in battle."[22] In all its years of Egyptian enslavement, Weil
complains, Israel remained impervious "to faith either in Osiris, in immor-
tality, in salvation, or in the identification of the soul with God through
charity." It is clear, in other words, that any social or communal aspect of
religion is unacceptable to Weil. The collective is anathema; the individual

spiritual experience remains definitive. Weil understood well that the politicization of religious truths into institutions weakens their discrete impact and meaning. Her concept of charity is thus a restricted one. Nonetheless, her startling but perhaps not unexpected conclusion regarding Israel is that "this refusal made possible the putting to death of Christ."

The fourth theological point is also negative. All that is truly spiritual in Christianity derives from its Egyptian, Greek, and other ancient roots. The negative elements in Christian thought evolve from "Hebrew prejudice,"[23] because fledgling Christianity was not sufficiently strong to detach itself from an abominable heritage, whose leaders were "enemies of the Hellenic tradition."[24] That Weil finds Judaism culpable for the separation of the religious and secular in the modern world due to the lingering "Hebrew prejudices" latent in Christianity is yet another manifestation of her anti-Judaism. It echoes much of nineteenth-century antisemitic ideology as found, for instance, in Karl Lueger, the Catholic press, Houston S. Chamberlain, and *The Protocols of the Elders of Zion*. The very basis of Judaic theology is that all life is holy and is to be sanctified by human beings, a principle which effectively eliminates any division into religious and secular, especially in biblical and early rabbinic texts. However, some Christian views of the body, with an emphasis on otherworldliness, imply much more directly the separation Weil criticizes. Intellectual history does make clear, however, that Jews were ardent supporters of the rise of liberal political philosophy and the increasing conceptual undergirding of the separation of church and state. The influence of these ideas was realized in granting citizenship to French male Jews in 1791.

For Weil, Noah's revelation is a paradigm of the religious experience because Noah's physical nakedness, according to Weil, symbolizes a deeper spiritual nakedness in the face of necessity. The realm of necessity, in all its "wretchedness, distress . . . poverty . . . labour . . . cruelty . . . disease" is what other philosophers term "nature" or "social systems" or "human weakness." Yet for Weil "relentless necessity," characterized by all of the above, "constitutes divine love."[25] Necessity is the screen of the material and human worlds through which the individual must pass in order to "cease to be."[26] Noah's revelation is the contemplation of the mysterious unity of necessity and the goodness of God: "The genuine religious life is the contemplation of this unknown unity," Weil writes.[27] Noah's revelation is also a union with God, a surrendering of his identity as a creature of necessity, the acceptance of powerlessness. From this description, as well as from Weil's other writings, one may summarize the central components of her theology. First, since the realm of necessity is completely indifferent to the good, there is no teleological purpose at work in the universe; there is no divine providence, either individual or general. Second, the genuine religious life consists of the contemplation of the mysterious unity of a good God and a world of necessity, and is, strictly speaking, singular and individual. While its attainment is best facilitated in a society structured to encourage its development, there is no religious community as such; the collectivity is a beast. And third, the content of the authentic religious life is the diminishment of oneself as a personality. As God created by self-denial,[28] human beings strive for and reach godly holiness and union with the supernatural by sacrificing the self. An individual becomes, in a sense, a non-person, undoing the work of creation. This is termed, in some of Weil's writings, "decreation." The notion of erasing the self, the center of agency and free will, resonates with certain traditional religious concepts of the feminine, usually identified with submission.

In sharp contrast is the theology of the Hebrew Bible, which must be considered together with rabbinic thought as embodied in the Talmud and midrashic texts. Weil chooses to neglect these, even as she ignores much of the biblical text itself. The broad sweep of her writings seem to revolve exclusively around the problem of theodicy. The Hebrew Bible, in contrast, affirms teleology intrinsic to the universe and divine providence as integral to human history, both individual and historical. The formulations of this providence and how it operates in the world are theological issues with a variety of resolutions, none of them authoritative. Certainly one may see the Bible as a record of divine providence, both general and individual, but there is no one theory or philosophy or analysis agreed to untangle the theological knots in an orderly and unproblematic fashion.[29] Rather, ambiguity and complexity characterize the diverse attempts to deal with theodicy.

In addition, although there is a tradition of mysticism in Judaism (which in some respects is similar to Weil's, a comparison beyond the scope of this discussion), the genuine religious life, according to mainstream biblical and rabbinic thinking, is one in which a person recognizes both heteronomous and autonomous moral behavior. These govern not only the individual's relationship with God, but also his or her relationship with other persons. Thus, in Judaism, all civil and criminal codes are also religious codes. One becomes holy not by denying oneself, but by recreating in oneself, through study and action, the highest possible duplication of God. This *imitatio Dei* is also present in Weil, but her version assumes decreation, erasing of self, as the very essence of godliness and therefore of human spirituality. Weil's emphasis on Christian mysticism leads to annihilation and affliction of the self as essential components in reaching religious ecstasy and self-realization, aspects of all mystical thinking. Yet to be human is to live within the realm of necessity; to be godly is to sanctify the necessary through internalization and external following of God's ways. In Judaism, there is speculation on and contemplation about the suffering of the innocent and the seemingly infinite distance between the goodness of God and the evils (or necessities) of this world. But these do not constitute the sole religious experience or even a major part of one's religious life. Weil, however, incorporates deeply embedded interpretations of Christian theology, emphasizing the holiness of a meta-life, decreation, and focus upon the individual rather than a historical religious community.

All religious life, however, even that which emphasizes individual salvation, contains an intrinsic dialectical tension between the individual and the religious community as well as between one's own community and those outside it. A person's religious life is singular from one perspective. But it is constantly opposed to, part of, and enriched by the significance of an historical collective, the covenantal community (in Judaism), which in turn is part of the universal and diverse community of all human beings. The Catholic Church, whose notion of historical community is very different from that of Judaism, nonetheless also maintains a deep sense of "tradition," the "tradition" of the historical Church. But despite Weil's allegiance to significant aspects of Catholicism, her individualism is so radical as to separate her from this central premise, a notion she ascribes to its Judaic roots.

The short, intensely provocative essay "The Three Sons of Noah" is paradigmatic of Simone Weil's thought. According to Weil, Noah, Melchisedec, and Christ are threads of spirituality in a historical trajectory otherwise characterized by materialism, nationalism, and established social norms. Weil's exegesis attempts to recast the biblical text in order to attain a reading in accord with her presuppositions. Her central underlying assumption is that the unique spiritual heritage of Ham lit up, from time to time, the darkness of the millennia, until it was almost obliterated in the Albigensian Crusade of the thirteenth century. In this crusade, a twenty-year (1209–1229) military campaign in Languedoc initiated by the Church to eliminate what it called the Cathar heresy, Christians massacred Christians for holding what Weil considers the "correct" belief. That which the Church considered heretical is for Weil the true spiritual legacy of Ham. Weil's radical theology, her rejection of Judaism as carnal, non-spiritual, and collective, is rooted in an unusual and contorted reading of early Mediterranean history and selected biblical texts. Indeed, the characterization of Judaism as carnal parallels not only antisemitic literature (e.g., Chrysostom, Luther, Wagner), but also anti-female statements found in various Catholic writings.[30] The denial of femaleness is inextricably bound up with Weil's theology: she worships the figure of Jesus and does not mention Mary; she adores the sacrifice of Jesus, failing to see in that adoration the typical female sacrifice of her own autonomy. As God allowed the murder of Jesus out of love for his declared son, she wishes to un-create herself as a sign of her love of God. Weil's rejection not only of Judaism but also of the Judaic roots of Christianity strongly emphasizes her use of Greek interpretations of Christian doctrine. Perhaps Weil's rejection of Judaism and the Hebrew Bible is founded on her understanding of what she saw as an unbridgeable gap. And perhaps her interpretations of Christianity are a daring, ecstatic, and distorted vision of how that gap might be crossed.

One might understand Weil's negative attitudes toward Judaism in a narrow intellectual sense. Yet the vituperative language in which they are articulated indicates the depth, intensity, ambivalence, even anger that clothe her seemingly rational analyses. It is not that the Hebrews erred in their version of the Noah story, but that they did so "out of hatred."[31] The Hebrew tale stands accused of being a deliberate falsehood motivated by self-interest and base materialism. At the conclusion of the Noah essay, Weil writes,

> Today . . . the sons of Japheth and of Shem make the most noise. The former are powerful and the latter persecuted. Though separated by a terrible hatred, they are brothers, and there is a resemblance between them. They are alike in their refusal of nakedness, in their need for clothing made of flesh and warm with the collective warmth of numbers, clothing to protect the evil each one bears within him from the light. Such clothing renders God harmless, it makes it equally possible to deny or acknowledge him . . . it makes it possible to pronounce his name without the soul being transformed by its supernatural power.[32]

Here, Weil laments the "evil" within Shem, the ancestor of Judaism, an evil deriving from Judaism's communal, collective aspects, which keep it warm. Instead, were the descendants of Shem to truly honor God, they would be painfully cold, exposed to the elements, so that the "God of love" could demonstrate this love through true affliction. This quotation articulates an ambiguity in Weil. It is anti-Jewish, much in the way John 8:44 is ("your father is the devil"); at the same time, it clearly expresses ideas of Christian mysticism, especially the medieval mystics. It is difficult to ascertain the extent to which Weil's concepts of religious evil and spiritual purity derive primarily from her own speculations rather than from the influences on her of specific spiritual mentors. Certainly the mysticism she describes is widespread in Christian thinking, and its connection to the Passion story intimate. Jesus became spiritually naked by agreeing to submit himself to Roman punishment; his maleness offers a possible explanation for Weil's denial of her femaleness in a way similar to the Catholic Church's persistent denial of ordination for women. In that light, Weil's conflicts with her femaleness and Jewishness are more understandable: Jesus (in her view) was the ultimate, authentic Christian, and of course, he was male. His spirituality, male though it was, becomes for Weil a paragon of practical ethics, leading to her absence of concern for Jews in Europe.

OTHER WRITINGS

Weil's implacable stance against Judaism is manifested as well in several other writings. She does not recognize, even superficially, the length, breadth, and depth of Judaism and seems not to have known of Kabbalah. Judaism, as she describes it, is incompatible with her conception of an authentic, mystical, centered religion. Moses knew and had refused the wisdom of Egypt "because he conceived religion as a simple instrument of national greatness."[33] Thus, Judaism became associated with particularism, power, and violence. The human sacrifices made to Baal, the wars of the Greeks and other ancient peoples: none is as evil, carnal, violent, conniving, and manipulative as the Hebrews. Weil's indictment is total. There is not even a minor acknowledgment that the very moral and ethical standards by which Weil judges the Hebrews derive from the text she despises, the Hebrew Bible. Indeed, here is an anti-female woman worshipping the love that led to the affliction and murder of Jesus, the zenith of spirituality and maleness. Since that love is, for Weil, the ultimate and supreme value, continued existence of Jews in the world would be of little consequence. If the death of Jesus gave meaning to the world, perhaps the death of Jews— even so many—would anchor and corroborate the eternal and ultimate meaning of humanness. Weil's supersessionism, grounded in an apocalyptic perspective, is thus connected to the Holocaust. Weil's anti-female, anti-Judaism posture and the Holocaust come together in a contorted, complex tangle. These attitudes, both overt and covert, are encapsulated in four writings from different periods of Weil's life.

First is Weil's response to the August 1940 legislation that barred all Jews from teaching. In October of that year, when the *Statut des Juifs* defined a Jew as anyone with three Jewish grandparents, she sent a letter to the secretary of state for public education, Jerome Carcopino, arguing that she was not a Jew.[34] Two of her grandparents, she contended, had been freethinkers. Moreover, she asserted that she had no link with the people who resided in Palestine in ancient times. Heredity, she argued, had no connection with religion, and she acknowledged no religious doctrines or beliefs. Some of the arguments expressed to Carcopino are echoed in an October 1941 letter to Xavier Vallat, Vichy's antisemitic minister of Jewish affairs. "I do not consider myself a Jew," she writes, having "never entered a synagogue" nor followed any Jewish practices. "I regard the Statute on Jews as generally absurd and unjust."[35] Notably absent from this epistle is any expression of compassion for those who are Jews. One might say this statement articulates an anti-compassion directed solely to her brethren. Weil's statement, as a self-identified Christian, expresses the anomaly of the Gospel of John, which contains the command to love, yet espouses hatred toward Jews.

Then, in New York in 1943, Weil advises her brother to have his daughter Sylvie baptized. In her letter, she lists varying religions, but only Judaism is called "fanatical." Why? Does this description indicate a view of Jews as the appropriate victims of the Church, a negative connection to those already riding the trains to Drancy? With a sense of desperation, Weil desires to protect one for whom she cares and has affection.

Another example is her writing for a rightist Free French group that in postwar France there should not be too many Jews in educational or civil positions, Jewish immigration should be halted, and non-French Jews should be expelled. These suggestions echo the persistent undercurrent of antisemitism from the nineteenth century, the Third Republic, and the Dreyfus Affair. Some of Weil's phrases even recall Richard Wagner's

"Jewry in Music," in which Jewishness is a disease, a bacillus, a contagion,[36] a set of terms and a concept that became a staple in nineteenth-century antisemitic literature and that was used extensively in Nazi propaganda. Jews are, according to Weil, a "handful of uprooted individuals" and "have been responsible for the uprooting of the whole terrestrial globe. The part they played in Christianity turned Christendom into something uprooted with respect to its own past . . . Jews are the poison of uprooting personified."[37] Weil's anti-Judaism, her wish that the world be free of Jews, is intertwined with the anti-female woman espousing an ideology dear to Nazism, which itself saw the female only in terms of her sexual productivity. The Hebrews and Moses are blamed for a lack of spirituality and a nationalistic attachment to the land of Israel. Yet Weil was a passionate French patriot and would write from New York, in one of her last letters, "because for me the separation is from a whole country and a country which contains nearly everything I love."[38] She understood her own French patriotism but, to her, Jewish nationalism was anathema.

Another letter, composed during Weil's fairly brief stay in New York, constitutes the final example; it also names Moses. Writing to a prominent philosopher in France, Weil restates her view that the ancient thought of China, India, Egypt, and Greece share a common thread of truth that finds its ultimate and final expression in the truths, absolute and universal, of Christianity. Then she states, "As to the Jews, I think Moses knew the wisdom and refused it because . . . he conceived religion as a mere instrument of national grandeur." Then Weil lists several books of the Hebrew Bible that she considers highly spiritual and therefore non-Jewish in origin (e.g., Job, Daniel, Tobit, Song of Songs), and concludes with "Almost all the rest of the Old Testament is a tissue of horrors."[39]

CONCLUSION

How is Simone Weil's aversion to Judaism to be understood? Weil lobbied for the oppressed, fighting in the Spanish Civil War and working as laborer in the French countryside. Her social and political tracts are rich in insights about labor, the impact of technology, the needs of simple folk. Yet she ignores the many verses in the Hebrew Bible that accord deep respect both to labor and the laborer and that emphasize social justice, the ethical core of which is the holiness of the individual. She helped the Free French and supported the Spanish Civil War by traveling there to fight. But she did not write about the Jewish victims of Nazism or lament their fate, although she surely knew of their persecution.

It is inadequate to claim Weil's anti-Judaism as that of a self-hating Jew. Her fierce independence and drive for autonomy—especially intellectual autonomy—remain significant. Perhaps Weil wished to suffer on her *own* terms, not as a consequence of artificial categories created by pseudo-racial theories; affliction, after all, is a central concept in her theology. Thus she could disassociate herself from "them," the Jews. Weil's conception of Christianity viewed Jews as evil and as a threat to the pure spirituality she espoused; Judaism was carnal and materialistic. At the same time, her knowledge of Jewish traditions was superficial. Weil ostensibly did not realize, as one Catholic theologian has stated, that the "Hebrew Bible is not . . . a long Book of Joshua" and that "the ancient Hebrews . . . were not the ancient Romans."[40] In an otherwise sophisticated thinker whose writings are permeated by a demand for compassion and a deep sense of justice, her limited reading of Judaism is both surprising and painful. Indeed, her philosophy of compassion, derived from a Gnostic Platonism, is one that can lead toward genocide, much as, in European Christianity, it did. Weil denounces Christianity's role in the Crusades and the Inquisition, but is impervious to the continued violence in Nazi Europe done to those targeted by European culture, a culture defined by its deep roots in Christianity. She silently assents to the destruction of those whose ideas and practices she understood as working against the stripped and naked Christian spirituality she espoused.

I do not wish to reduce religious experience to psychological need or personality structure. How these play out in individual lives is subject to many influences, both of nature and nurture. The concatenation of circumstances that led Weil to embrace an extremist Christian mysticism and vilify Judaism has puzzled many. Can one say that her identity search undermined her considerable intellectual gifts? That is too reductionist. We are all swayed by subjective and unconscious motivations. Weil's thinking must be examined on its own merits, whatever puzzling aspects remain unresolved.

Thinkers such as Albert Camus, Armaud Lundi, Martin Buber, Jean Améry, and Emmanuel Levinas—philosophers and theologians both Jewish and not—have praised Weil's insights into politics, philosophy, and speculative theology but lamented her harsh assessments of Judaism. Weil deliberately starved herself to death in England, refusing to consume more calories than the Nazis permitted captured members of the French Resistance. Was this manifestation of a kind of anorexia a search for spiritual purity or for control or for realization of decreation? Although she died prior to the end of World War II, Weil's critique of Judaism constitutes a kind of historical deterioration, a lack of sustained moral and intellectual judgment rooted in historical awareness. Weil mourned the Cathars, or Albigensians, but could not grieve for the Jews of Europe; she was not concerned with the rations of Jews in ghettos or camps. Jean Améry, himself a survivor who, like Weil, tried to evade his Jewish identity and eventually committed suicide in 1978, makes an astute observation. He writes, regarding Weil, "She lost from her sight all that's really beautiful, good, and just only because it can never be perfect."[41] This insight fits with Weil's voluntary starvation and attraction to suffering and with her repeated resistance to baptism. Weil writes brilliantly about the Catholic Church in whose theology she was deeply enmeshed, but the Church, too, was insufficiently perfect for her ultimate religious commitment. David Tracy calls it Weil's search for "the Impossible."[42] She remained outside, both as a Jew, as a Christian, and as a woman. Outside is the place—emotionally—where she found the greatest meaning and the deepest comfort. Weil resisted both physical and spiritual nourishment, thus demonstrating again the denial of femaleness. Weil clung to separateness, loneliness, and the literal emptiness of persistent hunger, not life, nourishment, and nurturing.[43]

Using a psychological profile in order to understand an intellectual position is fraught with danger. On another level, however, to conjecture causality or explanation is not to devalue the insights formulated as their result. Robert Coles's study of Weil, attempting to deal with Weil's utter turning from Judaism, notes the possible reductionism implicit in searching out causes of personality traits and intellectual patterns of thinking. Yet he persists, even including in his work an interview with Anna Freud about Weil. He says: "Simone Weil pays no attention to those Jews who followed Jesus, the disciples and authors of the Gospels. Risking psychological reductionism, one wonders at times whether a few ancient fishermen didn't present a challenge to her—sibling rivalry of sorts, triggering old competition and self-hate."[44] Anna Freud reminds one to take historical context into account. Weil could not have avoided dealing in some way with "the Jewish question," which gained a certain legitimacy once Hitler came to power. Freud declares, "I suspect that had Weil lived [after Hitler's defeat] she might have found other matters to preoccupy her than this one of her Jewishness, or she would have altered the way she thought about that part of herself. I hope so!"[45]

Professor George Grant wrote a response to Coles's chapter on the Jewishness of Weil. Titled "In Defence of Simone Weil," it refers to Weil as a "gnostic saint" who appropriated the claims of Marcion regarding God and the Hebrew Bible. As he notes, Catholic thinkers have indicted Weil for her criticisms of the Hebrew Bible, recognizing that her views do not align with Western Christianity, but rather with that which has been rejected by official Western Christianity. Coles, Grant claims, might be obligated to protect and guard Judaism. If Coles is a Jew, he writes, "he obviously had the duty to defend Judaism."[46] (Coles was raised Episcopalian, although his father was half-Jewish). Or, as Professor Grant said to me, "But you know, Simone Weil is right." His words showed me that Weil's anti-Judaism, no matter its source, remains justified among some Christian thinkers.

For Grant, a Christian Platonist like Weil—the vertigo of spirituality she espouses; the ecstatic understandings of the Incarnation, the Cross, the Trinity, the figure of the suffering Jesus; the notion of Christian Truth traversing India, Greece, China, and Egypt before rooting itself in a first century Jew and his followers—these sufficiently filled his soul so that he, like Weil, could accept, intellectually and emotionally, the invective and canards she used to describe her people. Simone Weil's spiritual hunger led her on a most unusual journey, one accompanied by a decision not to satiate, or even nourish, the physical hunger of her body. In a sense, Weil wanted to be—and to an extent became—pure spirit, a Platonic ideal, a lover of suffering; in her intended purity, she saw herself as neither Jewish nor female. For a Jew to perish from starvation in 1943 was, alas, a most common occurrence. It happened in France and Poland and Holland and the Ukraine. But for it to be the chosen fate of an assimilated Jewish woman whose family was alive and, until then, had mostly been able to protect her from extreme actions makes Simone Weil's journey an unusual and lamentable Holocaust tale.

NOTES

1   See Thomas R. Nevin, *Simone Weil: Portrait of a Self-Exiled Jew* (Chapel Hill: University of North Carolina Press, 1991), 241.

2   Richard H. Bell, *Simone Weil: The Way of Justice and Compassion* (New York: Rowman and Littlefield, 1998), 88–89.

3   Nevin, *Simone Weil,* 245.

4   Simone Weil, "The Three Sons of Noah," in *Waiting on God,* trans. Emma Crau-
     furd (London: Fontana, 1974), 177.

5   Weil, "The Three Sons of Noah," 177.

6   Ibid.

7   This question is carefully analyzed in U. Cassuto, *A Commentary on the Book of
     Genesis, Part Two: From Noah to Abraham,* trans. Israel Abrahams (Jerusalem:
     Magnes Press, Hebrew University, 1964), 149–62.

8   Cassuto, *Commentary on Book of Genesis,*152.

9   Ibid., 154.

10   It is interesting that the Pelagians of the fourth century stoutly defended rabbinic
     interpretations of the first three chapters of Genesis, arguing that human nature
     was basically good and human beings had free choice. Augustine, however, argued
     for a negative view of human nature and his formulation triumphed in the Chris-
     tianity of the Roman Empire and ever after in Christian-dominated cultures. See
     Elaine Pagels, *Adam, Eve, and the Serpent* (New York: Vintage, 1989), esp. chapter
     V.

11   See Genesis 10:6; Ramban (Nachmanides), *Commentary on the Torah, Genesis,*
     trans. Charles Ber Chavel (New York: Shilo Publishing House, 1971), 148–49; Cas-
     suto, *Commentary on Book of Genesis,* 206, 209, 212. Also, "Semites" in *Encyclope-
     dia Judaica* 14: 1148 (Jerusalem: Keter Publishing, 1972).

12   For instance, Deucalion, "The Noah of Greek Mythology," is cited on page 179 of
     "The Three Sons of Noah." Cf. Cassuto's discussion of Deucalion and the Amphic-
     tyon Council of Delphi in Cassuto, *Commentary on Book of Genesis,* 160, 172, 178.

13   The verse Weil refers to is found in Genesis 14:18. She writes about it in "The Three
     Sons of Noah," 179. Cf. Simone Weil, *Letter to a Priest* (London: Routledge &
     Kegan Paul, 1953), 108. My thanks to Barbara Kaiser for pointing out the reference
     to Melchisedec in Psalm 110.

14   Simone Weil, "The Pythagorean Doctrine," in *Intimations of Christianity Among
     the Ancient Greeks,* trans. Elizabeth Chase Geissbuhler (Boston, MA: Beacon
     Press, 1959), 152.

15   Weil, "The Three Sons of Noah," 179.

16   Weil, *Letter to a Priest.*

17   Weil, "The Three Sons of Noah," 179–80.

18   Ibid., 182.

19   Ibid.

20   Weil, "The Pythagorean Doctrine," 163. Cf. "The Pythagorean Doctrine," 183f, in
     which Weil writes of the Trinity in Greek thought.

21   Weil, "The Three Sons of Noah," 185.

22   Ibid., 185.

23   Ibid., 186.

24   Ibid., 187.

25   Simone Weil, "Decreation," in *Gravity and Grace,* trans. Emma Craufurd (Lon-
     don: Routledge & Kegan Paul, 1972), 28. See also pages 29, 30, 33, 34.

26 Ibid., 28.

27 Weil, "Is There a Marxist Doctrine?" in *Oppression and Liberty,* trans. Arthur Wills and John Petrie (Amherst: University of Massachusetts Press, 1973), 174.

28 Weil writes, "On God's part creation is not an act of self-expansion, but of restraint and renunciation." Weil, *Waiting on God,* 102.

29 For example, see Zachary Braiterman *(God) After Auschwitz* (Princeton, NJ: Princeton University Press, 1998).

30 See Elizabeth Clark and Herbert Richardson, eds., *Women and Religion: A Feminist Sourcebook of Christian Thought* (New York: HarperCollins, 1977).

31 See Clark and Richardson, *Women and Religion,* 3.

32 Weil, "The Three Sons of Noah," 188.

33 Simone Weil, *Seventy Letters,* trans. Richard Rees (London: Oxford University Press, 1968), 160.

34 Some say this letter was never sent. See Nevins, *Simone Weil,* 28.

35 Quoted in Nevins, *Simone Weil,* 241.

36 See Richard Wagner, "Jewry in Music," in Paul Mendes-Flohr and Jehuda Reinharz, *The Jew in Modern World: A Documentary History.* 2nd ed. (New York: Oxford University Press, 1995), 327–30.

37 Simone Weil, *Notebooks,* trans. Arthur Wills (London: Routledge and Kegan Paul, 1971), 576–77.

38 Letter, September 10, 1942, quoted in J. M. Perrin and G. Thibon, *Simone Weil as We Knew Her* (New York: Routledge, 2003), 125.

39 Quoted in Nevins, *Simone Weil,* 247–48.

40 David Tracy, "Simone Weil: The Impossible," in *The Christian Platonism of Simone Weil,* ed. E. Jane Doering and Eric O. Springsted (Notre Dame, IN: University of Notre Dame, 2004), 235.

41 Quoted in Nevins, *Simone Weil,* 257n.91.

42 Tracy analyzes Weil as a Christian Platonist, one who brings the Greek category of tragedy to her understanding of Christian doctrine. He calls her Christology "odd" (240).

43 Francis du Plessix Gray, *Simone Weil* (New York: Viking/Penguin, 2001).

44 Robert Coles, *Simone Weil: A Modern Pilgrimage.* Radcliffe Biography Series (Reading, MA: Addison-Wesley Publishing, 1989), 61.

45 Quoted in Coles, *Simone Weil,* 57.

46 George Grant, "In Defence of Simone Weil," *Idler* 15 (January-February 1988), 36–40.

4

Patriarchy, Objectification, and Violence against Women in *Schindler's List* and *Angry Harvest*

AMY H. SHAPIRO

It is not uncommon for Americans to look to film as a way to understand and imagine historical events. Witness such films as *The Deer Hunter*; *Born on the Fourth of July*; *Good Morning, Vietnam*; *Saving Private Ryan*; and *Gone with the Wind*. Not only is film a common medium for historical reenactment and the representation of moral conflict, it is often used to help students at the secondary and college levels to engage issues and contextualize historical fact. Many of my students have watched *Hotel Rwanda* in high school classes, for instance. Whether educators and scholars like it or not, film is a source of knowledge for many Americans. What might specific films reveal about Americans' perceptions of the Holocaust? What might the work that has been done in feminist theory and film tell us about gender perceptions and the Holocaust?[1] How are understandings of the Holocaust constructed for unsuspecting audiences?[2]

Film as an art form allows us a unique means of entry into the investigation of Holocaust-related issues, and individual films offer general and specific perceptions of these issues. Film may also provide us with a glimpse into the cultural assumptions at work in an artist's vision. Though I will not directly address the artistic dimensions of film in this chapter, it is important to consider the influence of film as both art and commodity. As I show in this chapter, the way specific films render interpretations and represent identities can be very revealing.

Perhaps the most widely used and known Holocaust film is Stephen Spielberg's *Schindler's List*, an American film. Though most Holocaust scholars[3] view *Schindler's List* without much concern (after all, it is "just a Hollywood film"), its use in high school and college classrooms and its significance in the American film landscape make it a touchstone for both introductory and advanced study of the Holocaust. Additionally, many people now view *Schindler's List* as the definitive film/story of the Holocaust. Having viewed the film, many suppose they have attained a comprehensive understanding of the Holocaust and its significance in history, a misperception that should be of some concern to historians and Holocaust scholars.

Some may dismiss my complaints by saying that *Schindler's List* is just a film, one of many such films Americans use as sources of knowledge without questioning the meaning or the treatment of facts. Precisely this sort of film, however, is ultimately contrary to what many in Holocaust Studies are trying to achieve.[4] The danger of *Schindler's List* is that it feeds the public a framework that disposes of questions and disrupts the creation of new questions; such a film invites viewers to conclude falsely that they have acquired all the knowledge needed to understand the events and circumstances of the Holocaust. The film reinforces gender stereotypes and the objectification of women for its own purposes (rather than as an examination of Nazi attitudes, as it purports). It asks viewers not to question the links between the Nazis' murderous actions and gender discrimination; rather, viewers are asked to accept gender inequality as a given. My intention is not to blast *Schindler's List*; it is to show how the film's objectification of women helps us to recognize a failure in our understanding of gender in relationship to the Holocaust. Viewing the film from a feminist perspective, we can see that the film is anti-feminist in its approach to the Holocaust.

Schindler's List was released in December of 1993. Not since the 1961 *Judgment at Nuremberg* and, before that, the 1959 *Diary of Anne Frank*, had a film on the Holocaust received such attention and importance in the United States. Though numerous Hollywood-made Holocaust-related films preceded it (for instance, Costa Gravas's 1989 film *The Music Box* and the 1978 television docudrama *Holocaust*), many of the best (more complex) films on the Holocaust have been foreign and little known. For example, consider the brutal and elaborate but little seen Russian film, *Come and See*, which tells the story of the Nazis in the Soviet territories from a wandering adolescent's perspective.[5]

For those few who have not seen *Schindler's List*, the film, based on the book *Schindler's List* by Thomas Keneally, tells the story of Oskar Schindler, a German industrialist, who used his position and personality to acquire wealth from German government contracts during the war. [6] Eventually, he learns of the fate of the Jews and first rescues them by employing them in increasing numbers in his factory. Eventually, he compiles a list of over 1,000 names of Jews and saves them by moving them to a new factory in Czechoslovakia, where they produce poor grade products for the Nazi war effort.

WOMEN AND *SCHINDLER'S LIST*

A number of scenes in *Schindler's List* demonstrate a particularly problematic and unforgivable objectification of women that reveals a profound flaw in the way the film approaches the Holocaust. These scenes simultaneously romanticize and sexualize the women in the film, using familiar constructs to engage viewers. In various scenes throughout the film, we see nude women—both Schindler's and S.S. Officer Goeth's lovers are naked before the camera. At least twice we encounter Goeth's lover, breasts and body exposed, juxtaposed against Goeth's morning shooting of Jews in Plaszow. Though this scene is meant to convey a confusion or contortion of sexuality and cruelty in Goeth's character, the frontal nudity of his anonymous lover is superfluous to the viewers' comprehension. It seems to be meant as "eye candy" for the (male) viewer.

Even more distressing and problematic is the scene in which Goeth seeks out Helen Hirsch, his personal Jewish slave, in his cellar, and beneath her wet slip her nipples and breasts are revealed to the camera. Though her flimsy clothing is understandable in light of her status and the context, the focus of the camera causes the viewer to see Helen Hirsch not only in terms of Goeth's desire but also in terms of our own. She is exposed to us in her near nakedness and, together with the other scenes with Schindler's and Goeth's mistresses, their visible shapeliness, breasts, and beauty invite us to see these women as objects of our own filmgoers' gaze. Why else are they visible to us? Why must we see them naked and exposed? Skimpy clothes and beautiful women form a construction in film history that cannot be escaped by the claim that it is only meant in this particular film to show us Goeth's desire or Helen Hirsch's fragility and precarious circumstances. (Are we to detect some desire in her? Are her nipples erect? Why the wet slip?) As Laura Mulvey states, "Traditionally, the woman displayed has functioned on two levels: as erotic object for the characters within the screen story, and as erotic object for the spectator within the auditorium, with a shifting tension between the looks on either side of the screen."[7]

These scenes raise some interesting questions about the success of the film. Could it have been successful without those scenes? Could it have even been conceived without them? The answer is most likely "no" to both questions. Judging from the use of frontal female nudity in an exceptionally large number of Hollywood films from the 1990s forward, the assumed expectations of the viewing audience and the orientation of American filmmakers seem almost to require these visual renderings. Given that Spielberg chose a subject for his film that many critics believed would turn people away and that he was perceived to have taken a huge risk (though this is questionable in light of film and gender issues), one might imagine he could have risked a different film language as well.

Initially, the scenes themselves may appear innocuous in relationship to the bigger picture (and larger issues) of the film. But the scenes actually reflect a deeper problem, and they should lead one to rethink both the film itself and, through examination of the intersection of American cinema and knowledge of the Holocaust, what Schindler is meant to become for its viewers. *Schindler's List* provides us with a heartbreaking insight into the nature of human violence against the Other as a result of objectification and dehumanization. Yet this insight is revealed not in terms of what the film intends, i.e., the experience of the Jews, but in terms of the female Other.

OBJECTIFICATION OF THE OTHER

Objectification is a useful framework for understanding the role of perpetrators in the Holocaust on many levels. Feminist scholarship recognizes the complexity of objectification and the way it can be used both to dehumanize the female Other and to configure as the feminine Other everyone from children to foreigners to male athletes ("don't be a girl").[8] Understanding the feminine Other also helps us to recognize the feminization of the Other that occurs in the objectification of individuals on the basis of race or class.[9] Holocaust scholars use this insight to understand the use of objectification to dehumanize the Jewish Other.[10] Of course, when one speaks of the "Jewish Other," the reference already entails the othering of the female, since what is assumed to be represented is the Jewish male whom the Nazis feminized through victimization. This feminization initially took the form of removing all avenues to a livelihood, positioning Jewish males as women to be viewed as useless, dependent, weak, and powerless.

It is incongruous that Spielberg employs objectification to encourage audiences to envision the Holocaust. What is probably even more disturbing is that the understanding he had to have gained of the Holocaust in order to make the film failed to bring him insight into traditional gender constructs and their relationship to the issues with which he was dealing. This failure helped make the film wildly popular and allowed audiences to ignore its dangerous reification of objectification of the Other in service of some sort of (monetary and self-congratulatory) gain.

One might dismiss Spielberg's use of gender objectification as a nod to typical American filmmaking, but to dismiss it would miss the true significance of its task in the film. Reflection on the use of objectification for the viewing "pleasure" of an American audience reveals the film's principal flaw: an anti-feminist organization as its central approach to the Holocaust. *Schindler's List* allows us to "view" the Holocaust and provides us with constructed explanations—explanations of both what the Holocaust was and "what it is to act morally" in such dire circumstances. Such explanations act as conclusions in a context where few conclusions can be drawn about what the Holocaust is or what constitutes acceptable moral human behavior in its context. Additionally, the film does not ask itself the question of whether, as a film about the Holocaust, it has a moral responsibility; it behaves as if the answer is provided in the character of Schindler. If we examine *Schindler's List* in this way, we see that we do not need to learn anything more about the Holocaust than what the film superficially states. Never mind that there might be historical or cultural inaccuracies. We could easily correct those, and as Holocaust scholars we are well aware that the film can be an easy springboard for historical inquiry. The character of Schindler and the moral that the film sets forth let the viewer off the hook for self-examination and engagement with moral complexity and, in turn, reject the gendered analysis that begs to be heard.

Perhaps another way to understand this point is to reflect on the way inequities are portrayed as hierarchical rather than seen as interrelated. I would argue that the film makes a moral decision to "sell" itself by objectifying women because of what it sees as a bigger story: the murder of the Jews and the story of Schindler. If the objectification of women is seen as less significant, it is morally permissible to employ objectification to sell the bigger issue. Part of the point here is that objectification of the Other is a construct that has multiple dimensions that are worth exploring and articulating, but using them to sell a film is duplicitous, to say the least.

In order to elucidate the problems of *Schindler's List*, I will contrast it with a starkly different film that deals with some similar Holocaust related themes. Co-written and directed by the celebrated filmmaker Agnieszka Holland and released in 1985, *Angry Harvest* provides an approach to issues of the Holocaust that directly challenges the assumptions behind the "entertaining" *Schindler's List*. *Angry Harvest* tells a story about gender that challenges viewers to raise questions about the relationships between gender, violent ideologies, and what we accept as givens about the world in which women and men live. Understanding what *Angry Harvest* prompts its viewers to do, in turn, challenges *Schindler's List* and its failure to raise moral and epistemological questions. *Schindler's List* leads us to accept ideologies that objectify the female Other, and these are the sorts of ideologies that form the foundations of movements that lead to genocide, group rape, and the destruction of cultures. It not only fails to recognize feminist issues but also invites the viewer to ignore the questions or analysis that could be raised through examination of the objectified female Other.

Both films are set in Poland and aim to depict significant aspects of the country and its people; both deal with people's relationships to one another during the Holocaust. But their stark differences, and the questions and frameworks posed by *Angry Harvest*, shed light on the place of power both within and in terms of the position of *Schindler's List* in Holocaust filmography and for students of introductory courses on the Holocaust.

ANGRY HARVEST AND PATRIARCHY

In *Angry Harvest*, we encounter head-on the traditional structure of the male-female relationship in patriarchal societies, exposed by the circumstances of war. Leon, once a peasant and a former student for the priesthood whose father was a groom for a local aristocratic family, has grown rich with the war and become a landowner. Clearly uneducated and socially uncomfortable with women, he is vested by those around him, including the wife and daughter of his father's former employer, with a social rank to which he is unaccustomed. Throughout the film, the viewer becomes aware that Leon, initially confused in his status, is eventually schooled in the responsibilities and position that come with being rich. When, in his woods, Leon discovers Rosa, an upper class Jewish woman from Vienna (class and culture play a role here), and later finds out that she has escaped a transport with her husband and child and has been separated from them, opportunity comes in the guise of moral goodness. Leon hides Rosa and eventually "falls in love" with her.

I pause here at the lack of language available to discuss Leon's feelings for Rosa. These feelings are embedded in a limited world of raw sexuality, in which Leon's desire is tempered by a severe Catholic upbringing that prompts him to punish himself for masturbating and for having sexual desire. His interest in and desire for upper-middle-class Jewish Rosa is fueled by her status as a Jew and a woman within the patriarchal Nazi and Polish constructions of the world of Christians and Jews. He clearly views her as both someone below him (because she is a Jew and a woman) and someone above him (because she is Viennese and upper class and beautiful), the former encouraging him to act out of his response to the latter. Together, these perceptions allow him to recast his anxieties and ambivalences about women. As her savior (both as rescuer and as he schools her in Christian doctrine), Leon allows himself to entertain notions of his own moral goodness (he feeds her, heals her, provides bedding for her in his dirt cellar, and teaches her his limited Catholic understanding, about which she seems to know more than he does), gradually coming to view her as a "wife."

Leon's sense of himself as Rosa's savior complicates his moral identity. He has played the role of rescuer in spite of the risks involved (and revealed an unwillingness to engage in the antisemitism of his countrymen and women). This is further complicated in the film when he chooses not to deliver a package for the Polish Underground (is he worried, as the viewer might suppose, that it will put Rosa at risk?) and asks the priest's sister to carry out the task, manipulating her romantic interest in him. Her estimation of his goodness, like the film viewer's, rises when he makes this request. Not only is he a good Christian, he has also involved himself in a noble and risky undertaking in her eyes. His goodness is countered, however, by her resulting death and her priest-brother's insinuations of Leon's culpability.

Angry Harvest is a disturbing movie on many levels. It deals with issues of religion, class, and gender as a complex whole, showing not only how male-female relationships are constructed but also how this construction inevitably leads to power, control, and destruction when left unchecked and marred by ignorance and objectification. Leon's relationship to and perception of Rosa are determined by his rescuer position, which allows him to use his Christianity (race/religion) and his position as a landowner (class) to fortify his goodness as a male while objectifying her as the temptress who has caused his fall from grace through the pleasure he derives from having sex with her. Because he perceives her as the cause of this fall, he must rectify his situation either by teaching her the right way and making her his wife or by casting her out.

Throughout the film, viewers are allowed to experience the brutality that lies below the surface of social relationships and are prompted to check their own understanding of how good intentions can justify acts that feed the evils embedded in our social structures. Leon is no simple protagonist and Rosa's choice to commit suicide does not help us feel better about the path to freedom. Her dependence on Leon, the reduction of her emotions to "love" for the man who has rescued and harbored her, no matter who he is, leaves the viewer shattered at the potential horror that lurks within male-female relationships and the way that objectification and brutality within these relationships fuels the decisions of individuals (men, in particular) to participate in genocide.

It has been suggested that *Angry Harvest* can be read as an allegory of Poland's ambivalence toward its Jews.[11] I have focused here on the compelling personal and gendered relationship between Leon and Rosa, but the connection with this allegorical dimension may help us even better understand how the male/female construction sinks its teeth into the objectification of the Other.[12]

Over the years, I have been intrigued by students' responses to the film. Many have suggested that Rosa manipulates Leon as much as he manipulates her. At first, though I wondered if my students had seen something I had not, I perceived this attitude as a consequence of my failure to successfully convey the context of the film—Poland's position in the war and the dire circumstances of Europe's Jews. What is now clear to me, however, is that the ability to "read" *Angry Harvest* depends upon an awareness of patriarchal society.[13]

The complexity of Armin Mueller-Stahl's portrayal of Leon produces a strong sense of compassion for this lonely peasant who, at risk of his own life, rescues a Jewish woman (and might even lead us to momentarily forgive him when he withholds information regarding her husband). Rosa's psychologically authentic identification with Leon helps foster this compassion. Some viewers, who identify with Leon and want Rosa to accept his romantic overtures, may even feel anger at her profound grief and despair at having lost her child and husband in the jump from the transport (not to mention her home, community, and trust in the decency of her fellow human beings). After all, he offers her a new, Christian world where she is "safe." Furthermore, the film's perspective belongs to Leon: we see not only him but what he sees. Through this perspective, we are invited to hope that Rosa appreciates how much Leon, as naïve and innocent rescuer, has done and risked for her.

Although Rosa does give in to Leon's sexual advances, Elisabeth Trissenaar's amazing performance shows that she never really submits to him out of romantic love as much as out of a psychological identification with a captor and complete and utter dependence on him for her survival. The way that Rosa offers herself up as objectified Other reinforces the film's portrait of the sexualization of male-female relationships in a patriarchal society. But instead of seeing her sexual surrender to Leon as motivated by a combination of resignation and gratitude, many students see Rosa on equal footing, using her sexual wiles to maintain her place in his home. This interpretation misses the fact that the circumstances that create the opportunity for Leon's goodness as Christian rescuer are the same circumstances that create the conditions for genocide. The students' perception reveals the power of patriarchy to use the perception of the woman as the objectified Other to hide from view the violence that results from inequality between men and women. So even though Leon sees Rosa as a thing he can have because of her status as a Jew, viewers might see Rosa as powerful because they fail to understand the status of Jews and women as another aspect of this same objectification—a double whammy so to speak: the woman as objectified Other and the objectified Other as feminized.[14]

Leon's control over Rosa is nearly total. She is able to hold onto her dignity as an individualized self only through a numbness she both describes and portrays, suggesting that the only way to retain one's dignity when a victim of such complete objectification is as a numbed individual (not unlike the *muselmänner* of the camps[15]). There is nowhere for her to escape and the longer she remains in the dirt cellar, the more disoriented and disconnected she is from the world around her. Leon compounds her disorientation by drunkenly acting out his fears of being caught by the Nazis. He yells and behaves as if he is fighting Nazi intruders, but when Rosa questions him a day (or is it days?) later, he denies that anyone entered the house. (His weakness complicates the viewers' perceptions since the deception is not portrayed as intentional.) On another occasion he forces her, while letting her take in a little sun, to hear the shots from the distance that kill a local man and the Jew he harbored so as to make her understand the gravity of the circumstances (as if she does not already understand what it means to be a Jew in a Nazi-Polish world). Rosa is forced to appreciate his goodness as her rescuer because of such risks, while he regards her completely in terms of his own experience, unattached to a life or a world outside of his perception.

It should be no surprise that one evening an inebriated Leon rapes Rosa on the kitchen table. His desire for her has become emboldened by alcohol and his need to see her as his—which she is, given her profound dependence on him. The rape solidifies his ownership. Harboring a woman who has become his gives him the confidence to finally "be a man." He becomes forceful, consciously controlling, and able to act on his desires. He feels he has neutralized her challenges to his religion, which, in turn, have challenged his sense of his own moral goodness.[16] He must also control her in order to maintain his superiority to her base female Jewishness.

After the body of a collaborator killed by the underground is found in the newly appointed house for the daughter of Leon's former employer, she begs Leon to let her live with him. He agrees but he cannot have a refugee/Jew living in the basement. In what seems to be an inevitable result of objectification, Rosa eventually outlives her usefulness, and Leon notifies her that he will move her to another shelter. This is an opportunity that Leon cannot ignore and one that is hastened by the suggestion of his friend that others know he is hiding Rosa. It becomes an opportunity to cast her out of his view, to get rid of the perceived cause of his base desires, desires which threaten his sense of his own goodness. At the same time, he is clearly ambivalent about his loss. Acting on her perception that he is getting rid of her, Rosa commits suicide.

The ambiguity at this moment in the film is striking. While Rosa lies dead in his basement, Leon has sex with a local maid who is readying the house for Leon's new guest. Yet he seems to despair when he discovers that Rosa is dead in his basement. His ambivalence allows the viewer to feel some forgiveness, especially since it might seem easier for him to be angry at Rosa for giving up. He has certainly loved Rosa, though whatever he feels toward her does not prevent his rape, dishonesty, and coercion (another version of the way the objectified Other is seen as cause for his downfall). Leon is temporarily devastated by Rosa's suicide partly because he cannot comprehend his own part in it. He successfully erases her life by feigning ignorance to the inquiring husband who shows up at his door. Denying knowledge of her death, he finalizes the annihilation of her individual being.

Leon's rescue and protection produces a violent end for Rosa, similar to the one she would have met in the gas chamber had she not leaped from the train: it is anonymous, unaccounted for, and violent. One may argue that Rosa's death is by her own hand so it is a choice and, having made that choice, she maintains some dignity. I am not sure this point can be successfully argued. Since Rosa's rescue has brought about her loss of perspective and desolation, it has become her prison. She is ultimately another victim of the Holocaust and the Polish collaboration.

Perhaps the most stunning moment in the film is the end when Leon receives a letter from America from Rosa's husband. The letter seems meant to represent the way the memory of Rosa will plague Leon. Her suicide in his house extinguishes his ability to free himself morally to think of himself solely as a rescuer. His house will forever remind him of her and consequently he cannot so easily recover from his own actions and feelings; he cannot easily dismiss Rosa as base temptress. Her suicide directly challenges him to reflect on his relationship to her.

On the other hand, his new wife (the former maid) is pregnant and running to him with the letter. She is outside and visible. And the viewer is left with the sense that, had Rosa not entered his life, Leon Wolny would not have a wife. Her memory is tangible because her individuality has broken through his objectification of her, if only to challenge the validity and righteousness of his actions. Perhaps her memory is meant to represent the stain on and the gash in Europe and Poland resulting from the eradication of its historical Jewish communities.

SCHINDLER'S LIST AS FEMININE CURRENCY

As a historically compelling film that offers information about and a visual representation of the Holocaust, *Schindler's List* is unselfconscious about its limitations There is no question that as a film it is powerful. However, it provides no sense of the complexity of its choices in creating a sense of historical reality: for instance, the choice to use black and white to convey documentary likeness and associate an emotional lack of color with the time, not to mention the uncritical portrayal of Schindler as a moral hero. I am troubled by this dimension of the film insofar as the film serves as a feminine construction, an object passed between people and thought to exemplify knowledge of the Holocaust and to provide insight into moral goodness.

In "Reading Ourselves: Toward a Feminist Theory of Reading," Patricinio Schweickart provides an extraordinary articulation of how the canon brings about androcentric reading strategies and how androcentric reading strategies sustain the canon.[17] She explores how female characters as object of the male gaze in androcentric texts help convert the text itself into an object that is passed as currency between men. The currency of the text is compared to the use of females as currency, e.g., brides passed from father to husband (literally in the marriage ceremony) as means of establishing family connections or acquiring land.[18] With this analogy, Schweickart argues that canonized texts become canonized partly (mostly) because they serve to validate male readers' dominant established positions in the world. The texts are "used" as currency to inform and reassure male readers of their relationship to the world and to each other while female readers are immasculated, a word she borrows from Fetterley.[19] In order to fully share in the reading experience, females are taught to identify with the universal male hero, usually against their identification with the female Other viewed by the male hero. Normally we speak of males becoming immasculated, that is, having their masculinity removed, their effectiveness taken away, and being weakened (feminized). Reading androcentric texts, on the other hand, females became immasculated—their femaleness is repressed as they learn to identify with the male subject. Schweickart asserts that the female is rendered particular, individual, and specific whereas the male represents what is not female, something that is general, universal, and shared. The female reader must relinquish her individual female identity to identify with the male hero and, through the canonized text, learns to value the male and that with which he is associated (including this notion of universality) and devalue herself.

It can be safely argued that *Schindler's List* has been canonized in American cinema. Steven Spielberg's status in American cinematic history, the broad viewing and use of the film, and its academy awards for Best Motion Picture and Best Director among seven others all attest to this. This canonization alone places the film in a problematic role. One of the reasons for its canonization is the traditional androcentric film language it employs to convey meaning. As the quintessential American film on the Holocaust and a portrait of a man who is both powerful and flawed, moral and immoral, it provides currency for knowledge of the Holocaust and the moral codes that can be attached to it. And as currency it is exchanged within a traditional patriarchal construct that not only allows but demands that we disregard the role of gender in the Holocaust.

SCHINDLER AS MORAL MODEL

The way *Schindler's List* asks us to view Helen Hirsch represents how we are supposed to treat the film itself: as object for our knowledge and our pleasure. Unlike in *Angry Harvest*, we are not asked to consider how violence is caused by gender inequities and the objectification of women. The feminization of the objectified Other is taken for granted and consequently rendered invisible as the film constructs Schindler as a moral model. We do not have to engage the struggles of Schindler in a context that, in reality, created incomprehensible moral ambiguities and conflict. In *Angry Harvest*, our perpetrator/rescuer is portrayed as a complex, ambiguous individual. It may be difficult to identify with him, but he appears complexly human both because of the moral dilemmas he struggles with and because these are understood in the particular context of his environs and the Holocaust.

Schindler's List tells us that Spielberg's Schindler (a phrase that would be a more honest title for the film) is complex. But what we are given to view is his daring and debauchery, and this characterization is not complex. He is instead fashioned as larger than life and as universal, presented not only as a character to be admired but as one with whom the film viewer should desire to identify. The film, if anything, presents his womanizing and the freedom that comes from his male position in the social milieu in an admiring light. At the same time, his flaws are meant to emphasize the extent of the heights he had to climb to become good, especially in contrast to Goeth, who is portrayed as pure evil. In many ways, the film works to make its viewers believe in redemption, in the goodness of even those who are unlikable and disagreeable.

I have had arguments with those who want to make a case that Schindler is portrayed in the film as a vividly complex character who invites intense sympathy and identification. The evidence often given to prove this complexity is Schindler's debauchery and attachment to the good life, his relationship with Plaszow Camp Commandant Amon Goeth, and his creation of the list. But all that these supposedly robustly contradictory elements really add up to is the image of a male who transcends what is bad about himself in extenuating circumstances. These circumstances may even, in turn, convert negatives like his womanizing and debauchery into positive dimensions of his personality. Is this not a universal (male) construction of what women are supposed to beg for in everyday life? And does it not play off the very thing those of us in Holocaust Studies disdain as minimizing the circumstances and delimiting the complexity of the events? The need for Schindler is the need for a forgivable male who is secretly admired for his womanizing, gambling, and debauchery. Because of his list, the film viewer is not only allowed but is even encouraged to admire him. The fact that this sort of objectification of women and abuse of the value of others' lives is part of the process is not only supposed to be forgivable because of his list; the former is supposed to make the fact of the list that much more profound. Such a portrayal allows for a cover-up of the gender, religious, and class objectification that is at the heart of patriarchy and its deadly categorizations.

The film encourages us not to question what makes Goeth see Schindler as a significant person with whom to challenge and gamble or to recognize the outrageous fact that in one instance what is gambled is a woman. When Schindler gambles for Helen Hirsch, we are not led to consider the representational significance of the trafficking of women so much as to admire Schindler's noble desire to rescue Helen Hirsch through such trade. Are we meant to view her as uniquely rescuable because she is beautiful? Because she is Goeth's? Because she has become significant to Goeth and Schindler knows this? Is she meant to represent the list as a "good in itself" as Itzhak Stern, Schindler's Jewish assistant, describes the list? Since beauty is so often seen to represent the good, so both the character of Helen Hirsch in all her beauty and Schindler's risks for her are meant to represent the list.[20]

The film locates Schindler's goodness in his ability to transcend both his negative qualities and his non-Jewishness to create the list and rescue so many people out of pure altruism. A plot summary from the Internet Movie Database articulates this view: "Oskar Schindler is a vainglorious and greedy German businessman who becomes an unlikely humanitarian amid the barbaric Nazi reign when he feels compelled to turn his factory into a refuge for Jews."[21]

Schindler becomes the moral archetype. A man who has singlehand-edly saved 1,100 Jews (we have fleeting glimpses of his wife but are given no real sense of the role she plays in the rescue, and Schindler as victimizer is nearly obscured) has become morally transformed by his actions and by his exposure to Jews as the objectified Other. By the very fact of the list, there is no question of how extraordinary a man the historical Schindler was. The film, however, idealizes his goodness in terms of his masculine power; it identifies the good with the male universal, thus linking good-ness with the use of power for "good" in a cinematic world that assumes and accepts objectification of the Other as a way to procure and maintain power. Schindler's transcendence is meant to make the film itself into a "good." It becomes currency for knowledge of the Holocaust and iconic for the goodness of rescue.

As film viewers, we are expected to accept the goodness of Schindler. We are not expected to question how the circumstances that gave Schindler his power arose to begin with, nor are we asked to reflect too much on who is placed on the list or why the film encourages us to believe that these choices were made by Stern. Helen Hirsch's objectified beauty is also pre-sented as a given that mirrors the beauty of the list, so that to question the film's portrayal of her is to challenge the goodness of the list itself. I have no doubt that viewers walk away from *Schindler's List* with the uplifting feeling that they have participated in the hell of the film and braved its horrors to become acquainted with the good that can come from the Holo-caust. It escapes their notice that the idea of moral goodness in a Holocaust landscape is implicitly problematic.

Once viewers realize that the film asks nothing more than this cathar-sis, it is easy to use the film as a sole resource for Holocaust knowledge. Schindler comes to represent what any person can do despite his or her flaws, without much regard to the different contexts in which we find our-selves. Not only does the film draw no connection between the violence that is part of our gender constructions and the violence employed by the Nazis, it succeeds in separating them by providing a neat resolution and a way to feel good about oneself for having seen the film. And the character of Schindler maintains the illusion of distance between power and objecti-fication by failing to clearly consider his position as a male in a society that is misogynist in its antisemitism. The male viewer can easily identify with the male universal and the female viewer is "immasculated," in Fetterley's phrase, to identify with the male universal and disregard any identification she might feel with the objectified female Other. One might also suggest that as currency representing Holocaust knowledge, the identification with the male universal subject also allows the viewer a sense of distance from the objectified Jewish Other, the victims of the Holocaust.

WHAT *ANGRY HARVEST* DOES / WHAT *SCHINDLER'S LIST* DOES NOT

Angry Harvest reveals the male objectification of the female Other through its examination of rampant ignorance and violent attitudes. The film shows us how Leon's inability to reflect on his circumstances—who he is and how he has come to be who he is—leads to Rosa's suicide. The fact that he studied for the priesthood and yet has only an elementary grasp of Christian theology pointedly bolsters the film's condemnation of the Church, Poland, and the individuals who carried out the Nazi agenda willfully or unconsciously. Additionally, the film lays bare the unwarranted but foundational attitudes that are informed by and can be found (not so latently) in male objectification of the female Other. Examining the relationship between Leon and Rosa, the film depicts the power of an ignorant and seemingly powerless man to control and dominate absolutely and to choose to do so without self-conscious awareness. The end of the film leaves the viewer ravaged by the unnecessary and insidious violence done to Rosa because she is both a woman and a Jew.

Schindler's List, on the other hand, unselfconsciously sanctions the status quo as it takes its place at the crown of the film canon (not just among Holocaust films).[22] In doing so, it creates, to paraphrase Schweickart, an androcentric viewing strategy that suggests a certain moral high ground on which to imagine Holocaust rescuers. The film celebrates the agency of the male: Schindler's virtue is in his having saved so many and changed into a moral being. He creates the list in direct contrast to his tendency toward debauchery, gambling, the acquisition of wealth, and notoriety, but also turns these flaws around and uses them to save people. No examination of his position in society, his privilege and its contribution to the wealth and aspirations of the Nazi agenda is demanded. Without examination of the power and privilege Schindler derives from being male and German, he is free to serve as a universal representation of goodness.

If we place Spielberg's Schindler and Holland's Leon Wolny side by side, we find that Schindler's successful heroism is a product of his social position. Both men are rescuers who derive significant self-identity through their choices to rescue; both are interested in rescuing women for their own gain; each gains money and status through the war. But in contrast to Leon, an ignorant villager with little grasp of his place in society, Schindler is a worldly entrepreneur and city dweller. If we look at Schindler through the lens of the character of Leon, we can see that Schindler's moral goodness extends only as far as his place in society, foremost as a male.

In her book *Transforming Knowledge*, Elizabeth Minnich emphasizes the need to recognize the assumptions and "mystified concepts" that lurk in our very ways of knowing.[23] Failure to recognize the contextual underpinnings and traditional concepts that maintain male positions within patriarchy, that made it possible for Schindler to create the list, and that prompted Spielberg to create a hero through classic moral archetypes allows the film to endorse the very assumptions that require exposure. To reassure ourselves through the film that moral choices lie solely within our individual selves and are within our grasp represents a profound failure to understand the role of the male universal gaze in regard to the objectified female Other and the violence and destruction it causes for those who are objectified by it. To disengage antisemitism and racism from sexism is itself an act of sexism that contributes to a status quo that fails to understand how all three—antisemitism, racism, and sexism—play a role in the very structures of our ways of knowing.

In this sense, *Schindler's List* not only has entered the canon of Holocaust films, it has reified the significance of individual roles of heroism as moral models for the masses, without any analysis of the structures that exist and maintain power and control. Taking Schindler as hero of the film eclipses the brutality and misogyny that wreak havoc in *Angry Harvest*. These, in turn, point to the undercurrents of brutality and misogyny in the world of *Schindler's List*. Disconnecting Schindler from the power of gendered objectification lets its viewer off the hook. Left with the story of Oskar Schindler and the list, we can pursue historical questions about the Holocaust and never need consider the more distressing questions of how similar to the conditions of the Holocaust are many aspects of present-day patriarchy. The Schindler of the film emphasizes the power of individual choices without recognizing the power that belongs to men of Schindler's position (non-Jewish, elegant, good-looking white males), thus reinforcing the idea that those who fail to choose the good always have the opportunity and are in a position to do so. Concealing the world of Leon and Rosa makes invisible the consequences of patriarchy for both genders.

NOTES

1 See, for example, E. Kuhn, *Women's Pictures: Feminism and Cinema* (London: Routledge & Kegan Paul, 1982); Lorraine Gamman and Margaret Marshment, eds., *The Female Gaze: Women as Viewers of Popular Culture* (Seattle, WA: Real Comet Press, 1991); a good collection of essays in feminism and film is E. Ann Kaplan, *Feminism and Film* (Oxford: Oxford University Press, 2000).

2 For comprehensive discussion of the Holocaust and film, see Annette Insdorf, *Indelible Shadows: Film and the Holocaust* (Cambridge, UK: Cambridge University Press, 2002) and Judith E. Doneson, *The Holocaust in American Film* (Syracuse, NY: Syracuse University Press, 2002).

3 For a discussion of the film, see *Spielberg's Holocaust: critical perspectives on* Schindler's List, ed. by Yosefa Loshitzky (Bloomington: Indiana University Press, 1997).

4 Some would argue with me that viewing *Schindler's List* prompts students to want to learn more about the Holocaust. I would not disagree with this assessment, but what interests me is that desire to learn about the Holocaust as a result of *Schindler's List* points students in the direction of learning about events and facts without questioning the very assumptions upon which the film rests. This will, I hope, become clearer later in the essay.

5 There are many films I could name here, some of which have had a wide distribution but were not viewed nearly as much as *Schindler's List*. For instance, the French films *Night and Fog* (1955), *Au Revoir, Les Enfants* (1987), *Train of Life* (1999); the Italian film *Garden of the Finzi Contini* (1971); the Russian film *Come and See* (1986); Verhoeven's German film, *The Nasty Girl* (1990); Hungarian films *My Mother's Courage* (1995) and the award-winning *The Revolt of Job* (1983); and a little known Czech film, *Distant Journey (Daleka Cesta)* (1950).

6 Thomas Keneally, *Schindler's List* (New York: Touchstone, 1982).

7 Laura Mulvey, "Visual Pleasure and Narrative Cinema," *Screen* 16, no. 3 (Autumn 1975): 6–18, especially 12.

8 Writings on objectification of the female are vast and too numerous to list. Specific texts that have had a significant influence on my thinking, especially philosophically, include Simone de Beauvoir, *The Second Sex*, trans. and ed. H. M. Parshley (New York: Alfred A Knopf, 1953); Sherry B. Ortner, "Is Female to Male as Nature Is to Culture?" in *Woman, Culture, and Society*, ed. Michelle Zimbalist Rosaldo and Louise Lamphere (Stanford, CA: Stanford University Press, 1974); Gayle Rubin, "The Traffic in Women: Notes on the Political Economy of Sex" in *Toward an Anthropology of Women*, ed. Rayna R. Reiter (New York: Monthly Review Press, 1975); Cheris Kramarae, "Proprietors of Language," in *Women and Language in Literature and Society*, ed. Sally McConnell-Ginet, Ruth Borker, and

Nelly Furman (New York: Praeger, 1980); Teresa de Lauretis, *Technologies of Gender: Essays on Theory, Film, and Fiction* (Bloomington: Indiana University Press, 1987); bell hooks, *Talking Back: Thinking Feminist, Thinking Black* (Boston: South End Press, 1989); Cherrie Moraga and Gloria Anzaldúa, eds., *This Bridge Called My Back: Writings by Radical Women of Color* (New York: Kitchen Table Women of Color Press, 1983); Judith Butler, *Gender Trouble: Feminism and the Subversion of Identity* (New York: Routledge, 1990); Uma Narayan, "Contesting Cultures: 'Westernization,' Respect for Cultures, and Third-World Feminists" in *Dislocating Cultures: Identities, Traditions, and Third World Feminisms* (New York: Routledge, 1997); and Chandra Talpade Mohanty, "Under Western Eyes: Feminist Scholarship and Colonial Discourses," in *Third-World Women and the Politics of Feminism*, ed. Chandra Talpade Mohanty, Ann Russo, and Lourdes Torres (Bloomington: Indiana University Press, 1991).

9   I owe the recognition of this point to an exchange with Elizabeth Minnich.

10 *Experience and Expression: Women, the Nazis, and the Holocaust*, ed. Elizabeth R. Baer and Myrna Goldenberg (Detroit, MI: Wayne State University Press, 2003), and Bergen, chapter 1 in this volume.

11 See Agnieszka Holland, interviewed by Gordana P. Crnković, *Film Quarterly* 52, no. 2 (Winter 1998–1999): 2–9, http://links.jstor.org/sici?sici=0015-1386%28199824%2F199924%2952%3A2%3C2%3AIWAH%3E2.0.CO%3B2-R.

12 The male objectification of the female Other is articulated through Poland's historical patronizing of its Jews and its ambivalent perceptions of the Jews as objectified Other within its polity. The Jew in Poland is a version of the objectified female. For more insight into the place of *Angry Harvest* within Polish filmmaking, see Gordana P. Crnković, "Inscribed Bodies, Invited Dialogues and Cosmopolitan Cinema," in *Kinoeye* at http://www.kinoeye.org/04/05/crnkovic05_no2.php (November 2004), vol. 4, issue 5.

13 And this helps us become even more aware of the insidious and veiled objectification of the female Other within patriarchy that so often escapes our perceptions and is dismissed when discussing genocide.

14 For a powerful discussion of Nazi ideology and the role of women, see Claudia Koonz, *Mothers in the Fatherland: Women, the Family, and Nazi Politics* (New York: St. Martin's Press, 1987). See also Marion A. Kaplan, *Between Dignity and Despair: Jewish Life in Nazi Germany* (New York: Oxford University Press, 1998).

15 See, for instance, Terence Des Pres, *The Survivor: Anatomy of Life in the Death Camps* (New York: Oxford University Press, 1976).

16 Perhaps we might even say that Rosa's existence represents the Jewish challenge to Christianity's idea of supersessionism.

17 Patrocinio P. Schweickart, "Reading Ourselves: Toward a Feminist Theory of Reading," in *Gender and Reading: Essays on Readers, Texts, and Contexts*, ed. E. A. Flynn and P. P. Schweickart (Baltimore, MD: Johns Hopkins University Press, 1986).

18 See Gayle Rubin "The Traffic in Women: Notes on the Political Economy of Sex," in *Toward an Anthropology of Women*, ed. Rayna R. Reiter (New York: Monthly

Review Press, 1975).

19 In addition to Schweickart, see Judith Fetterley's essay, "Reading about Reading," in Flynn and Schweickart, *Gender and Reading*.

20 It could easily be argued that Schindler gambles for Helen Hirsch in the film because he did so in real life, but it is important to keep in mind here the choices of the filmmaker in terms of what meanings Spielberg is trying to convey. My argument with the film has little to do with its historical accuracy.

21 Harald Mayr, "Plot Summary for Schindler's List," Internet Movie Database, http://www.imdb.com/title/tt0108052/plotsummary.

22 I might also add that it easily falls into place in the Holocaust curriculum, for many curricula have been developed for it, and it is widely used in high school courses in the United States.

23 Elizabeth Kamarck Minnich, *Transforming Knowledge* (Philadelphia: Temple University Press, 2005).

5

Sex-Based Violence and the
Politics and Ethics of Survival

MYRNA GOLDENBERG

The Holocaust "nearly destroyed Jewish life
and left the world morally scarred forever."
—John K. Roth

Jewish women were victimized as Jews. Simply because they were Jews,
they were subject to the Final Solution. Because they were women, they
were also subject to the physical abuses and sex-based violence that all
women face, particularly in wartime.[1] However, during the Holocaust,
the consequences of an act of rape by a German man differed from what
is often called wartime rape[2] because, in addition to violating a woman's
body and causing her both bodily and emotional harm and, in the process,
declaring Jewish men impotent to protect their women, the German who
raped a Jewish woman violated his own existential identity and damaged
his future identity as member of a separate and, indeed, in its own eyes, a
master race. Racial purity was an essential component of Nazi ideology,
and, accordingly, sexual contact with a Jew contaminated the bloodline
for several generations. The very act of violating the Law to Protect German Honor and Blood threatened the physical purity of a people and, in so
doing, set into motion a chain of long-term consequences that threatened
the ideology on which Nazism stood. Yet Germans, military and otherwise, raped and tortured Jewish women. It is obvious that Jewish women

were almost always powerless to save themselves from attacks by German men. On the other hand, in certain circumstances, they were able to use their bodies as commodities, as items of value to exchange for life.[3]

This chapter focuses on Jewish women who were subjected to unthinkable cruelties, including rape and torture, at the hands of the Nazis and who were also victimized by Jewish and other non-Aryan men. By no means can we equate the treatment by Nazis and their Eastern European allies with that by Jewish men, but neither can we ignore the fact that some Jewish women were "used" by Jewish men, particularly in ghettos and camps. I will briefly examine the sexual violence done to Jewish women by Nazis, including the policy on race mixing, or *Rassenschande,* and then discuss the situation in which Jewish women, though essentially powerless, responded to offers of food or shelter in return for sexual favors. The former involved rape and torture (and almost always murder of the victim) and reflected German betrayal of both the civil law governing the Third Reich and the higher laws that hold human life valuable.[4] The physical abuse of Jewish women by Jewish men was non-violent yet coercive as the circumstances were neither neutral nor balanced. I consider this type of sex for survival as another dimension of the "gray zone" in that the male further victimized the female, both of whom were victims of the same oppressor.[5]

It behooves us to acknowledge, at the outset, that the Holocaust was not about gender or sex. However, because Jewish women were vulnerable in different ways than men were, gender and sex cannot be dismissed by responsible scholars. Moreover, acknowledging women as victims of (sexual) violence also asserts that women's lives are as valuable as men's. To ignore or neglect the abuse and murder of women is to assert that the murder of women is less consequential than the abuse and murder of men. Though not totally ignored, the subject of women as well as the subject of rape during the Holocaust has not received serious attention until recently. Perhaps the fact that the Nazis prohibited sexual contact with non-Aryans and prosecuted it as a violation of the Law for the Protection of German Blood and Honor, one of the notorious 1935 Nuremberg Laws, led scholars to assume that rape was not an issue of importance. The Law, after all, was supposed to prevent rape and any other physical contact between Aryans and non-Aryans. It may also be that scholars saw race-mixing as an expression of legal theory rather than as expression of behavior, thus transforming physical violence into an abstraction. Perhaps, too, resistance to the inclusion of women into the study of the Holocaust, except as part of the population of Jews, contributed to the neglect of rape as a legitimate subject to examine when studying the Holocaust.[6]

THE LEGAL STATUS OF RAPE OF JEWISH WOMEN: *RASSENSCHANDE*

We know that sexual contact and violence between Germans and Jews occurred not infrequently and was sometimes subject to legal recriminations and sometimes ignored, often depending upon who was involved, on the part of the Reich in which sexual contact occurred, on the particular attitude of the court in which the violation was tried, and on the individual circumstances of the perpetrator and victim. Sexual violence against Jewish women involved breaking laws so fundamental that they defined the Nazi regime's ideology. Indeed, to an extent often unacknowledged, the Nazi regime fostered a preoccupation with sexuality,[7] sometimes as an expression of its ideals, such as the obsessive attention given to court cases involving race-mixing, and sometimes by using the complex structure of the camp system to accommodate sex, including the use of camp brothels to reward prisoners and officers.

Although the rape of Jewish women was clearly one proof of German men's power and a reiteration of their complete dominance, the fact is that Jews, both women and men, *had already been made powerless and had already been targeted for elimination*. Thus rape of Jewish women, unlike rape in the former Yugoslavia, Rwanda, Darfur, and the Congo, was not an instrument of genocide or ethnic cleansing. During the Holocaust, rape was eclipsed by the Final Solution. In the face of the systematic total elimination of Jews, rape and other forms of sexual violence were redundant tools of terror and racial dominance. Rape, whether in war or not, is an act of "extreme violence implemented . . . by sexual means."[8] The death camps, forced labor squads, planned starvation and overcrowding, psychological and physical torture, and inhuman medical experiments were effective and nearly successful means of achieving what they set out to do.

In Nazi Germany, rape and other forms of sexual abuse against Jewish women were not defined as crimes; *Rassenschande*, however, was a serious crime.[9] The crime of race defilement is defined in Paragraph 2 of the 1935 Nuremberg Law for the Protection of German Blood and Honor, which forbade marriage between Jews and Germans as well as "extramarital intercourse between Jews and subjects of the state of German or related blood."[10] Moreover, according to Hilberg, violation of this law included not only intercourse but covered "touching or even looking" because even such mild or passive acts could conceivably threaten German honor, though not German blood.[11]

Rassenschande forbade Jews and Aryans from having sex because, according to race theory, intimate contact would contaminate the Aryan bloodline for generations, thereby seriously subverting racial purity. It has been argued that one of the reasons Nazism is distinctive is that "in no other ideology has sexuality played such an important role."[12] Race mixing was a crime more serious than murder, according to an official report on Kristallnacht, because it violated a Nuremberg law.[13] Szobar cites statistics that state that nearly 2,000 cases of race defilement were prosecuted between 1935 and 1940, with 1937 and 1938 as the peak years. Trials attracted public attention and often became "sexual spectacles" because of the prosecutors' persistent focus on the details of the alleged sexual contact.[14] These trials continued, though at a declining rate, until the end of the war.

Despite the severity of the crime of *Rassenschande,* rape occurred on several levels of social and commercial interaction. We also have testimony that German bureaucrats, Wehrmacht soldiers, and SS officers demanded sex in return for favors. For example, posing as a pitiable Belgian mother who was smuggling food from Lille to Antwerp, Flora Singer's mother Fani Mendelowitz took a calculated risk and approached a German officer over dinner at an inn in which she usually stayed. She fabricated a story that her husband was a Belgian prisoner of war and that she was a helpless, innocent Belgian woman, desperately trying to feed her children. She needed his help to assure a safe crossing over an ever increasingly strict crackdown on smugglers. It was a transparent story told by a smuggler who undoubtedly was Jewish, but he agreed. Fani did not expect to see the officer till the next day, when they were to meet to cross the border, but that evening, after ordering Flora, ten years old at the time, to wait outside, he forced his way into Fani's room and raped her. From the stairwell where she was hiding, Flora saw the officer leave, his uniform disheveled and his face bloody, and returned to the room to find her mother sobbing.[15] While we cannot be certain that the officer knew that Fani was Jewish, he understood that either as a smuggler or as a Jew, she would not report the rape, and the possibility of violating the *Rassenschande* law did not deter him.

The prosecution of race defilement was both bizarre and inconsistent. Although Jewish women were treated as subhuman, at worst, and as commodities, at best, German law held that the man, not the woman, was responsible for race defilement. Jewish women involved in *Rassenschande* with German men were often charged as witnesses, not perpetrators, in race defilement cases and turned over to the Gestapo who held them in protective custody, which meant they were given a prison sentence or sent to a "retraining" or concentration camp. In cases of German women and Jewish men, the law granted the women complete immunity; it was usually presumed that the Jewish men had seduced them.[16] As we might anticipate, Jewish men, if convicted, were sent to prison, where they were subjected to "special forms of torture and death."[17] Thus, while intent—whether rape or consensual sex—was inconsequential, the act of *Rassenschande* was a grave crime, and the perpetrator faced punishment of some kind, the nature of which grew progressively more severe as the war continued. The burden of proof was entirely on the defendant. As Szobar points out, punishment in 1935 ranged from three months to one year, but within a few years, the "judiciary viewed 'race defilement' as seriously as 'high treason.'" The penalty grew even more severe and more inconsistent, depending on the case and the judge. This inconsistency is demonstrated by the only rape case reported in a Croatian concentration camp in the years 1941 and 1942, which resulted in sentencing the rapist, a German guard, to six months in prison for "desecration of the race."[18]

The Katzenberger-Seiler Case

Adjudication of *Rassenschande* cases was erratic, despite Hilberg's contention that the courts gave no leniency in these cases and did not allow for mitigating circumstances. He cites the case of Lehmann Katzenberger and Irene Seiler, dramatized in the 1961 Abby Mann film, *Judgment at Nuremberg*. In March 1942, Katzenberger, sixty-seven years old, owner of a wholesale shoe business that included a chain of shoe stores and an important member of the Nuremberg Jewish community, and thirty-two-year-old Irene Seiler, a German women, were accused of race defilement. Katzenberger had been a friend of Seiler's father for years; when Irene opened a photography shop in Nuremberg, her father asked Katzenberger to help her. He did so; she rented an apartment in a complex of buildings he owned, he gave her gifts of shoes, cigarettes, and flowers, and he apparently gave her money when she was short of cash. Her apartment doubled as her studio and his corporate offices were in the same building complex; they saw each other often and had an affectionate relationship that did not go beyond friendly fatherly kisses. Their relationship became the talk of nosy neighbors and fueled long time jealousies between Katzenberger and local party officials, including Julius Streicher, who attacked Katzenberger openly in *Der Stuermer*.

According to the author of a well-researched book on Seiler and Katzenberger, the trial was fixed—the presiding judge had made up his mind to execute Katzenberger despite lack of evidence, third hand gossipy witnesses, and attempts at intervention by members of the judiciary.[19] Like other trials, this one drew much attention, and, predictably, the defendants were found guilty. Since Seiler could not be convicted of race defilement because she was a woman, she was convicted of perjury and sentenced to two years in prison; she was released in June 1943 after serving nineteen months. Katzenberger was guillotined in June 1942.[20] It appears that in this case the severity of the punishment was a function of the court and, especially, judicial histrionics.

Rape in the Ghettos

Although the war preoccupied the Nazi bureaucracy, race defilement continued to be a concern because it threatened the myth of the superior, pure Aryan warrior. Nevertheless, trial and military records, witness accounts, and memoirs prove that German soldiers raped Jewish women. As early as June 1941, Mary Berg confided to her diary that people "from Lublin, Radom, Lodz, and Piotrkow—from all the provinces" poured into Warsaw and "all of them tell terrible tales of rape and mass executions."[21] Nomi Levenkron reports that an underground newspaper in L'vov told in October 1941 of rapes that occurred during pogroms: "Women were raped in the middle of the streets. The murderers dragged Jewish women out of their apartments and cut off their breasts. . . . It is estimated that the number of victims reached a few thousand."[22] In the eyes of the soldier rapist victor, rape was an acceptable, even a routine exercise of male superiority and aggression.[23] *Rassenschande* notwithstanding, for a substantial number of German soldiers, both SS and Wehrmacht, it would seem that rape was one of many acceptable steps toward establishing themselves as part of the master race and to "prove [themselves] worthy Supermen," a goal to be accomplished in part by "total humiliation and destruction of 'inferior peoples.'"[24]

Rape during Kristallnacht

For the female victim, the combination of elements in the phrase "Jewish woman" was lethal. The Nazis assaulted Jewish women through degradation, physical violence, and murder; in planned riots; at murder sites; in the ghettos; and in the camps. Though there are reports of degradation and violence coupled with rape throughout the Holocaust, as noted above, large scale "campaigns" of (sexual) violence started on Kristallnacht and continued for the next six and a half years throughout German-occupied territory.[25] Charlotte Opfermann relates one such example telling of the rape of her aunt Kaettel Hirsch during the vandalism of her home on Kristallnacht.[26] In Vienna, a woman who was raped during Kristallnacht sought shelter and pleaded for emigration papers in the American Embassy. The Ambassador refused to help her. She was raped again, and again sought refuge in the American Embassy. The Ambassador explained to her that she would need an American sponsor in order to emigrate. Her pleas continued, and the Ambassador, apparently exasperated, handed her the New York City telephone book and told her to search for a sponsor. She opened to a page that had numerous entries for Schiff. The first and only call she made was to Dorothy Schiff, publisher and owner of the *New York Post* and granddaughter of the successful Jacob Schiff. Schiff was sympathetic and sponsored her and nineteen other Jewish women before World War II began.[27]

SEX-BASED VIOLENCE AND THE *EINSATZGRUPPEN*

The several different editions of *The Black Book,* each of which records the actions of the German murder squads in different parts of Eastern Europe, contain contemporaneous accounts of the actions as witnessed by survivors. From these documents, we can deduce that rape and other forms of brutality were a routine part of the process of the murder squads or *Einsatzgruppen.*[28] The reports and photos show women stripped naked and abused in front of their husbands, fathers, and sons before they were shot into open pits or mass graves. Thus, terror was accompanied by the humiliation of public nakedness and made all the more painful by the presence of male relatives and friends who were forced to stand by helplessly. *The Black Book of Polish Jewry*, first published in 1943 and reprinted in 1999, includes proof that, despite the seriousness of *Rassenschande*, Berlin did not scrutinize sexual behavior in eastern Europe as it did in Germany proper: "The Nazi racial theory presented no obstacle to the behavior of the German soldiers toward the Jews, not even the Nuremberg law which prohibited sexual relations with Jewesses [sic]." Referring to a town thirty kilometers west of Warsaw, one affidavit given to a representative of the World Jewish Congress in Wilno reads:

> At night the Germans would force their way into Jewish homes and rape women and girls. The other members of the household would be locked up in another room. Some of the girls, those of the more educated type, would be taken by the Germans to their barracks where they were raped and killed."[29]

Testimony by a Romanian prisoner of war reported "merciless robbery and tortures . . . women and young girls were raped in the presence of mothers, husbands, and children, and then killed."[30] In these actions, both men and women suffered the leers and laughter of the killers. More often than not, the soldiers murdered their victims—no victim, no crime!

The Black Book also quotes a deposition given by a man identified as J. L. who arrived in Palestine in 1940 and testified to the Committee for Polish Jews in Jerusalem on October 9 of that year. His testimony relates conversations between Dr. Henryk Szoszkies, a member of the Executive Committee of the Jewish Community Council, and Unit Leader Wende, a member of the Gestapo, that began on November 2, 1939, barely two months after the Germans invaded Poland. Wende explained: "As you know, we have a large garrison of young, healthy men who are suffering from a lack of sexual relations. Casual meetings in the street have already resulted in many cases of venereal disease." Wende then ordered the Health Department to open a brothel for German soldiers, in fact, two brothels, "one for officers and a separate one for privates. He gave Szoszkies two days to present plans for the brothels, promising him the "best of linen and furniture" as well as a share of the profits. On the next day, however, Wende barged into the Council office demanding a "palatial two-story home for the officers' brothel . . . must contain 12 to 15 rooms" and gave Szoszkies permits to confiscate a Jewish or a Christian home for the business. Unwilling to fulfill this order and apparently taking Wende's threats of reprisal seriously, Szoszkies fled Poland and managed to come to the United States. Szoszkies gave his affidavit in New York City on January 14, 1940, and it was published in the *Contemporary Jewish Record* of March–April 1940.[31]

In a short section, "The Humiliation of Jewish Women," *The Black Book* relates more incidents of rape in Warsaw, in 1940, of Jewish women and young girls being snatched from the streets and raped, or raped in their homes or in shops:

> A mass rape took place in a mirror shop; "orgies" on the part of German officers took place in the house of M. Szereszewski, a well-known Warsaw Jew in Pius Street"; during a raid in Franciszkanska Street, "40 Jewish girls were dragged into the house which was occupied by the German officers. There, after being forced to drink, the girls were ordered to undress and to dance for the amusement of their tormentors. Beaten, abused and raped, the girls were not released till 3 A.M."

Another survivor/witness laments, "nor is it enough to tell of the camp in Tulchin, from which no one returned alive; the camp under the rule of the infamous Petekau, who asked each night for two Jewish virgins."[32]

Reports of many incidents of rape continued, including mass rapes, some of which were documented in pamphlets that described what was happening to the Jews.[33] We have no records that indicate that the rapes in Warsaw and other cities were reported to German authorities beyond Wende, but the brothels in Warsaw were never established.

Violence, including sexual abuse and rape followed by murder, became a pattern for the *Einsatzgruppen*. Brownmiller draws on the testimony of Sophia Glushkina, a Russian Jewish woman, in a war crimes deposition about the German assault in Krasny. After describing brutal beatings and humiliation in the course of several late-night SS attacks, Glushkina reported that soldiers entered the house of a man they had beaten and killed the night before and demanded his widow: "We thought that she would be killed, but the Germans acted more beastly [*sic*] than that; they raped her right here in the yard." After witnessing another incident of rape and torture in what became the Krasny ghetto, Glushkina escaped into the forest to join partisans.[34]

The Black Book of Soviet Jewry, another contemporaneous compendium of eyewitness reports, letters, and diaries of the victims and survivors of the *Einsatzgruppen,* tells harrowing tales of mass executions, rapes, and other sexual abuses that are not and would not have been covered in official reports to Berlin headquarters. For example, in early July 1941, in Riga, the Nazis celebrated their successful mass murders by herding

> several dozens of Jewish girls to their orgy, forced them to strip naked, dance, and sing songs. Many of these unfortunate girls were raped right there and then taken out in the yard to be shot. Captain Bach surpassed everyone with his invention. He broke off the seat cushions of two chairs and replaced them with sheets of tin. Two girls, students of Riga University, were tied to the chairs and seated opposite each other. Two lighted Primus stoves were brought and placed under the seats. The officers really liked this sport. They joined hands and danced in a ring around the two martyrs. The girls writhed in the torment, but their hands and feet were tightly bound to the chairs; and when they tried to shout, their mouths were gagged with filthy rags. The room filled with the nauseating smell of burning flesh. The German officers just laughed, merrily doing their circle dance.[35]

The Nazis combined mutilation of mothers with their murders and, in the words of one scholar, devised a process whereby "maternity was infected by atrocity where the established conventions of motherhood are deliberately ravaged and assaulted"[36]: "the German beasts snatched small children from their mothers' hands, seized them by the feet and killed them by dashing them against poles and fences."[37] Another witness testified: "In Demanevka, the fascists tore babies in half and smashed their heads against stones. Women had their breasts cut off,"[38] and further,

> they did not waste their lead on the children. They crushed their skulls against posts and trees and threw them alive into the bonfires. The mothers were not killed right away, so that first their poor hearts could bleed at the sight of the deaths of their little ones. . . . One German woman was . . . especially cruel. . . . "It was as if she were drunk with her own cruelty: screaming wildly, she would crush the skulls of little children with such blows of her rifle butt that their brains were scattered over a wide area."[39]

In the Minsk ghetto, *Hauptscharfuhrer* Ribbe selected thirteen beautiful Jewish women and led them down a street that led to the cemetery.

"The animals stripped the women naked and mocked them. Then Ribbe and Michelson personally shot them. Ribbe took Lina Noy's [one of the women's] bra and put it in his pocket: 'To remember a beautiful Jewess,'" he said.[40] In Brest, Osher Zisman testified that while he watched through a ventilation opening in a hiding place he "saw the Germans herd the young girls into a shed next to the graves and rape them before the execution. I heard one girl call for help; she hit the German in the snout, and for that the Germans buried her alive."[41] Part of a chain gang in Bialystok that was ordered to dig up and cremate the bodies, Nukhim Polinovsky reported digging up a "pit with 700 women. . . . The bodies were absolutely naked. The breasts of many of the victims had been cut off."[42] Mutilation is thus added to the list of Nazi crimes against Jewish women.[43]

Father Patrick Desbois conducted meticulous research to learn the fate of Ukrainian Jews. Through on-site interviews with witnesses and supporting documents from the Soviet Jewry files of the United States Holocaust Memorial Museum, he collected accounts of "infinite sadism . . . We had to calm ourselves down, catch our breath, drag ourselves out of the narrative, and detach ourselves from the obscenities performed on women and children."[44] In one particular interview, Anna Dychkant told him that after the dissolution of the ghetto,

> the young girls—there was one who went to school with me, Silva, who was very beautiful—weren't killed straight away. Silva had to live with the German commander. The other girls waited on the other soldiers. When the girls got pregnant, they were killed, because they couldn't have children with these people. They asked the Sokal police to take these girls, who were really beautiful, to a place 10 kilometers from Busk to kill them because they didn't want to do it themselves. There was half a truck-load of them.[45]

Rape in the Camps

One French survivor I interviewed was raped in Birkenau. After two years of hard labor and several months in Block 25, she was assigned to the Kanada commando after it was expanded in spring and summer 1944 to handle the belongings of Hungarian Jews. An older Wehrmacht soldier, as she described him, was returning from the Russian front and stopped in Auschwitz where he stayed for a day or two. He had been eyeing her, nineteen years old at the time, and even followed her. One day in September, her fellow prisoners in the commando warned her that he was after her; she fled to her bunk, where he found her and raped her. "It was the deepest defilement," and one of her loneliest moments, she told me.[46] One report from the Russian section of Auschwitz says that SS guards raped young, pretty, and healthy girls "until they were half dead. From there they went to the ovens." Father Joseph Tyl testified that a "certain SS guard" who was a "pervert who killed people for pleasure . . . was also a maniac who satisfied his lust with young, pretty Jewish girls, whom he murdered immediately afterwards."[47]

Apparently unafraid of retribution, the "Germans, most of them young bachelors . . . approached Jewish women." In the several labor camps of Radom, there were rumors of "forbidden sexual liaisons" with Jewish women. "The inmates . . . knew the identity of [their foreman's] lover but turned a blind eye because [he] had been decent to them."[48] Using Yad Vashem testimony, Karay describes other violations of racial purity. She tells us that "manager Walter Glaue . . . occasionally picked out a young woman in addition to his steady lover. When [one such woman] Bella Sperling was executed on charges of sabotage, rumor had it that Glaue had impregnated her and therefore wished to get rid of her." The charge of sabotage ensured Sperling's death. Without a victim, there is no crime. Karay reports another famous case in the labor camp: foreman Hugo Ruebesamen

> loitered excessively in the vicinity of the most beautiful Jewish woman in the department. The supervisor was informed, and he flayed the woman until she bled in an attempt to force her to admit that she had had sexual relations with Ruebesamen. When she would not, she was sent to the SS hq in Radom, from which she disappeared without a trace. Although Ruebesamen also refused to confess, he was sentenced to three months imprisonment.[49]

Survivor Susan Cernyak-Spatz, a university history professor, spoke almost casually about being raped in Birkenau. Indeed, the index to her memoir does not include a "rape" entry. Assigned to work in the construction department as a typist and cleaning woman, she was invited by Jupp, a German *kapo* imprisoned as a habitual criminal, to follow him to the storeroom where he said he would give her food. Because she was starved, she went: "What followed was a plain quick rape on the floor of the store-room and a bit of sausage thrown at me for payment." Jupp was not afraid that Cernyak-Spatz would report him, for to do so would incriminate her-self and she would assuredly suffer more consequences than he.[50]

A compilation of 1946 survivor interviews by David Boder also includes narratives that reveal episodes of sadism and rape. Before the Warsaw ghetto uprising in 1943, Roma T. was deported to Majdanek. She talks about being "processed" into the camp:

> Then in the bathing installation they proceeded with a selection. An SS man came—women also, men with dogs—we were completely naked, and they simply looked us over, like animals. Looked into our teeth, tested our muscles with their hands. And the dogs barked, and then some of the older women and the sick were pushed to one side. These did not come out of the bathhouse anymore. Afterward we were bathed, and we were . . . [she was unable to finish the sentence]. We had our turn in the bath; then we were given other clothes. Everything was taken away. In addition we were told that we should conceal nothing, because we would be exam-ined gynecologically. . . . Some women, out of excitement, standing for the first time stark naked in front of men, became hysterical. They cried terribly. But among us were those who said, "If they are not ashamed, why should we be ashamed?"[51]

Roma T. was then sent to a labor camp that manufactured munitions, guarded by SS and Ukrainians. Her workshop was supervised by Ukraini-ans and Germans: "There was a German foreman by the name of Krause, the most terrible in the factory. When Krause would go by, even the machinery would run differently. Sometimes he would get drunk, pick a few women and rape them, and later they were shot so that there would be no evidence of 'race pollution.' "[52]

Rape of a Hidden Child: A Case Study

The narrative of one child, Anne, is haunting. Born in Paris in 1937, she lost her parents and two siblings when they were picked up by French gen-darmes, maybe in 1941 or '42. She does not know for sure. The concierge of her building took care of her for a short while and then turned her over to an underground organization that hid Jewish children. Taken from one peasant family to another every three months, she was violated over and over again hideously and very painfully and to the point of torture. Each family received food and clothes coupons as well as a stipend for caring for her, but, in some of the homes that took her in, she was tied up to a chair in just her underwear all day, day after day. She was released each evening when the family returned from work and told to use the yard as her bathroom although they had indoor plumbing. At first, she accepted the abuse she suffered as the norm, but eventually she began to blame herself. However, after repeated incidents of painful and bloody vaginal, anal, and oral sex, she felt brutalized and began to distrust the adults with whom she was staying. She had had very little memory of "normal" life, but, at one point, she preferred to die than to keep suffering and so she cut her wrists. She was unaware of the war, had no notion of Germans, or, as she says, of anything in the world. At the war's end, she changed her name because she wanted to forget the nightmare that was her past. In 1948, when she was eleven years old and was adopted by an Australian family, she had never had fruit or chocolate and she could not read. She continues to suffer and, more than fifty years later, she still does not enunciate her name.[53]

Anne's experience was extreme, even in comparison to the extended world of "Planet Auschwitz," where the extreme was both the typical and the accepted norm. It deserves retelling in part to prove the point that if we do not investigate the topic of rape, her experience is lost. While her trauma and guilt are likely to have shaped her memory of these experiences, undoubtedly she suffers extraordinary pain in the process of remembering. Her memory of the four years before she was orphaned is hazy, if not unreliable, and she cannot recall her parents' or siblings' faces. She says she endured all the neglect and violence because she was waiting for her parents, mainly her father, to retrieve her. She can recall the sound of her own voice, but not theirs. Her inability or unwillingness to say her name speaks to her difficulties about her identity.

BARTERED SEX OR SEX FOR SURVIVAL

Jewish women faced another type of exploitation from Jewish and non-Aryan men who were neither in the military nor in the German bureaucracy. Women's memoirs speak of using sex to barter with men in both ghettos and camps for food or some other necessity of survival. Without corroboration by these men, whether Jewish or not, we cannot assign motives with any certainty, but their behavior invites analysis. The Nazis reversed the traditional hierarchy of the Jewish family soon after they came to power, by stripping the men of their roles as protectors and providers. This diminution of status was, in effect, emasculation, and they were powerless and unable to fulfill the most basic obligations of husband, father, brother, and son. Even when husbands and fathers were not conscripted into forced labor or deported to labor and concentration camps, for the most part, they were denied the means of taking care of their families. Thus Jewish women were left vulnerable and unprotected. Not only did they have to take on unfamiliar and previously male responsibilities to provide for themselves and their children and sometimes even their parents, but they were also prey for German men and, as the war progressed, non-German men.

Sex for Survival in the Camps

Perhaps Jewish men were unconsciously responding to their humiliation and trying to restore or reassert their dominance by requiring sex in return for food or a similar necessity—a sweater or a bowl, for example. Again, we see sex as an instrument of power—only now, without overt physical violence. In her memoir, Dr. Gisella Perl describes the appalling conditions in Birkenau under which bartered sex occurred:

> The latrine also served as a "love nest." It was here that male and female prisoners met for a furtive moment of joyless sexual intercourse in which the body was used as a commodity with which to pay for the badly needed items the men were able to steal from the warehouses. . . . Sexual desire was still one of the strongest instincts and there were many who lacked the moral stamina to discipline themselves. . . . Detachments of male workers came into Camp C almost daily, to clean the latrines, build streets, and patch up leaking roofs. These men were trusted old prisoners who knew everything there was to know about camp life, had connections in the crematories and were masters at "organizing." Their full pockets make them the Don Juans of Camp C. They chose their women among the youngest, the prettiest, the least emaciated prisoners and in a few seconds the deal was closed. Openly, shamelessly, the dirty, diseased bodies clung together for a minute or two in the fetid atmosphere of the latrine—and the piece of bread, the comb, the little knife wandered from

the pocket of the man into the greedy hands of the woman. At first, I was
deeply shocked . . . revolted. I begged, preached. . . But later when I saw
that the pieces of bread thus earned saved lives, when I met a young girl
whom a pair of shoes, earned in a week of prostitution, saved from being
thrown into the crematory, I began to understand—and to forgive.[54]

Perl's use of the words "greedy" and "prostitution" betrays her judgmen-
tal attitude and her assumption that these women needed to be forgiven.
Olga Lengyel, an infirmary worker, describes similar scenes of "busy lovers" when she tells the story of rejecting a proposition of food—two potatoes and a promise of other food—in return for sex. She prides herself on
retaining her morality.[55] We see here, in the condemnation of victimized
women, another dimension of the "gray zone."

In the latrines of Auschwitz-Birkenau, surely starved, filthy, scab- and
lice-covered women were not sexually attractive, but the situation rendered them vulnerable to fellow prisoners who had access to food and
other vital items, such as sturdy shoes and sweaters. These men stole or
traded for these items while working as roofers, electricians, carpenters, or
plumbers. Sex bartering was particularly common when these work crews
visited the women's camp at Auschwitz-Birkenau to do necessary repairs.
Exchanging food for sex was, for some Jewish men on these crews, a measure of control or a means of restoring themselves as head of the house, as
primary provider, as a person of status. Although such trades may have
enabled Jewish men to regain their status as protectors and dominant figures in a heterosexual relationship, consciously or otherwise, they did so
at the expense of women.

Bartered sex also occurred between men in the work crews and the
non-Jewish women who were the *Blockelste* or *kapos* or in similar positions of relative power or importance, i.e., "prisoner-functionaries." In
these cases, according to Pawelczynska, "more or less permanent relationships started up among the prisoner-functionaries . . . who had food sup-
plies and separate quarters, and the men [on the work crews] who were
interested in the material aid (regardless of the allure of an erotic relationship)." For those men interested in bettering the living conditions of
women prisoners, these relationships helped them achieve their goal: "The
men used their influence to shelter the mass of women prisoners from the
functionaries' aggression and also to see that camp functions were handed
out to the prisoners."[56] Work crews also delivered messages to and enabled

visits between family members who were in parts of the camp that were separated by barbed wire. These connections and fleeting visits "fortified the prisoners' inner strengths and hardened their resistance to camp destiny."[57]

In all of these prisoner relationships, the competing pressure of two basic drives is clear, but we must note that for some women the "sex drive was completely subjected"[58] and supplanted or rendered irrelevant by hunger and thirst. These men, on the other hand, had access to food and therefore were less likely to be as motivated by hunger as were the women. Hunger, the ubiquitous topic of discussion as well as the unrelenting physical need, was the primary motive of "survival sex" and accounts for the willingness of Jewish women prisoners to accept food for sex.[59] In essence, the men had food and other necessities and the women had their bodies. At the most basic level, bartered sex completes a transaction of equivalence: each party experiences a benefit, one psychological and the other physical. The woman, though a victim, may experience shame but, at the same time, has the choice of using her body to save herself and thereby become an agent of her own survival.

Bartered Sex and the Gray Zone

Sex in exchange for food is neither rape nor prostitution, but it is not exactly consensual sex. Terminology appropriate for normal society can hardly be applied to the world of the concentration camp. While sex for money or its equivalent may have similar motivations in both the concentration camp and the peacetime worlds, it must be remembered that Jewish women who accepted food for sex were victimized and scheduled for death—in other words, women whose control of their lives was forcibly taken—and had few to no alternatives in order to live.[60] On the other hand, some women who used their bodies to survive strain our sense of morality. How does one judge a Jewish *kapo* who used a "little cubicle at the end of the barracks" to save herself. In an interview for an oral history project in 1990, Lucille Eichengreen relates a story about this *kapo*, explaining that an SS man came to see her each night, but, because it was dark, the prisoners in that barrack could never determine whether the rumor was true or merely gossip. In 1946, Eichengreen accidently met the former *kapo,* whose beatings she remembered, at the glove counter in B. Altman's, then an upscale New York department store. After a short conversation, she learned that not only was the rumor true but also that the SS officer pursued the *kapo* from DP camp to DP camp and even to New York, professing his love. "He was a decent sort," explained the *kapo*, and she married him.[61]

Thus, "normal" is relative. The normal morality of pre-concentration camp days was not the morality of the camps. Starvation and other life-threatening deprivations drove some prisoners to behave ruthlessly or immorally according to pre-Nazi standards.[62] However, except in the case of partisan groups in which women sought male partisans to protect them in return for sexual favors,[63] non-Aryan and especially Jewish male prisoners who took advantage of the weakness of their sister prisoners added to their misery. Their opportunism was not benign; it was humiliating and degrading.

On the other hand, Charlotte Opfermann complicates the matter of consensual sex and adds ambiguity to the word *consenting*. She writes that

> there was some sexual activity in Theresienstadt, also. . . . As for sexual activity between (often consenting) prisoners: this depended to a large extent on the work and housing assignment of the individual prisoners. Their penalty for pregnancy was instant re-deportation to the death camps in the East. My roommate (one of 36) Reni became pregnant and Dr. Walter Freund performed an abortion. As for such voluntary sexual activity, I would like to call your attention to the fact that this was often motivated by a sense of *Torschlusspani* (fear of impending death).[64]

Possibly because of embarrassment and shame about the measures they felt forced to take in order to survive, women almost always relate these occurrences as happening to some other woman. They describe these "trades" from the perspective of a casual onlooker. But the fact that these experiences are part of the narrative indicates that they were part of their suffering. Clearly, bartered sex is as old as civilization and not limited to times of war, but the devastation of war "normalizes" the exchange of sex for food and shelter. The circumstances in Nazi Germany and its occupied countries, however, were different. Although the Nazi machine made them its enemy, Jews were not a conquered nation. Jewish women were not an enemy's lifeline to the future, in the form of a labor force that would, in time, support the victorious nation. Jewish women were targeted because they were Jewish. Succinctly stated, Jewish women were a danger to Aryans and were left without the resources necessary for life.

THE IRONY OF INNOCENCE AND
THE PRESENCE OF "GOOD" MEN

Some Jewish women, who were not caught and deported, were able, for a time, to pass as non-Jews and possibly avoid rape or bartered sex. After a succession of short stays in various Polish towns and cities to dodge the Gestapo, Hannah Bannett found a job with Sep Wirth—a good friend of Hans Frank, Governor of the General Government based in Krakow. Wirth complimented her work, but when he made advances, she had to leave. She then got a job with Dr. Prof. Helmut Sop, a psychiatrist and director of a hospital, and he permitted her and her daughter to move into his house. When Dr. Sop told her to dress better, she explained she could not afford to because she needed money to pay the people taking care of her son in the country. She pleaded with Sop to let her bring her son to the house. Sop agreed. On one occasion when both Dr. and Mrs. Sop were not home, she went into the living room to straighten up. Facing her was a "Gestapo man half dressed, sprawled on sofa." He teased her and when she tried to leave the room, he demanded not only food but also her presence while he ate. He began to interrogate her about her husband, who by then had been picked up in an action, never to be seen again. In order to escape what she knew would be rape, she said she had to prepare lunch for the mistress of the house and the children. "'Well done,'" he said, and then I understood that he knew I was Jewish."[65]

Not only were adult Jewish women vulnerable to abuse and worse, young Jewish girls also faced horrors, but a few found "protection" through their innocence. Eva Slonim and her younger sister Marta were the only children without parents in the train that took them from Sered to Auschwitz-Birkenau, a journey which, she remembers, lasted seven days. They "felt alone, orphaned. A man offered to throw me out of the train wrapped in a blanket in return for a sexual favor which at the time I did not understand." She was about ten or eleven. She and Marta were taken to the *Familienlager* and there the *blockelteste*, a Jewish man, "approached [her] to sleep with him." Again, she did not know what he was asking for.[66]

After her parents died of starvation in the Lodz ghetto, seventeen-year-old Eichengreen was left to take care of her twelve-year-old sister Karin. Trying to find her a place in one of the factories, she encountered a manager who was willing to "hire" Karin but demanded something in return. When Lucille "explained that [she] had neither money nor valuables, he laughed and said that that was not what he had in mind." She was "stunned. The realization was sudden and painful: there were favors to be bought, but they had to be paid for one way or another—even among our own." Later, as a prisoner in a labor camp, she could not resist stealing a "dirty piece of cloth in splashy shades of rust red and olive green" from the rubble she was supposed to clear. She hid the cloth between her thighs, intending to use it later to cover her bald head. When her SS guard ordered her to a secluded place where he could rape her unseen, he found the scarf and disgustedly flung her aside with the words, "You filthy, useless bitch! Pfui! Menstruating"![67]

Judgment of either the women or men, if it is at all appropriate, is complicated by the awareness that there were Jewish and non-Jewish male prisoners who did not exploit sister prisoners and by Jewish women who were able to resist bartering. For example, born in Bialystock and deported to Majdanak and later to Blishjen, a work camp, Helen Schwartz needed shoes. "The man who usually made shoes for us would not give any to me unless I would have intercourse with him. At Blishjen, if a man had extra food, he would ask a girl for sexual pleasures and pay her in food. This was common, but not for me. This shoemaker could not understand that I wanted only shoes and nothing more . . . Some of the girls were so desperate that they used their body to pay for the bare necessities they needed."[68]

Eva Brewster remembers kindnesses of a German male:

We now had the opportunity to meet with privileged, mostly German male prisoners who worked in another building within the complex [Laundry Detail]. They traded for food and other items required by the SS in the town of Auschwitz, accompanied by only one guard, often a guard who could be bribed to keep his mouth shut if the prisoners did a little trading for themselves. Some of these men brought us their washing and paid with food. Some fell in love with a girl and would look after her, keeping her supplied with almost anything she needed.

Otto, the [German] man who singled me out, was the men's Capo. He had been in various concentration camps since 1933 for having been involved in a street brawl between Hitler Youth and young Communists shortly after Hitler came to power. He befriended my mother first and was old fashioned enough to ask her permission to meet and talk with me. Unlike many of the other men, he never asked for any favors in return and if he had any plans for the future which included me, he never once talked about them. All he wanted to do was to see us through ordeals to come, to feed and clothe us adequately and to keep us fit and strong enough for the exodus he foresaw once the Russians advanced into Poland.[69]

Sophie Sohlberg, also in a Laundry Detail, tells a similar story. Her barrack was close to the railways, where Willy Reich, a Jewish friend from Neuendorf, a camp to prepare people for emigration from Germany to Palestine, worked pushing wagons. Her story is touching but sad.

> Several times he brought me little presents, such as food and other things.
> I remember that on my birthday he gave me Quaker Oats with sugar . . .
> I knitted gloves for him. [She got the yarn and knitting needles from one
> of other girls in the *Flickstube*, or Mending Room.] One of the things
> he gave me was a prayerbook. Because it was quite big, I could not take
> it with me everywhere and hid it under the mattress of some bed at the
> back of the dormitory (Block II).

On September 14, 1944, the camp was attacked by either British or Russian planes. When bombs fell, the prisoners and the SS went to an inner hall. She continues: "A bomb made a big hole in the floor exactly through the roof and the floor in front of the bed with my prayerbook, and it was impossible to get there to retrieve it. When I told Willy that my prayerbook was 'bombed' . . . he brought me a new one, a very small one which I could hide on my body—and I have it still. I met Willy on the first night of the Death March. He gave me a loaf of bread and a stick of margarine. That was the last time I saw him. He did not live to see the liberation."[70]

POST-HOLOCAUST LISTENER RESPONSE

Regrettably, because of the aging and deaths of many survivors and the scant number of gendered interview questions until recently, much information is irretrievable. We do have limited information from David Boder, who asked direct questions about sexual violence and abuse. Apparently, sexual violence was one of the topics that interested him and about which his subjects were willing to speak. Micheline Maurel's experience proves the listeners' interest in sex-based violence. In her 1958 memoir, Maurel narrates her experiences in the camps and her return home. When she finally arrived home she was bombarded with questions.

> The questions I was asked were always the same: "Tell me, were you raped?" (This was the one question that was most frequently asked. In the end, I regretted having been spared this. Seemingly, by my own fault, I had missed one part of the adventure, to the great disappointment of my audience. However, I could at least tell them of the rape of others.)[71]

In the preponderance of memoirs by women, sex-based abuse is seldom reported in the first person. Considering the environment from which most of the victims came, it is likely that many women were too embarrassed to reveal such abuse as happening to themselves.

This distancing from direct personal experience is exacerbated by the fact that at least two decades passed before there was widespread interest in the survivors and even less interest in women survivors. When interest returned, sex-based dehumanization discomfited the interviewers and the subjects. After a hiatus of about forty years during which time such questions were not asked, questions about rape and other sexual abuses are occasionally being asked of survivors.

Scholars, however, have larger questions to consider: Why was the issue of rape so marginalized in the history of the Holocaust? Is this vacuum evidence of the presumed marginalization of women? Does it protect men from culpability? Was it simply that women of that generation were unlikely to describe rape because of the shame attached to it—then and now?[72] What accounts for the energetic research about Nazi reproductive policies and the impact of this and other Nazi policies on German women and on sexuality, but comparatively little work on or analysis of sexuality and the prisoner victims? How are we to understand the Nazi "obsession" with sexuality in the context of mass murder? Or the voracity of Nazi courts with sexual details? These inquiries will not diminish the fact that Jewish women were victims first of racial theory and secondly of misogyny. Indeed, they deepen our base of knowledge and help contextualize what we already know.

At one point in his book, Father Desbois terms the murder of Ukrainian Jews a confrontation with unspeakable horror. He refers to his discoveries as "everyday evil."[73] Investigations of the intersections of sexuality and violence in the context of mass murder and genocide appear to be everyday evil under the cover of war. Our approach to sex-based violence should focus on aggression rather than on sex because rape is not the "aggressive manifestation of sexuality but rather a sexual manifestation of aggression."[74] Although its victims were either silent or silenced and recovery of more victim voices is unlikely, careful scrutiny of victim and witness testimony—where it exists—coupled with new archival documents make new information and perhaps understanding entirely possible.

NOTES

My colleagues Elizabeth R. Baer, Dorota Glowacka, and Amy Shapiro shared their comments about this chapter with me, and my work is the better for their ideas and generosity.

The chapter epigraph is from *Gray Zones: Ambiguity and Compromise in the Holocaust and its Aftermath*, ed. Jonathan Petropoulos and John K. Roth (New York: Berghahn Books, 2005), 383.

1   I adopt the term "sex-based violence" here and in the title over the more common term "sexual violence" because it encompasses a "variety of violent and victimizing acts directed at women because of their gender." In the context of the Holocaust, sex-based violence includes forced nudity; verbal abuse (the favorite name for women prisoners in the camps was "whore"); fear of amenorrhea; threats of rape and being sent to brothels; forced sterilization; fear of reprisals and actual reprisals for rejecting sexual favors from *kapos*, soldiers, and others in authority; forced abortion; rape; and consenting to sex in order to survive. Fionnuala Ni Aolain introduced the term to discuss sex-based violence from the legal perspective. See Fionnuala Ni Aolain, "Sex-Based Violence and the Holocaust—A Reevaluation of Harms and Rights in International Law," *Yale Journal of Law and Feminism* 12, no. 1 (2000): 43. http://www.law-lib.utoronto.ca/diana/fulltext/aola1.htm.
Among other related issues, Aolain discusses the paucity of "our vocabulary of violation" in the pre-war years, which inhibited discussion and particularly legal action. See page 49 in the printed version of the text. However, I use the phrase "sexual violence" throughout most of this chapter to accommodate readers who are likely to be more familiar with term. In reference to verbal abuse, see Marlene E. Heinemann, *Gender and Destiny: Women Writers of the Holocaust* (New York: Greenwood, 1986), 29: "The term 'whore' is one of the first and most common insults applied against female deportees, even by female *kapos*." Heinemann's work is one of the earliest extended analysis of literary memoirs and fiction that focuses on women and discusses works by both men and women.

2   Wartime rape is a "ritual" of war, an act that communicates from the men in one group to the men in the other group that they are incapable of protecting their women. It is a physical manifestation of the domination of vulnerable victims,

both male and female. See Rhonda Copelon, "Surfacing Gender: Reconceptualizing Crimes against Women in Time of War," in *Mass Rape: The War against Women in Bosnia-Herzegovina,* ed. Alexandra Stiglmayer (Lincoln: University of Nebraska Press, 1994), 197–218; and Catharine A. MacKinnon, "Turning Rape into Pornography: Postmodern Genocide" and "Rape, Genocide, and Women's Human Rights," in Stiglmayer, *Mass Rape,* 73–81, 183–96. Although MacKinnon describes it as "extracurricular, as just something that men do as product rather than as a policy of war," rape is not the inevitable product of war. Rather, it is the insatiable demand for domination that leads to rape. Susan Brownmiller, in *Against Our Will: Men, Women, and Rape* (New York: Bantam, 1967), explains that "rape is considered by the people of a defeated nation to be part of the enemy's conscious effort to destroy them. . . . Rape by a conquering soldier destroys remaining illusions of power and property for men of the defeated side. The body of a raped woman becomes a ceremonial battlefield, a parade ground for the victor's trooping of the colors. The act that is played out upon her is a message passed between men—vivid proof of victory for one and loss and defeat for the other" (31). In this context, rape is public and a source of pride for the male rapists. See, for example, William I. Hitchcock's discussion of British and American soldiers' raping local women after D-Day, in *The Bitter Road to Freedom* (New York: Free Press, 2008). See also Jonathan Gottschall, "Explaining Wartime Rape," *Journal of Sex Research* 41, no. 2 (May 2004): 129–36, an analysis of four theories of wartime rape: feminist theory, cultural pathology theory, strategic theory, and the biosocial theory, which, he concludes, is the most reasonable explanation for wartime rape.

3   One example is the well-known story of the "dancer" who resisted the SS orders to undress in the anteroom of the gas chamber and "uses her sexuality as a form of resistance," killing one SS officer (Schillinger) and wounding another. See Kirsty Chatwood, "Schillinger and the Dancer," in *Sexual Violence against Jewish Women during the Holocaust,* ed. Sonja M. Hedgepeth and Rochelle G. Saidel (Waltham, MA: Brandeis University Press, 2010), 61–74. Chatwood analyzes the various sources of this story and then contrasts it with resistance to sexual assault and "sex for survival" as narrated in various memoirs. See also Judith Dribben, *A Girl Named Judith Strick* (New York: Cowles Book Company, 1970). Heinemann writes, "Dribben lures Nazi officers to their deaths in a partisan headquarters" (*Gender and Destiny,* 29).

4   Of course, murder of Jews, men and women, was not a crime in the Third Reich. The commodification of Jewish women during the Holocaust is a subset of the commodification of all Jews before they were annihilated, but commodification is also part of the process of annihilation in that men and women were often worked to death or to near death before they were murdered.

5   Primo Levi, "The Gray Zone," in *The Drowned and the Saved,* trans. Raymond Rosenthal (New York: Summit Books, 1988), 36–69. See also Petropoulos and Roth, eds., *Gray Zones.*

6   See Elizabeth R. Baer and Myrna Goldenberg, "Introduction," in *Experience and Expression: Women, the Nazis, and the Holocaust* (Detroit: Wayne State University

Press, 2003), xiii–xxxiii, for an analysis of the controversy over the issue of including women in the study of the Holocaust.

7   Helga Amesberger and Brigitte Halbmayr, "Nazi Differentiations Mattered: Ideological Intersections of Sexualized Violence during National Socialist Persecution," in *Life, Death and Sacrifice: Women and Family in the Holocaust,* ed. Esther Hertzog (Lynbrook, NY: Gefen Books, 2008), 181–96.

8   Ruth Seifert, "War and Rape: A Preliminary Analysis," in Stiglmayer, *Mass Rape,* 55: "In the perpetrator's psyche it serves no sexual purpose but is the expression of rage, violence, and dominance over a woman. At issue are her degradation, humiliation, and submission. To be sure, the violent act is carried out by sexual means."

9   Oddly, until very recently, *Rassenschande* had not captured much historical attention. A quick survey of the indexes of standard Holocaust history books suggests that rape and sexuality are not considered as a significant part of Nazi history although most historians devote at least a paragraph to the topic of racial purity. For example, in Walter Laquer's *The Holocaust Encyclopedia* (New Haven, CT: Yale University Press, 2001) there is no mention of rape or any other type of sexual coercion. There is, however, a body of feminist literary analysis of memoirs and fiction that addresses sex-based violence. See, for example, Heinemann, as well as Sara Horowitz, *Voicing the Void: Muteness and Memory in Holocaust Fiction* (New York: SUNY Press, 1997), and Elizabeth R. Baer, "Rereading Women's Holocaust Memoirs: Liana Millu's *Smoke Over Birkenau,*" in *Lessons and Legacies: From Generation to Generation,* VIII (Evanston, IL: Northwestern University Press, 2008); Lucille Eichengreen, *Haunted Memories: Portraits of Women during the Holocaust* (Exeter, NH: Publishing Works, 2011) and the introduction to the German translation of *Frauen und Holocaust: Erlebnisse, Erinnerungen und Erzähltes* (Bremen: Donat Verlag, 2004). See also the *Journal of the History of Sexuality* 11, no. 1/2 (2002) for a gender-based analysis of the issues related to sexuality during the Holocaust.

10 See "Nuremberg Law against intermarriage between Jews and German citizens, 15 September 1935," in *Sources of the Holocaust,* ed. Steve Hochstadt (New York: Palgrave / Macmillan, 2004), 44.

11 Raul Hilberg, *Perpetrators Victims Bystanders: The Jewish Catastrophe 1933–1945* (New York: HarperPerennial, 1993), 72.

12 Amersberger and Halbmayr, "Nazi Differentiations Mattered," 182.

13 William Shirer, *The Rise and Fall of the Third Reich* (New York: Simon & Schuster, 1959), 431.

14 Patricia Szobar, "Telling Sexual Stories in the Nazi Courts of Law: Race Defilement in Germany, 1933–1945," *Journal of the History of Sexuality* 11, no. 1/2 (2002): 131–63. Szobar details the confusion in carrying out the law over the period of the Third Reich, including the difficulties of enforcing the law on couples in mixed marriages.

15 Flora Singer, *Flora: I Was but a Child* (Jerusalem: Yad Vashem, 2007), 33–35.

16 Saul Friedlander, *Nazi Extermination and the Jews 1939–1945: The Years of Extermination* (New York: HarperCollins Publishers, 2007), 50–51. See also Szobar, "Telling Sexual Stories."

17 Szobar, "Telling Sexual Stories," passim.

18 Narcisa Lengel-Krizman, "A Contribution to the Study of Terror in the So-Called Independent State of Croatia: Concentration Camps for Women in 1941–1942," *Yad Vashem Studies* 20 (1990): 15.

19 See Christiane Kohl, *The Maiden and the Jew: The Story of a Fatal Friendship in Nazi Germany,* trans. John S. Barrett (Hanover, NH: Steerforth Press, 1997). Kohl's research, based on scores of interviews as well as meticulous readings of court and other documents, reveals the influence of "malevolent" neighbors in a city with a long record of hostility to Jews coupled with a legendary antisemite (Julius Streicher) bent on destroying the wealthy and prominent Katzenberger. Seiler and Katzenberger, Kohl makes clear, acted inappropriately. She was high-spirited and flirtatious, and Katzenberger was foolish and incredulous that he would be victimized. He felt safe. This case drew Hitler's attention because of the court's verdict against Seiler. He "insisted from the very beginning that women should not receive sentences when 'racial offenders' were tried. In keeping with that, the section relevant to the severity of punishment mentioned only men, not women. The decision had a certain amount to do with Hitler's warped sexual views—he considered the man active and responsible; the woman was merely the innocent object of masculine desire" (144). Hitler intervened in such cases as early as 1939, and women were not punished except in cases of "false testimony not given under oath [which] was excluded from punishment—perjury under oath was not mentioned, and thus not excluded from sentencing. Hitler thought the two year sentence was too high" (145). Moreover, "the investigating judge, Hans Groben, did not feel entirely happy about the proceedings against Lehmann Katzenberger. Groben later asserted, 'It went counter to my feelings for justice.'" Katzenberger was tried in Special Court where sentences were "more severe than in other courts." He was also charged with violating the Law Concerning Acts Detrimental to the People, "a sort of martial law that severely punished even minor crimes if they were carried out through the exploitation of wartime conditions," e.g., carried out under blackout condition when it was dark, thereby violating the blackout orders. Katzenberger's and Seiler's meetings at night were therefore violations of this law. Judge "Rothaug concluded that the 'offense against racial purity' most certainly had occurred at night, in other words, during darkness" (127–29).

20 Raul Hilberg, *The Destruction of the European Jews* (New York: Holmes and Meier, 1985), 44–47; and Friedlander, *Nazi Extermination and the Jews,* 365–67.

21 Mary Berg, *The Diary of Mary Berg: Growing Up in the Warsaw Ghetto* (Oxford, UK: Oneworld Publications Limited, 2007), 60.

22 Nomi Levenkron, "Death and the Maidens," in Hedgepeth and Saidel, *Sexual Violence against Jewish Women,* 17–18.

23 Szobar, "Telling Sexual Stories," 59.

24 Brownmiller, *Against Our Will,* 44.

25 Ibid., 45.

26 Email correspondence from Charlotte Opfermann to Richard Levy, February 2, 1999, and forwarded to Myrna Goldenberg, February 3, 1999. The subject of these emails was rape during the Holocaust.

27 Gregory Weeks, conversation with author, Seventh Biennial Conference, "Responding to Genocide Before It's Too Late: Genocide Studies and Prevention," International Association of Genocide Scholars, Sarajevo, 2007. Note too that the 1978 television series *Holocaust* depicted a rape of one of the lead characters during Kristallnacht. The series was a fictionalized interpretation of the Holocaust that began with Kristallnacht and ended with liberation. It was not intended to be scholarly history, but its narrative is based on historical events.

28 After the Nazi invasion of the Soviet Union, the Nazis sent Murder Squads, or *Einsatzgruppen,* to four regions of the Soviet Union to annihilate Jews. Atrocities by these squads were relentless. See Brownmiller, *Against Our Will,* 51–52, for her summary of the Molotov Note, a list of Nazi atrocities committed against Jewish women and girls.

29 Jacob Apenszlak, ed. *The Black Book of Polish Jewry: An Account of the Martyrdom of Polish Jewry Under the Nazi Occupation,* American Federation for Polish Jews, 1943 (Westport, CT: Brohan Press, 1999), 8–9.

30 *The Black Book: The Nazi Crime Against the Jewish People* (New York: Duell, Sloan, and Pearce, 1946), 301. From the book jacket: "The entire manuscript was submitted to the juridical authorities of the UN War Crimes Committee meeting at Nuremberg, Germany, as evidence of the crimes committed by the Nazis against the Jewish people."

31 *The Black Book of Polish Jewry,* 25–28.

32 *The Black Book: The Nazi Crime Against the Jewish People,* 164.

33 *The Black Book of Polish Jewry,* 28–29.

34 Brownmiller, *Against Our Will,* 46. Sophia Glushkina's statement is included verbatim in *The Black Book: The Ruthless Murder of Jews by German-Fascist Invaders Throughout the Temporarily-Occupied Regions of The Soviet Union and in the Death Camps of Poland During the War of 1941–1945,* ed. Ilya Ehrenburg and Vasily Grossman, trans. John Glad and James S. Levine (New York: Holocaust Library, 1980), 254–56. See also *The Complete Black Book of Russian Jewry,* ed. Ilya Ehrenburg and Vasily Grossman, trans. David Patterson (New Brunswick, NJ: Transaction, 2002), 212–13. *The Einsatzgruppen Reports: Selections from the Dispatches of the Nazi Death Squads' Campaigns Against the Jews in Occupied Territories of the Soviet Union July 1941–January 1943,* ed. Yitzhak Arad, Shmuel Krakowsi, and Shmuel Spector (New York: Holocaust Library, 1989), 101, corroborates the presence of partisan groups in the area.

35 *The Black Book: The Ruthless Murder,* 302. (Report by USSR Capt. Yefim Gekhtman, war correspondent for the newspaper *Krasnaya Zvezda* during the war.)

36 Aolin, "Sex-Based Violence," 52.

37 *The Black Book: The Nazi Crime against the Jewish People,* 330.

38 *Complete Black Book of Russian Jewry,* 16.

39 *Ibid.,* 62.

40 *The Black Book: The Ruthless Murder* (based on information provided by A. Machiz, Grechanik, L. Gleyzer, and P. M. Shapiro. Prepared for publication by Vasily Grossman). See also *The Complete Black Book,* 132–33.

41 *The Black Book: The Ruthless Murder*, 221.

42 Ibid., 244.

43 The record of sadism by the *Einsatzgruppen* is not to be found in official German reports. Those reports cited above as *The Einsatzgruppen Reports*, found by American soldiers in the Gestapo offices of Berlin, detail the trumped up charges of crimes that Jews perpetrated on the Germans, the Ukrainians, the Belorussians, and so forth. These charges include not wearing the yellow star in public places and apparently justify the murder of the offenders. Most of the reports use the passive voice to detail the death of Jews: 20 Jews were shot for not wearing the star or for not reporting to work or for encouraging others to not work. One report dated September 21, 1941, from Smolensk to Berlin admits that the civilian (non-Jewish) population "complains constantly to military headquarters about burglaries and rapes committed by members of the German army." See especially page 146. Of course, *Reports* also boasts about the statistics—the lists of the number and place of dead Jews and, in most cases, the crimes for which they were shot or otherwise executed. *The Black Books* are more reliable and precise: Jews were shot, beaten to death, hanged, mutilated to death, or set afire.

44 Father Patrick Desbois, *The Holocaust by Bullets: A Priest's Journey to Uncover the Truth Behind the Murder of 1.5 Million Jews*, trans. Catherine Spencer (New York: Palgrave / Macmillan, 2008), 109.

45 Desbois, *Holocaust by Bullets*, 126.

46 Interview, Philadelphia, 1996. The subject does not wish to be identified in any way.

47 Eugene Aroneanu, comp., *Inside the Concentration Camps: Eyewitness Accounts of Life in Hitler's Death Camps* (Westport, CT: Praeger, 1996), 30, 34.

48 Felicja Karay, "Women in Forced Labor Camps," in *Women in the Holocaust*, ed. Dalia Ofer and Lenore Weitzman (New Haven: Yale University Press, 1998), 289.

49 Ibid., 290.

50 Susan Cernyak-Spatz, *Protective Custody: Prisoner 34042* (Cortland, NY: N and S Publishers, 2005), 178–79.

51 Donald Niewyk, ed. *Fresh Wounds: Early Narratives of Holocaust Survival* (Chapel Hill, NC: University of North Carolina Press, 1998), 217. The interviews were conducted in 1946 by David Boder, an American psychologist who went from one DP camp after another to collect the unexceptional or typical stories of survivors. See http://voices.iit.edu. One hundred and nineteen interviews in their original and English translations are well-indexed and easily accessible.

52 Niewyk, *Fresh Wounds*, 221.

53 Paul Valent, ed. *Child Survivors of the Holocaust* (New York: Brunner-Routledge, 2002), 249–65.

54 Gisela Perl, *I Was a Doctor in Auschwitz* (1948; Salem, NH: Ayer Company, Publishers, Inc., 2005), 78–79. Earlier in her memoir, she describes rejecting a trade of sex for a string she needed to fasten her shoes. Willing to give her bread ration for the string, she was shocked by his demand for sex and rejected him, 57–58.

55 Olga Lengyel, *Five Chimneys* (1959; London: Granada Publishing, 1972), 60–64.

56 Anna Pawelczynska, *Values and Violence: A Sociological Analysis* (Berkeley: University of California Press, 1980), 99.

57 Pawelczynska, *Values and Violence*, 99.

58 Elie A. Cohen, *Human Behavior in the Concentration Camp* (New York: Grosset and Dunlap/The Universal Library, 1953), 134.

59 See, for example, the discussion of sex and survival of Fania Fenelon's *Playing for Time*, a memoir in which two women in the women's orchestra in Auschwitz have sexual liaisons with *kapos*, which appears to be "a free act," in Heinemann, *Gender and Destiny*, 31 and passim.

60 Cohen, *Human Behavior*, 135.

61 Lucille E., transcript of interview, August 14, 1990, Holocaust Oral History Project, San Francisco. Lucille E. also relates the experience of a Jewish camp leader at Sasel. An SS corporal from "another camp came every week to visit and bring food. But she paid in return. . . . They locked themselves up in some storage room. Sex."

62 Cohen, *Human Behavior*, 139.

63 Nechama Tec, *Resilience and Courage: Women, Men and the Holocaust* (New Haven, CT: Yale University Press, 2003), 146, 305–35.

64 Opfermann, email to the author, February 3, 1999.

65 Brana Gurewitsch, ed. *Mothers, Sisters, Resisters: Oral Histories of Women Who Survived the Holocaust* (Tuscaloosa: University of Alabama Press, 1998), 58–62. Gurewisch's book includes several stories of lucky breaks in the face of propositions.

66 Valent, *Child Survivors of the Holocaust*, 23–25.

67 Lucille Eichengreen, *From Ashes to Life: My Memories of the Holocaust* (San Francisco: Mercury House, 1994), 48–49, 105–7.

68 Helen Schwartz, "Personal Reflections," Parts III and IV. *www.womenandtheholocaust.com*. Judy Cohen, owner.

69 Lore Shelley, *Auschwitz: The Nazi Civilization*. Studies in the Shoah, vol. 1 (Lanham, MD: University Press of America, 1992), 158.

70 Shelley, *Auschwitz*, 170.

71 Micheline Maurel, *An Ordinary Camp* (New York: Simon and Schuster, 1958), 136–37.

72 Note: Comfort women of Korea finally went public about sex slavery for Japanese in 1992—nearly fifty years later.

73 Desbois, *Holocaust by Bullets*, 203.

74 Seifert, "War and Rape," 55.

PRACTICE OF FEMINIST THEORY AND GENDER ANALYSIS OF THE HOLOCAUST

Each of the essays in Part II directs us to consider gender not so much as a focal point but rather as a context through which we can examine specific issues; such examinations expand and enrich our understanding of the specifics of the Holocaust. Thus, while Part I emphasizes history and theory, the chapters in Part II focus on the impact of the Holocaust on personal and intellectual identities, female relationships, and the experiences of children and mothers.

One way to consider the chapters in this section is to see them as a response to the ways in which gender differences are used to maintain the notion of the Other and to affirm male dominance. Attention to gender has the capacity to challenge assumptions that in the past have been ignored. Those whose purpose it is to delegitimize the experiences of women have successfully done so by suggesting, as if this were a natural opposition, that legitimizing women's voices opposes the legitimacy of men's voices. Such oppositions are self-serving. The "Other" is a consequence of constructing a relation of opposites where oppositions do not exist except as hypotheses for social, political, or rhetorical purposes. Why even consider the idea that giving voice to individual experiences would somehow delegitimize other voices? This would be like suggesting that examination of the experiences of French Jews, for instance, would delegitimize the experiences of Romanian Jews—a completely absurd statement.

The first chapter in this section is a bridge between the two parts of the book. Björn Krondorfer's chapter, written with Karen Baldner, "From Pulp to Palimpsest: Witnessing and Re-Imagining through the Arts," demonstrates two dimensions of the undertaking of this book and, in particular, of this section. On the one hand, Part II is meant to show how theory becomes praxis. On the other hand, we can see that theory not only leads to application but can lead to a change in methodology and the result can be discovery of new theoretical perspectives. Krondorfer's chapter is a description of a multi-layered dialogue. The result is a series of artworks that continues the dialogue in new ways and leads to new methods of intellectual self-discovery with the potential to create new theory. Krondorfer illustrates the role of discomfort and personal morality when we have to consider the ways we are inscribed by gender constructs.

The two chapters that bookend this section construct narratives in which the authors reflect on their moral and intellectual identities in relation to the Holocaust and the lives of those who were affected by it. In Krondorfer's chapter, it is through a personal encounter with the child of German Jews; in Britta Frede-Wenger's chapter, it is in an imagined encounter with Ruth Klüger based on a reading of both the German and English versions of Klüger's memoir. Both authors, in different ways, confront their German identities.

Between these two chapters are works that represent several disciplines and perspectives. In his compelling examination of Nazi attitudes toward the Jewish mother and its consequences for Jewish women, David Patterson's chapter, "The Nazi Assault on the Jewish Soul through the Murder of the Jewish Mother," considers the way gender perspectives can help interpret Nazi behavior; he contextualizes Nazi policy toward Jewish women within Jewish theology and leads us to understand the devastating consequences of such policy on Jewish motherhood. His essay is a wrenching and mystical one.

Patterson's essay is followed by "*Wiedervereiningung Ersehend: Gender and the Holocaust Fate of the Müller and Gittler Families*," in which Suzanne Brown-Fleming considers the correspondence of a German-Jewish family, with close attention to the particularities of gender in both experiences and perceptions. From her investigation of this series of letters, we can see how gender influenced decision-making and, therefore, experience. In her case study, a German Jewish mother appears to be weak, almost invisible, in a time when the burden of sustaining a household generally fell on the women. Hence, gender is one among several characteristics that determine the choices one makes in extreme as well as in "normal" situations.

Because of her focus on the experiences of both girls and boys in the *Kindertransport*, Mary Gallant concludes that "gender differences were important to understanding the experience of traumatic loss and its impact on survival in boys and girls." By enlisting gender as a framework, Gallant gives us a broadened view of the children of the *Kindertransport* and of the motivations and aspirations as well as challenges faced by the rescuers. "The Kindertransport: Gender and the Rescue of Jewish Children 1938–1939" reflects her comprehensive research and intellectual insights. Gaby Glassman, in "Survivor Mothers and their Daughters: The Hidden Legacy of the Holocaust," reveals the rupture in memory between survivor mothers and second-generation daughters and the expectations that the latter be "memorial candles." Glassman finds that consideration of gender in the experiences of the second generation allows insight into individual lives; she demonstrates the influence of female identity on these women's experiences of the world in light of the Holocaust. This chapter is a direct consequence of her work as a therapist running short-term groups for children of survivors. The reader might find that Glassman's essay has connections to Krondorfer's in the light they shed on the second generation.

Britta Frede-Wenger's chapter, "Talking to Ruth Klüger," concludes the book but by no means ends the study of gender and the Holocaust. One of the insights Frede-Wenger has gleaned from Ruth Klüger's *weiter leben* is that we bring ourselves, our own questions, problems, and emotions, in particular, into our work on the Holocaust. Frede-Wenger makes herself uncomfortable as she engages her imagined dialogue with Ruth Klüger. As someone who studies the Holocaust and who unsentimentally confronts difficult questions regarding her own interpretations of Klüger's experiences, Frede-Wenger challenges her sense of herself as a woman, a German, a scholar, and as a young person as she imagines asking Klüger and herself about responsibility to the past.

We, the editors, hope that the readers of this section and the book as a whole will not only be left with a new set of questions to consider but will recognize that consideration of gender engages them in the practice of *tikkun olam* ("repair of the world") as we use gender as a legitimate and necessary dimension of our work.

6

From Pulp to Palimpsest

Witnessing and Re-Imagining Through the Arts

BJÖRN KRONDORFER

IN COLLABORATION WITH KAREN BALDNER

Since the summer of 2002, Karen Baldner and I have been engaged in a collaborative project creating objects about our German and Jewish family histories. We are transforming the cultural messages we have received from our familial and social networks into material representations. As descendants of a persecuted Jewish-German family and a non-persecuted German family, respectively, we have ventured into the haunted spaces left by the legacy of the Shoah and the war. As a Jewish woman and gentile man, we understood early on that rendering ourselves vulnerable in the face of the Other is the most promising way to create a dialogue that would remain true to our quest of accounting for the past without having the past determine our friendship in the present. We collected, assembled, and arranged scraps of memory in response to discomfiting details of family lore and history. A landscape of ruptured lives eventually began to unfold in front of our eyes, and each of us looked at this materialized vista through the lens of our cultural, gendered, and familial dispositions. Because of those differences and because the distance between our residences prevents regular face-to-face encounters, our collaboration seemed an unlikely candidate for success. Yet over the years we have created a small body of work that has received a modicum of public recognition through exhibitions at galleries and museums.[1]

This chapter describes the collaborative process between a woman artist and male scholar that has led to the creation of "material witnesses"
(as we like to call our book art installations). We actively transform personal conversations about the fragility of traumatic memory into material
objects available for public viewing. In quite literal ways, we mix our dialogue into the wet pulp for papermaking; once pressed and dried, the pulp
becomes the parchment onto which we record voices from a fragmented
past. Upon further cutting, arranging, layering, printing, lithograph-
ing, and framing, parchment turns into a palimpsest of collected, faded,
erased, and recombined memories. From pulp to palimpsest: the material level merges with the metaphoric, the personal with the historical,
the traumatic with the visionary, the idiosyncratic with the communal.
Metonymically, pulp becomes our inherited legacy, parchment resembles
our skin, and palimpsest-like installations mirror anxieties that have been
inscribed into the biographies and bodies of our families and ourselves.

RUPTURE

Karen's training and profession is that of a visual artist. She comes from
a Jewish-German family persecuted during the Nazi era. She grew up in
post-Shoah Germany but today resides in Bloomington, Indiana. Art is
her life. She knows about the tradition of bookmaking. She knows how to
turn pulp into paper, how to print and etch, and how to wrap book covers
in fine leather and plain felt. She has the patience to cut, fold, sew, glue,
stitch, and press. She has the artist's courage to discard pieces when they
do not satisfy her aesthetic standards. She is familiar with the art history
of books and with binding techniques. She knows how to prepare the surface of paper, how to turn iron into rust, how to scratch and corrode mirrors. She knows about lost homes. She knows about the loss of trust and
innocence. Between the European World Wars, her maternal grandparents owned one of the largest literary publishing houses in Germany. As
assimilated Berlin Jews, they were an integral part of Germany's cultural
life. They published Rainer Maria Rilke, Thomas Mann, Arthur Schnitzler,
Franz Werfel, Hugo von Hofmannsthal, Hermann Hesse, Alfred Döblin.
In 1935, they managed to rescue part of their publishing house from the
Nazi encroachment by resettling in Vienna. In 1938, they had to abandon
their Austrian apartment overnight and escape to Stockholm. Even Swe-
den turned out to be an inhospitable place. They fled again, this time to

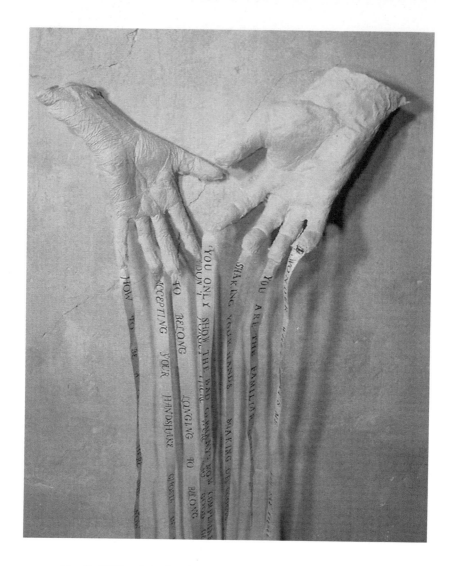

FIG. 1. Detail of *Tikkun/Mending* (2006). Baldner and Krondorfer. Paper-sculpture, c. 60 x 25 inches. From the papercast of our hands, stripes cascade downwards from the top of our fingers, stamped with incomplete phrases.

Moscow and from there with the Trans-Siberian Express to Wladiwostok, to Japan, to Santa Monica, to Connecticut.

I come from a non-persecuted German family. I grew up in postwar West Germany and now am a religious studies professor at a college in Maryland. I teach, I do research, I write. I have patience with words. I facilitate intercultural encounters between people divided by an antagonistic past. I am an imaginative person but not an artist by profession. I have neither the training nor the techné required for book binding, papermaking, or printing, and I have a low tolerance for solving the technical hitches in the artistic process. Yet I thrive when I find opportunities that allow me to think and act creatively. Earlier in my life, I was enthralled by performance art and co-founded the Jewish-German Dance Theatre, a company of American-Jewish and non-Jewish German dancers. Delving into the fragile relationships of a generation born after the Holocaust, the company created an original performance—a kind of movement memorial—that we staged for audiences in Germany and the United States. Concentrating on the expressiveness of body and voice, we crafted a tapestry of images and reminiscences with minimal props, embodying on stage our apprehension about what it means to inhabit a post-Shoah world.[2]

In 1992, Karen and I met for the first time at my college. When I saw Karen exiting the library with a book on Holocaust art tucked under her arm, we discerned a common interest. We started a conversation—tentatively, hesitantly, cautiously. At that time, Karen did not want to talk about her grandparents. Her family biography seemed of little interest to her American environment. Unlike most Jewish refugees, her maternal grandparents had decided to return to Germany after 1945, gathering and rebuilding what was left of their publishing enterprise. Toward the end of their active and embattled lives, they retired and retreated to Italy. The wounds of betrayal never healed. Both grandmother and grandfather wrote extensive autobiographies, testifying to their love of German culture as well as to their lingering suspicion toward a nation that they once called home.[3] In Karen's eyes, I was a descendant of those who, by collectively belonging to the German nation, had expelled and then alienated her grandparents from their *Heimat* (home nation). I was inquisitive, she was reticent. Why talk about her family to me? Why open her past to this German man? It took almost ten more years before we decided to embark on a collaborative project.

Born in 1952 and 1959, we grew up in a world ruptured by the Holocaust and the war. As children of different families and circumstances, we knew that the effects of historic trauma would make impossible any unencumbered, innocent meeting. Hence, we have searched for ways to negotiate the sensitive nature of our encounters by anchoring our dialogue in the materiality of artistic objects. By unpeeling layers of family memories and cultural histories, reassembling them and eventually publicly displaying

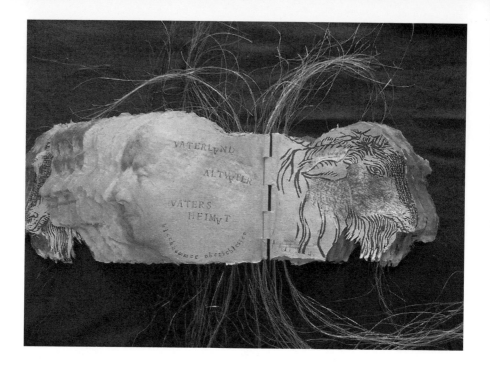

FIG. 2. Detail of *pushmepullyou* (2007). Baldner and Krondorfer. Piano hinge binding with horse hair, linoleum cut, text transfer, digital print on handmade paper, unique book; 7 x 11 x ¼ inches. First exhibited in the show *Sündenbock* (Scapegoat), Neue Synagoge, Berlin, 2007. Each page is individually designed and contains recollections of our cultural and familial legacies

them, we make visible a subjective experience. Our objects leave tangible and touchable traces of personal conversations. Mirroring back to us partial and incomplete truths, our material witnesses mediate, facilitate, and deepen our dialogue. Once placed into public environments, they can also be seen, touched, and witnessed by others, inviting audiences into the privacy of our haunted space.

In the center are stories of our families of origin and the accumulated layers of emotional and political baggage of generations: experiences of conquest and exile, of forced flights and voluntary migration, of refugees and immigrants, of assimilation and defeat, of lost childhoods and interrupted lives, of new beginnings and unfinished business, of bodies violated and restored, of men and women, of Jews and Germans, of Karen and me. Unearthing old longings, we revive worn stories. We discover anew the intimate Other in our families, often catching a glimpse only of shadows.

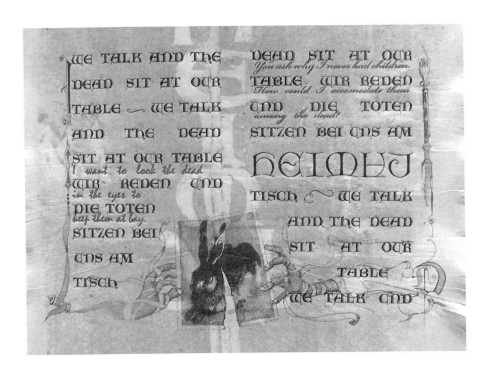

FIG.3. De. *Ghosts* (2010). Baldner and Krondorfer. Mixed media print in handmade paper with text stencil; 40 x 18 x 24 inches. Edition.

We greet the dead sitting at our tables. We decipher handwritten testimonies on forgotten postcards, diaries, and letters. We talk to those still among us. We recall family utterances about Jews and about Germans that leave us with a visceral discomfort in the act of summoning them. We recall resentment and love expressed in the familiarity and fragility of kinship. We mix the contradictory richness of family lore into the wet pulp like precious spices and embed them in sheets of paper like traces of a fragrance.

We quote from visual and oral family archives, sometimes with the approval of loved ones, at other times against their reticence. We arrange retrieved fragments of the past in light of the here-and-now. We make transparent to the public the material that emerges, and we become, in the process, transparent to each other: beyond shame, beyond guilt, beyond recriminations. Not that these feelings don't exist, but they do not dominate our aesthetic exploration. We juxtapose memories like a palimpsest that reaches back to the injuries of the past while pointing to the possibilities of the future.

We have worked with crude iron frames surrounding fragile revelations transposed on Plexiglas panels. Like wooden wings on a triptych, these transparent panels swing open, squeaking in their rusted metal hinges. Even when closed, they make visible the (family) secrets scribbled onto their surface. We code those secrets as memories that are both personal and collective.

We have written marginalia onto fabric and Plexiglas, onto strings of handmade paper and lithographed snap shots. As if adding commentary to Talmudic pages, our marginalia examine past choices made by our families and communities. We remain aware of the incompleteness of our endeavor to restore the past to the present.

We have created written testimonies that cannot be pressed between the covers of a book: strings of words flowing out of fingertips of papercast hands—the blood and ink of our lives. Each word, each phrase that streams out of our fingers is part of how we articulate ourselves into being. As these printed strings entangle and intertwine, they become part of an assemblage that does not insist on isolation. Acknowledging that our roots are found in a shared historical and geographical space—a space filled with hurt, betrayal and losses—we begin to bond to each other.

HOME

Books are important to Karen and me. Not only are books rooted in the German and the Jewish traditions, they are also personally significant to us. Books were the livelihood of Karen's grandparents, books are part of my livelihood. Karen likes to make pages from pulp, I like to put words on those pages. She likes to play with the book format, I like to play with language. She likes to bind them, I like to write them. Books contain worlds: intimate notes and dogmatic declarations; prayers and business records; stories and prohibitions; memories and visions. They contain destructive ideologies and give testimony to suffering. You can close worlds by closing books. You can burn books. You can lock them away. You can enshrine them. You can carry them suspended from around your waist. You can make them transparent. You can hide messages in them or adorn them with marginal notes. You can erase words. You can turn pages into mirrors so that you may encounter yourself. Karen and I are experimenting with such possibilities, exploring the quality of different materials and searching for the style that befits the stories we have to tell.

In homage to a particularly German binding style, we have created medieval girdle books. These are pocket-size books that can be carried suspended from a waist belt. They are intimate and inconspicuous, and yet add weight to your body. They are a little piece of "home" you can take along wherever you go. And so we called our first girdle book "Heimat."

Bound in smooth yellow leather, "Heimat" is constructed from handmade paper, some pages the color of earth, others the color of ashes. Embedded are scraps of European maps. Handprinted black letters dance on ocher paper, and lithographed negatives of family snapshots gild black surfaces. Strings of yellow, red, and black wire thread pour out of "Heimat," uncontainable by the cover. The pages recall conflicting bits of memories, citations, and ideas, unfolding like a stream of consciousness. "Heimat"

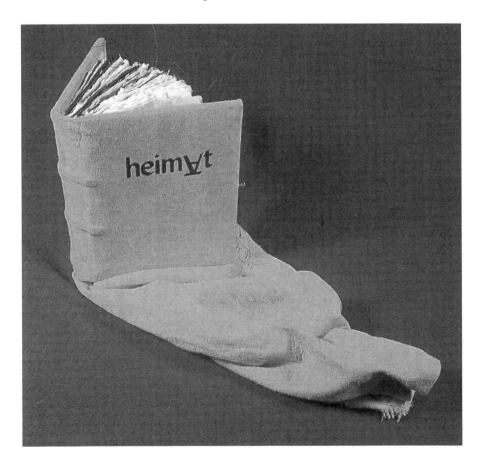

FIG. 4. *Heimat* (2005). Baldner and Krondorfer. Girdle book; 5 x 4 x 1 inches.

documents our uncertainties about our German homes of origin—an uneasiness already visible in the printed title on the leather cover. Referencing Albrecht Dürer's signature A, we place it on its head in allusion to the upside down B in the phrase "ARBEIT MACHT FREI" of the infamous entrance gate to Auschwitz.

Our family stories are saturated with experiences of uprootedness: stories of *Exil, Flucht, Vertrauensbruch, Versteck, Assimilation, Kriegsgeschichten, Vertreibung*. Uprootedness is loss of home, of *Heimat*. It is the pained awareness of that loss. It is a nostalgic yearning that throbs like a heartbeat under the surface of the present. To be uprooted is less the result of a deliberate cutting of one's roots than a response to unsettling forces greater than oneself: exile, expulsion, emigration. Replanted into new soil, the soul remains strung to a past that now lives on only in the imagination. What is lost cannot be recovered. The awareness of loss, however, can settle into one's present life, expressing itself in sentiments that oscillate between resentment and bereavement, public regrets and private tears. Nostalgia: the pain (*algia*) for the nest (*nostos*). While yearning for a lost home immobilizes, a lived sense of at-homeness is restorative.

"Home is memory of irretrievable childhood," writes postwar German novelist Bernhard Schlink. "It is a scent, the most fleeting of sensations."[4] I am easily swayed by his poetic sentimentalism. It is the sweet pain of nostalgic yearning, not marred by the bitterness of those who have been forcibly expelled as non-citizens.

For Jean Amery, nostalgia is privilege. "One must have a home in order not to need it," he writes. And: "Traditional homesickness" is nothing but "comforting self-pity." Like other Holocaust survivors, Amery had to realize that the country he had once called home "had never been ours." What is left, Amery laments, is the hurt that arises from a "combination of hatred for our homeland and self-hatred."[5] Karen relates to Amery's disenchanting realism. In the beginning of our project, she did not refer to Germany as home and she would rarely speak German to me—as if she had cut off any ties to the country of her childhood, a place she perceived as unwelcoming.

For Karen, *Heimat* is something that others may possess, but not her. Her assimilated German-Jewish grandparents had been forced out of Berlin. They lost their private home and their publishing house, their citizenship, and their trust. Karen, who was born to one of their daughters, did not experience the expulsion personally. But she grew up with a loss that had become her family's *unheimlicher* companion—the uncanny presence of not-at-homeness.

NAKED

We feel at home in our bodies. Skin demarcates the boundaries of this home, the boundary between me and the other. Skin repels and absorbs, invites and rejects, tickles and burns, protects and gets torn. It is a permeable membrane that facilitates the exchange between inside and outside. Skin channels sensuality, yearned for at times, unwelcome at others. If trespassed and intruded, that which ought to be truly ours turns into an alienating place. Instead of providing comfort, pleasure, and safety, the body-as-home becomes a storage room filled with anxiety.

Uncannily, the ideology of racial hatred Karen's parents and grandparents had experienced recurred as physical assault in her own life. The inherited anguish of her family's severed national roots returned in the form of a bullet that sliced the flesh below Karen's ribcage and struck the wooden floor of her American home. The scars are still visible today, both in her body and her house. The assailant—her husband—killed himself after the attack. Instantly, her house and her body had become unstable, violated places.

A woman's home twice betrayed.

A Jewish woman's triple betrayal.

Just as Karen's ancestors' at-homeness had been plundered and ransacked, her American home was desecrated and her skin ripped open. The experience of many Jews became the experience of many women. Expelled from the metaphoric womb and assaulted by an intimate male Other, Karen began to draw her flayed body in charcoal on torn paper. Lifeless skin that lacks skeletal and muscular support; a limp integument devoid of any belonging.

Years later, Karen became victim of yet another assault, this time by a man unknown to her, who broke into her house and raged against her body. De-skinned. Flayed. Raw. Naked. Karen needed to draw bodies unprotected, but beyond shame, in order to restore herself—to restore what seemed like a chain of violations: from her maternal grandparents' flight from Berlin and her paternal grandfather's imprisonment in a Nazi forced labor camp to her ravaged American home.

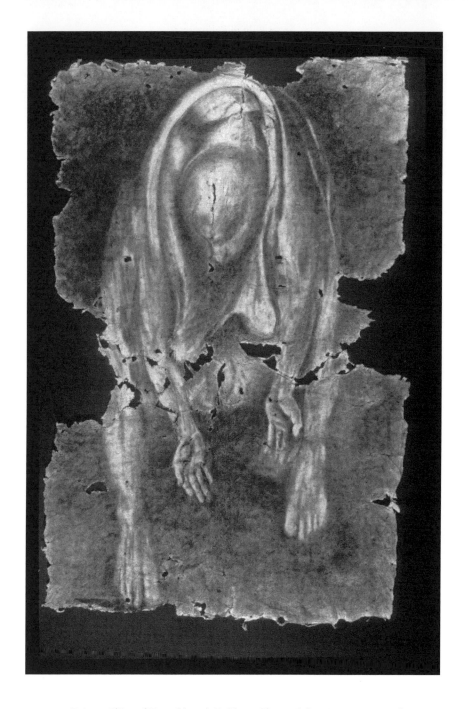

FIG. 5. *Privacy Skinned/Boned* (1992). Baldner. Charcoal drawing; 60 x 50 inches.

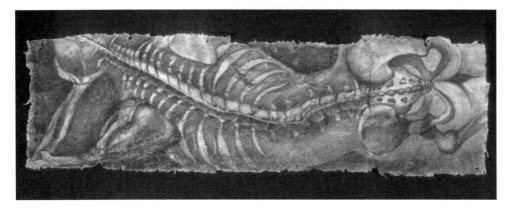

FIG. 6. *Private Backache* (1993). Baldner. Drawing; 22 x 77 inches.

When I met Karen—a book on Holocaust art tucked under her arm—
the assaults had been in the past, but the road to recovery was not yet
completed. When Karen met me, she saw a smiling man who spoke with
a German accent: "Let's open our past to each other. Let's become vulnerable in each other's presence." I did not know about Karen's shattered
sense of safety, and my body had never experienced the kind of violations
she survived. When I suggested that we should continue our conversation through the unconventional means of movement improvisation—the
way I had earlier worked in the Jewish-German Dance Theatre—she was
intrigued. We tried it, but the experiment did not last long. For Karen, the
idea of exploring through movement the mistrust that had accumulated
between Jews and Germans over generations was hitting home too closely.
It frightened her; only much later did she tell me about the sexual assaults.

Years passed before we embarked on our collaborative project. We
stayed in contact through email, occasional phone conversations, and
the rare visit. During this period, Karen's art focused on the female body
to express the loss of physical integrity, while my scholarship shifted to
questions of masculinity and religion. While I completed a book on the
intersection of the religious imagination and the male body, Karen completed a series of drawings that rendered the body of the "other"—male
and Christian—wounded and vulnerable. Her images seemed a perfect fit
for the cover of my book, and so began our first non-intentional collaboration. Karen writes: "My new body of work followed on the heels of a cycle
of drawings that looked at my own wounded body. In an attempt to widen

FIG. 7. Krondorfer performing in *The Jewish-German Dance Theatre* in 1988. The company experimented with techniques that often required imaginative identification.

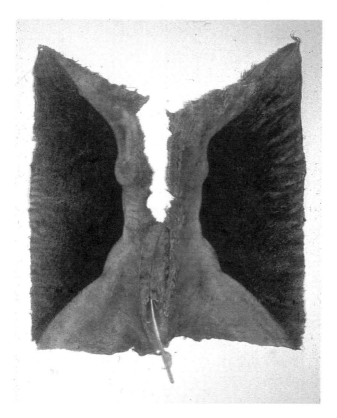

FIG. 8. *Feathered Privacy I* (1992). Baldner. From a series of fifteen charcoal drawings; 15 x 11 inches. The *Privacy* cycle is a self-portrait of a personal healing process.

FIG.9. *Stations OFF the Cross* (1992). Baldner. From a series of eight charcoal drawings; 60 x 50 inches.

my circle from my own gendered female wound it made most sense to me to look at the wounded male body through the lens of an iconic body, such as the Christ figure."

Naked and exposed, her male bodies stretch across torn parchment in the pose of crucifixion, radiating pain and ecstasy. An eerie mood of violation and sensuality is exuded from these broken bodies. Ordered sequentially, her *Stations OFF the Cross* drawings show a limp penis rising to visible signs of erection. Karen states that "while the tradition of depicting Christ seems to allude to him as heroic and divine, it also seems to point distinctly to his maleness while, at the same time, making an effort to suppress his sexuality. What would happen, I wondered, if such images were just left to play themselves out to their hidden intentions? What would be left of the depiction of the heroic and divine?" I would later write in the introduction to *Men's Bodies, Men's Gods*, "The theological insistence on the simultaneity of Jesus' maleness and Christ's asexuality seems to have been experienced as a continuous source of frustration, for it produced a paradoxical notion of male spirituality by insisting on phallic power while denying the sexual penis."[6] Other books followed that feature Karen's work as cover art.

 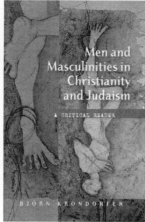 

FIG. 10-12. Books authored by Björn Krondorfer, with cover art by Karen Baldner. From left: *Men's Bodies, Men's Gods* (New York University Press, 1996); *Men and Masculinities in Christianity and Judaism* (SCM Press, 2009); and *Male Confessions: Intimate Revelations and the Religious Imagination* (Stanford University Press, 2010).

Below the surface of conscious effort, serendipity shaped our nascent dialogue. Our parallel interest in the male and the female body—pursued through distinct professional venues—influenced how we began exploring our Jewish and German identities. Nakedness as the deleterious effect of forced intrusions; nakedness also the result of deliberate peeling away of sacrosanct layers of cultivated misinformation and distrust. Sensitized to the vulnerability of gendered bodies, we queried our Jewish and German acculturated bodies: How has history written itself into and onto our skins? Are our bodies "memory texts"? Would we be able to decipher the codes of communal belonging chiseled into our very beings? Would it require the gaze of the Other to realize that what we take as our natural identity is actually sculpted by the cultural ethos of our families and communities?

BEGINNINGS

Long after our failed movement improvisation and after years of intermittent correspondence, Karen unexpectedly said, "I am ready now. Would you still want to work together?"

Karen's wish to return to dialogue through the medium of art was motivated by several factors. For one, her search for understanding of her family origins had taken on an urgency she had not felt before. With her grandparents dying (and having already lost both her mother and her brother), Karen felt called to become the visual scribe for her family's legacy. She gently urged her reluctant father to talk about his survival during the war years in Berlin. In the terminology of Nazism, her father had been classified a *Halbjude*: his mother was from a renowned Jewish family, owners of a German department store chain, and had married a non-Jewish classical musician.

Karen also realized that her own victimization was somehow linked to the ambience of victimhood in her childhood home. She writes: "My own wounded body fit right in with the familiar wounded 'family body.' It is this awareness that brought me to seriously immerse myself in my family history." The torment she experienced in her female body became entwined with the anguish of her Jewish-German family origins. To that effect, she identified increasingly as a "second-generation" artist.

Wanting to restore her at-homeness again, Karen probed the coincidental significance of her birthday of November 9, 1952. Onto a wall-sized panel of handmade paper, into which she wove strands of black hair, she printed over and over again, "November 9." Karen was born on the day on which—fourteen years earlier—Jewish stores had been smashed, synagogues burned, and people beaten, arrested, and killed. The Night of Broken Glass in 1938 foreshadowed the genocidal killing that was about to be implemented as a policy across Nazi-occupied Europe. Raised by Jewish re-émigrés in postwar Germany, Karen would celebrate her birthday each year while across West Germany the annual rituals of commemoration inevitably took their course. On this day, public representatives would feel moved to recite the political wisdom and moral certitude of "never again." Each year, Karen would sense the gap between the smoothness of public memorializing and the emotional turmoil of family memories. Then, on November 9, 1989, the wall in Berlin fell, ending the postwar division between East and West Germans.

"November 9" is Karen's attempt to link her individual birthday to momentous historical events. The hairy surface, suggestive of the privacy of skin, blends intimate fragility with collective experience. Permeable and temporary as aging skin, the wall-size parchment recalls Berlin's graffiti-covered wall, Jerusalem's Wailing Wall (as Karen says), and a gigantic scroll containing a very personal midrash.

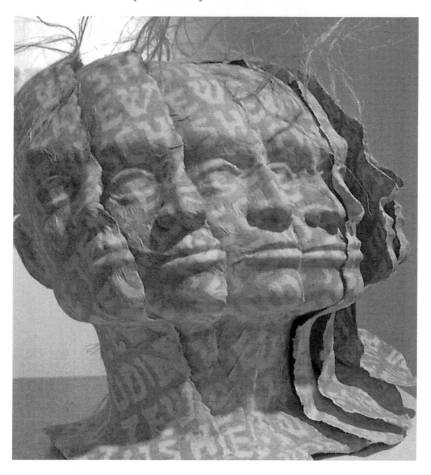

FIG. 13. *German/Jew* (2004). Baldner. Book structure; 12 x 12 x 12 inches. Multiple paper casts of Karen's portrait. Peeled away, each layer reveals "Jew" on one half of the head and "German" on the other, stenciled into the paper as watermarks. The face's enigma: Does it portray the bursting of a unified personality or the birthing of a new self?

Slowly, Karen's acute woundedness and personal uncertainty gave way to communal concerns. In her drawings, she left behind depictions of de-skinned individual bodies and, instead, moved toward a communal project, in which women explored intimate aspects of the female body. Karen organized the Bloomington Breast Project, in which women of all ages and walks-of-life created paper casts of their breasts and exhibited them as installations in public spaces. Instead of private interiority, public outreach. Karen writes:

> Somehow, through all the emotional haze of growing up in a trauma-infused home I wished nothing more than to be heard by another German, to tell the perpetrator about the outrage that I felt beneath the lines of my family's persecution story. When I revisited Björn's offer for an encounter, it was at a point when, similar to the rape healing, I was ready to integrate my identity as a Jew and a German into a larger post-Shoah context. I think it was the Bloomington Breast Project that helped me get to that point. Through it I firmed up my sense of security and identity as a woman and built a vocabulary of communicating as a woman. I also gained confidence in the language of collaborating. Meanwhile, my understanding of Shoah history grew as I became more steeped in family history and identified as a member of the second generation after the Shoah. What attracted me to Björn was his reconciliation work, his personalized and subjective involvement with history, and ultimately his willingness to be vulnerable. I felt a strong need to go beyond verbal dialogue because it invariably felt like it allowed for escaping responsibility. The creative process, however, always leaves traces that make the creators accountable. From Björn's work as a performer I knew he had the courage to leave such traces.

When Karen asked me to re-ignite our dialogue beyond the occasional conversation, I was hesitant. Having worked for many years on issues of post-Shoah relations, both in facilitated encounters and in my research, I was unsure of whether to enter yet another round of intensely personal exchanges. In my own search for family history, I had earlier reached a pivotal point when discovering a perplexing aspect of my father's life. At the age of seventeen, he had been stationed in a military unit in close proximity to a Jewish slave labor camp. I learned this fact only coincidentally from a casual remark in a conversation with my father. When he mentioned the camp's name, I recalled the testimony of Edward Gastfriend, a Jewish survivor born in Sosnowiec, Poland. Edward had survived several camps, among them Blechhammer (Blachovnia in Polish) in Upper Silesia, about forty miles west of Auschwitz. Decades later, during a casual dinner conversation, my father made a brief reference to Blechhammer when talking about his adolescence, not knowing that I would recognize this location.

In this instance, worlds collided that had hitherto seemed apart: my own family biography and the history of the Shoah unexpectedly overlapped.

My father and Edward are of the same age. They were both teenagers when the war uprooted them. My father had been stationed in the vicinity of Blechhammer in order to be trained in an anti-aircraft unit. Edward Gastfriend, during the same time, struggled to keep alive under the severe conditions of the slave labor camp. Dropped in the forested region of Upper Silesia, where the Germans were building a sizeable industrial complex to produce synthetic gas, my father and Lolek (as Edward was called back then) lived parallel lives. For several months, between 1943 and 1944, each of them experienced the region of Blechhammer from different sides of the fence. My father protected the chemical plant as a German soldier from the bombing raids of American warplanes, while the very same factory exploited the labor of a Jewish teenager.[7]

When my father turned seventy, he and I traveled to Poland in search of Blechhammer. With the help of historic maps, we eventually found the camp's remnants overgrown in a remote forest. We even found the spot where the big anti-aircraft gun had been positioned that my father's military unit operated. As I moved with my father through this landscape, the geography of Blechhammer became part of my own world. I also began to realize that my father and Lolek—unbeknownst to each other—must have

FIG. 14. *Blechhammer, 1943-44* (2007). Krondorfer. Linocut; 6 x 6 inches. Based on a photo from a family album, now part of *pushme-pullyou* (see fig. 2).

seen each other back in 1943 on a road leading to the industrial site. Both of them describe the same road in their separate narratives.

When Karen asked me to return to our family stories, I felt I could go no further.

This was the situation when Karen and I began our collaborative journey: she reached out at a moment when I was about to withdraw from soul-searching with respect to Jewish-German dialogue. I felt that I had exposed myself enough. I had also become more protective of my parents.[8] The allure of art, however, persuaded me, and I said yes.

WIT(H)NESS

"Recovering from the rape experience and mending my relationship to the Shoah happened concurrently," Karen writes.

> When I met Björn, these two identities were still deeply steeped in victim experience and far from being teased apart. On the horizon I could see the contours of a broader, more positive and integrated self, but Björn's offer to connect through contact improvisation posed a huge discomfort. It challenged me into exactly the kind of intimacy that I feared: the revealing of vulnerability toward each other. In my sense of victimhood at the time, I was not willing to entrust my feelings toward him, a German and a man. His physical proximity was suspicious to me, just as any man's closeness. Björn's efforts to clarify my feelings toward him as a German seemed like a philosemitic gesture. This was a judgmental attitude I had inherited from my parents, which I had not yet replaced with my own views. Along that line, I paradoxically felt intimidated by his vast knowledge of the Shoah, of Jewish traditions and of reconciliation efforts between Germans and Jews. I felt like I had to own this knowledge myself first before I could consider his offer for a thorough encounter. I did not, however, forget the offer. It felt like a life-long wish come true.

We retreated for five days to a studio in Manhattan. During these days, we mostly talked, interrupted only by simple drawing exercises. We told each other our family histories in frank and detailed openness. We sketched our family trees on poster-sized papers and pinned them to the wall. We added names and dates, drew arrows between family members, appended our emotional relations to them, and identified cultural topoi replicated in familial experiences.

What Karen had appreciated about my earlier offer of dialogue she now reciprocated with kind generosity. Without judgment, she listened to the stories I knew about my family. She allowed herself to see my father as a teenager—beyond the Wehrmacht uniform. She teared up when I showed her a postcard I had retrieved from the family archive. It had been written by my grandmother to my mother in January of 1945, when she had stayed behind as the last person of her family at her home near Königsberg, East Prussia. The Soviet Army had already encircled this region and my grandmother did not expect to survive. To her seventeen-year-old daughter, whom she had sent off to find her own way westward, she penned the following words: "Facing the inevitable separation, I greet and I kiss you one last time. I submit to the inevitable and pray for your future destiny. Hour by hour, the situation grows worse, rescue is hopeless. In eternal love your loving mother." Luckily, they both survived the chaotic flight in the winter of 1945—but they did not know this when my grandmother sent these lines, which she must have believed to be her last testament. Karen remembers, "There were moments when I felt really touched, sometimes in tears, but happy tears. For example, when you read to me from materials that must have been difficult for you; yet you read them to me word for word."

I felt similarly touched when Karen shared documents from her family archive. For example, her father, hitherto reticent to bring up the past, handed her a journal of the war years in Berlin, and I read parts of these handwritten pages in Karen's home in Bloomington.

In a small installation called "Obituaries/Nachrufe," we arranged family documents about our grandfathers, who had died before we were born. Presented as fragments of our unknown grandfathers, "Obituaries/Nachrufe" has the feel of *objets trouvé*: haphazardly retrieved scraps from family archives, collected at the mercy of coincidence and caprice, and displayed as a mosaic of war mementos. My "unknown" maternal grandfather had been a Wehrmacht officer who died of stomach cancer in 1941. As a young man, he had fought in the First World War and volunteered, twenty years later, in the Second World War. Karen's "unknown" paternal grandfather Max, the musician, married into a Jewish-German family. He died in 1946 from the effects of his imprisonment in the forced labor camp of Leuna. As a mixed family, he and his Jewish wife and children found temporary refuge at the Silesian estate of Yorck von Wartenburg. When von Wartenburg got involved in the failed July 20 plot to assassinate Hitler, the family returned to Berlin. Refusing to divorce his Jewish wife, Max was sent to Leuna. He never recovered from his deteriorated health and died a year after liberation.

The personalities of "the grandfathers we never knew" (as Karen and I often call this piece) surface through obituary materials affixed between Plexiglas panels. Snippets of letters of consolation from former comrades, public eulogies from friends, and various symbolic materials (fabric, hair, straw, sand) allude to their personalities and deaths. By combining the panels at random, two different sides of German society are made transparent in surprising synchronicity and non-linear chronology.

In another installation, stories emerge from a set of three typewriters arranged waist-high above the floor. Ghost-like hands, cut at the wrist, feed each typewriter with scraps of recollections that rise from a messy heap on the ground. From a pile of fabric, hair, and strings, memories wind their way upward, dangling freely in the air, inchoate, often illegible. Eventually, these memory strings find themselves pressed into the mechanics of the

FIG. 15. *Obituaries/Nachrufe* (2005). Baldner and Krondorfer. Panel mounted on wood; 13 x 30 x 25 inches. The work relies on relatively small materials and a collapsible structure that people can move and manipulate.

typewriter, where they are bent to the rules of technology and grammar. A tellable story is imprinted onto the tangled mess of what is remembered and what is forgotten. "When I was a child, JUDE was a word that triggered extreme discomfort . . ." begins the legible sentence of the typewriter administered by ghostly German hands. Jewish hands, floating in midair, write, "I grew up among you but how could I call myself one of you . . ."

At times, it seems that the friendship between Karen and me evolves because of our Jewish and German identities; at other times, our collaboration moves us beyond this legacy. Our dialogue is not limited to an *ars memoria* but also expresses bonds of affection. We are not prisoners of the unresolved lives of our families of origin but live auspiciously in the presence of our families of choice. When my wife and I welcomed our first-born into this world, Karen was a witness to this moment of bliss. Later, my daughters learned bookmaking and printing from Karen at her studio during a summer arts camp.

Occasionally, Karen and I share our concerns about the flourishing of a Holocaust memorial culture that seems to suppress nuances of life. During a life crisis, I wrote these thoughts to her:

> I sometimes wonder whether my involvement in Holocaust related issues
> over so many years—with its heavy, traumatizing content—has begun
> to rob me of a joy of life and whether it has stalled my ability to be fully
> in the present. I feel the same about family history—not in general, but
> specific to me—in the sense that I've done enough to try to work out
> unresolved issues of previous generations. I can't go any further because
> these issues resist resolution. I won't really get any more insights from my
> parents and their generation. Hence, I wonder how wise it is to focus on a
> new idea about a book object that again looks at the *unbewältigte Vergan-*
> *genheit* (unresolved past) of our families' past.

Karen responded:

> Since your life crisis began I have felt out of sync with our tenacious ideas
> for this book. Instead, what emerges for me is how much I like our title,
> *Wit(h)ness*. And how drawn I feel to the bottom line of what our project
> has always meant to me: that it is about us today, against the backdrop
> of the Shoah, and ultimately about two people who are sharing in each
> others lives. I am wondering if we could make the book about what is

FIGS. 16 AND 17 Details of *with-drawing the line: Triptych* (2008). Baldner and Krondorfer. Installation; c. 50 x 50 inches.

happening to us right now. Our work has always been a kind of witnessing process and certainly a "withness." My point here is that there is a subtext: the need to move away from the Shoah and the struggle to find a shape for this urge. You may remember that I felt attracted to using your article on "Forgetting"[9] as a springboard for our book last summer. There are profound life processes at work for each of us and we are actually witnessing them to each other. The title "wit(h)ness" is beautifully serendipitous and beckoning.

We created a unique exemplar called "wit(h)ness," in which we queried the value of remembering and forgetting. Bound in felt fabric, we chose again the girdle book format (later, we produced a numbered edition of this work). Each of the white pages is embossed with letters. Sunken into the texture of handmade cotton paper, words leave tangible evidence of the intangible, traceable with either fingers or eyes: "remembrance is betrayal of the totality of memory"; "with hold"; "can I redeem my parents' past?" On another page, the negative space left by the hollowed-out letters reads,

FIG. 18. Page from *wit(h)ness* (2010). Baldner and Krondorfer. Letterpress embossed text on handmade cotton paper; 5 x 4 inches.

"white memory." Wit(h)nessing, we circumambulate the *terra incognita* of a trauma-laden, guilt-ridden, elusive past: the imprint of fading post-memory, the white lies of remembrance, the white fire of etched forgetfulness.

MATERIALS

Our choice of material—handmade paper, fabric, leather, horse hair, felt, Plexiglas, plastic, twine, colored wire threads, mirrors, rusted steel—blends contemporary sensibilities with cultural histories. In "Who Am I in Your Presence/*Wer bin ich in deiner Gegenwart*," our first work, we placed a scratched mirror into a crude, rusted steel frame, with Plexiglas panels attached to each side. The movable panels outline the profile of our faces. Surfacing from behind the scratched mirror, a map of Europe reveals locations of lost and abandoned homes.

Karen and I work with maps. We cut out maps of Europe from historical atlases. On them, we mark the birthplaces of parents, grandparents, and great-grandparents. Surprisingly, the geographies of our families overlap

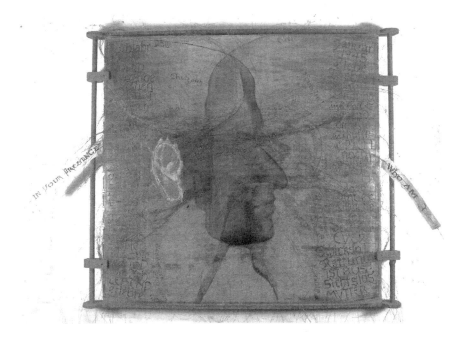

FIG. 19. *Who Am I in Your Presence / Wer Bin Ich in Deiner Gegenwart* (2004). Baldner and Krondorfer. Wall-mounted panels; 20 x 72 x 20 inches..

in several places. Connecting the dots, we trace the migration patterns of our Jewish and German ancestors, and the European landscape becomes crisscrossed like a spider web. Despite the many losses of homes—from Transylvania to East Prussia, from Moravia to Berlin—we sense something like *Heimat* when immersing ourselves into geographies.

A map's surface gains in depth as we dig beyond the smooth print and unearth the smell of our roots. The pock-marked landscape becomes a staging ground for our post-memories. We trace the silhouettes of our faces as if tracing geographical patterns. Our faces become like maps, genetic contours of ideological landscapes. Patterns imposed on maps, words imposed on silhouettes, memories imposed on the present.

The choice of material, which occasionally challenges our personal aesthetic, has gender implications. "Some materials are beyond my physical realm as a woman, a short woman for that," Karen states.

> I would not gravitate toward rusted steel, mirrors, even wood and Plexiglass, let alone a combination of these. Not to mention packing, crating and shipping such materials all over the country and abroad. I had to force myself to familiarize myself with lifting, cutting, welding and sandblasting metal. I had to learn about table saws, varieties of blades, specialty glues. I had to befriend the workshops that dealt with metal fabrication and solicit help from a world that I found was mostly dominated by men. In the end I was grateful for having learned a lot about a new language of materials and the particular synergy of matter that has become our signature vocabulary. Because of our joint work I have become more sensitized to the material choices in my own work as being feminine. I have sometimes felt myself internally chuckling when Björn came up with something I would never think about. His choices felt particularly masculine, which I enjoyed as they would surprise me. I guess I didn't want to admit my delight as I was afraid it would make him—creatively—self-conscious. His idea about steel frames is a case in point. I really liked the idea, but steel continues to be foreign to me. In the end it is part of the process of listening to each other.

Karen once asked me whether papermaking seemed foreign to me, as a man. It doesn't. Getting my hands wet in the pulp has been one way to actively partake in the act of creation. Lacking the skills and technical know-how, I am largely sidelined in the actual labor with the material aspects of our work. If anything ever feels like a challenge to my masculine identity, it is the humbling realization of my technical inadequacies.

"Materials" also come in the form of inspiration. Although we refrain from making deliberate references to other second-generation artists, our dialogue takes place within contemporary aesthetic sensibilities. Our "material witnesses" are no islands. Inspired by the monumental work of the visual maestros of German *Vergangenheitsbewältigung*, like Joseph Beuys, Gerhard Richter, and Anselm Kiefer,[10] Karen and I create our installations on a far more humble scale. Listening closely, one can hear echoes of Jean Amery, Paul Celan, Shimon Attie, Christian Boltanski, and Rachel Whiteread—each of them struggling differently with the presence of absence.[11] At times, the discovery of unintended affinity to other artists is uncanny. Only recently did I learn of Bracha Ettinger's artistic and theoretical testimony to the ineffable trauma of her parents' survival. It was not until Karen and I had completed the unique exemplar of "wit(h)ness" that a colleague made me aware of Ettinger's use of the neologism "wit(h)nessing." Building upon Levinas's philosophy, the Israeli artist and feminist theorist applies the term to the act of bearing witness as a shared experience with others. Ettinger creates an "intersubjective zone of closeness and togetherness, in which fractured subjects continuously engage," writes Dorota Glowacka. "For Ettinger, the skin-parchment is first and foremost the site of contact, vulnerability and sharing, of sensuousness and touch."[12] I was stunned by the parallel to our collaboration when I was reading these lines.

TRANSFORMATION

Language as home: for a long time Karen found it difficult to speak with me in German. When I once confided to her that I felt a familiarity between us because of our common German roots, she balked at the idea and insisted on difference, not sameness. Her response puzzled me, for I truly felt that—around her, while surrounded by Americans—I was in the presence of a fellow German, who, like me, happens to live in the United States.

Karen writes in a letter: "My relatives were ever vigilant towards the 'German other,' paranoid about being lashed out against, prepared to be victimized yet again, scrutinizing almost everyone around us. When you led me into German colloquialisms (and I allowed myself to be led into them) I simultaneously hated and enjoyed the language. In one of the pages of 'Heimat,' I wrote that you are re-teaching me the German language, and

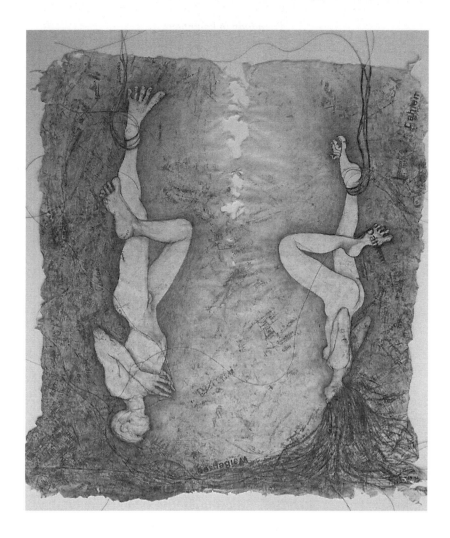

FIG. 20. *The Presence of Your Absence XXI* (2008). Baldner; 18 x 12 inches..

you answered that my admission is painfully embarrassing to you. Yet, for me a huge hurdle was crossed in this interaction."

We have changed since: Karen now allows herself to indulge in longings for German culture while I have adopted U.S. citizenship. We are comfortable conversing in German and English indiscriminately, often switching languages in mid-sentence. However, we keep agonizing over the use of language in our objects. What language should we speak? Since blending image and text is important to us, should we inject and insert ourselves in our mother tongues? Would we estrange an audience unfamiliar with

German? Would foreign words add a layer of enigma, like the patina of old photographs? If we were to provide translations, would we sacrifice our aesthetic vision for educational objectives? We are constantly reminded of how challenging it is to transform the particulars of intimate memory to the universals of contemporary recognition.

Today, we embrace our bilingualism as both a blessing and a burden: we can feel home in two worlds but we are never completely *complete* in either.

In the end, our *ars memoria* yearns for transformation rather than documentation: separate memories morph into visually unified pieces, open to interpretation and inspiration. We have taken the risk of listening to each other and we have moved beyond the inherited skin that traps us in the roles of descendants of victims and perpetrators. There is no longer a fixed and predetermined position from which we speak. When our material witnesses stare back at us like mirrors, they prompt us to ask again whether we have accomplished the level of honesty we are striving for. What might have previously fallen through the cracks of interpersonal tension may now be revealed in the tangible objectivity of our art.

Standing at a threshold, a wind is blowing from a topography of hungry ghosts behind us, pushing us into a landscape of inquisitive spirits. The dead might be sitting at our table, but we do not have to continue eating from the same anxious memories. Our act of bearing wit(h)ness happens in a forum where cultural secrets can be exchanged, personal memories appreciated, the past accounted for, and the present re-imagined.

NOTES

1   Shows at galleries and exhibits include *Trifold* (Williamsburg Art & Historical Center, Brooklyn, New York, 2010), *remembering* (Herron School of Art & Design, Indianapolis, 2010), *Bookish* (Harrison Center for the Arts, Indianapolis, 2009), *Witnesses* (Center for Book Arts, New York, 2008); *Sündenbock* (Meshulash Exhibit, Neue Synagoge, Berlin, 2007); *book bodies* (Indy Art Museum, Indiana, 2007); *Conflict/Peace* (Columbia Art Center, Maryland, 2007); *Annual National Affiliate Show* (Soho 20 Chelsea, New York City, 2010, 2006, and 2005); *Homeland/ Heimaten* (DAI, Heidelberg, Germany, 2004); and *Monologues/Dialogues* (Arthur M. Glick Jewish Community Center Gallery, Indianapolis, 2004). At the opening of our solo exhibit *pushmepullyou* at Mathers Museum (Indiana University, Bloomington, 2008), a symposium of scholars discussed our work. The symposium included art historian Lisa Saltzman as keynote speaker, followed by a panel with Susan Gubar, Alvin Rosenfeld, Edward Linenthal, and David Thelen.

2 The Jewish-German Dance Theatre was founded in 1985. For description of this group, see Krondorfer, *Remembrance and Reconciliation: Encounters between Young Jews and Germans* (New Haven, CT: Yale University Press, 1995).

3 Gottfried Berman-Fischer, *Bedroht—Bewahrt: Weg eines Verlegers* (Frankfurt: Fischer, 1971); and Brigitte B. Fischer, *Sie schrieben mir, oder was aus meinem Poesiealbum wurde* (München: dtv, 1981).

4 Bernhard Schlink, *Heimat als Utopie* (Frankfurt: Suhrkamp, 2000), 25.

5 Jean Amery, "How Much Home Does a Person Need?" in *At the Mind's Limits* (Bloomington: Indiana University Press, 1980), 41–61.

6 Björn Krondorfer, ed., *Men's Bodies, Men's Gods: Male Identities in a (Post-)Christian Culture* (New York: New York University Press, 1996), 8.

7 Edward Gastfriend, *My Father's Testament: Memoir of a Jewish Teenager, 1938–1945*, ed. Björn Krondorfer (Philadelphia: Temple University Press, 2000).

8 See also Krondorfer, "Ratner's Kosher Restaurant," in *Second Generation Voices: Reflections by Children of Holocaust Survivors and Perpetrators*, eds. Alan and Naomi Berger (Syracuse, NY: Syracuse University Press, 2001), 258–69.

9 Krondorfer, "Is Forgetting Reprehensible? Holocaust Remembrance and the Task of Oblivion," *Journal of Religious Ethics* 36, no. 2 (June 2008): 233–67.

10 On postwar German painting, see Lisa Saltzman, *Anselm Kiefer and Art after Auschwitz* (New York: Cambridge University Press, 1999), and Matthew Biro, "Representation and Event: Anselm Kiefer, Joseph Beuys, and the Memory of the Holocaust," *The Yale Journal of Criticism* 16, no. 1 (2003): 113–46. See also Astrid Schmetterling, "Archival Obsessions: Arnold Dreyblatt's Memory Work," *art journal* (Winter 2007): 71–83.

11 On poetic voices, see, for example, Susan Gubar, *Poetry After Auschwitz: Remembering What One Never Knows* (Bloomington: Indiana University Press, 2003); on visual and conceptual artists, see Lisa Saltzman, *Making Memory Matter: Strategies of Remembrance in Contemporary Art* (Chicago: Chicago University Press, 2006); Dora Apel, *Memory Effects: The Holocaust and the Art of Secondary Witnessing* (New Brunswick, NJ: Rutgers University Press, 2002); *Absence/Presence: The Artistic Memory of the Holocaust and Genocide*, edited and curated by Stephen Feinstein (exhibition catalogue, Katherina E. Nash Gallery, University of Minnesota, 1999); and Leslie Morris, "Berlin Elegies: Absence, Postmemory, and Art after Auschwitz," in *Image and Remembrance: Representation and the Holocaust*, ed. Shelly Hornstein and Florence Jacobowitz (Bloomington: Indiana University Press, 2003), 288–303.

12 Dorota Glowacka , *Disappearing Traces: Holocaust Testimonials, Ethics, Aesthetics* (Seattle: University of Washington Press, 2012), 184, 191.

7

The Nazi Assault on the Jewish Soul
through the Murder of the Jewish Mother

DAVID PATTERSON

> The silent face of my mother—
> With her last glance turned to the sky;
> And her last thoughts, most likely of her children;
> Mother was set ablaze. A mother burns!
>
> Ka-tzetnik 135633, *Kaddish*

What did the Nazis set out to exterminate in their extermination of the Jews? The Nazis themselves provide us with a clue. Nazi ideologue Alfred Rosenberg, for example, writes, "This heroic attitude [of National Socialism], to begin with, departs from the *single* but *completely* decisive avowal, *namely from the avowal that blood and character, race and soul are merely different designations for the same entity.*"[1] Thus, Rosenberg insists, "Our race has been poisoned by Judaism,"[2] and not merely by Jewish blood, since "blood and character" are synonyms, the -ism is *in* the blood. Therefore, the Nazis saw to it that they understood very well the religious and metaphysical implications of their actions against the Jews. Herman Kruk attests to this point in his diary from the Vilna Ghetto, where he often refers to the Gestapo's "Jew Specialists" such as the infamous Dr. Pohl, director of *Judenforschung ohne Juden*, that is, "Research on Jews without Jews."[3] It was the responsibility of certain Nazis to be thoroughly familiar with Jews and Judaism, with Jewish teachings and traditions, and to use their knowledge to destroy Jewish souls and the testimony that enters the world through the Jewish people.

From the standpoint of the Nazi *Weltanschauung*, its all-encompassing worldview, "race" is not about color or physiognomy or anything else that meets the eye. No, it is a *metaphysical* category: *race* means *soul*. The notion has a name: it is *Rasenseele*. Explaining the concept of *Rasenseele*, or "race-soul," Rosenberg writes, "Soul means race viewed from within. And, vice-versa, race is the externalization of soul."[4] In Nazi thinking, race is tied to the nature of thought, which, in turn, determines the substance of one's being. Inasmuch as Nazi thought is expressed in Nazi teaching, it cannot tolerate the thought expressed in Jewish teaching. And since Jewish teaching lies in Jewish blood, *every* Jew must be eliminated. For the slightest trace of Jewish thinking—of Judaism—can infect both the Aryan *Geist* and the Aryan blood. There lies the existential threat of the Jew. Hence, writes Rosenberg, "It must be emphasized that the situation would not be altered if the Jew denied the Talmud, because the national character . . . remains the same."[5] And the national character lies in Judaism.

Judaism represents a view of God, world, and humanity that is diametrically opposed to the Nazi *Weltanschauung*. Nazi economist Peter Heinz Seraphim insisted, therefore, that National Socialism was not based on prejudice or racial hatred or anything as banal and vulgar as ethnic or religious difference; rather, the racial foundations were grounded in an all-encompassing philosophical outlook.[6] They rest upon a difference in first principles, upon a *metaphysical* difference. Which means: the Nazis were not antisemitic because they were racists; rather, they were racists because they were antisemitic. If the Nazis are to be Nazis, then they *have to* eliminate the notion of a higher, divine image within the human being that places upon each of us an infinite responsibility for the *other* human being. In order to eliminate this Hebrew sense of reciprocal responsibility, the Nazis were driven to eliminate the Jewish people, whose very presence in the world signifies this responsibility that derives from the divine spark.

And the source of the Jewish people? It is the Jewish mother. If the crime of the Jew is being alive, then the most heinous of criminals is the Jewish mother. In order to better understand what is exterminated in the extermination of the Jewish mother, however, we should consider Jewish teachings concerning the manifestation of the feminine in this realm. For the assault on the Jewish mother is an extension of a broader assault on the feminine.

JEWISH TEACHINGS ON THE FEMININE

What the feminine signifies in the Jewish tradition can be seen in the first woman.[7] Exceeding the ontological landscape "nature," the Eve signifies what transcends the ontological projects of conquering and possession. Created from the side of man, which is hidden even when he stands naked, she consists of the hidden: she is the one beyond our grasp (see *Bereshit Rabbah* 80:5). Woman, then, is not just the "Other"; beyond all ontological categories, she opens up the very otherness of the interrelation that defines humanity, as well as the mystery of divinity, as a giving, over and against a conquering. Forever sought and eternally future, woman is the one through whom holiness enters the world. Therefore, says the Talmud, only through a woman does blessing come to a home (*Bava Metzia* 59a). In fact, says the Midrash, without woman a man is not an *adam*, not a human being (*Kohelet Rabbah* 9:9:1).

In the Jewish tradition the feminine manifestation of the Holy One is represented by the *Shekhinah*. Says the thirteenth-century mystic Rabbi Joseph Gikatilla, the *Shekhinah* "in the time of Abraham our father is called Sarah and in the time of Isaac our father is called Rebecca and in the time of Jacob our father is called Rachel."[8] Therefore, says the *Zohar*, "When a man is at home, the foundation of his house is the wife, for it is on account of her that the *Shekhinah* departs not from the house" (*Zohar* I, 50a)—or from the world. And what comes into the world, through this origin that is woman? It is Torah, as the Maharal of Prague has taught: "If the home possesses Torah it possesses that which sustains it. Understand this."[9] Which is to say: if a home possesses Torah, it possesses the feminine presence of the Holy One.

As the feminine presence of the Holy One, the *Shekhinah* accompanies Israel into exile, so that the Jews are able to endure life without succumbing to the alienation of exile. What is the sign of this accompaniment? It is the Torah itself, which the Jews bear with them in their wanderings. According to an ancient teaching, the Torah had to be accepted first by the women at Mount Sinai before it could be received by the men. For the House of Jacob mentioned in Exodus 19:3 precedes the reference to the Children of Israel, and the House of Jacob refers to the women among the Hebrews (see, for example, Rashi's commentary on Exodus 19:3; see also *Mekilta de-Rabbi Ishmael*, *Bachodesh* 2; also *Zohar* II, 79b). Through the women of Israel, who embody the mystery of value and meaning, we have the Torah and a dwelling place in the world. Indeed, the meaning of Torah is given in the first letter of Torah, in the *beit*, which also means home or dwelling place: the task for which we are created is to transform creation into a dwelling place for holiness, and that task is accomplished most fundamentally through the feminine. It is not for nothing that the Nazis rendered the Jews homeless before they murdered them: living in a camp, a ghetto, or in hiding, *every Jew in Nazi Europe was homeless*. This homelessness is a manifestation of the Nazi assault on the feminine, which is an assault on the *beit*—on the home—that is the origin and essence of the Torah.

"At the level of Divinity," Rabbi Yitzchak Ginsburgh points out, "the house symbolizes the ultimate purpose of all reality: to become a dwelling place below for the manifestation of God's presence. Not as Abraham who called it [the Temple site] 'a mountain,' nor as Isaac who called it 'a field,' but as Jacob who called it 'a house.' "[10] Hence women of Israel are known as the *House* of Jacob. Thus linked to the Creator and the dwelling He makes possible, the feminine lies at the origin of Creation and the center of the dwelling place. Only with the House of Jacob is there room for a world and a space for dwelling. The mystery of meaning unfolds wherever we make room for another—that is the meaning of dwelling: we do not usurp the place of another. As the one who harbors a womb, woman is the one who precisely does *not* usurp the place of another but rather makes room for another to dwell in the world, quite literally and quite graphically, by conceiving and giving birth. There is no giving more profound than giving birth, no giving more profoundly holy. Dwelling happens where a woman is present because a woman represents a dwelling *place* or *Makom* that does not usurp the place of another but rather opens up a place *for* the other. That is why *Makom* is one of the names of God. Like God in the mode of the Creator, the feminine in the mode of mother—or of anyone who, as a female, *might* be mother—is *other*-oriented. What, then, does Judaism teach about the mother?

JEWISH TEACHINGS ON THE MOTHER

According to Jewish tradition, to have an origin—to have a mother—is to be already marked for a mission: origin implies destiny, when that origin is seen as a *mother* and not as some primeval ooze. Situated at the origin of human sanctity, the mother represents not the primeval but the immemorial, the remembrance of something that transforms everything, prior to everything, and forever afterward into something *meaningful*. Therefore, it is a Jewish mother, and not a Jewish father, that makes a Jew a Jew.

Defining the mother is the "womb," that is, *rechem*; it is a cognate of *racham*, which means to "love" or to "have compassion" as only a mother can love and have compassion. Joined with *rachamim*—that is, "compassion" or "love"—the father becomes the Holy One, as in the expression *Av HaRachamim*, "the Father of love and compassion" or "the loving and compassionate Father"—the Father who is also Mother. Without God the Mother we have no access, no relation, to God the Father. The Oneness of God is a singularity that entails the Oneness of the Supernal Mother and the Heavenly Father; when these two origins are *uniquely* One, the purpose of reality becomes clear: to create a home. The one created in the image of the Holy One is created both male and female—and then that one is separated into two (see *Bereshit Rabbah* 1:1) because both are required to make creation into a dwelling place for the Creator. Both are required for bringing life into the world.

One may understand more clearly now what it means to say that through the mother we have the Torah: bearing life into the world, she bears Torah into the world. For the Torah *is* life; it is the *Etz Chayim*, the "Tree of Life" that sustains all life (see, for example, Proverbs 3:18). Thus in the *Zohar* it is written: "First came *Ehyeh* (I shall be), the dark womb of all. Then *Asher Ehyeh* (that I am), indicating the readiness of the Mother to beget all" (*Zohar* III, 65b). The "I shall be" posits the yet-to-be that is the horizon of meaning; the "That I am" or "What I am" is the manifestation of meaning along that horizon: begetting all, the mother begets meaning. Begetting all, the *Zohar* says further, the Supernal Mother begets all of humanity: "The [Supernal] Mother said: 'Let us make man in our image'" (*Zohar* I, 22b). From the depths of the mother's compassion—from the *rechem* within the *rachamim*—human life itself begins to stir. Thus the mother links us to the Creator, to the absolute origin and meaning of all things. That is what the Nazis set out to murder in the murder of the Jewish mother. That is what the memory of the assault seeks to recover.

THE MEMORY OF THE ASSAULT ON THE MOTHER

One of the most horrific expressions of the Nazi assault on the Jewish soul through the murder of the Jewish mother can be found in a vision from

Ka-tzetnik's *Shivitti*, a vision in which he beholds what his novels could not contain:

> My mother. I see her naked and marching in line, one among Them, her face turned towards the gas chambers. "Mama! Mama! Mama!" A voice comes rolling down to me out of the Auschwitz sky. . . . It's my mother, naked. She's going to be gassed. I run after her. I cry out, "Mama! Mama!" I, outside that line, run after her: "Mama! Listen to me! Mama!" My mother naked. Going to be gassed. I behold my mother's skull and in my mother's skull I see me. And I chase after me inside my mother's skull. And my mother is naked. Going to be gassed.[11]

In Ka-tzetnik's vision, we have a revelation of the primal mother of all the children of the earth, a vision of the Supernal Mother, who is buried with the ashes of her children, herself reduced to ash. It is a vision of the *Shekhinah* herself going to be gassed.

In the *Tanya*, Rabbi Schneur Zalman maintains that loving kindness in the form of charity is maternal, for "it receives a radiation from the light of the *Ein Sof* [the Infinite One] that [like a womb] encompasses all worlds."[12] From a Jewish perspective, therefore, maternal love is not just a feeling or a state of mind but is the manifestation of the Most High in our very midst. Like the light created upon the first utterance of Creation, the mother's love is the mainstay of life, even and especially during the reign of death. If, as Olga Lengyel declares, "Inhumanity was the natural order of things at Birkenau,"[13] it is because Birkenau was, in its essence, the antithesis of the maternal. For in Birkenau motherly love was systematically eliminated from the order of being: in Birkenau motherly love was a capital crime. And yet, one finds the discourse of motherly love at work in this realm where mothers were murdered for being mothers: women in the camps who took others under their wings would refer to the protected ones as their "camp daughters."[14]

Signifying love in its holiest aspect, the mother signifies a difference that is a radical non-indifference, a love that comes from beyond the human being to awaken a non-indifference within the human being. Maternal love is not part of the fabric of being—it is a breach of being. Through that love the mother opens up a path through which the divine reveals itself from beyond the mute and indifferent neutrality of all there is. "Mothers never thought of themselves," writes Holocaust survivor Ana Vinocur.

"They were sublime, special beings, divine!"[15] Only where we have a connection to these "special beings" do we have a connection to life. Why? Because their love commands us to love. The memory of the mother's love is a memory of the divine commandment to love (Leviticus 19:18); indeed, the Holocaust memoir's remembrance of the mother is itself an act of love *for* the mother. That memory breathes life into the one who remembers, just as the very sight of the mother sustained life in a time of death.

Leon Wells provides us with an illustration of this point. "Nothing could disturb me," he writes in his memoir. "I had seen my mother again. It had been the happiest day in my life for a long, long time."[16] Similarly, Kitty Hart writes, "One thing I needed very much: regular visits to my mother."[17] Why? Because everything else in Auschwitz declared that she was a non-entity, not a human being but a shadow about to be swallowed up in the Night. Through her mother's eyes she could retrieve some trace of herself as a *someone*, who is loved and is therefore alive. When Kitty fell ill with typhus, her mother once again was the source of her life: "Mother talked to me, though all she got in return was rambling nonsense. I did not even recognize her. But she persevered, slowly and steadily drawing me back to life."[18] In these lines, we see that maternal love is as unconditional as it is deep, absolutely unconditional, and therefore—inasmuch as it might be an expression of the love of the Supernal Mother, and not just the love of a close friend—a reflection of the Absolute.

"Mother talked to me": the mother speaks, which is to say, the mother loves, without reinforcement or reciprocity, without response or recognition. She loves without ground or limitation, infinitely and eternally, as God loves. And so she summons from the child a love that also transcends the boundaries of time and death; she summons from the child the word *mother*, in a most fundamental restoration of meaning to the word. Thus the memory of the mother re-establishes a bond not only between mother and child but also between word and meaning. Like maternal love, memory is itself a manifestation of Someone on high: it is . . . a visitation. For Isabella Leitner, this visitation assumes the form of an epiphany. "My mother's face," she writes in a remembrance of the moment when she saw her mother led to the gas, "her eyes, cannot be described. . . . She knows that for her there is nothing beyond this. And she keeps smiling at me, and I can't stand it. I am silently pleading with her: 'Stop smiling.' I gaze at her tenderly and smile back."[19] One swoons at this silent exchange! The commandment to love that signifies the Divine Presence is a commandment to live. More than the remnant of a life, the survivor is the bearer of a life. For she bears the loving gaze of the mother who bore her—and who, like the Torah, commands her to choose life.

Because maternal love is transcendent, the *presence* of the mother manifests itself despite death, across the boundaries of death. Eugene Heimler lost his mother just prior to his deportation to Auschwitz. Yet while riding the train he notes, "Everybody to whom I belonged was either unconscious or dead. . . . And then I saw my mother's face approaching from the distance."[20] Once more the epiphany maternal love overcomes the ferocious isolation that the Nazi would impose upon the Jew in an assault upon the soul of the Jew. Once more the memory of maternal love invokes a moment in life over which death has no power. Saul Friedländer also recalls an instant of horror and panic during the time when, as a child, he was hiding from the Nazis. It too happened on a train; although the train was not bound for the camps, the incident took place after his mother and father had been deported. "I screamed in terror," he writes. "But suddenly, by a miracle, my mother, who had set out in search of me, appeared. I ran to her. . . . I opened my eyes: it was Madame Chancel stroking my forehead to calm me."[21] Once again we have the maternal visitation of a loving caress reaching across the chasm of death, as though his mother moved the hands of his protector Madame Chancel.

Here we begin to sense on a deeper level what it means to recover a link between word and meaning in memory's recovery of the mother. Thomas Geve's memoir takes us even deeper. There he recalls receiving a message from the women's camp in Birkenau: "News of my luck spread quickly and soon I was surrounded by dozens of roommates who . . . wanted to hear details—but above all to see the word 'mother.' "[22] Here the word *mother* is itself a message, a conveyor of meaning and of love. It appears in the midst of an anti-world calculated to annihilate the Jewish soul by murdering not just Jewish mothers but any Jewish teaching regarding the Jewish mother, a teaching that is part of the Judaism that Alfred Rosenberg insisted was poisoning the Aryan race. Just as Geve's friends gathered around this word, so do we gather around this memory rendered through the word. Just as they see in this message not only *his* mother but *the* mother, so do we see in this memory a trace of maternal love as such. For if this love succumbs to the annihilation aimed at it, then this word loses its meaning. But if the word is there, then, if only for an instant, the block assumes the air of a home.

But what about the block to which the Jewish mother is confined? There we collide with perhaps the most radical assault on the soul in the Nazis' calculated murder of the Jewish mother. Let us consider why.

CHOICELESS CHOICES

In November 1941 Emmanuel Ringelblum noted in his diary that "Jews have been prohibited from marrying and having children. Women pregnant up to three months have to have an abortion."[23] In the concentration camp at Ravensbrück, Germaine Tillion recalls, "The medical services of the *Revier* were required to perform abortions on all pregnant women. If a child happened to be born alive, it would be smothered or drowned in a bucket in the presence of the mother."[24] (Yes, *in the presence of the mother!*) And in the murder camps, pregnancy was neither a medical condition nor a blessing from God—it was the worst of crimes against the German Reich. The testimony of these two witnesses alone reveals a unique aspect of the Holocaust as the murder not only of human beings but of the very origin of human life and of human sanctity, which is substance of the soul: the murder of the very being of the Jewish woman and the Jewish mother.

But there is more. On February 5, 1942, Vilna Ghetto diarist Herman Kruk wrote, "Today the Gestapo summoned two members of the Judenrat and notified them: No more Jewish children are to be born."[25] Six months later, in his diary from the Kovno Ghetto, Avraham Tory noted, "From September on, giving birth is strictly forbidden. Pregnant women will be put to death."[26] There lies the murder of the soul. Perhaps better than anyone else, Emil Fackenheim understood the implications of this murder of mothers and motherhood. "The very concept of holiness," he argues, "must be altered in response to the conjunction, unprecedented in the annals of history, of 'birth' and 'crime.'"[27] And with the unprecedented conjunction of these categories there arises within the murder camps a singular, unprecedented dilemma, a dilemma that exceeds all moral dilemmas, a dilemma that consumes the soul.

Isabella Leitner offers us a devastating description of that impossible dilemma, of the choice that is no choice. It is a description of what transpired upon the birth of a child in Auschwitz:

> Most of us are born to live—to die, but to live first. You, dear darling,
> you are being born only to die. How good of you to come before roll call

though, so your mother does not have to stand at attention while you are being born. . . . And now that you are born, your mother begs to see you, to hold you. But we know that if we give you to her, there will be a struggle to take you away again, so we cannot let her see you because you don't belong to her. You belong to the gas chamber. Your mother has no rights. . . . She is not a mother. She is just a dirty Jew who has soiled the Aryan landscape with another dirty Jew.[28]

Of course, the little one born here is born not just to die but to be murdered: in order to save the mother, the mother's closest friends, Jewish women, must kill the infant who makes the mother a mother. They must kill something of themselves, part of their own souls, part of the essence of the feminine. There lies the horror of the Nazi assault on the Jewish soul.

"For a moment, for just a moment," Leitner recalls, "we touched the dear little one before she was wrapped in a piece of paper and quickly handed to the *Blockelteste* so the SS wouldn't discover who the mother was, because then she, too, would have had to accompany the baby to the ovens. . . . Are we ever to know what life-giving feels like? Not here. Perhaps out there, where they have diapers, and formulas, and baby carriages—and life."[29] *There are no diapers in the anti-world*—that is what makes it an anti-world. The babe was hidden from the SS, but who could hide the mother from herself? And where were the others to hide, those women who gave the child over to death?

When a woman named Esther announced to Sara Nomberg-Przytyk that she was going to have a baby, her reaction was: "I turned to stone."[30] Not "Oh, how wonderful!" or even "How could you be so foolish?" but the silence of turning to stone. That is the response elicited by these glad tidings in the midst of the anti-world. "Our procedure is to kill the baby after birth in such a way that the mother doesn't know about it," Nomberg-Przytyk recalls. "The mother is told that the baby was born dead. After dark, the baby is thrown on a pile of corpses, and in that manner we save the mother."[31] When Esther gave birth to her baby, the head of the block was supposed to have reported the birth, "but somehow she delayed. She had pity on Esther."[32] The result of this pity was that three days later both Esther and her baby were gassed. What sort of pity, then, is one to have?

The metaphysical horror that defines the Shoah is that one is led to kill, not to destroy but to save, to kill out of love, both for the mother and for the child. Says Gisella Perl, who served as a doctor in Auschwitz, "I loved those newborn babies not as a doctor but as a mother and it was again and again my own child whom I killed to save the life of a woman."[33] My own child: to destroy one's child is to destroy a defining dimension of one's soul. For the child signifies meaning in the life of the mother, as well as in the life of the one who loves the child like a mother. More than the biological distinction of being a mother, that *love* is what comes under assault in the Nazi assault on these Jewish women, whether they themselves are mothers or not.

On one occasion, Dr. Perl tried to save a baby born to a woman named Yolanda. After two days, however, she says, "I could hide him no longer. I knew that if he were discovered, it would mean death to Yolanda, to myself and to all these pregnant women whom my skill could still save. I took the warm little body in my hands, kissed the smooth face, caressed the long hair—then strangled him."[34] The incongruity of the caress of love coupled with the touch of death is staggering. The maternal embrace of the child consecrates the relation that imparts sanctity to the human being. But in a realm where that relation is expressed by killing the child, both the relation and the meaning it consecrates are turned on end.

What is the greatest mitzvah, the most profound utterance to God in the form of a deed, the mitzvah that overrides all other mitzvot? It is the saving of a life, which is the saving of a world. Thus the *Mishnah* teaches that saving a single life is like saving the entire world (*Sanhedrin* 4:5). In the same verse, it says that to destroy a single life is like destroying the entire world. Where, then, is the mitzvah in killing an infant to save the mother? What does *this* prayer in the form of a deed say to God? And what becomes of Dr. Perl's maternal love in *this* act of loving kindness? The key to the assault on the soul lies in this perversion, this twisting, of the mitzvot. For the soul is made of mitzvot, beginning with the mitzvah that prohibits murder. Thus Olga Lengyel laments, "The Germans succeeded in making murderers of even us. . . . Our own children have perished in the gas chambers and were cremated in the Birkenau ovens, and we dispatched the lives of others before their first voices had left their tiny lungs."[35] But have the Nazis indeed succeeded in recreating these women after their own image? Are these women who killed the children they loved like a mother made into murderers? To these questions, we must answer No. Even in the antiworld, Jewish mothers retain their sanctity. For that sanctity is inviolable, despite the Nazi assault.

But does the world retain its sanctity in the aftermath of the Nazi assault on the very holiness of life? Has a world that stood by during the Nazi assault on the soul lost its soul? If so, it is a world in which the soul is in exile. It is an orphaned world.

IN CLOSING: EXILED TO AN ORPHANED WORLD

By now we can see that the Nazis' assault on Jewish women, particularly their calculated murder of Jewish mothers, was tied to the murder of the Supernal Mother, the One whose four-letter Name ends in the feminine vowel sign *kamats*. With the assault on the Supernal Mother, a people and a world are ontologically orphaned, and not simply because the vast majority of Holocaust survivors *were orphans*. No, we are orphaned because we have all been accomplices in this assault on the feminine.

In Sara Zyskind's memoir, we find a premonition and a dread of this ontological turn, in the memory of an outcry that rises to the surface of her page: "I don't want to be an orphan, Mother!"[36] The orphan's memory is the memory of the loss of the one who will never forget her name, even if she should forget. The emptiness the orphan experiences is the void of being forgotten. Losing those hands and that face—*through the murder of the mother*—the child loses her own hands and face, her own deeds and words. She is left alone not in the world but in the anti-world. When the mother is thus turned to ash, creation is returned to the *tohu vevohu*, to the chaos and the void, antecedent to every origin. Who among us does not have a sense that the world teeters on that edge? That is where we are in the aftermath of Auschwitz. That is what it means to be orphaned: it is to be turned over to the world as a wilderness, homeless and aimless.

In the Jewish tradition, as in most traditions, the mother is associated with the earth. The pervasive sense that the earth itself is threatened—that it is poisoned and burning beneath our feet—lies as much in the eclipse of Planet Earth by Planet Auschwitz as in any "scientific data." For Planet Auschwitz rests not upon the earth but upon several feet of Jewish remains, on the ashes that now eclipse Mother Earth. The ashes that cover the Mother abide in the alienated earth from which we harvest our bread, in the bread that we put into mouths, in the blood that flows in our veins, and in the soul that abides in our blood. What does it mean to live in an orphaned world? It means living in a state of exile, in which the soul itself is lost.

NOTES

1   Quoted in Max Weinreich, *Hitler's Professors: The Part of Scholarship in Germany's Crimes against the Jewish People* (New Haven, CT: Yale University Press, 1999), 26.

2   Alfred Rosenberg, *Race and Race History and Other Essays*, ed. Robert Pais (New York: Harper & Row, 1974), 131–32.

3   See Herman Kruk, *The Last Days of the Jerusalem of Lithuania: Chronicles from the Vilna Ghetto and the Camps, 1939–1944*, ed. Benjamin Harshav; trans. Barbara Harshav (New Haven, CT: Yale University Press, 2002), 311.

4   Rosenberg, *Race and Race History*, 34.

5   Ibid., 183.

6   See Weinreich, *Hitler's Professors*, 78.

7   While the word *feminine* refers to a learned characteristic and the word *female* to a biological feature, in Jewish teachings on the *Shekhinah*, for example, as well as in Hebrew discourse, the two terms are often synonymous.

8   Joseph Gikatilla, *Sha'are Orah: Gates of Light*, trans. Avi Weinstein (San Francisco: HarperCollins, 1994), 204.

9   Yehuda Loeve, *Nesivos Olam: Nesiv Hatorah*, trans. Eliakim Willner (Brooklyn, NY: Mesorah, 1994), 322.

10 Yitzchak Ginsburgh, *The Alef-Beit* (Northvale, NJ: Jason Aronson, 1991), 46.

11 Ka-tzetnik 135633, *Shivitti: A Vision*, trans. Eliyah De-Nur and Lisa Herman (New York: Harper & Row, 1989), 100–101.

12 Schneur Zalman, *Likutei Amarim Tanya*, trans. Nissan Mindel (New York: Kehot, 1981), 593.

13 Olga Lengyel, *Five Chimneys* (London: Granada, 1972), 94.

14 See, for example, Myrna Goldenberg, "Memoirs of Auschwitz Survivors: The Burden of Gender," in *Women in the Holocaust*, ed. Dalia Ofer and Lenore J. Weitzman (New Haven, CT: Yale University Press, 1999), 328.

15 Ana Vinocur, *A Book without a Title*, trans. Valentine Isaac and Ricardo Iglesia (New York, Vantage, 1976), 88.

16 Leon Wells, *The Death Brigade* (New York: Holocaust Library, 1978), 86.

17 Kitty Hart, *Return to Auschwitz* (New York: Atheneum, 1984), 104.

18 Ibid., 106.

19 Isabella Leitner, *Fragments of Isabella*, ed. Irving Leitner (New York: Thomas Crowell, 1978), 6.

20 Eugene Heimler, *Night of the Mist*, trans. André Ungar (New York: Vanguard, 1959), 31.

21 Saul Friedländer, *When Memory Comes*, trans. Helen R. Lane (New York: Avon, 1980), 101–2.

22 Thomas Geve, *Youth in Chains* (Jerusalem: Rubin Mass, 1981), 82–83.

23 Emmanuel Ringelblum, *Notes from the Warsaw Ghetto*, trans. and ed. Jacob Sloan (New York: Schocken Books, 1974), 230.

24 Germaine Tillion, *Ravensbrück*, trans. Gerald Satterwhite (New York: Doubleday, 1975), 77.

25 Herman Kruk, "Diary of the Vilna Ghetto," trans. Shlomo Noble, *YIVO Annual of Jewish Social Science* 13 (1965): 20.

26 Avraham Tory, *Surviving the Holocaust: The Kovno Ghetto Diary*, trans. Jerzy Michalowicz (Cambridge, MA: Harvard University Press, 1990), 114.

27 Emil L. Fackenheim, *The Jewish Bible after the Holocaust* (Bloomington: Indiana University Press, 1990), 87.

28 Leitner, *Fragments of Isabella*, 31–32.

29 Ibid., 49.

30 Sara Nomberg-Przytyk, *Auschwitz: True Tales from a Grotesque Land*, trans. Roslyn Hirsch (Chapel Hill: University of North Carolina Press, 1985), 68.

31 Nomberg-Przytyk, *Auschwitz*, 69.

32 Ibid., 71.

33 Gisella Perl, *I Was a Doctor in Auschwitz* (New York: International Universities Press, 1948), 82.

34 Ibid., 84.

35 Lengyel, *Five Chimneys*, 111.

36 Sara Zyskind, *Stolen Years*, trans. Margarit Inbar (Minneapolis, MN: Lerner, 1981), 44.

8

Wiedervereiningung Ersehend

Gender and the Holocaust Fate of the Müller

and Gittler Families

SUZANNE BROWN-FLEMING

"People go into a tunnel in a mountain, and along the way
there is a great hole and they all fall in and disappear."
— Marion Samuel (seven years old), 1938

On April 21, 1943, Harry and Theresia Müller of Leobschütz and Ziegenhals (Upper Silesia) were among forty-six persons deported on Gestapo
transport XVIII/5 from the town of Oppeln (Opole, Oppein) to Theresienstadt.[1] Gestapo authorities deported a total of 294 victims from Oppeln
to Theresienstadt between November 13, 1942, and March 21, 1944.[2] On
October 28, 1944, Harry and Theresia Müller were deported on transport
"Ev" from Thersienstadt to Auschwitz—the very last of the ten autumn
transports—where, presumably, they were murdered upon arrival.[3] Weeks
later, gassings ceased at Auschwitz. Harry Müller was sixty-six. Theresia
Müller was fifty-nine.

International Tracing Service (ITS) documents refer to both as among
those Jews who "perished in Auschwitz" (*gestorben in Auschwitz*).[4] On
the transport list from Theresienstadt to Auschwitz for the single day of
October 28, 1944, Theresia Müller, listed as number 1066—number one
thousand and sixty-six among the thousands of others transported on that

single day—is identified as a housewife (*Haushalt*); Harry Müller, number 1067, is listed as a doctor (*Arzt*).[5]

Wilhelm and Gertrud Gittler of Breslau were deported to Block 8-1414 in Izbica Lubelska,[6] a town in the Krasnystaw district (Kreis Krasnystaw) of Lublin (Lublin Distrikt), part of the Nazi-run *Generalgouvernement* (Poland). They might have been among the 1,871 Jews deported from Nadrenia and Breslau in two separate transports arriving from Germany on March 20, 1942.[7]

Two sets of family letters, the first set written by Harry and Theresia Müller between April 1939 and September 1941, and the second set written by various members of the Gittler family between 1938 and 1941, allow for a partial reconstruction of the daily lives of these two families, related by marriage. Recently, Holocaust scholars have begun to recognize the dignity and value of reconstructing the experiences of heretofore forgotten Jewish individuals and families at the micro level. The recent book *Into the Tunnel: The Short Life of Marion Samuel* by Götz Aly[8] uses documentation scattered across German archives to trace the life of a single German-Jewish child murdered in Auschwitz. To rescue hundreds of thousands of Jewish families from the kind of oblivion Marion Samuel already felt in 1938, new works, such as *Every Day Lasts a Year: A Jewish Family's Correspondence from Poland,* try to capture "everyday family life" for "those who hovered between hope and despair."[9]

Marion Kaplan points out aptly that "there is no single story of Jewish daily life."[10] Each family's story was affected by many factors, one of which, argues Kaplan, was gender.[11] In her groundbreaking 1998 book *Between Dignity and Despair: Jewish Life in Nazi Germany*, Kaplan chronicles the lives of German-Jewish families as they "endured the living nightmare of Nazism."[12] For these families, physical death, she argues convincingly, was preceded by "social death."[13]

The letters of the Müllers and the Gittlers allow us to reconstruct the daily experiences of two German-Jewish families and challenge us to examine the implications of gender in their daily lives after 1938. Harry I. Müller was born in 1878 in Neustadt, Upper Silesia.[11] ITS records indicate that he lived in Leobschütz until 1938.[15] His wife, Theresia S. Müller (Süssmann), was born in 1885 in Cosel (Kosel), Upper Silesia. ITS records confirm that she too lived in Leobschütz until 1938.[16] In 1938, the couple relocated to Ziegenhals (Upper Silesia; today Głuchołazy, Poland).[17] From their address in Ziegenhals (Gartenstrasse 22), they penned a series of letters to their four children: Hans Gert, or "Gert" (Gerd), born in 1908; Lieselotte, or "Lilo," born in 1910; Ursula, or "Ursel," born in 1913; and Klaus, the youngest of the siblings.[18]

Gert was a physician like his father. By April of 1939, he had already emigrated and begun a medical practice in America. He, his wife Ilse Gittler, and their first-born son, Steven, lived in Lysander, New York. Gert spent the war as a physician with the United States Army (10th Mountain Division). Lilo was a nurse. In August 1938, she was living in Munich (Hermann Schmidstrasse 5), where she received notification from the American Consulate in Stuttgart that she had been given the number 9,857 on the waiting list for emigration to the United States.[19] By July 1939, she had left Munich for Plymouth, England, where she was head nurse at the Prince of Wales hospital on Greenback Road.[20] By December 1940, she had married an American, Morris Lassman, and had moved with him to Phoenix, New York.[21]

Ursula married Gerhardt Steinitz, a physician, in March 1936. On March 11, 1938, the American Vice Consul in Berlin issued Ursula Steinitz Quota Immigration Visa Number 2,813. Her German-issued passport bears the stamp "*ausgereißt* [emigrated] 7 April 1938."[22] She and Gerhardt settled in Fulton, New York. From their home on 403 Oneida Street in Fulton, they worked desperately to try and secure passage for their parents to England.[23] They had a daughter named Karen who was born in November 1940.[24] Klaus Müller also emigrated to the United States.[25] By May 1941, he, too, was living in Fulton, New York.[26]

The Müller and Gittler families were linked by marriage. Gert Müller's wife, Ilse Lotte Gittler,[27] or "Ilselein," as she was affectionately called by her brother Franz (and "Ilschen" by her parents), was born in Kattowitz on April 28, 1915.[28] She was one of three children born to Gertrude Rehfeld (maiden name)[29] and Wilhelm Gittler,[30] a lawyer by profession. Ilse had an older sister, Marie, born in 1909, who died at the age of twelve.[31] The Gittlers of Kattowitz moved to Breslau (Silesia), where Wilhelm Gittler established his own law practice.[32] Franz Ludwig ("Frank") was born on March 12, 1924, a Thursday at 7 p.m., in Breslau.[33] One of the greatest highlights of his childhood was his close relationship with his sister, Ilse.[34]

DAILY LIFE AND GENDER ROLES

Wilhelm Gittler lost his license to practice law in 1937. "When my father [Wilhelm] lost his license to practice law and my brother-in-law [Gert] lost his license to practice medicine, it became obvious to my parents that even though their lives may not be saved . . . their children's lives should be," wrote Franz Gittler, reflecting on these events years later.[35] The Gittlers were a wealthy family: Franz recollected having a cook, three to four servants, a laundress, and a Christian governess.[36] They were, in Franz's memory, "assimilated Jews," German and Prussian to the core. His father employed four or five legal secretaries, and his mother administered the household, managed several apartments owned by the family, and entertained. Theirs was a proper German bourgeois household: "If I wanted to see my father," Franz Gittler said many years later, "I made an appointment." He had supper with his father once per week. Franz saw his mother daily, in the morning, when she came to the *Kinderstube* (the area of the house designated for the children) to give instructions to the governess for that day.[37]

For Harry Müller, the ability to practice medicine was a primary concern. The purge of Jews from the medical profession began in March 1933, when Munich general practitioner and longtime Nazi Dr. Gerhardt Wagner initiated the process of dismissing Jewish functionaries from national, regional, and local medical associations.[38] "This idle time is difficult for me," Müller wrote to his children in April 1939. Despondency did not appear to claim him; rather, he wrote of continued efforts to find work in Breslau and also in Munich. In such efforts, familial and social networks counted for much. In one example, Lilo introduced her father to a Munich-based Jewish physician named Dr. Meyer:

> Dr. Meyer in Munich, Lilo's friend, is waiting for a visa to the USA and is attempting to wait out the time in England. . . . He thinks it might be possible for me to become his successor in Munich, since most of the doctors there have emigrated. Most of those remaining are older and unwilling to do without their pensions, and they therefore choose not to register their practices. . . . Meyer has such a big practice that he can barely manage it; furthermore, he has no incentive to stay, since he can't take the money with him to England anyway. His wife and daughter are staying here [in Germany] for the time being and would gladly offer me lodging in their large apartment.[39]

Several features of this passage are striking: first, as late as April 1939, some Jewish Germans nearing retirement age retained their optimism that they would still receive pensions, implying their belief that living decently in Germany was still feasible. Also, the option of emigration was available to and exercised by Dr. Meyer and by many of his colleagues. Finally, Lilo's own position as a nurse in Munich prior to her emigration allowed her to cultivate this potentially helpful contact for her father. Harry Müller referred to his desire to work for a second time in one of his last available letters to his children, remarking that "this forced idleness has been anything but pleasant, and I'll be truly happy when I'm able to work again."[40]

Inability to practice a profession meant financial hardship. In April 1939, the Müllers' financial situation was still solvent. Harry Müller remarked that he and Theresia still had 3,000 Reichsmarks (RM) in cash, and, as a precaution, dismissed their housekeeper in order to add to their cash assets her salary of 1,600 RM monthly. The Müllers had set aside 700 RM for the Punitive Tax (*Judenvermögensabgabe*), meaning that their net property value totaled 5,000 RM at the time of the November 21, 1938, decree,[41] and still expected a 300 to 400 RM refund from the previous year's income tax.[42]

Later letters indicate a change in their financial security. In August 1939, Theresia Müller noted in a letter to Lilo that her daughter would have to send the postage fee to Stuttgart for a package from Ziegenhals "since we can't afford it ourselves."[43] Still, they had the means and generosity to send 250 marks to their daughter that same month for the purpose of helping another emigrant.[44] As of October 1, 1939, they were compelled by the state to pay rent for their living quarters, an added expense.[45] By December 1940, they depended on their children to supplement their basic living necessities. "We want you to know the package finally arrived," they wrote on December 8. "Its contents were very welcome to us." They remained close to Wilhelm and Gertrude Gittler in Breslau, remarking that "as ordered, we sent half of [the package's contents] to Breslau."[46] When an additional package arrived days later, they would remark, "We . . . saw that you went above and beyond what we had asked for . . . We're already looking forward to receiving the things you mentioned in [your] last letter."[47]

Despite retaining a housekeeper, Harry and Theresia Müller expected their daughters to have a hands-on role in their own households. Both Theresia and her husband believed it was important for a woman to know how to cook. Upon Lilo's marriage, her parents wrote that "Mom is especially happy that Morris enjoys your cooking, Lilo. It is important that a housewife (*Hausfrau*) be able to cook well. . . . Surely you have both heard the famous saying, 'How do I keep the love of my husband? Feed him well.' "[48] That they took the time to write such a note indicates their feeling that, as parents, they had a responsibility to impart this advice to their newlywed daughter, even under the circumstances in which they found themselves in January 1941. On February 27, responding to a letter from Lilo, the Müllers wrote with evident pride, "We are especially happy about your letter, Lilo. Every line proved to us that you are happy. It is surely a big step to have and care for your own home, and Mother is happy to know that she raised you and Ursel to be good housewives and to satisfy your husbands."

Both parents wished to know more about the household: "Naturally, we want to know all about how you managed this new home of yours. . . . Did you both have to buy all new things? We're glad the knick-knacks that were in our room are well-used in your rooms. Whenever you see them, you can think of our beautiful apartment in Leobschütz."[49] Lilo, too, seemed to find comfort in the furnishings of her childhood home. "You asked about the embroidery covers, Lilo," her mother wrote on May 19, 1941. "They're still here. . . . They're actually not embroidered yet, because we don't have any thread. . . . We've received approval to have them on our list of things to take with us. Then you and I can embroider them together."[50]

Harry and Theresia Müller appeared to adhere to their traditional roles as late as January 1941. In an interesting passage, Harry describes his wife's bout of illness and its impact on the household:

> Mother [Theresia] has just today recovered from a mild case of the flu. . . .
> She's feeling quite well again. Tomorrow, she plans on again taking on the
> housework. Our housemate, Mrs. Sachs,[51] has been taking care of every-
> thing here since Mom has been sick; she's taken care of Mom, cooked for
> all of us, etc. We don't know what we would have done without her.[52]

One can surmise that after his own disenfranchisement barring him from practicing medicine, Harry Müller did not take on cooking or household chores in the absence of their housekeeper and in the event of his wife's illness. Rather, Mrs. Sachs, their housemate, took up Theresia Müller's duties.

THE STRUGGLE TO EMIGRATE

Admonishing against the thoughtless question, "Why did German Jews not leave sooner,"[53] Kaplan writes that "even in mid-1938, as Jews endured second-class citizenship and privation, the situation looked unclear to many. . . . After 1939, however, the rapid escalation of persecution . . . left German Jews scrambling to flee."[54] In fact, writes Kaplan, "Emigration became the highest priority within the Jewish community" in the period following the November 1938 pogrom.[55] The elderly had the most difficulty in managing to emigrate. Between June 1933 and September 1939, the number of Jews in Germany under age thirty-nine decreased by eighty percent. The elderly and women were disproportionately left behind.[56]

The Müller and Gittler families demonstrate these statistics vividly. On August 31, 1939, Gertrude Gittler accompanied her youngest child to Berlin and watched him board the train as one of approximately 10,000 Jewish children leaving Germany on the Kindertransport. "I still . . . see in front of me and will never forget my mother's face as the train pulled out, waving and holding back her tears since both she and I knew we may never see each other again," wrote Franz.[57] His father did not accompany him due to illness and the risk of random arrests.[58] Franz Gittler's testimony, poignantly told in his 1996 Shoah Foundation interview, bears out the idea that the Kindertransport "could be terribly wrenching, a considerable adventure, or both."[59] His own journey began in Berlin and ended in Boston, Massachusetts, via the circuitous route of Cologne, Amsterdam, London, Ingatestone (Essex, UK), Edinburgh, Birmingham (UK), and New York Harbor.[60]

Harry and Theresia Müller were also among the thousands of German-Jewish parents who made the agonizing decision to send their children abroad to safety. *"Aus Kindern wurden Briefe"* (children turned into letters) was a common expression in Jewish circles during these years; Harry and Theresia Müller would have frequent chance to use it.[61] Young adults by the time of the Nazi period, their children, Gert, Lilo, Ursula, and Klaus, all had emigrated from Germany to the United States by 1941.

On April 2, 1939 (the first available letter in this collection), Harry and Theresia wrote to their children indicating that a Franz Süssman (presumably related to Theresia) had written them offering to inquire with the American consulate as to the Müllers' status on the waiting list. Their letter relayed a sense of guarded optimism about their future: "The consequences of the earth-shattering events (*weltbewegende Ereignisse*) that have been taking place have not yet reached us here, and we hope that everything will settle down again (*Alles wieder beruhigen wird*) and that we can wait out this time until departure without any trouble."[62] Harry Müller also expressed support for his son Gert's life in his new country (the United States), writing, "We assume that a good life can be had in a place where one can work in calm, freedom, and with respect of one's fellow man (*Ruhe, Frieden und Achtung von Seiten seiner Mitmenschen*)."[63]

This theme—the willingness to leave Germany behind for a better life with their children—appears consistently throughout these letters. Harry and Theresia Müller expected to emigrate to England in the summer of 1939, together with Wilhelm and Gertrude Gittler, with the aid of the London-based Jewish Aid Committee, and sought the help of their daughter Ursula and her husband, Gerhardt. Ursula and Gerhardt were optimistic about borrowing $2,000 from friends in Syracuse, the Bakers, for the necessary security deposit.[64] "It doesn't matter where [Harry and I] go over there [in England] as long as we're near you and are able to provide for you some comforts of home. . . . We'll be glad when we, too, can leave [Germany]," the Müllers wrote to Lilo on August 8.[65] Harry and Theresia Müller fully expected to be able to join their daughter in England within a short time. "We're moving forward with our preparations," Harry Müller wrote on August 15. "We already received the transport documents of compliance (*Unbedenklichkietsbescheinigungen*), but we had to send them back; we want to make sure that they also apply to Mother, and they did not express as much. . . . We're sure we won't have to wait as long as you did and that everything will go smoothly for us."[66] They received their *Unbedenklichkietsbescheinigungen* three days later, according to a letter from Theresia Müller to Lilo dated August 18.[67]

Wilhelm and Gertrud Gittler, however, had less reason to be optimistic, and, at least in the memories of their son, Franz, were not entirely enthusiastic about emigrating.[68] Theresia Müller learned from her son Gert and his wife Ilse that they had been unable to afford the $2,000 deposit for Ilse's parents, nor was the Jewish Aid Committee willing to forgive the shortfall. At that point, Theresia considered taking young Franz Gittler, not yet assured a place on the Kindertransport, with them. "[Gert and Ilse] have asked us whether we want to take Franz with us to England. Of course we want to take him, without question . . . we are closer to the Gittlers than we are with our immediate relatives," Theresia wrote to Lilo on August 18.[69] Their eagerness to go to England was palpable, as they wrote eight days later, "[We] spend the days waiting for our permit. In the meantime, we've already gotten preparations underway . . . because once the permit arrives, we don't want to be held up any longer than we have to be."[70]

Weeks later, frustration set in. On October 8, 1939, Harry Müller wrote to Lilo asking her to contact the Jewish Aid Committee in London: "Brit [a family friend] got in touch with the Jewish Aid Committee and inquired about whether or not they have received the [$2,000] security deposit from [Ursel's husband] Gerhardt, but she hasn't heard back from them. Perhaps it's possible for you to get more concrete information about this; my reference number is 10040," he wrote.[71] Why their plans to emigrate to England in 1939 failed is not clear in this series of letters. What is clear is that throughout 1940, Ursel and Gerhardt worked feverishly to book passage for Harry and Theresia Müller to America, then to Norway, then to Shanghai, and then to Spain, all without success.

On March 14, the Aid Society of Jews in Germany (*Hilfsverein*) in Breslau sent a Western Union telegram to Gerald and Ursula Steinitz directing them to remit $1,600 to the Committee for the Assistance of European Jewish Refugees in Shanghai for the Müller's passage. On March 15, Gerhardt Steinitz wired this enormous sum. Following another urgent Western Union telegram from Nansen Aid on April 3, he cabled $1,000 to the Creditbanken Oslo as a deposit for his in-laws. On June 6, he wired $100 to Mr. Egmont Pollak in Shanghai.[72]

But Harry and Theresia Müller remained in Ziegenhals. By December 1940, bleakness set in. On December 8, Harry and Theresia wrote their children that "regarding emigration to the USA, one hears nothing at all now."[73] Four days later, Harry Müller wrote to his children, "We . . . looked on the map to see where the setting of the book [*Northwest Passage*] is located, and we saw that it's not at all far from you. Hopefully we'll also be able to go there sometime to see it for ourselves." He was, by this point, open about his doubts, writing, "We'll have to wait a long time until then, because there has been no progress in terms of our emigration."[74]

Their daughter Lilo's 1940 marriage to Morris ("Fritz") Lassman gave them some renewed hope. In January, 1941, remarking on pictures of the Lassmans' new home in Phoenix, New York, Harry and Theresia wrote, "We continue to hope that we'll be able to be with you soon." They marveled at the apparent ease of achieving American citizenship, continuing in their letter, "It is said here that foreigners (*Ausländerin*) who marry an American can receive American citizenship in just two or three years. How can that be? Gerd [Gert] wrote to us that you [Lilo] have now become an American citizen. How does that work? Is it authentic?"[75] Harry and Theresia went on to suggest the possibility of obtaining a travel visa (*Ausreise*) sponsored by Morris Lassman. They contacted the *Hilfsverein* for aid in (once again) submitting their affidavits, and this time they included Morris Lassman as a sponsor. "Perhaps this will make our emigration proceed more quickly," they wrote.[76]

They had good reason to hope, and then to despair: Harry and Theresia Müller received word that they would be booked for a June 1941 departure to the United States, via Lisbon. Because they did not receive their transit visa on the expected date (May 6) and their deposit failed to come through, they had to await another summons.[77] When they received confirmation of a booking on the Hapag-Lloyd steamship line, departing in July, they were skeptical: "We have now read, in a letter from Lisbon to Hapag, that two places have been booked for us, [but] we don't believe it. Other sources have told us that the routes to Lisbon, as they are to Spain, are closed off."

Regarding their delayed transit visa, they "received assurance from the consulate" that they could pick up the visa in July.[78] This would not come to pass; they did not receive their visa in time for a July departure. On July 11, they wrote to their children, "We suppose you have learned in the meantime of our misfortune hindering us to be with you. There still remains a vague hope that everything will come out all right. . . . You can be sure of course that we are very disappointed, because we have arranged everything for our emigration and our hopes are shattered again. . . . we have been in the same situation twice or three times already before. It is . . . hard to bear such disappointments and we hope this will be the last."[79]

They now pinned their hopes on receiving the necessary visas in time for a passage departing on September 12, 1941, via the Hapag-Lloyd steamship line bound for America.[80] "It looks as though there is a good chance of our coming to you before the end of the year," wrote Harry and Theresia to Morris Lassman on July 31. "Everything depends now on the authorities in Washington and their consideration of your request." They waited also for the necessary transit visa from the consulate in Madrid or Lisbon. "Oh, it is all so difficult, and additional hindrances continually pile up," wrote

Harry and Theresia to Lilo. "When you left here, it was much easier, and you don't understand the half of what we go through now," they added, openly expressing frustration.[81]

By August 1941, they acknowledged that emigration for them seemed impossible: "After all this back and forth, we have no hope of leaving here before the end of the war. The fact is that, without a travel visa to the USA, we will not be granted a transit visa. In other words, a transit visa would only be granted to us if we already hold a travel visa. So this game just continues back and forth," they wrote to their children on August 20.[82] Still refusing to give up, they pursued tourist visas for Cuba. These efforts would also come to naught, though in September 1941 they were unaware that this would be yet another blind alley. "Concerning the passage to Cuba, there are no more obstacles. This is due to the July closure of the U.S. Consulate, allowing for the chance for a few more people to leave. We now just have to wait," they wrote on September 8.

As late as September 1941, even in their frustration and impending sense of the impossibility of their emigration, they continued to hold out hope that the United States Department of State would respond favorably to the efforts undertaken by their son-in-law.[83] At the same time, they worried about the impact their continued attempts had on their children, who had all successfully started new lives for themselves in America. "We don't want you to take on our emigration issues; we're concerned that it would become a financial burden for you," they wrote late in 1941.[84] But their letters acknowledged for the first time that they might not see their children again.

"Dear Morris," Harry and Theresia wrote to their son-in-law in January 1941, "we would prefer to learn your [American] tongue in your triangle—Phoenix, Lysander, Fulton. But our hope is [a] little one."[85] Their letters took on a tone of finality, of gravity, of an urgency to express parental hopes and dreams for their children:

> We're writing today to congratulate you, Lilo, on your [31st] birthday on March 29 . . . This past year has brought you the happiness that we always hoped for you. We hope, from the bottom of our hearts, that it will remain with you forever and, most of all, that you both remain healthy. You surely plan on celebrating your first birthday together in your new home, and know that we will be with you in spirit.[86]

As postal communication became increasingly difficult and unreliable, the Müllers made their feelings of disconnection and frustration clear. In an August 1941 letter to their children, they wrote, "Our receipt of mail is quite irregular. Consequently, we don't understand some of the things that you mentioned in your letter . . . you can imagine how uneasy [*unruhig*] we feel. . . . So, we ask that you take the time to clearly explain [happenings in your lives that you have already written about] to us again. It's always possible that a letter never arrives or arrives very late [and] we have no control over this."[87] Only in one letter do they openly state their personal unhappiness, speaking plainly about their burdens, writing, "Our life here has been really unpleasant [*denn es ist wirklich keine schönes Leben, das wir hier führen*]."[88]

Further available communication between the Müllers and their children is limited to four messages transmitted through the International Red Cross. In an undated message received at American Red Cross Headquarters in Washington, D.C. on February 19, 1942, and transmitted to the Comite International de la Croix-Rouge at the Palais de Conseil Général in Geneva over five months later on July 28, 1942, Gert wrote to his parents in Ziegenhals, in English. Per the restrictions placed by the Red Cross on these messages (the English-language Form 1616 states explicitly: "message to be transmitted not more than twenty-five words, family news of strictly personal character"), he wrote exactly twenty-five words: "We are ok and hope the same of you. Steven calls Opi and Omi when seeing your pictures. Klaus does well and is okay too."[89]

Limited also to twenty-five words, and penning exactly that number, Harry Müller replied to his son on September 20, 1942: "[We] simultaneously also [received] your first letter, [we are] very happy, especially about Steven. Why does Lilo not write? We are in the meantime still here [in Ziegenhals], healthy, [and] hope to see [you] again soon. Greetings, kisses."[90]

In December 1942, Harry Müller sent another message to his children, addressed to his son Gert in Lysander—first via the German Red Cross Committee (*Präsidium*) foreign office (*Auslandsdienst*) in Blücherplatz a, Berlin, received there on January 8, 1943; then sent on to the International Committee of the Red Cross Agence Centrale des Prisonniers de Guerre, received there on February 18, 1943; and finally received by the American Red Cross in Washington, D.C., nine months later, on September 1, 1943:

Beloved children! [We are] still here [in Ziegenhals], [and] in good health. [We are] most happy [concerning] the addition to your family in the middle of the month, [we] send heart-felt good wishes to the other children, unfortunately from whom we have not received news. Write soon. One thousand greetings. [Your] parents.[91]

They would send one final cable from Ziegenhals. "Dear Children! [We] again await [our] departure to Theresienstadt (*Geliebte Kinder! Wider erwarten Abreise nach Theresienstadt*)," Müller wrote to his son Gert in Lysander on April 19, 1943.[92] "[We] hope for [the] soonest connection with you. [We are] in good health. [We] wish all [our] heartfelt best, and are with you in spirit (*Hoffen baldigst Connex mit Euch. Sind wolauf. Wünschen Allen herzlichst Bestes, im Geiste stets bei Euch*)," he continued. With only two more words to spare before reaching the twenty-five word maximum, he concluded: "[Whether we] reunite remains to be seen (*Wiedervereinigung ersehnend*)." His message was received by the German Red Cross in Berlin on May 5, and by the American Red Cross in Washington, D.C., on August 19, 1943.[93] By the time this message reached the United States, Harry and Theresia Müller had been living in Theresienstadt for nearly four months.

Harry and Theresia must have been able to correspond with Gert at least once from Theresienstadt. After the war, Gert inquired about them via the Czech Red Cross and listed them as residing in 12 Seestrasse,[94] Theresienstadt.[95] Harry's brother Kurt received a card from him dated September 1944, confirming receipt of a package of soap, potatoes, cigarettes, and other items that Kurt Müller sent to his brother monthly from Bautzen, Germany.[96] Kurt Müller would learn of his brother's fate in January of 1946. He wrote to Gert and Ilse:

> An acquaintance of mine told me he knew someone who was in Theresienstadt with your father. [This person] told me that he knew my brother and that in 1944 he was sent to Auschwitz with about 1,000 other doctors. I now have to abandon all hopes of seeing your father again.[97]

As a single case study, the Müllers appeared to have been a strong couple who actively pursued emigration and did not cease in their efforts despite repeated setbacks and difficulties; who pursued their respective work—-he as a doctor and she as a housewife—as best they could, with little effect despite their efforts. Most clear is the great value they placed on their children and reuniting with them. The available documentation demonstrates much of the trajectory described so eloquently by Marion Kaplan: their "social death" via the abrupt removal of Harry Müller and Wilhelm Gittler from their professional lives; the expropriation and impoverishment of both couples; the loss of household servants, furnishings, and ultimately their homes; the pain of losing their children to emigration, tempered with the pleasure of knowing their children were out of the reach of the long Nazi arm; and their inability to emigrate despite every effort to do so.

Marion Kaplan argues that housewives and mothers "strove to preserve a sense of normality in the midst of desperation while learning to cope with less and expect even worse," and that "women maintained their dignity amid their despair by remembering who they really were, not who their enemies said they were."[98] In the case of the Müllers, certainly all of these things were true about Theresia, but they were also true of her husband, Harry. Their letters to their children convey a sense of partnership in which Harry and Theresia shared all of their burdens with dignity.

NOTES

The views expressed are the author's alone and do not necessarily represent those of the United States Holocaust Memorial Museum or any other organization. I wish to thank Nicole Frechette for her hard work in translating and transcribing this series of letters and Jennifer Rodgers for her aid in locating the International Tracing Service documents relating to the Müller family in a timely way. This essay would have been long delayed without their efforts. I would also like to thank Karen Andolora, Renee and Mitchell Gittler, and their extended families for sharing these materials with the USHMM. To work with them has been a privilege.

1   *Theresienstädter Gedenkbuch: Die Opfer der Judtransporte aus Deutschland nach Theresienstadt, 1942–45* (Theresienstadt Memorial Book: The victims of the Jewish transports from Germany to Theresienstadt, 1942–1945), 82 (Institut Theresienstadter Initiative Academia, 2000

2   Transportliste des Ghettos Theresienstadt (Transport list for the Ghetto Theresienstadt), OCC 26/50 (Outer Concentration Camps/Theresienstadt/Shelf 50), Ordner (file) 31, Seite (page) 131, ITS Digital Collection, USHMM; Transportlisten aus dem Gestapo-Bereich Oppeln (Transport list from the Gestapo District of Oppeln), 13.11.1942-21.3.1944; Inventarisierung von Neumaterial (Inventory of new material), KL documente (Concentration camp documents), Datum der Eintrag, 4 April

1997 (date of receipt), Eingangsbuch (Entry book) lfd. 7164, Ablagort Gestapo-Bereich Oppeln (Deportations from the Gestapo District of Oppeln), VCC 155/XVIII, Ordner 36, ITS Digital Collection, USHMM. Among those deported from Oppeln, only 61 survived the war. *Theresienstädter Gedenkbuch*, 756. Dr. Harry Müller and Theresia (misspelled Therese in this source) are listed on page 758.

3   Transportliste des Ghettos Theresienstadt (Transport list for the Ghetto Thersienstadt), OCC 26/50 (Outer Concentration Camps/Theresienstadt/Shelf 50), Ordner 31, Seite 131, ITS Digital Collection, USHMM.

4   Tracing Document Number 86798; Tracing Document 100615, ITS Digital Collection, USHMM. On January 31, 1986, inquiries as to the fate of Harry and Theresia Müller were made by the Bundesamt für Wiedergutmachung (Neustadt-an-der W.) (Federal Office for Reparations in Neustadt-an-der-Weinstrasse) for a Hamburg-based lawyer named Rosenhaft. I am working to obtain copies of their case ("TD") file.

5   Transport: "Ev" am 28.10.1944 zum KL-Auschwitz (Transport, Ev departing October 28, 1944 to Auschwitz), Blatt (pages) 75-163, ITS Digital Collection, USHMM.

6   Robert Kuwałek, "Izbica Lubelska," translated from the Polish by Steven Seegel. In Martin Dean, ed., *Encyclopedia of Camps and Ghettos, 1933-1945*, vol. 2, *German Run Ghettos* (Bloomington: Indiana University Press, 2011). The Germans first occupied Izbica on September 15, 1939. At the end of 1939, the Germans began resettling Jews into Izbica from Polish towns farther to the west that had been incorporated into the Third Reich Protectorate of Bohemia and Moravia, Germany, Austria, and Slovakia, due to its location on the main line between Lublin and the extermination camp Bełżec, established in November 1941. In total, there were seventeen transports to Izbica between March 11, 1942, and early June 1942.

7   Kuwalek, "Isbica Lubelska."

8   Götz Aly, *Into the Tunnel: The Brief Life of Marion Samuel, 1931-1943*, trans. Ann Millin (New York: Metropolitan Books, in association with the United States Holocaust Memorial Museum, 2007).

9   Christopher R. Browning, Richard S. Hollander, and Nechama Tec, eds., *Every Day Lasts a Year: A Jewish Family's Correspondence from Poland* (New York: Cambridge University Press, 2007), x.

10   Marion A. Kaplan, *Between Dignity and Despair: Jewish Life in Nazi Germany* (New York: Oxford University Press, 1998), 6.

11   For several decades, Myrna Goldenberg, Nechama Tec, and other scholars have studied and written about the differing experiences of Jewish men and women across Europe as they faced the unprecedented challenges Nazism presented. See Myrna Goldenberg, "Different Horrors, Same Hell: Women Remembering the Holocaust," in *Thinking the Unthinkable: Meanings of the Holocaust*, ed. Roger S. Gottlieb (New York: Paulist Press, 1990), 150–66; and Goldenberg, "Women's Voices in Holocaust Literary Memoirs," *Shofar: An Interdisciplinary Journal of Jewish Studies* 16, no. 4 (Summer 1998): 75–89.

12   Kaplan, *Between Dignity and Despair*, 3.

13   Ibid., 236.

14 His father's name was Salomon Müller. Harold G. Müller, Lysander, New York, to Dr. Harry Müeller, Ziegenhals, Germany, February 19, 1942. American Red Cross #14962. Letters from the estate of Lieselotte Müller, in the custody of her niece, Karen Andolora of Conesus, New York (hereafter cited as Lieselotte Müller Letters and Documents, Conesus, NY).)

15 Tracing Document Number 86798, International Tracing Service Digital Collection, USHMM.

16 Tracing Document Number 100615, International Tracing Service Digital Collection, USHMM. According to her card in the ITS Central Name Index, Theresia's parents were named Jacob and Fanny (Brauer) Süssmann.

17 Secondary source literature on Ziegenhals includes Werner Bethge, *Entfaltung jeder Form des Massenwiederstandes. Die Bedeutung der illegalen Funktionärstagung der Kommunistischen Partei Deutschlands am 7. Februar 1933 in Ziegenhals im Widerstreit der Meinungen* (GNN Verlag, 2001).

18 Gert changed his name to "Harold" when he arrived in the United States. After surviving World War II with no injuries, Gert died at the age of thirty-eight after contracting meningitis from one of his patients. As of September 2002, Lieselotte, who spelled her name "Liselotte" after she arrived in the United States, was living in Syracuse, New York. Ursula died of cancer in her forties. Klaus Müller, still alive in September 2002, was living in Yonkers, New York. Source: Letter from Karen Andolora, 5405 West Lake Road, Conesus, New York, to Suzanne Brown-Fleming, 14 September 2002.

19 American Consulate, Stuttgart, to Liselotte Müller, August 8, 1938. Lieselotte Müller Letters and Documents, Conesus, NY. In June 1939, Liselotte Müller was still living in Munich, as indicated by a June 29, 1939, notice she received from the Oberfinanzpräsident of Munich (Devisenstelle) regarding her property. See Oberfinanzpräsident (Devisenstelle) Liselotte Sara Müller, June 29, 1939, Lieselotte Müller Letters and Documents, Conesus, NY.

20 Harry and Theresia Müller, Ziegenhals, to Liselotte ("Lilochen") Müller, Plymouth, England, August 8, 1939. Lieselotte Müller Letters and Documents, Conesus, NY. Though this letter is signed "Mutti und Vati," several references within the letter indicate that Theresia Müller is the author.

21 Harry and Theresia Müller, Ziegenhals, to their children, December 8, 1940. Lieselotte Müller Letters and Documents, Conesus, NY.

22 I thank Ursula's daughter, Karan Andorola, for supplying me with a copy of her German passport.

23 Harry and Theresia Müller, Ziegenhals, to Liselotte ("Lilochen") Müller, Plymouth, England, August 8, 1939. Lieselotte Müller Letters and Documents, Conesus, NY. Though this letter is signed "Mutti und Vati," several references within the letter indicate that Theresia Müller is the author.

24 Harry and Theresia Müller, Ziegenhals, to their children, December 8, 1940. Lieselotte Müller Letters and Documents, Conesus, NY.

25 A letter dated July 24, 1939, from Harry Müller, Ziegenhals, to Liselotte Müller, Plymouth, England, refers to Klaus Müller's address as KWM Trondanger, Inter-

ocean Line San Cristobal Panama. Lieselotte Müller Letters and Documents, Conesus, NY.

26 Harry and Theresia Müller, Ziegenhals, to Mr. Morris L. Lassman, DDS, Phoenix, New York, May 19, 1941. Lieselotte Müller Letters and Documents, Conesus, NY.

27 Gert and Ilse Müller had three children: Steven, Nancy (married name: Belkowitz), and Theresa (married name: Freind). Today, Nancy Belkowitz, an attorney, is a volunteer at the United States Holocaust Memorial Museum.

28 Frank Gittler, interview by Margarita Gilbo, August 2, 1996, in Allentown, PA, Code #18143-38, 5 tapes, University of Southern California Shoah Foundation, Institute for Visual History and Education, United States Holocaust Memorial Museum, Washington, DC.

29 Gertrud Gittler was born October 6, 1887, in Allenstein (East Prussia). Central Name Index (CNI) Card for Gertrud Gittler, ITS Digital Collection, USHMM.

30 Wilhelm Gittler was born June 12, 1877, in Kattowitz. Central Name Index (CNI) Card for Gertrud Gittler, ITS Digital Collection, USHMM. Wilhelm Gittler was one of ten living children and the only one of his siblings to attend university (he attended the universities of Heidelberg and Breslau). Frank Gittler, interview.

31 Frank Gittler, interview.

32 In the Gittler family correspondence, Wilhelm Gittler's professional letterhead lists an address of Höfchenstrasse 1, Breslau 5. Their home address was Viktoriastrasse 118, Breslau. See Gittler Family Correspondence, #2009.176, Archives of the United States Holocaust Memorial Museum.

33 The day and time of his birth remained significant in the memory of Frank Gittler because his mother was "superstitious" and was afraid her son would be born on Friday the 13th, a sign of bad luck. Frank Gittler, interview. Once in the United States, Frank Gittler had four children: Jeffrey, Mitchell, Susan (Musselman), and William. I am grateful to Renee and Mitchell Gittler for their donation of Frank Gittler's letters to the United States Holocaust Memorial Museum.

34 Frank Gittler, interview.

35 Frank Gittler, interview.

36 In Franz's recollection, his grandfather owned a large shoe manufacturing business, which made shoes for the German Army, and his grandmother on his mother's side was heir to a department store. Frank Gittler, interview.

37 Frank Gittler, interview.

38 Michael H. Kater, *Doctors under Hitler* (Chapel Hill: University of North Carolina Press, 1989), 183. Chapter 6, "The Persecution of Jewish Physicians," is still the best essay on the topic to date.

39 Harry Müller, Ziegenhals, to his children, April 2, 1939. Lieselotte Müller Letters and Documents, Conesus, NY.

40 Harry and Theresia Müller, Ziegenhals, to their children, September 8, 1941. Lieselotte Müller Letters and Documents, Conesus, NY.

41 Following Kristallnacht (November 9–10, 1938), those German Jews who still retained private property were subject to a punitive tax. Its purpose was to raise one billion Reichsmarks in payment for the damage wrought during the pogrom.

Within fifteen months, the punitive tax raised over 1.1 billion Reichsmarks. See Joseph Walk, *Das Sonderrecht für die Juden im NS-Staat. Eine Sammlung der gesetzlichen Massnahmen und Richtlinien—-Inhalt und Bedeutung,* 2nd edition (Heidelberg: C. F. Müller Verlag, 1996), 257–307.

42 Harry Müller, Ziegenhals, to his children, April 2, 1939.

43 Harry Müller, Ziegenhals, to Liselotte Müller, Plymouth, England, August 15, 1939. Lieselotte Müller Letters and Documents, Conesus, NY.

44 Harry and Theresia Müller, Ziegenhals, to Liselotte ("Lilochen") Müller, Plymouth, England, August 8, 1939. Lieselotte Müller Letters and Documents, Conesus, NY. Though this letter is signed "Mutti und Vati," several references within the letter indicate that Theresia Müller is the author.

45 Harry Müller, Ziegenhals, to Liselotte ("Lilochen") Müller, Plymouth, England, October 8, 1939. Lieselotte Müller Letters and Documents, Conesus, NY.

46 Harry and Theresia Müller, Ziegenhals, to their children, December 8, 1940. Lieselotte Müller Letters and Documents, Conesus, NY.

47 Harry Müller, Ziegenhals, to his children, December 12, 1940. Lieselotte Müller Letters and Documents, Conesus, NY.

48 Harry and Theresia Müller, Ziegenhals, to their children. January 23, 1941. Lieselotte Müller Letters and Documents, Conesus, NY. References in the letter indicate that it was written by Harry Müller, though it is signed "Vater und Mutti." The passage reads: "*Mutti freut es ganz besonders, dass Morris Deine Küche so gut schmeckt. Es gehört eben schon mit zu den Pflichten einer Hausfrau, kochen zu können das ist bei Euch ganz besonders wichtig, wo die Hausangestellten-Frage ein besonders schwieriges Problem its. Euch ist doch die zur Zeit preisgekrönte Antwort auf die Frage bekannt: 'Wie erhalte ich mir die Liebe meines Mannes? Füttere die Bestie gut.'*"

49 Harry and Theresia Müller, Ziegenhals, to their children, February 27, 1941. Lieselotte Müller Letters and Documents, Conesus, NY.

50 Harry and Theresia Müller, Ziegenhals, to their children, May 19, 1941. Lieselotte Müller Letters and Documents, Conesus, NY.

51 No further information is available concerning "Mrs. Sachs."

52 Harry and Theresia Müller, Ziegenhals, to their children. January 23, 1941. Lieselotte Müller Letters and Documents, Conesus, NY.

53 Kaplan, *Between Dignity and Despair,* 3.

54 Ibid., 6.

55 Ibid., 129.

56 Ibid. 142

57 Frank Gittler, "The Kindertransport," 1. Unpublished manuscript supplied to the author courtesy of Nancy Belkowitz.

58 Ibid.

59 Kaplan, *Between Dignity and Despair,* 117.

60 Gittler, "The Kinder Transport," 1–6.

61 Kaplan, *Between Dignity and Despair,* 117.

62 Harry Müller, Ziegenhals, to his children, April 2, 1939. Lieselotte Müller Letters and Documents, Conesus, NY.

63 Ibid.

64 Harry and Theresia Müller, Ziegenhals, to Liselotte ("Lilochen") Müller, Plymouth, England, August 8, 1939. Lieselotte Müller Letters and Documents, Conesus, NY.

65 Ibid. Though this letter is signed *"Mutti und Vati,"* several references within the letter indicate that Theresia Müller is the author.

66 Harry Müller, Ziegenhals, to Liselotte Müller, Plymouth, England, August 15, 1939. Lieselotte Müller Letters and Documents, Conesus, NY.

67 "We received clearance for both of us to leave [for England]," wrote Theresia. Theresia Müller, Ziegenhals, to Liselotte Müller, Plymouth, England, August 18, 1939. Lieselotte Müller Letters and Documents, Conesus, NY.

68 "It appeared to me that my parents were not too eager, my father did not want to go through another law school education, and he certainly did not wish to leave our properties and money," writes Franz Gittler. Gittler, "The Kindertransport," 1.

69 Theresia Müller, Ziegenhals, to Liselotte Müller, Plymouth, England, August 18, 1939. Lieselotte Müller Letters and Documents, Conesus, NY.

70 Harry and Theresia Müller, Ziegenhals, to Liselotte Müller, Plymouth, England, August 26, 1939. Lieselotte Müller Letters and Documents, Conesus, NY.

71 Harry Müller, Ziegenhals, to Liselotte Müller, Plymouth, England, October 8, 1939. Lieselotte Müller Letters and Documents, Conesus, NY.

72 See series of Western Union Telegrams and financial receipts belonging to Gerhardt and Ursula Steinitz. Lieselotte Müller Letters and Documents, Conesus, NY.

73 Harry and Theresia Müller, Ziegenhals, to their children, December 8, 1940. Lieselotte Müller Letters and Documents, Conesus, NY.

74 Harry Müller, Ziegenhals, to his children, December 12, 1940. Lieselotte Müller Letters and Documents, Conesus, NY.

75 Harry and Theresia Müller, Ziegenhals, to their children, January 23, 1941. Lieselotte Müller Letters and Documents, Conesus, NY. References in the letter indicate that it was written by Harry Müller, though it is signed "Vater und Mutti."

76 Ibid.

77 Harry and Theresia Müller, Ziegenhals, to Mr. Morris L. Lassman, DDS, Phoenix, New York, May 19, 1941. Lieselotte Müller Letters and Documents, Conesus, NY.

78 Ibid.

79 Harry and Theresia Müller, Ziegenhals, to Mr. Morris L. Lassman, DDS, Phoenix, New York, July 11, 1941. Lieselotte Müller Letters and Documents, Conesus, NY. According to an added note to this letter written by Harry and Theresia in German, it appears that they had booked passage on a steamship departing on September 12, 1941 (further details are not available in the letter), but awaited their visas.

80 Harry and Theresia Müller to Lassman, July 11, 1941, Müller Letters.

81 Harry and Theresia Müller, Ziegenhals, to Mr. Morris L. Lassman, DDS, Phoe-

nix, New York, July 31, 1941. Lieselotte Müller Letters and Documents, Conesus, NY. The ease with which problems arose was evidenced also by an anecdote they relayed about some acquaintances: "The Krämers' [transit] visa expires at the end of the week, and without it, they'll be unable to leave [Lisbon]. They were not finished getting everything in order, and additionally, their money for the passage arrived a few days late in Lisbon. Therefore, the shipping company canceled their reservations."

82 Harry and Theresia Müller, Ziegenhals, to his children, August 20, 1941. Lieselotte Müller Letters and Documents, Conesus, NY.

83 Harry and Theresia Müller, Ziegenhals, to his children, September 8, 1941. Lieselotte Müller Letters and Documents, Conesus, NY.

84 Harry and Theresia Müller, Ziegenhals, to their children, January 23, 1941. Lieselotte Müller Letters and Documents, Conesus, NY.

85 Harry and Theresia Müller, Ziegenhals, to their children, February 27, 1941. Lieselotte Müller Letters and Documents, Conesus, NY. The awkward phrasing is explained by the fact that the Müllers wrote to their new son-in-law in English.

86 Ibid.

87 Harry Müller, Ziegenhals, to Morris Lassman, Phoenix, New York, August 20, 1941. Lieselotte Müller Letters and Documents, Conesus, NY.

88 Harry Müller, Ziegenhals, to Morris Lassman, Phoenix, New York, September 8, 1941. Lieselotte Müller Letters and Documents, Conesus, NY.

89 Harold G. Müller, Lysander, New York, to Dr. Harry Müller, Ziegenhals, Germany, n.d., message American Red Cross #14962. Lieselotte Müller Letters and Documents, Conesus, NY.

90 Ibid.

91 In the original German: *Geliebte Kinder! Noch hier, wolauf. Hocherfreut erflihren Monatsmitte euren Familienzuwachs, senden herzlichste Glückwünsche von den anderen Kindern leider ohne Nachricht. Schreibt bald. 1000 Grüsse. Eltern.* Dr. Harry Müller, Ziegenhals, Germany, to Harold G. Müller, Lysander, New York, December 1942, message German Red Cross #445133. Lieselotte Müller Letters and Documents, Conesus, NY.

92 Dr. Harry Müller, Ziegenhals, Germany, to Harold G. Müller, Lysander, New York, April 19, 1943, German Red Cross #516937. Lieselotte Müller Letters and Documents, Conesus, NY.

93 Ibid.

94 12 Seestrasse was a small house located in the former "L1." The street is now called Dukelskych hrdinu and the house is still number 12. I thank Ms. Anna Hájková, PhD candidate in history at the University of Toronto, for this information. I thank Till Hilmar for photographing this residence for me in August 2008.

95 Marína Pauliny (vice chairman, Czechoslovak Red Cross), London, to Captain Harold G. Müller, c/o Division 10th Mountain (Medical Branch), July 19, 1945. Lieselotte Müller Letters and Documents, Conesus, NY. The short response from Miss Pauliny reads: "In reply to your letter of the 3rd, we write to tell you that we have sent the enclosed letter to your parents Dr. and Mrs. H. Müller, 12 Seestrasse,

Terezín to our headquarters in Prague. We asked them to find out the present whereabouts of your parents. As soon as we receive a reply, we shall not fail to notify you."

96 Kurt Müller, Bautzen, Germany, to Gert and Ilse Müller, July 26, 1946. Lieselotte Müller Letters and Documents, Conesus, NY.

97 Ibid. Kurt and his wife Meta Müller, who was not Jewish, were the owners of a factory in Bautzen. They had a son named Helmut, who would later marry against the will of his parents and attempt to emigrate to Brazil (Harry and Theresia Müller to their children, February 27, 1941. Müller Letters and Documents, Conesus, NY). Kurt reports to his nephew that he was arrested on November 9, 1938, and sent to Buchenwald for fourteen days. Forced to sell his business to pay the punitive tax and having what remained of his income confiscated by the county's revenue service, he was left in poverty save "a monthly allowance for sustenance." In August 1941, he took an accounting job in Bautzen for a small business "not owned and run by Nazis" and remained in this job until April 1945. He remarked that "besides a period of two days in which Aunt Meta and I were imprisoned, banned from restaurants, and living in fear, we were able to live our lives freely to an extent." In February 1945, Kurt was called to Dresden, but the air attacks of February 13 and 14, 1945, destroyed the building to which he was to report. After a brief period in April, when he and Meta were forced to leave Bautzen for the Sudetenland, they returned to Bautzen on May 19. At the end of that month, "the Russian town mayors appointed [him] as councilor for business and industry."

98 Kaplan, *Between Dignity and Despair*, 236.

9

The *Kindertransport*

Gender and the Rescue of Jewish Children,
1938–1939

MARY J. GALLANT

The close family ties fostered in Judaism continued to provide a haven for its members despite the antisemitism that inflamed the social and political climate in Germany between 1919 and 1929. However, from 1933 onward, the Jewish experience of persecution in Germany was unrelenting, straining the practical basis of everyday life for families. From the beginning there was a gendered dimension to the persecution.[1] Until full scale deportations started during the war years, men were far more vulnerable to physical assault and arrest than women. Husbands, with their careers threatened or ruined and their businesses subject to confiscation by the state, often tried to leave Germany or were taken to concentration camps. Wives switched to a more active role outside the home. Mothers had to expand their roles, to quickly learn how to be proactive for their families in getting them some form of safety; many took paid employment for the first time. Jewish women rescued and supported their husbands, fathers, uncles, and brothers. They struggled to keep their families intact at a time when their community was under assault. They were often the last to leave, if they escaped at all.

In German state education, Jewish children of both genders had to make unprecedented structural and personal adjustments.[2] Each day they faced pernicious assaults on their self- esteem from teachers and fellow students. To save their lives, from 1934 onwards, using a variety of means, 18,000 unaccompanied children left Germany. This number represented 10 percent of the Jewish children in Germany in 1933. By 1939, 82 percent of children aged fifteen and under, and 83 percent of youth aged sixteen to twenty-four, had managed to escape. By 1941, there were only 25,000 Jewish children still in Germany; most did not survive. After Kristallnacht, November 9–10, 1938, the British Refugee Children's Movement (RCM) put together the Kindertransport operation, which brought close to 10,000 children to safety before Britain went to war with Germany on September 3, 1939. This chapter is about the Kindertransport and the rescue of these Jewish children—how it was accomplished, who was involved, the roles played by women and men in making it a success, and the effects of displacement on the children saved by it from certain death under Nazism.

Why was it that Britain undertook this kind of rescue,[3] and how did the organizing group, the Refugee Children's Movement (RCM), get past the hurdles of immigration, organizing transports out of Germany and into England, obtaining and managing funds, then making the necessary adjustments when it became clear that the rescue effort would be long term rather than what temporary visas had allowed? As repression of European Jews intensified in 1938, public opinion polls in Britain showed an increased alienation from Germany, and, between 1938 and 1945, 71,000 Jews from the continent found refuge in Britain.[4] Nevertheless, rescue and resistance to Nazi repression worldwide was never commensurate with the need.[5] Kristallnacht was the spill point for directing goodwill efforts toward imperiled Jews in Germany, Austria, Czechoslovakia, and Poland.[6]

Kushner and Knox mark the radio broadcast of former Prime Minister Lord Stanley Baldwin in December 1938 as the starting point for the rescue effort. In this broadcast, he highlighted the need for funds to get "the most helpless and innocent" of Nazism's victims out of harm's way. The response was half a million British pounds.[7] There had been a smaller effort by the British Inter-Aid Committee for Children from Germany, formed in 1936, which brought 471 children from Germany to Britain. Lord Baldwin's appeal was the start of a much more developed effort. It led to the formation of 166 local committees in Britain. These were organized into 12 regional committees under the general supervision of one central committee, the RCM. The largest of these committees was the regional committee in Oxford, covering Oxfordshire, Buckinghamshire, Berkshire,

Surrey, Hampshire, and the Isle of Wight, and overseeing twenty smaller committees. In Hampshire, six counties provided between 100 and 250 refugee children with homes. While most counties accommodated fewer than 100 children, seven counties had between 250 and 1,000 children.

Although critics of the rescue movement today emphasize problems in the long-term care of those rescued in the Kindertransport, the lives of thousands of Jewish children who may otherwise have perished were secured by the RCM working together with rescue organizers in Berlin, Vienna, and Prague. The number of visas open to the children was at first unlimited, with the expectation that Britain would be taking from 500 to 50,000 children at any one time. That only about 10,000 children were finally rescued is largely attributable to the outbreak of the war on September 1, 1939.[8]

THE RESCUE ORGANIZERS

The Kindertransport seemed to emerge unexpectedly, yet such an outreach must have been on the minds of many who were in situations of influence. Gillespie notes that

> after the infamous Kristalnacht [*sic*] in November 1938 . . . International Finance Houses realized that they must raise a central fund for German-Jewish Aid. Prominent British bankers all contributed money, and so did men and women important in Whitehall including the Foreign Minister at that time, Sir Samuel Hoare, a Quaker; Eleanor Rathbone, MP; Ellen Wilkinson, MP; Sir Wyndham Deedes; and Mr. Norman Bentwich, a colonial civil servant who had worked in Palestine as Attorney General.[9]

Other early promoters were Englishmen like the stockbroker Otto Schiff; Norman Bentwich, Hebrew University Professor of International Relations and former Attorney General of Palestine; Dennis Cohen, founder and publisher of Cresset Books; Sir Wyndham Deedes, National Council of Social Service director; Viscount Herbert Louis Samuel, former High Commissioner of Palestine; banker Lionel de Rothschild; members of parliament Philip Noel-Baker and Major Victor Cazalet; Home Secretary Sir Samuel Hoare; Former Prime Minister Lord Baldwin; and Sir Charles Stead, the first executive director of the Refugee Children's Movement (RCM).

The determined and sustaining roles of women played an important part in the success of the Kindertransport.[10] Not only did they make the arrangements and keep records on each of the nearly 10,000 children, they also saw to their care throughout the war years. They came from different class and religious backgrounds. Among the women Oldfield mentions were volunteers such as the Quaker interventionist Bertha Bracey; the Headmistress of Bunce Court School in Kent, Anna Essinger; three chairwomen of the regional and local committees of the RCM, Greta Burkhill, Professor Edith Morley, and activist Ruth Simmons; RCM treasurer Elaine Blond and her younger sister, the activist Zionist leader Becky Sieff; Ms. Blond's friend, Lola Hahn-Warburg, sister of Kurt Hahn; and RCM administrator Dorothy Hardisty.

Most remarkable among the British organizers were two individuals, Dennis Cohen and Nicholas Winton, both of whom actually left Britain to head up specific efforts to reach Jewish families and endangered children. Cohen and his wife were sent to Berlin to choose the children for the first transport. He handled over 600 applications, going specifically to places known to have Jewish children already in jeopardy: disenfranchised children awaiting deportation to Poland, children in state orphanages due to the destruction of Jewish orphanages during Kristallnacht, and those in small towns where there were no Jewish community agencies or Quaker Emergency Committee representatives. Winton went to Czechoslovakia in late 1938 at the invitation of a friend working at the British Embassy and, after visiting a refugee camp run by the British, began to organize the eastern arm of the Kindertransport. Winton managed to set up the Czech Kindertransport in early 1939 before returning to London. Initially, he had 200 parents who interviewed with him. In London, he began searching for sponsors and foster-parents for those already on his list. He obtained entry permits and visas, got the Home Office to arrange a safe passage for each train transport, and drew together organizations to help out in the effort. Working with colleagues in Prague, he finally got over 660 children out of Czechoslovakia in eight transports.[11] Those rescued were thereafter referred to as Winton's children. Another 250 children were due to leave Prague on a ninth transport the day the war broke out. It never left the station and none of the children survived the war.

Cohen and Winton were joined in their efforts by a host of organizers in Berlin, Vienna, and Holland. The determined character of these organizers saw matters through rough spots. Norbert Wollheim, one of the organizers in Berlin, writes of escorting the first transport out of Berlin and finding that it was the Nazi SS, not German customs officials, who were boarding the trains. They tore into the children's luggage, "looking for jewels and foreign currency. . . . It was awful."[12] Though they could find nothing, they could and did harass the children with their viciousness, delaying the train and removing the children. Under strong protest from the Dutch Committee, and one vociferous woman organizer in particular, Truus Wijsmuller-Meijer, the children were put on an express train a few hours later and did leave as scheduled on the ferry for England.

VICISSITUDES OF MANAGING LONG-TERM MASS RESCUE

At the start of the Kindertransport, immigration authorities expected a two-year turnaround for each child, rather than a permanent stay. Children on each of the train transports coming to Britain had to be sponsored either by a British subject or by block sponsorship through one of the German-Jewish Aid funds.[13] Britain had waived the need for passports for them and instead required photo-identity cards stamped by the Home Office in London and counter-stamped by German police. The funds for handling all this came from a variety of sources, including Jewish banking houses all over the world, the Save the Children Fund, Inter-Aid, and the Baldwin Fund, which contributed half a million pounds, half of which was given to the finance department of the Children's Movement at Woburn House.

The first transports coming from Berlin and Vienna in early December 1938 continued on a weekly basis until late August 1939. There were at least two transports every week. The British government eased immigration restrictions to permit an unspecified number of children under seventeen years of age to enter Great Britain from Germany, German-annexed Austria, and Czech lands. Organizers sought to get the most brutalized and endangered children to safety on the first transports. Stateless children under constant threat of expulsion, children in orphanages, children alone at home (because their parents had to work), and children whose families were in insecure positions were given priority status. About two-thirds of the children leaving Vienna on these first transports were teenage boys; because circumcision made boys vulnerable to discovery and apprehension, they were seen to be in the greatest danger. Later transports included an increasing number of girls because factors relating to the host country began to take precedence over a simple calculation of who was most at risk. British refugee policy required that a fifty pound sterling bond had to be posted for each child, and rescue workers at the point of origination would meet with each child to create a file that included information on appearance, family background, personality, talents, and communication ability. Children with personality profiles closer to British middle and upper middle class norms were favored by organizers, making class at least as important a factor as gender in the second stage of the Kindertransport.

The rescue effort started on December 1, 1938, and ran until September 1, 1939, when WWII began. During that time, it stopped only once, in February 1939, when the RCM ran short of funds. The breakout of war meant children could no longer be treated as on a temporary stay. Volunteers as well as regular workers adapted to a longer term model of care. Children reaching adulthood in this period variously got jobs, entered the military, or pursued their education, and gender became a more powerful source of inequality. During the war years, the RCM, perennially low on funds, was aided by the British government, which donated one million pounds, and the United States, which provided two million dollars, in support of job programs.

THE EXPERIENCE OF PERSECUTION, EXILE, AND RESCUE: EFFECTS ON THE *KINDER*

Rescue meant safety for the children who had lived under persecution in Germany during the 1930s, but it also held upsets and challenges. It severed children's connection to past community and left a radical disorientation of their social frame. England was a welcome change from persecution and repression; policemen, for instance, normally did protect and serve rather than violate human and civil rights,[14] and of the 10,000 children the RCM brought to England, only fifty had to be moved to different homes. Nevertheless, leaving home involved something of a sense of abandonment.[15] By 1940, communication with the continent ceased, and many of the *Kinder* faced additional emotional strain in balancing the competing worlds of past and present. Interview and other data on *Kinder* show that they were torn between gratitude and bitterness. After the war, like children who survived in hiding, *Kindertransport* children had a kind and degree of survivor's guilt not present in child survivors of the concentration camps.

The first arrivals on the *Kindertransport* trains to Britain were 200 children who entered Harwich from Berlin on December 2, 1938.[16] They were housed at Dovercourt Holiday Camp nearby, which normally would have been closed for the winter. The winter of 1938–1939 was one of the coldest on record and, with no way to heat the chalets in which the children slept, they were given hot water bottles. During meal times or when they took English lessons or recreation in the dining rooms, they did have some heat. *Kinder* on the first transports were more likely than later ones to overlook these difficulties, as safety held a strong visceral meaning for them. Many were already damaged by the trauma of persecution, anxiety, and unbearable loss. By the second phase, many of the earlier organizational difficulties had been resolved. Children who had been carefully selected to blend with their new families came from comfortable middle-class lifestyles. For them, there were other kinds of concerns. As Wolfgang Benz points out, assimilated German Jews identified themselves as Germans first. Emigration grated on them, even though it saved their lives. They were up against new odds in a new social hierarchy.[17]

The length of exposure to persecution had a definite impact on all the *Kindertransport* children. Having endured at least five years of society set against them, they compared poorly with a different group of Jewish children that Anna Essinger brought over from Germany to Britain earlier in the 1930s.[18] In 1933, some parents and supporters of these children foresaw that things would only get worse for Jews in Germany and allowed their children to leave for England. All of Essinger's students hailed from the New Herrlingen School, a prestigious private school in South Germany, where she taught. Anna, as one of the teachers there, had personally taken charge of the children's removal to England. At the Kentish mansion Bunce Court, she found accommodation for the children. The New Herrlingens endured difficulties but remained confident, well-spoken, and courteous. Though exiled, they were high spirited and upbeat. Children rescued in the *Kindertransport* were by contrast old beyond their years from the persecution they left behind. Some were timid and mumbled; others had physical or interactive problems. The RCM needed this remarkable woman and sought her help.

Essinger had a talent for making children feel safe and sure, and in 1938, as a supervisor at Dovercourt, she was particularly attentive to bridging the distance between the *Kinder* and the New Herrlingens. She and her staff of six advanced students inspected the reception process for children on their arrival. They noticed that there was something of a cattle-market at Dovercourt, for instance. Each day, local committees acting on behalf of adopters searched along rows of children during meal times, picking whomever they fancied and cruelly leaving the less attractive behind. To replace this, Essinger inaugurated a system that put children together with specific foster families at Liverpool station, immediately after they got off the ferry. Not all pairings were happy, but most were successful. Essinger also arranged new preliminary accommodations for the *Kinder* which were much more agreeable than Dovercourt. St. Felix School for girls at Southwold provided space for 200 boys over the December holidays, and its staff gave over their vacations to look after them. Girls were housed at Grammar School in Lowestoft. Hostels were set up, some of which housed ten to twelve children in comfortable appointments with a house-mother, cook, and two assistants, all of whom were refugees themselves. A senior physician at the Great Ormond Street Hospital for Children provided funds for one such hostel, and there were also others. Small hostels were often the happiest places for refugee children because they were with others who could share their feelings.

Though the rescue transport to England represented an extraordinary success for the organizers and a piece of good luck for the children,[19] there were unanticipated effects. Charlie Hannam,[20] one of the rescued children, notes that while some of the children were unaware of their feelings about their persecution, perhaps because of their very young age, many others felt self-hate or saw themselves as ugly and unworthy. They experienced suppressed grief and an acute fear of being killed or maimed even after rescue had removed the direct source of the threat. Edith Milton's recollection of leaving behind her parents and country of origin are quite different from Hannam's. While both had positive identifications with their home of refuge, Hannam stayed in Britain and at adulthood became a soldier in the British forces; Milton was among the re-emigrants to America.[21] Differences in the worlds of women and men cast a long shadow. Boys were more likely to be trained for a variety of paying jobs in the labor force; girls were more likely to be used in domestic service to their sponsors and their families. Job training was delayed for girls and they were less likely than boys to be given the option of a higher education.

When we compare two of the *Kinder*, a girl and a boy, we see gender differences intertwined with personality and developmental uniqueness. Vera Gissing, for instance, came from an upper-middle-class home and a close-knit family; Walter Fulop was a teenage boy on one of the first transports. For Gissing, the first nine years of her life were a time of warm family love and security; indeed, she failed to understand how dangerous it was to be a Jew until her parents took what seemed to her to be the startling precaution of having both her and her sister baptized. That was in 1938.

In the spring of 1939, Gissing left Czechoslovakia with other "Winton Children." Her father gave her a diary just before she left, and her first entries read much as if she and her sister were on holiday. She notes that Holland was a beautiful sight for both of them and that they watched the sunrise together on the ship they boarded for England. Other diary entries mention things like "our first English breakfast, which most of us fed to the fishes," the early morning train rolling through the sleeping countryside, and, in London, proudly riding on a double-decker bus.[22] This tourist gaiety, however, may have been a hedge against a deeper sense of vulnerability.

At Liverpool Station, she and her sister were separated, with her sister going on with her host family while Gissing had to wait. That shocked them. Each of them felt unceremoniously ushered into new living arrangements, knowing next to nothing about how things might actually work. The rule on arrival was that as each child's name was called, they left through a side door to meet their new guardians. When her sister's name was called, Gissing felt terribly alone—"with a kiss and a hug she was gone." Gissing's new family could not get there that day; her spirits plummeted. The delay increased her anxiety over not being able to converse in her mother language while believing that she spoke English poorly. Her loneliness, especially for her mother, worsened. But the *Kindertransport* effort had been guaranteed by wealthy backers and so, that day, in the midst of feeling greatly displaced, she was chauffeur-driven in a limousine to a beautiful house, the home of a Church of England bishop, while she waited for her foster parents to arrive. Her distinguished host had twin daughters who made her feel very much at home. When, on the following Monday, she met with her English foster mother, they ran toward each other, "laughing and crying at the same time." Words that stayed in her memory for a lifetime were spoken at that turning point. Her foster mother, "Mummy Rainford," hugged her and said as they entered their new quarters at Bloomsbury House, "You shall be loved."

Walter Fulop's experience contrasts with Gissing's. He had been in hiding in Vienna after Kristallnacht and left for London on one of the first

*Kindertransport*s in January 1939. Looking older than his years, once he entered Britain he was not treated in as sheltered a way as the younger children. He held a job and lived in group housing wherever any could be found. As war broke out and France fell, the older *Kinder* not in foster care had to be either interned or sent to areas in the country to await jobs and housing. Fulop reports that Kempton Park Race Course, where hundreds of internees, young adults of various ages, were sent, did not even have toilet facilities. Holes had been dug in the ground to serve as latrines. Makeshift bedding was all they had. Internees became incensed and threatened a revolt, which led to having the situation questioned in Parliament. A general inspection ensued, and English hosts were as flummoxed as the internees. The whole incident was off-putting and alienating; complete dependency on their rescuers exacerbated the internees' sense of injury and neglect. However, they eventually were sent on to an empty boarding house at Onchan on the Isle of Man. In contrast with the situation they had at Kempton Park Race Course, at Onchan they developed a bourgeois lifestyle. Before exile, many internees had come from families of artists, scientists, business persons, and teachers. They gave lectures and concerts as part of their weekly fare. When Fulop's stepfather arrived in England, he was able to arrange for a house the two could share. It is something of a positive commentary on the sincerity and far-sightedness of his rescuers that for Fulop the most unsettling part of his experience in exile came after the war, when he found out that in 1944 most of his Romanian relatives had been deported by Hungarian security forces to Auschwitz where they had perished.

Michael Geyer's work reconstructs the experience of *Kindertransport* children from family letters, especially those of two sisters, Ruth and Esther, "Winton Children" who left Prague on June 30, 1939, and arrived in England July 1. He portrays them as very resilient, determined to continue communication with their families and cultivate a life "together in separation."[23] Families saw the rescue as giving their children a future that would otherwise have been denied them. The practical work rescuers did to deal with the daily worries of getting each transport of children settled in with their caretaker families shows that the women of the RCM seemed to have put their very best efforts into making a daunting and bitter time bearable for the *Kinder*.

SOCIAL FACTORS AND CHILDREN'S WHOLENESS IN EXILE

Wartime conditions in Britain left everyone greatly stretched. As the Battle of Britain ensued, nightly bombing runs by the Nazi Luftwaffe imperiled the southern and southeastern cities and manufacturing areas of the country. Eisenbruch points out that between 1939 and 1945 in Britain, eight million children were abandoned or left homeless.[24] Refugee children were a small part of this number, but the safety measures employed were the same for all—city children would be sent to safety in the countryside. For the *Kinder*, evacuation amplified the woes of displacement and separation. Freud and Burlingham examined the impact of war on children and found that bombings, for instance, were much less likely to trouble children who remained with their parents or parent surrogates than children separated from family. Though evacuation and removal to the countryside may have spared the lives of the *Kinder*, as it did their hosts, it increased the anguish of having left their own parents and family far away, still persecuted, and ever more out of reach.[25] After the war, although the *Kinder* as a group received no more inpatient treatment than the general population, rates of mental illness treated on an outpatient basis at hospitals were far higher for *Kinder* than for native-born Britons of the same age group. Studying other displaced children in exile, Eisenbruch suggests that as a result of uprooting alone, they might have suffered personal and cultural bereavement, loss of identity, and disrupted development. Children did, however, receive some comfort from items their parents had given them. These formed precious bridges to the past, joining the social worlds of childhood and adulthood and helping the child survivor affirm a positive sense of identity. Mona Korte points out that the items placed by loving parents in the one little suitcase children were allowed to take with them became "keepers of memory"—a means to mourn and identify otherwise un-nameable feelings.[26]

Scars from loss and displacement had multifaceted effects that are only just coming to light as research on the *Kindertransport* grows. Variables of age, gender, and class configured these scars in different ways. Separation anxiety often fell harder on girls than boys of similar ages, especially if they experienced many caregivers and were evacuated to the countryside during the German bombing of Britain. Ute Benz examined the case of the Behrendt children. The boy was fourteen when he left Germany for Britain, and his sister was ten. The boy adjusted well and was allowed to visit his sister, then living in Scotland, in 1943. When he saw her, she shocked him by turning away—she was afraid of him. Being taken away from home and torn from her closest bonds had scarred her while, though he also missed his family, it had not harmed him. As a self-protective strategy, she had not kept in touch. Benz notes that the younger the child at separation from loved ones, especially for those barely able to express themselves verbally, the greater the negative impact on their sense of self. Moreover, the younger a child at separation, the slower his or her social development.[27] Anna Freud's work with difficult children in exile further supports Benz's findings and indicates that profound change brought on through separation and exile can lead to serious disruption of normal psychological growth.

Looking at exilic writing, Hammel followed child survivors into adulthood. This study, with almost twice as many women writers as men, shows that there is great situational variation in life after the great rupture in childhood. Gender is a prism through which boys and girls in exile experienced separation differently, with boys making instrumental adjustments focused on getting a job or moving ahead in a career, while girls, following the gender model of the times, were expected to be reflective and focus on relationships and values.[28] Finnan connects acculturation with the ability to narrativize experience. Female children torn from their families may initially adjust less well than males of similar age, but at adulthood, their predilection for narrating and writing proves to be an advantage. While these results cannot be conclusive, as they are based on autobiographical insights rather than research designed for causal modeling, they are strongly suggestive.[29]

LESSONS FROM THE *KINDER*

Lessons from all parts of the Holocaust are written in pain. In the memoirs and narrative literature of the Kindertransport, social scientists note that the *Kinder* are likely to iconize their sense of anxiety and displacement right from the start in terms of discomfort with a second language. While many did speak at least two languages, they frequently refer to language insufficiency as being an issue.[30] The children worried that they might not be able to express themselves as well in their new contexts as they had in their past and believed a command of the new language was essential to success. With their taste in food being so different from the English, they also feared that cultural distinctions could translate into personal distance, widening the gap between being "rescued" and being "wanted." Evacuation from large urban centers due to the German bombings was also a source of difficulty.

Kinder were comfortable with diversity; an urban context was important to many because there they could at least find synagogues and join Jewish community centers. Being close to others who openly shared a rich attachment to faith was an acute need especially for children of Jewish Orthodox background. Nevertheless, Kleinman and Moshenko suggest that, based on their research, social class may have had more bearing on the adaptation of *Kindertransport* children than did either gender, religion, or language.[31] Letters from home were initially helpful for both genders, but, as Laura Selo's letters from her family show, later on, as these letters painted a painful struggle of conditions closing in on loved ones, they were equally horrifying for both boys and girls.[32] Yet gender differences were important to understanding the experience of traumatic loss and its impact on survival in boys and girls; the comparison between Gissing and Fulop is instructive. Interaction with loved ones through letters helped feeling, memory, and reflection enter the pattern of daily survival for girls. In boys, these were sidelined by a focus on instrumentality, weaving them less intensely into their practical daily awareness and routines.

FINAL THOUGHTS: TERROR AND DISPLACEMENT EFFECTS OF PARENTS AND CHILDREN

Wolfgang Benz notes that in the winter of 1938–39 the anguish of parents was immense as they agreed to their children's rescue.[33] Benz quotes from the diary of a physician from Berlin, Hertha Nathorff, whose thirteen-year-old son was leaving on the *Kindertransport*. Nathorff's diary entry of March 2, 1939, reads

> My child is gone! Early this morning at 6 o'clock we brought him to the Schlesischer Bahnhoff and put him on the *Kindertransport* to England.... Amazing who I met.... A colleague deeply in mourning; her husband died three days after being released from a concentration camp. She is sending her boy.[34]

This situation of *Kinder* and their parents strikes a contrast with other exiles of Nazism. While many political exiles returned to their points of origin to make new lives, *Kinder* had left their homes in childhood, identifying more with parents than place. At the end of the war, with their parents murdered, most felt no wish to return. Most became fully vested in their social worlds of rescue, expressing gratitude toward their rescuers and developing rich bonds with teachers and foster or adoptive parents. The felt losses they suffered were mostly borne in silence, and their threatened selves occluded by the "saved" identity of rescue. The image of a child moving away from a group of family members standing at a train station in Germany, Austria, or Czechoslovakia symbolized for them the meaning of persecution. The rupture of separation from parents in their early lives came out in dreams, reflections, and irrational fears in adulthood.[35] There were few happy endings and for many there would never be complete closure. Once war ended, parents had simply not returned. Only one in five *Kindertransport* refugees was ever reunited with his or her parents. Delayed closure in adulthood paralleled delayed grief in childhood.

Unlike other Holocaust survivors, *Kinder* rarely met each other and did not exist as a social category. They were rarely legitimized in collective memory by reunions or monuments until, in 1999, a statue commemorating the *Kindertransport* was erected at Liverpool Street Station. Smaller in number than the survivors of the camps, and less well known as a survivor category than those who hid, the *Kinder* had invisibility more than identity; their search for help in dealing with any lingering problems had no structural support. Only in the 1980s were they able to share a common thread with other *Kinder*, when large reunions were organized and sponsored in Britain and North America so that they could exchange memories with other exiles like themselves for the first time. This formal acknowledgement brought a sense that they belonged to something larger than their individual experience of rescue. However, it came late, and its potential for healing was diminished by years of neglect.

What sustains survivors of chronic childhood trauma from descent into despair is even the smallest evidence of an ability to form new loving connections. Being part of a vitalizing group, finding the means to remediate generational loss by establishing fulfilling relationships of various kinds in a new context, close solidarity, camaraderie and esprit de corps with new friends and associates—all are important for an untroubled adulthood. *Kinder* were not only survivors of traumatic upheaval but also lived with a compromise in the foundation of trust that forms in childhood. Effective therapy after the war was not available. Their narratives reflect a contained horror and with it a related, very measured, discipline that holds back a consuming sadness.

A lonely search for solutions during a time of persecution characterizes the pain that *Kinder* and their parents experienced. As a woman, a mother, and a widow, Charlotte Levy writes that, after trying unsuccessfully to have her family flee Germany, only her child escaped. She felt an unbearable degree of contradiction and despair in deciding to put her son on one of the *Kindertransports*. To feel relieved was impossible; she was sending her little boy of nine away to a foreign country whose language he did not speak, to strangers and an uncertain future. Getting the last things ready for the child to take on his journey, she discovered the diary he had left behind. As she flipped through the pages, she understood what he had faced each day on the trams to school, in the classrooms, and on the streets. He had not spoken to her about the antisemitic jeers, the filthy epithets, and constant humiliations he noted in the diary. She wanted him to be far away from that; his diary became her comfort when she missed him most. She had chosen wisely after all, one positive act in a sea of vulnerability and terror.[36]

NOTES

1   Marion A. Kaplan, *Between Dignity and Despair: Jewish Life in Nazi Germany* (New York: Oxford University Press, 1998), 5–7, 94–118, 119–44. Kaplan looks at emigration and gender as variables in the Jewish experience of persecution under Nazism. She explains that women expressed their opposition to Nazism mainly by articulating family ties to ameliorate the constraints of persecution. See also Michael Geyer, "Virtue in Despair: A Family History from the Days of the *Kindertransports*," *History and Memory: Studies in Representations of the Past* 17, nos. 1–2 (2005): 323–65.

2   Kaplan, *Between Dignity and Despair*, 54–62, 94–118; see also Phyllis Lassner, *Anglo-Jewish Women Writing the Holocaust: Displaced Witnesses* (New York: Palgrave/Macmillan, 2008), 19–20. Both Kaplan and Lassner take the position that gender is an important dimension in surviving persecution, differently impacting the lives of women and men survivors. Michael Burleigh, *The Racial State* (New York: Cambridge University Press, 1991) emphasizes that racism had a substantial impact among all the persecuted but that gender had an influence on how the sanctions and perils played out. Both women and men were tortured and killed; the differences related to where, when, and how. In *The Jewish Women of Ravensbrueck Camp* (Madison: University of Wisconsin Press, 2006), Rochelle Saidel

shows that in this women's concentration camp on German soil, in operation from 1938 to 1945, gender configured the practice of torture. Supporting the position that gender significantly affected the experience and remembrance of persecution and suffering during the Holocaust, Myrna Goldenberg maintains that distinctions in our gendered social worlds affected the manner of survival in the concentration camps in "Different Horrors, Same Hell: Women Remembering the Holocaust," in *Thinking the Unthinkable: Meanings of the Holocaust*, ed. Roger S. Gottlieb (New York: Paulist Press, 1991), 150–66.

3   There were other places and times in the 1930s when the rescue of Jews was attempted. See also Olga Drucker, *Kindertransport* (New York: Henry Holt, 1992); Drucker points out that about twenty thousand more children immigrated to Palestine; twelve thousand children did so through the Youth Aliyah movement. Sixteen thousand others were taken to France by the OSE (*Organisation pour la sante et l'education*). Considered adults and responsible for their own welfare, refugee children under German immigration law were subjected to harsh medical examinations and subsisted on their own for indefinite periods of time. In fact, millions of people were displaced by National Socialism between 1933 and 1945 and most were not welcomed anywhere. See Michael Marrus, *The Unwanted: European Refugees in the Twentieth Century* (New York: Oxford University Press, 1985). He notes poignantly that there had never been a nation or a time that gave rise to more panic, dislocation, or injury than that generated by National Socialism. During World War II, even more were displaced by what Christopher Browning refers to as ideological warfare; see *The Origins of the Final Solution: The Evolution of Nazi Jewish Policy, September 1939–March 1942* (Lincoln: University of Nebraska Press, 2004).

4   William Rubenstein and Hilary L. Rubenstein, *Philosemitism: Admiration and Support in the English-Speaking World for Jews, 1840–1939* (New York: St. Martin's Press, 1999), 98; the authors note that in a 1943 Gallup poll, 78 percent of British respondents supported helping Jews escape Nazism; see also Martin Gilbert, *Jewish History Atlas* (London: George Weidenfeld and Nicholson, 1985; orig. 1969), 97. Gilbert details antisemitism and the flow of Jewish emigration to certain points of refuge between 1870 and 1943; Britain was strongly represented among them. Extending this point, Louise London suggests that official immigration policy in Britain was somewhat at odds with the determined efforts of citizens to bring Jews to safety from Nazi persecution. See Louise London, *Whitehall and the Jews, 1933–1948: British Immigration Policy and the Holocaust* (Cambridge, UK: Cambridge University Press, 2000), 13, 58–96.

5   Britain, though criticized for not doing more, nevertheless strikes a contrast with this pattern. Looking only at refugees entering Britain, Kushner and Knox note that among the main refugee groups between 1933 and 1939, there were 55,000 refugees from Germany, Austria, and Czechoslovakia and 60,000 from the rest of the continent, particularly Belgium and Holland. See Tony Kushner and Katherine Knox, *Refugees in an Age of Genocide: Global, National and Local Perspectives during the Twentieth Century* (London: Frank Cass, 1999), xiii, 154–71. In

1945–46, children of mixed nationalities from the concentration camps were given refuge in Britain as well. See also Nora Levin, *The Holocaust Years* (Malabar, FL: Kreiger, 1990), 27–36, which argues that the battle of annihilation for German Jews depended on the emigration process. Without some legitimate emigration source, Jews died. Britons helped where others did nothing.

6   There was an upscaling of anti-Jewish activities in Germany in 1938 that reached a crisis point on Kristallnacht, November 9–11, 1938. In *Kristallnacht: Prelude to Destruction* (New York: Harper Collins, 2006), Martin Gilbert details the extreme violence. In Wiesbaden, the violence began at six in the morning. The British embassy there reported to London that the burning of all the synagogues in that city started at that time. In Regensberg, which had the oldest Jewish quarter in Germany, dating back 918 years, shop windows were smashed and Jewish men were taken off to Dachau. Diplomats and foreign correspondents estimated that ninety-one Jews were killed, and thousands imprisoned. The caretaker of the synagogue at Prinzregenstrasse in Berlin was burned to death with his family, and two Jews were lynched in Berlin's East End. See David Cesarani, "Introduction," in *Into the Arms of Strangers: Stories of the Kindertransport*, ed. M. Harris and D. Oppenheimer (New York: MJF Books, 2000), 1–19, for more statistics related to 1938–39 Germany. Paul Kuttner, *Endless Struggle: Reminiscences and Reflections* (New York: Vantage Press, 2009) gives a richly detailed look at Berlin in the 1930s. Labeled *mischlinge*, he was aware of both the Christian and the Jewish worlds in Berlin and was among those on the first of the Kindertransports from Berlin. Amy Zahl Gottlieb, *Men of Vision: Anglo-Jewry's Aid to Victims of the Nazi Regime, 1933–45* (London: Weidenfeld and Nicholson, 1998) fills in a lot of missing details connecting the British and German refugee efforts at this time.

7   Kushner and Knox, *Refugees*, 154–71, notes that roughly six thousand of the 1938–39 Kindertransports were issued entry permits to England. These permits required a fifty pound deposit and a guarantor of stable financial means for each child.

8   Rebekka Gopfert and Andrea Hammel, "Kindertransport: History and Memory," *Shofar* 23, no. 1 (2004): 3. As Aimee Bunting points out, despite falling short of the RCM's own expectations, the Kindertransport accomplished more than ten times what was actually planned before war eventually broke out. It was the largest rescue of Jews in Europe or elsewhere in the 1933–45 period. Aimee Bunting, "Representing Rescue: The National Committee for Rescue from Nazi Terror, the British and the Rescue of Jews from Nazism," *The Journal of Holocaust Education* 9, no. 1 (2000): 65–84.

9   Veronica Gillespie, "Working with the Kindertransport," in *This Working Day World: Women's Lives and Culture(s) in Britain 1914–1945*, ed. Sybil Oldfield (London: Taylor and Francis, 1994), 123.

10 Sybil Oldfield, "It is Usually She: The Role of British Women in the Rescue and Care of the Kindertransport Kinder," *Shofar* 23, no. 1 (2004): 57–70.

11 Vera Gissing, *Pearls of Childhood: The Poignant True Wartime Story of a Young Girl Growing up in an Adopted Land* (New York: Pan Books, 1990), 10.

12 Harris and Oppenheimer, *Into the Arms of Strangers*, 112–13. Many other sources

also attest to the same facts about Winton, as do USHMM, Radio Prague, BBC News September 18, 2010; internet sources like, for instance, Louis Bulow, *Sir Nicholas Winton, or, A Man of Courage, Baruch Tenenbaum,* 2009, as well as those from other credible sources like the International Raoul Wallenburg Foundation (IRWF), the Imperial War Museum of Britain, Yad Vashem and USHMM provide trstworthy insight; newspapers like *Haaretz,* the *Guardian, Reuters,* the *London Gazette* provide recent credible and copyrighted sources of information that contribute to collective memory of a beloved and reclusive historical figure like Winton.

13 Claudia Curio, "'Invisible' Children: The Selection and Integration Strategies of Relief Organizations," *Shofar* 23, no. 1 (2004): 42, 41–56; Gillespie, "Working with the Kindertransport," 125–29; see also Martha Blend, *A Child Alone* (London: Mitchell Vallentine & Company, 1995), 104–5.

14 Barry Turner, . . . *And the Policeman Smiled* (London: Bloomsbury, 1990), 52–53; Gillespie, "Working with the Kindertransport," 129.

15 Marianne Kroger, "Child Exiles: A New Research Area?" *Shofar* 23, no. 1 (2004): 9–10, 22; Ruth Barnett, "The Other Side of the Abyss: A Psychodynamic Approach to Working with Groups of People who came to England as Children on the Kindertransport," *British Journal of Psychotherapy* 12 (1995): 175–94; Gopfert and Hammel, "Kindertransport," 21–27; Bertha Leverton and Sarah Lowensohn, eds., *I Came Alone: The Stories of the Kindertransports* (Sussex, England: Book Guild, 1990), 108–11. Phyllis Lassner, *Anglo Jewish Women Writing the Holocaust,* 48–76, looks at *Kindertransport* survivors who are now writers and shows this focus on abandonment in their writing. Having lost both her parents in the Holocaust, one of the *Kinder,* Karen Gershon, deals with the burdens of loss as the "primary shaping force" in her writing. It makes the child a stranger in a strange land, exiled forever.

16 Caroline Sharples, "Kindertransport," *History Today* 54, no. 1 (2004): 23–35; Gertrude W. Dubrovsky, *Six from Leipzig* (London: Valentine Mitchell & Company, 2004).

17 Wolfgang Benz, "Emigration as Rescue and Trauma: The Historical Context of the Kindertransport," *Shofar* 23, no. 1 (2004): 2; Gillespie, "Working with the *Kindertransport,*" 123–32.

18 Gillespie, "Working with the *Kindertransport,*" 123–32. Essinger is joined by Dorothy Hardisty, another legacy builder within the RCM. Essinger's personal commitment and skills in dealing with the children directly on a daily basis were as critical to the success of the rescue process in 1938–39 as they were in 1933.

19 In Karen Gershon, *We Came as Children: A Collective Autobiography of Refugees* (New York: Harcourt, Brace and World, 1989); Leonard Smith, "Thank God for the Kindertransport (A Letter)," *History Today* 54, no. 5 (2004): 92.

20 Charles Hannam's work, *A Boy in That Situation: An Autobiography* (New York: Harper and Row, 1977), elaborates on how the children felt. Emotions like self-hate, low self-esteem, and loneliness are evident in many of the memoirs; also see Hannam's, *Almost an Englishman* (New York: Harper and Row, 1977).

21 Edith Milton, *The Tiger in the Attic* (Chicago: University of Chicago Press, 2005), 84–103. Gissing, *Pearls,* 37–41, is also rich in material that allows for comparisons and insights of various kinds. As the *Kinder* became adults they felt the sting of being identified by the state as "enemy aliens" and interned unless they were defined under some other rubric or had become part of an adoptive family. Miriam Kochan, "Women's Experience of Internment," in *The Internment of Aliens in Twentieth Century Britain,* ed. David Cesarani and Antony Kushner (New York: Routledge, 1993), 147–66, shows women being discussed in the press, parliament, and in general as a threat to the nation in times of war.

22 Gissing, *Pearls of Childhood,* 37–41, 129, and Walter Fulop, in Leverton and Lewenshon, eds., *I Came Alone,* 108–11. Quotes throughout this comparison, like Mummy Rainford's "You shall be loved," come from Gissing, *Pearls of Childhood,* or, in the case of direct reference to the death of Fulop's relatives during the Nazi offensive on the eastern front, from Fulop. See also Smith, "Thank God for the *Kindertransport*"; and Turner, . . . *And the Policeman Smiled,* 1–53.

23 Geyer, "Virtue in Despair," 323–65; Gillespie, "Working with the Kindertransport," 129.

24 Maurice Eisenbruch, "The Mental Health of Refugee Children and their Cultural Development," *International Migration Review* 22, no. 2 (1988): 292–300; Anna Freud and Dorothy Burlingham, *War and Children* (London: Medical War Books, 1943), xx.

25 Judith Grunfeld's book *Shefford: The Story of Jewish School Community in Evacuation 1939-1945* (London: Soncino Press, 1980) addresses the difficulties of evacuation for those who had already been displaced. John Bowlby is among a host of scholars concerned with the effect of rupturing the parent-child and especially the mother-child bond due to displacement of various kinds (John Bowlby, "The Nature of the Child's Tie to His Mother," *International Journal of Psychoanalysis* 39 (1958): 1–23). See also Anna Freud's discussion of John Bowlby's work on separation, grief, and mourning in her *Research at the Hampstead Child Therapy Clinic and Other Papers* (London: International Universities Press, 1970), 169, where she explores many different facets of problems associated with displacement from parents and forms of social isolation that have long-term impact. Roger Rosenblatt, in his work *Children of War* (Garden City, NY: Anchor Press/Doubleday, 1983), puts the whole discussion of trauma and emotional wounding in a wider context.

26 Mona Korte, "Bracelet, Hand Towel, Pocket Watch: Objects of the Last Moment in Memory and Narration," *Shofar* 23, no. 1 (2004): 118–20.

27 Ute Benz, "Traumatization through Separation: Loss of Family and Home as Childhood Catastrophes," *Shofar* 23, no. 1 (2004): 85–95. See also Freud's discussion of John Bowlby's work, 169.

28 Andrea Hammel, "Representatives of Family in Autobiographical Texts of Child Refugees," *Shofar* 23, no. 1 (2004): 121–30; Ruth Klüger, *Still Alive: A Holocaust Girlhood Remembered* (New York: Feminist Press, 2000), 106.

29 Carmel Finnan, "Gendered Memory? Cordelia Edvardson's *Gebranntes such der Feuer* and Ruth Klüger's *weiter leben*," in *Autobiography by Women in German,* ed.

M.P. Cavies, B. Linklater and G. Shaw (Oxford: Oxford University Press, 2000); Hammel "Representatives of Family," 278–80.

30 Blend, *A Child Alone,* 58, 61, 104–5. For a further exploration of language and connection, see Eva Hoffman, *Lost in Translation: A Life in a New Language* (New York: Dutton, 1989).

31 Susan Kleinman and Ghana Moshenska, "Class as a Factor in the Social Adaptation of the *Kindertransport Kinder,*" *Shofar* 23, no. 1 (2004): 28–40.

32 Caroline Sharples in "Kindertransport" and Laura Selo, *Three Lives in Transit* (New York: Excalibur Press, 1992) are both among the many sources that mention the desperate struggle of those who were saved as they watched their parents and loved ones lose their battle to escape Nazism. Phyllis Lassner's study of *Kindertransport* memoirs identifies clear differences in the experience of females and males and addresses the role of "lifewriting" in her chapter "Other People's Houses: Remembering the *Kindertransport,*" in *Anglo-Jewish Women Writing the Holocaust: Displaced Witnesses* (New York and London: Palgrave / Macmillan, 2008) 28, 19–47. Gender differences among the *Kinder* orchestrated the configuration of self and identity, memory and meaning, as they became adults.

33 Benz, "Emigration as Rescue and Trauma," 5.

34 Hertha Nathorff, *Das Tagebuch der Hertha Nathorff, Berlin-NewYork, Augzeichnungen, 1933-1945* [The Diary of Hertha Nathorff, Berlin-New York Recordings, 1933-1945] (Frankfurt am Main: Fischer Taschenbuch, 1988), 149. The diary provides information on German immigrants from Berlin living in New York as well as general conditions on this time of oppression for Jews.

35 Several sources (such as, for instance, David Cesarani, "Introduction," in Harris and Opppenheimer, *Into the Arms of Strangers,* 18 and "A Teacher's Guide to the Holocaust," The Florida Center for Instructional Technology, College of Education, University of South Florida, 2005, http://fcit.usf.edu/holocaust) report that most of the *Kinder* never saw their parents again after joining the *Kindertransport* to Britain. This form of loss could be survived, but not without an emotional toll. For an example of loss and shock in the narrative of a hidden child, see Mary Gallant, "Rene," in *Coming of Age in the Holocaust: The Last Survivors Remember* (Lanham, MD: University Press of America, 2002), 57 and 66–67. Other significant works examine the impact of loss and shock, e.g., Yael Danieli, "Treating Survivors and Children of Survivors of the Nazi Holocaust," in *Post-traumatic Therapy and Victims of Violence,* ed. F. Ochberg (New York: Brunner/Mazel, 1988), 278–94, and the importance of connectedness for trust, as in Judith L. Herman, *Trauma and Recovery: The Aftermath of Violence from Domestic Abuse to Political Terror* (New York: Basic Books, 1992), 194. See also Benz, "Emigration as Rescue and Trauma," 204.

36 Harris and Oppenheimer, *Into the Arms of Strangers,* 84–85.

10

Survivor Mothers and Their Daughters

The Hidden Legacy of the Holocaust

GABY R. GLASSMAN

My prime focus on women in this chapter enables us to look at the generational line grandmother-mother/daughter-granddaughter, which the Holocaust ruptured in so many cases. Second, I draw on some of the findings from attachment theory studies to aid our understanding of why some people seemed to cope when others did not. The focus of these studies tends to be mainly on the attachment patterns between mothers and daughters. Third, I note that at the time that survivor mothers brought up their children, many of them were at home as the primary caregivers in these families. Consequently, a special identification based on their common gender had time to develop. Fourth, as in therapy generally, there seems to be a preponderance of women attending my second generation groups and, therefore, this gender concentration has given me a substantial opportunity to become aware of the ramifications of insecurities in mother-daughter attachments.[1]

In her introduction to *After Such Knowledge*,[2] Eva Hoffman writes. "The guardianship of the Holocaust is being passed on to us. The second generation is the hinge generation in which received, transferred knowledge of events is transmuted into history, or into myth." However, Chief Rabbi Sir Jonathan Sacks, argues that

Judaism was organised around something other than history. Its key word was memory. Perhaps the simplest way of describing the difference is this. History is what happened to someone else. Memory is what happened to me. Memory is history internalised, the past made present to those who relive it.[3]

In the first book on children of Holocaust survivors, published in 1979, Helen Epstein's opening words are:

> For years it lay in an iron box buried so deep inside me that I was never sure what it was. I knew I carried slippery, combustible things more secret than sex and more dangerous than any shadow or ghost. Ghosts had shape and name. What lay inside my iron box had none. [4]

Epstein describes a history that she did not live through but had, nevertheless, been affected by. Since then, numerous papers and books on the psychological aspects of transgenerational transmission have been published, written in the main by psychologists and psychotherapists,[5] and the topic has been articulated in the autobiographies of the second generation.

My observations are based on the several hundred children of Holocaust survivors and refugees who participated in second-generation groups I have conducted in London since 1989. The mothers to whom I refer in this chapter are the mothers of daughters who took part in my groups. These mothers either managed to escape Nazi persecution and come to England before the war—some bore children during the war—or survived in hiding or in concentration camps and arrived in England after the liberation. In most cases, the mothers left close relatives behind, many of whom did not survive. When survivors' worst fears about the fate of their relatives proved to be true, mourning for their loved ones was often inhibited by distance in time and geography and by the absence of a body, a burial ground, and, frequently, other relatives with whom to share their grief.[6] For many, having lost all or most of their families, procreation was paramount, as without children there could be no family continuity and, for some, no Jewish future.

As relatively few camp survivors and former hidden children settled in the United Kingdom,[7] there were insufficient numbers of second-generation survivors to form separate groups for only children of survivors. Whether the mothers were survivors or refugees, however, the impacts on the second generation were similar enough for the daughters to explore these impacts together in one group, in spite of marked differences between them. Considering the 65,000–70,000 Jewish refugees who came to Britain prior to WWII,[8] the total number of children of survivors and refugees might exceed 70,000.[9]

Although the second generation seems to be successful, both academically and professionally, I address in this chapter some of the implications of the attachment problems I have noticed second-generation children have experienced with their survivor parents. However, I believe with other authors that the legacy of parental trauma has also had an impact on their offspring in positive ways, as has been evident in the resourcefulness and creativity of many second generation individuals I have known.[10]

My comments are based on my work with second-generation daughters who have sought psychological help.[11] The focus of these self-selected groups was the impact of parents' Holocaust experiences on daughters' lives as children and into adulthood. My formulations can only be tentative, as their validity has not been tested against a control group. However, as the theme is not unique to the children of Holocaust survivors and refugees, I hope that what is described here will contribute to our understanding of other second-generation populations whose parents have been exposed to trauma.

All potential group members attended a two-hour preliminary individual meeting with me to help them decide whether to join a second-generation group. They had to commit themselves to attending all twelve sessions (eighteen hours over twelve consecutive weeks) unless there were special circumstances. They also had to agree to the fee for participating in a group, as well as to rules of confidentiality and to having no contact with other group members outside of the group.[12]

These groups took place in the library of a synagogue founded in 1939 by refugees; although independent, it is regarded as a progressive synagogue. The synagogue is in Swiss Cottage, an area of London home to many refugees from Nazi Germany. Some group members lived there as children before their families moved away, and a number of participants commented that going back to the synagogue and the area was like coming back home. The groups consisted of five to eight sons and daughters of survivors and refugees; occasionally, if no men applied, a women's group was formed. To qualify, a group member had to have a parent who had been persecuted because of having been born Jewish. Group members were heterogeneous: ages ranged from early twenties to late sixties, religious observance from strictly orthodox to completely non-practicing, including, in two instances, *Charedim* (ultra-orthodox Jews). The majority of group members were either not maintaining traditional Jewish practices or were affiliated with a liberal or a reform synagogue. Some had not been aware that they were Jewish until they were in their forties.[13]

The groups described here have, to my knowledge, been the only facilitated groups for the second generation in the UK. A few self-help groups meet once a month or once every two months, with a changing composition. The function of these groups tends to be supportive as well as social. The groups I facilitate have a therapeutic purpose. In spite of each group convening for only eighteen hours, group members have achieved insights and understanding and changed behavior to an extent that far exceeded their expectations.

Because of the general lack of awareness, it is not surprising that members of the second generation who experience psychological problems do not necessarily connect these to their parents' Holocaust background. Even for those in therapy, the second-generation component of their problems was not always detected, considered important, or addressed sufficiently, with the therapist possibly colluding with the client in keeping it hidden.

Attachment figures are usually part of a kinship network that persists from birth to death. In many cases, however, survivors lost all their natural attachment figures and therefore had to set up a new attachment network, often of a different sort. If they were the only survivors of their generation, their children grew up with no cousins, denying these children a sense of belonging they might have enjoyed. Unable to mourn their multiple losses, survivors dissociated from their emotions and suppressed them.

Infants have an innate disposition to form attachments through a mutual attuning process with their mothers or other caregivers.[14] If it feels safe, then getting close will be a rewarding experience for the infant. In secure attachments, traumatic attachment experiences have been worked through by the caregiver. However, based on what my group members reported, their mothers were often not able to come to terms with why they survived when their parents, brothers and sisters, and aunts and uncles did not, or they blamed themselves for not having been able to save their loved ones. Their survivor guilt seemed to impede the mourning process which, consequently, remained unresolved. This irresolution influenced their ability to provide the unconditional love sought by the children born following their trauma.

During the first twenty or so years after the war, wider society was not ready to listen to survivors' stories,[15] nor were those working in the mental health professions in the different countries in which survivors settled. Survivors responded by not talking about their experiences and feelings and instead focused their energy on rebuilding their lives. In this rebuilding, they lacked role models for the various life stages, as their parents' generation did not live to reach that stage in their own lives. Survivors' postwar coping ability depended on a variety of factors: on their pre-war experiences and personality, on the nature and severity of their wartime fate, and on the support they received after the war. Many who survived the war as children experienced a complete rupture in the relationship with their primary caregivers and, afraid to lose new close attachment figures, were unable to tolerate closeness again: the fear of being hurt by a new loss was to be avoided at all costs. In view of the losses survivors suffered and their concomitant feelings of abandonment, it nonetheless seemed unbearable for many to face the future alone. In order to fill the void the Holocaust left behind, they formed new lasting relationships, often based on their shared background or common fate rather than on mutual love, the so-called "marriages of despair." On the other hand, marriages that were built on practical and emotional support received from a kind person, completely unconnected with their Holocaust past, could forge a strong union.

By the time their children were born, parents had usually formed a family dynamic of speaking or not speaking about the Shoah, a tacit agreement about the extent of openness in the family and the range of feelings to be shared. This often included a non-articulated understanding regarding who had suffered most. This hierarchy of suffering demanded that family members do their utmost to protect that person and spare him or her further hurt. It left a gap in the family discourse that children were implicitly required to respect and, consequently, the children were obliged to suppress their feelings. Of course, in cases where both parents were survivors, the hierarchy of suffering also meant that survivor parents who were perceived as having suffered less—hidden children or those who came over on a Kindertransport—also suppressed their own feelings. In some cases, it took over forty years for these individuals to identify openly as Holocaust survivors and give voice to their traumatic past. At the start of a new second-generation group, too, a similar hierarchy of suffering always seemed to surface, with children of refugees feeling that their suffering did not match the suffering endured by children of survivors. It was crucial to the survival of each group to recognize this difference early on; once it was addressed, it ceased to be a problem.

Only some of the parents of my clients spoke openly about their Holocaust experiences. Mostly, the topic was avoided in order to protect the children, since survivors did not wish to burden their offspring with their suffering, and perhaps they preferred not to rake up old wounds for themselves. Children, for their part, were afraid to ask questions for fear of hurting and upsetting their parents. Although they wanted to know, they also did not want to know, unsure as they were as to whether they would be able to cope with their parents' emotional responses.

However, mothers still passed on their legacies unconsciously. Children picked up messages—mainly of fear—indirectly, through overheard conversations and nightmares, as well as non-verbally, through their mothers' facial expressions, sighing, and crying, as well as through witnessing their mothers' heightened state of aggravation. Silence also communicated feelings and fears, which were absorbed. These non-verbal transmissions occurred through daughters' identification with the suppressed part of their mothers' consciousnesses. Some daughters developed fearful fantasies that seemed almost worse than the reality had been, with Holocaust imagery in which they, themselves, felt persecuted by the Nazis. What made matters worse for them was that they realised they were not to talk about the family-created secrets outside the family.

Survivor mothers were perceived and described as seeming to be lacking ability to express feelings openly, if they were able to show feelings at all. Some mothers were reported not to "do feelings." However much was spoken, much remained unspoken. Having avoided their own painful feelings and thoughts, mothers also seemed to find it almost impossible to be attuned to their daughters' needs and wishes. I was struck by the daughters' accounts of their mothers' inability to empathize with them. Mothers often seemed to draw the wrong conclusions or respond in ways that their daughters took as deeply hurtful. Daughters, on the other hand, felt that, although they were attentive in trying to accommodate their mothers' wishes, their attempts remained mostly unacknowledged. Relationships with their mothers were, on their side, largely driven by guilt. Daughters unconsciously deferred to their mothers out of fear of rejection or of letting their mothers down, and found it extremely hard to arrive at decisions, even on relatively small matters. They developed anxieties about their mothers' sense of abandonment, perhaps representing the internalization of their mothers' projections of this fear.

For members of the second generation, belonging to a special group of people with whom they could identify generally created relief and validated and normalized their experience. Feeling different from their Anglo-Jewish peers has probably been the single characteristic mentioned most frequently by group members. Not only did they feel different, they felt neither British nor anything else. This left a lacuna in their identity which some found hard to fill. Most second-generation children were not raised in their parents' native tongue: German and Austrian refugees chose to speak English, as they wanted to leave their past behind them and because the language of the enemy was to be avoided. Additionally, those children who grew up, often by parental choice in order to help the family assimilate, in parts of the UK with few Jews could feel like fish out of water.

In recent years, there has been much discussion among researchers in attachment theory about the intergenerational impact of trauma. Van IJzendoorn and colleagues cite clinical studies of survivor mothers who lost both parents and were in occupied Europe during the war.[16] These studies report problematic family relationships, with children lacking emotional space to achieve separation and individuation. Epidemiological studies, on the other hand, have revealed little impact on the psychological functioning of the second generation and, therefore, no evidence of secondary traumatization. Thus, it is important to establish whether we can speak of secondary traumatization, i.e., of transmission of trauma from survivors to the second generation.

Van IJzendoorn reports findings from a meta-analysis.[17] From a total set of 32 samples of 4,418 families, more than 50 percent of the survivor mothers showed insecure attachment representations (psychic structures of attachment regulation based on past experiences). In particular, a significantly higher number of these representations were characterised by unresolved loss or unresolved other trauma, compared with only 18 percent in the control group of women who had immigrated from Europe to Palestine just before World War II. The authors of the studies considered interpret the difference as evidence that a large percentage of children of survivors grew up in an environment in which their survivor mothers were not able to work through the multiple losses of the deaths of their loved ones. In spite of this finding for survivor mothers, a subset of adequately designed studies of non-clinical, non-select samples of second-generation

Holocaust survivors showed that these individuals did not differ from the children in the comparison group in terms of attachment or unresolved trauma; in these terms, second-generation survivors could be considered well-adapted.

Van IJzendoorn and colleagues conclude tentatively from the same meta-study that when children of survivors functioned under *normal* circumstances, there was no transmission of trauma. However, when confronted with *extreme* stress, especially events over which they had no personal control such as life-threatening illnesses or war situations, the children of Holocaust survivors showed significantly more psychological problems than did the control group. This diminished psychological functioning in situations of extreme stress seemed to occur in both clinical and non-clinical second-generation survivors, although the difference was more pronounced for the clinical group. The authors suggest that, in the second generation, a latent vulnerability to maladaptive and prolonged posttraumatic responses may surface under certain circumstances.

In a study on mourning by Sagi-Schwartz et al,[18] 42 percent out of forty-eight female child survivors who were orphaned during the war displayed *unresolved* loss when the Adult Attachment Interview (AAI) was administered to them.[19] The discourse of these child survivors, who were young mothers at the time of the interview, was characterized by "shallow speaking; lack of expressions of sadness, pain," the sense that something was "missing," or of a "need"; and by "no indications of integrating the loss to a new representation." According to these attachment theory researchers, the survivors' lack of ability to reflect on their experiences and relationships was apparent.

I mention these findings in some detail to show the impact that survivor mothers' unresolved mourning had on their relationship with their daughters. They do not account for the secondary traumatization I observed in my clinical sample, which consisted of second-generation survivors as well as second-generation refugees. Whereas in the meta-study the occurrence of secondary traumatization was established only in *extreme* situations, particularly in the clinical group, my observations reveal the presence of *more subtle* yet traumatizing attachment insecurity in everyday family life among many of my group members. These could be triggered by the slightest incongruence of feeling between the second-generation children and their survivor mothers. The problems often provoked a sense of dread that could become embedded within the children's psyches.

Many of my group members never knew their grandparents. They also knew very few details about the circumstances of their grandparents' deaths or, indeed, about their lives; talking about it would have been too painful for their mothers. The little that children were told as they grew up was often full of euphemisms. Grandparents were said to have "perished" during the war; the why and how was not explained. The words "killed," "murdered," "shot," or "gassed" seem to have been perceived as too strong for mothers to use and for daughters to hear, and this avoidance of words stating what really happened also extended to the general discourse about the Holocaust in society at large. The word "perish" was intended to help shield both the survivor and the listener from the sheer horror of knowing details of how they died and to prevent the listener from feeling guilt. This lack of explicitness may perhaps indicate how little working through and mourning of the fate of their loved ones parents were able to do, troubled as they were by feelings of guilt that they had not been able to prevent them from being deported and murdered.

Like all infants, children of Holocaust survivors sought nurturing from their parents, their primary attachment figures. Many group members felt that their mothers had not been emotionally available to them; they felt they did not really know what unconditional love was as they had not experienced it. Often they believed that love was not forthcoming because they had done something wrong, or they blamed themselves for matters for which they carried no responsibility. Thus, they grew up feeling inadequate and generally lacking in confidence. Still hoping to receive approval and unconditional love, they tried to be kind and were often over-accommodating in trying to please their parents. Particularly if a mother's attachment to her parents had been severed during childhood, she often tended to cling to her daughter, with the daughter having to meet the mother's needs. This close identification made daughters highly sensitive to their mothers' inner worlds. Adult daughters reported that their mothers found it hard to acknowledge them as people with feelings and needs of their own.[20] Daughters, sensing that their mothers felt threatened, developed strategies that resonated with what they perceived to be the sentiments their mothers would tolerate. Instead of the normal wide range of positive and negative emotions, only a narrow band seemed permissible. The mother's "tunnel vision" allowed little or no room for learning by trial and error or for a broader scope or *Weltanschauung*. Sometimes the entire family colluded to avoid challenging the survivor's susceptibilities. Some mothers continued to treat their daughters as children who had to do as they were told, to the extent that some adult daughters still found themselves sucked into their mothers' mindsets and ambiguities. Even if their mothers were no longer alive, their powerful and omnipresent internalized voices seemed to drown daughters' own voices.

In my groups, it became apparent that as daughters grew up they found it harder to let go and separate emotionally from their mothers than did their non-survivor peers. By remaining dependent on them, these daughters fed their mothers' neediness. They became the containers for their mothers' unresolved feelings, the survivor's "memorial candle"[21]—the child in a survivor family designated to carry the burden of the legacy, at times without realizing it. A first-born or only child was naturally more prone to becoming a "memorial candle," and survivor parents would also sometimes identify with one child in particular who was of the same gender or physical appearance as a dead relative. A son could become a "memorial candle" if he was the firstborn, an only child, one in a family of sons, or if the father was the survivor. However, "memorial candles" were more common in mother-daughter relationships, in view of the common gender and because mothers, as the primary caregivers, were at home more than fathers were.

Sometimes, a survivor mother—or father, for that matter—associated a daughter with a murdered female relative whom the daughter was then destined to replace. The daughter was often named in memory of the person. Some daughters were aware that they resembled a grandmother or aunt, or that they shared a talent. To the parent, this resemblance brought solace, a delusional proof that the relative was living on. For the daughters, though, it felt like having to live someone else's life. References to family resemblances were often covert, and not every parent had photographs of their loved ones to show their children. Children were told after whom they were named but, apart from that, received little or no additional information about the person or the circumstances of their death.

In my twenty-five years of experience, it has been rare for more than one second-generation member of a family to seek help. Siblings seldom contacted me with a wish to join a group. My clients generally felt that although they believed their siblings to be affected by their parents' legacies, siblings were less affected because they were better able to distance themselves from the parents' experiences. Not infrequently, my clients mentioned that they considered their siblings to feel differently or to be less feeling. If the latter was the case, this difference in feeling would have helped the sibling identify less closely with their parents and avoid absorbing their parents' pain as readily.

Jewish mothers have been known to have high expectations of their children. Many of my group members felt pressure from their parents to achieve excellence academically and professionally: being successful was paramount and, consciously or unconsciously, perceived as justification for a family's survival. Mothers' unrealistically high expectations could also be a way of compensating for their own failed aspirations, often because their education had been cut short or because they lost out on a proper education altogether, depending on their age at the time of the Holocaust. Many daughters did manage to become high achievers, but some among them felt that their mothers, not they themselves, owned their successes. Further, while being a high achiever helped to develop a more confident professional self, it did not necessarily imply personal happiness. Those who always felt unable to meet their mothers' idealistic expectations still did not feel good enough in spite of their successes. Others felt so inadequate that they underachieved.[22]

Pressure on daughters to get married and have children appeared heavier on second-generation girls than on their Jewish peers. This pressure was linked to parental requirements that potential husbands possess the right faith, family, sect, and cultural background, thus leaving the choice for second-generation girls more restricted than for their contemporaries. At the same time, some daughters felt confused and burdened by their mothers' contradictory messages about their personal ambitions. On the one hand, it was extremely important for these mothers that daughters get married and give them grandchildren; on the other hand, mothers found it difficult to let daughters lead their own lives. Accepting that daughters had needs different from their own implied to the mothers a sense of rejection or abandonment. A significant number of daughters in my groups were not married or in any long-term relationship and, therefore, felt they had failed to provide their parents with grandchildren and the family with continuity.

As adults, many of my clients believed they had to be available at their mothers' beck and call. They had problems meeting the increasing demands their mothers made on them, still aspiring to do the right thing in their mothers' eyes. Afraid to hurt their mothers, they tended to avoid conflict of any kind, not only with their mothers but also within their own familial, social, and professional circles.[23] Consequently, they felt pulled in all directions and often saw themselves as failures as children, partners, mothers, friends, and workplace colleagues. Not recognizing their ability to make their own choices, they were still driven by trying to meet their mothers' expectations, whatever the cost to their other relationships, let alone to themselves.

On the occasions that daughters did not support their traumatized mothers but tried to stand up to them, mothers seemed to experience the challenge as rejection and to feel totally desolate. In response, daughters soon learned not to do it again. Daughters would rather submit than rock the boat, aware of the anguish the latter would cause. It was also easier for them not to assert themselves against their mothers and deal with any ensuing conflict. It seemed that their sense of guilt and disloyalty in opposing their mothers was too unbearable a price to pay for thinking and acting independently. Although mothers' sensitivities may have been confined initially to issues related to the Holocaust, they gradually spread to other emotionally charged topics. For daughters, too, the unspoken dread they had internalized could escalate to a fear of transgression and of beliefs of any kind that were contrary to those of their mothers. Emotional separation would often not happen in the usual, gradual way or at the usual time: some daughters achieved it by breaking away, while for others it came only after many years of adulthood, not infrequently with the help of therapy.

In comparison with their mothers, whose views were accepted as dictates, daughters' opinions and feelings were considered less important or of no value at all. If asked for an opinion, they preferred to remain silent rather than to expose their views and risk opprobrium. Their coping mechanisms depended on being peacekeepers and achieving consensus. They were "people pleasers" who automatically conceded their own interests and obliged what they perceived to be the wishes of others, even if those wishes had not been expressed.[24]

Boundaries for children's behavior were often left unclear, presented without explanation, and enforced inconsistently. Daughters could not understand why, sometimes, they were reprimanded by their mothers and sometimes not. Attempting to make sense of their mothers' overt and suppressed emotional responses, they would invent explanations based on their own negative self-image and low self-esteem. This served to reinforce their perceptions of their mistakes and shortcomings. To ensure their protection, these daughters would attempt to mold their behavior to their mothers' approval and to keep their antennae constantly attuned.

Sometimes when a daughter trespassed over an unstated boundary, her mother would resort to emotional blackmail and say things like, "You are giving me a heart attack." This would leave the daughter in a state of bewilderment and panic, unsure of the mother's real state of health. In attachment terms, the inconsistent responsiveness of caregivers is associated with a lack of confidence in the reliability of others. It leads to a susceptibility to fear, anxiety, and loneliness. Even when in a relationship, sufferers may devote much effort and mental energy to keeping others close by, for insecurity in the relationship can cause increased anxiety about separation.

Group members generally considered themselves more fearful than their non-survivor peers. Anxious and insecure in their attachments, they had no trust that things would work out for the best. They found it hard to relax and anticipated disaster at all times. If life ran smoothly, second-generation daughters were convinced that this would not last. They were active in preparing themselves and, particularly, for those who had them, their children for catastrophe. Although, rationally, they were aware that others had granted increasing autonomy to their children of similar age, they needed to know that their own late-adolescent children, the third generation, were safe. If they could, some would want to control every aspect of their children's lives.

In the stories group members related, I often noticed their mothers' reported difficulty in accessing the full range of emotions as well as the impairment of their ability to empathize. "We did what was best for you," daughters were told, and they accepted it without questioning, at least initially. When daughters realized that what their mothers had done was not necessarily best for them, they often did not see any point in having an argument about it with their mothers and also, because of their emotional state, lacked the words to articulate their stance. The subjugation by my group members of their own feelings and needs in order to support the unconscious needs of their survivor mothers was striking and inhibited the development of the second generation's ability to think independently, let alone to presume to act without full parental endorsement. Naturally, this kind of protracted mutual dependency between mothers and daughters inhibited the development of the daughters' identity, individuality, and autonomy.

The daughters in my groups had issues of intimacy and closeness. Close parent-child identification resulted in the most extreme cases in a symbiotic relationship. The internalized survivor parent seemed to be omnipresent, whereas some daughters wanted to be both close and more distant to the parent at the same time. Too much closeness and intimacy was often perceived as stifling and could make a daughter feel breathless. One of my group members, Angela, reported that she had always had a very soft voice and would become short of breath and start coughing whenever she used it.[25] She confessed that she had a fear of suffocating and worried that she would not survive the attack of breathlessness. It emerged that she did not feel heard by her mother. She added, "Isn't this terrible, what I am saying?" Angela exemplifies the difficulty survivor daughters have in making their own voices heard and in expressing their own emotions when their identification with their mothers is so powerful.

In most cases, only those daughters who had been in therapy for some time were able to show signs of anger and resentment. Some daughters resented the anger directed in the groups toward survivor mothers. For example, Theresa felt quite concerned about the anger being expressed and said that she was certainly not going to criticize her mother. She was very surprised at the extent to which other group members did criticize. She felt that parents had had to cope with horrendous experiences, and she did not wish to add to their burden. Rosemarie, another group member, mentioned that she, like Theresa, was very close to her mother, but that she had realized at some point that that degree of closeness was not healthy because it carried the cost of not knowing her own feelings. Whereas Rosemarie had been able to feel very angry with her mother during a rebellious period in her somewhat delayed adolescence, Theresa confessed that she had never gone through such a rebellious phase. Her mother, as a five-year-old, had been in hiding during the war. Required by the circumstances to hide her feelings, it seemed that she had remained stuck at the developmental level of a five-year-old, thus conveying a strong sense of vulnerability to her daughter. Rosemarie explained that it had come as a relief to her to realize, while in therapy some years ago, that she had to accept that that was the mother she had and should not expect her to change. In fact, she herself was the only person she could change and that, unless she did, everyone would dance the same steps and continue to repeat the same patterns. She mentioned that once she had stopped being angry with her mother she had found it easier to empathize.

One might better understand the silences between mother and daughter by examining what Freud called a phantom. Abraham and Torok, themselves survivors, perceive the phantom as transgenerationally transmitted, and the family secret as "something that must never be revealed, unspeakable because of the pain and shame it would evoke" in the first generation.[26] They define the traumatic as that which "is found in every experience that is impossible to psychically metabolize, i.e., to know, think, verbalize, symbolize and thereby transform into a bearable aspect of the subject's experiential world."[27] These undigested experiential fragments, which Abraham and Torok name "psychic phantoms," feel like entities foreign to the ego, as they are split off and dissociated from the experienced self. The authors claim that "the existence of the phantom in a parent creates a psychically mute zone, unexpectedly inaccessible and incomprehensible to the small child, who, failing to understand the sudden psychic absence of the parent, attempts to metabolize and is thereby compelled to incorporate this mute aspect of the parent, at the price of creating a mute psychic zone in the child."[28]

Carole bore the burden of a psychic phantom. Born after the war, she grew up feeling unloved. The spirit of her dead sister who had been gassed in Auschwitz before she was born and whom she therefore had not known came to haunt her.[29] Her parents had a large photograph of her dead sister on the wall in their bedroom, but there was no photograph of Carole, the daughter who was alive. Although the sister was seldom mentioned, she was omnipresent, and Carole always felt that whatever she did could not match the idealized expectations her mother had of her sister. She grew up feeling helpless and alone and experienced her mother's absence even more at times when she was ill, as her being unwell evoked particularly in her mother a fear that she might lose her, too.

As in the case of Carole's mother, the phantom could appear, for instance, in the language mothers used, even unconsciously seeking to exclude or circumvent the censored topic from their discourse. At other times, mothers would avoid the issue by distorting, deferring, or denying. According to Abraham and Torok's theory of transgenerational haunting, "the buried speech of the parent will be [a] dead [gap] without a burial place in the child." It becomes like a tomb or crypt, and occupies "a definite place" in the child's mental topography. And it is this crypt which then contains the "unknown, unrecognized knowledge which the parent sought to conceal through the unspoken silence of his discourse. This crypt contains, therefore, not only the discourse which the child always heard his parent not-speaking but also the silence which the child heard spoken." Within the buried crypt resides the parent's phantom.[30]

The core of the phantom is not always the secret itself but rather the violation of an imposed taboo about speaking of it.[31] One of my group members, Rebecca, described a sudden personality change that had occurred when she was thirteen. She changed from cheerful and extroverted to introverted and sad. She referred to it as if a cloud had come over her. She still remembered it with clarity but had no idea what had caused the change.

It became obvious that she had, unknowingly, absorbed her mother's phantom and that it had attached itself to Rebecca's unconscious. Her mother had left Czechoslovakia in 1939, at the age of thirteen, and had never been able to talk to anyone about her fate as a Jew. Over the years, Rebecca had become aware that her mother would always seek, albeit unconsciously, to exclude or circumvent the censored topic from her conversations. When, finally, Rebecca did try to break the silence and confront her mother about her Jewishness, her mother froze.

Second-generation daughters tend to long for approval and often, because of their low self-esteem and tendency to take on blame, act in anticipation of not getting it. They then become self-focused, do endless soul-searching to find the reason for not being liked, and interpret other people's behavior as hostile. They use biased reasoning and jump to conclusions, based usually on a single explanation. They often do this by extrapolating negative external information ("I could tell from the way she looked") based on their own projections. Convinced that their assumptions are valid, they become completely absorbed in and ruminate on these thoughts. Even the slightest issue may cause them to become preoccupied by a fear of rejection and therefore not see the range of options available to them. They find it impossible to approach problems with an open and balanced mind, and they panic. It is as though their ability to think shuts down.

Maternal reflective functioning, a mother's capacity to hold her baby and the baby's mental states in mind, has been found to play a vital role in the intergenerational transmission of attachment.[32] The concept helps to put a name to the absence of basic empathic understanding in communications between survivor mothers and their daughters. The example of my client Anna is a good illustration of a mother's self-centeredness and lack of understanding of her daughter's needs. On her mother's birthday when Anna, an only child, was eight, her mother began crying bitterly, saying that no one had remembered her birthday. Anna's father had bought a present for his wife before going abroad on a business trip, but Anna had forgotten to buy a birthday card for her mother. Full of guilt, she begged her mother for forgiveness, but whatever Anna said to calm her mother did not work. In the end, though, her mother said, "Never mind, I suppose I have to learn to live with it." Anna was extremely upset and desperately wanted her mother to just put her arms around her and hug her, but her mother, unable to think about Anna's mental state, did not try to comfort her.

With my help, Anna began to realize that her mother's distress was not something she had caused, but the result of her mother's projection onto her of her own anger with her husband for not being there on her birthday. Her mother's sense of emptiness at the perceived abandonment by her close relatives who had died in the Holocaust added to her feeling of vulnerability on the day. Anna felt relieved when she recognized that she no longer needed to feel guilty or take on the blame. She understood that she could not be expected to compensate for her father's absence and for the loss of significant others.

A mother's capacity to imagine her baby's complex mental states is particularly crucial for a range of later developments in the child. According to the Parent Development Interview, secure mothers were found to have higher levels of maternal reflective functioning than insecure mothers.[33] They were better able to represent and understand the breadth of their child's internal experience. A reflective, empathic caregiver thus increased the likelihood of the child's security of attachment. Mothers who were able to describe coherently their own childhood attachment experiences were more likely to be able to make sense of the intentions and feelings underlying their children's behavior and to understand when the children were seeking closeness. When this reflective ability was absent, not only did the child feel insecure but it also seemed unable to develop reflective functioning in its own right and tended to misinterpret parental mental states.

One illustrative case involves Susan, who told the group that she was able to say that she loved her father but that she could not say the same about her mother, whom she felt had not been available to her. Susan said that she cried a great deal as a baby, so much so that her mother, oblivious to her baby's need for closeness and comfort, pushed her pram out of earshot. During therapy, Susan reflected on her mother's mental state and felt that her mother had been unable to empathize with her on any level. In relation to her own behavior Susan, like her mother, seemed to lack reflective and reasoning skills and often made decisions without considering the likely consequences. Had she been able to reflect, she would have realized that the past sequence of undesired outcomes would be perpetuated and that she would continue to feel that her life was being programmed by a malevolent force outside her ken or control.

Jewish second-generation daughters who have recognised and identi-fied with some of the issues described in this chapter may feel some sense of relief in realizing that they are not alone; that their concerns are the out-comes of others' circumstances; that their issues can be resolved although the path to separate and free themselves is not always easy; that they can break the existing family dynamic without necessarily damaging the respect for their parents whom they hold dear; that they *can* determine their own destiny; and that, therefore, they need no longer feel haunted by this hidden legacy.

NOTES

1   I use the term "second generation" as that is what has been adopted generally in the psychological literature as the term to identify the children of Holocaust sur-vivors and children of refugees from Nazi persecution.

2   Eva Hoffman, *After Such Knowledge* (London: Vintage, 2005), xv.

3   Sir Jonathan Sacks, Chief Rabbi of the United Hebrew Congregations of the Com-monwealth, "Only by Bringing the Past Alive Can We Be Sure to Keep Our Future Free" (monthly "Credo" column), *The Times*, April 22, 1995.

4   Helen Epstein, *Children of the Holocaust* (New York: Bantam Books, 1981), 1.

5   Paul Marcus and Alan Rosenberg, eds. *Healing their Wounds* (New York: Praeger, 1989); Aaron Hass, *In the Shadow of the Holocaust: the Second Generation* (Ithaca, NY: Cornell University Press, 1990); Dina Wardi, *Memorial Candles: Children of the Holocaust* (New York: Routledge, 1992).

6   In the studies quoted in this chapter, the term "survivor(s)" is used for those who were in occupied Europe during World War II either in concentration camps, in hiding, or in other situations. However, in my comments and observations in relation to the second-generation groups I conducted I use the term "survivors" to refer both to survivors as defined above and refugees from Nazi persecution, including those who came over on the *Kindertransport*.

7   The official figure quoted over the years has been 2,000 (Board of Deputies Demo-graphic Unit) and excludes those who came over during subsequent waves of emigration from Central-European countries (Czechoslovakia in 1948 and 1968; Hungary in 1956) as well as those who settled in the UK often for economic reasons or to live closer to their second-generation children who had moved there.

8   According to Sir Martin Gilbert, *The Holocaust: A Record of the Destruction of Jewish Life in Europe during the Dark Years of Nazi Rule* (London: Board of Depu-ties of British Jews, 1978), 65,000 refugees settled in Britain. The Association of

Jewish Refugees quoted a figure of 70,000 refugees.

9 This figure allows for those children who migrated to Britain much later and for survivor and refugee parents marrying one another.

10 Shamai Davidson, "Psychological Aspects of Holocaust Trauma in the Life Cycle of Survivor-refugees and their Families," in *The Psychosocial Problems of Refugees: Collected Papers from the International Conference on the Psychosocial Problems of Refugees*, ed. Ron Baker (London: European Consultation on Refugees and Exiles/ British Refugee Council, 1983), 21–31; Yael Danieli, "Differing Adaptational Styles in Families of Survivors of the Nazi Holocaust: Some Implications for Treatment," *Children Today* (September–October 1981): 6–36; Axel Russell, Donna Plotkin, and Nelson Heapy, "Adaptive Abilities in Nonclinical Second-Generation Holocaust Survivors and Controls: A Comparison," *American Journal of Psychotherapy* 39, no. 4 (October 1985): 564–79.

11 Referrals to the groups came from advertisements I placed in second-generation journals; distinctively colored flyers displayed at events and locations likely to be frequented by second-generation Holocaust survivors and refugees; information on the web about my group work; the Holocaust Survivors' Centre; the Association of Jewish Refugees; rabbis; psychotherapeutic organizations and colleague psychotherapists; past group members; and attendance at lectures and workshops I presented.

12 The level of fee was designed to cover my professional time and expenses and also to enable me to provide bursaries to deserving participants (those with low incomes and the unemployed). All were required to make a contribution even at a token level.

13 No data are available for Jewish refugees as a whole on religious affiliation or on the percentage who married non-Jews. A survey of refugees who came over on the Kindertransport, *Making New Lives in Britain*, revealed that 19 percent of the respondents were Orthodox in their affiliation. In response to the question on "Spouse" to determine the percentage who intermarried, out of a total of 949 respondents, 653 (68.8 percent) answered that they had married Jews, whereas 137 (14.5 percent) stated that they married out of the faith, and 82 (8.65 percent) answered "other." Seventy-seven (8.11 percent) gave an answer that was indeterminate. This information was obtained from Hermann Hirschberger, MBE, former chairman of the Association of Jewish Refugees Kindertransport special interest group, who led the survey, published in 2008 in the form of a statistical database available at www.ajr.org.uk/kindersurvey.

14 Hirschberger, *Making New Lives in Britain*.

15 Yael Danieli, "Psychotherapists' Participation in the Conspiracy of Silence about the Holocaust," *Psychoanalytic Psychology*, no. 1 (1984): 23–42.

16 Marinus H. van IJzendoorn, Marian J. Bakermans-Kranenburg, and Abraham Sagi-Schwartz, "Are Children of Holocaust Survivors Less Well-adapted? A Meta-Analytic Investigation of Secondary Traumatization," *Journal of Traumatic Stress* 16 (2003): 5, 459–69.

17 Marinus H. van IJzendoorn, "Drie Generaties Holocaust? [Three generations

Holocaust?]," *Koninklijke Nederlandse Akademie van Wetenschappen* (Amsterdam, 2002): 1–32.

18   Abraham Sagi-Schwartz, Nina Koren-Karie, and Tirtsa Joels, "Failed Mourning in the Adult Attachment Interview: The Case of Holocaust Child Survivors," in *Extreme Life Events and Catastrophic Experiences and the Development of Attachment across the Life Span*, special issue, *Attachment & Human Development* 5, no. 4 (December 2003): 398–408.

19   The Adult Attachment Interview is a semi-structured interview that takes about one hour to administer. It involves twenty questions and has extensive research validation to support it. Mary Main, Ruth Goldwyn, and Erik Hesse, "Adult Attachments Scoring and Classification System," version no. 7.2 (2003), manuscript, Department of Psychology, University of California, Berkeley.

20   Anne Karpf, *The War After* (London: Heinemann, 1996), 3–4. Karpf gives a vivid account of her mother's insistence that she must be cold: "My family was big on coats. Throughout my adolescence and well beyond we'd spontaneously combust into spectacular rows about them. My parents, always convinced I was a season behind . . . would . . . openly lambast me for the thinness of my coat: 'You can't go out like that, you'll freeze . . . You'll catch pneumonia.'" Although Karpf believes that to her parents cold "wasn't just a meteorological fact but also a psychic state," reflecting the postwar outside world, in my view, her parents' fear of her becoming ill with pneumonia if she did not wear a (thick enough) coat was the sentiment that led them to be so pre-occupied and persistent—after all, in their minds becoming ill was equated with dying.

21   Wardi, *Memorial Candles*.

22   In a recent article, a Dutch cultural and organizational sociologist, Wanya Kruyer, assesses how, in her view, the Dutch-Jewish postwar generation will cope with the aging process. She makes the observation that, among the generation of Dutch Jews born after the war, there are more high achievers as well as more underachievers in comparison to other Dutch people of the same age group. The group of underachievers, she states, were not able to build up a career, start a family, or form long-term relationships. She forecasts that this group will cope less well with the aging process and will be faced with feelings of powerlessness to change the situation. She predicts that they will struggle with the meaning of life generally and with a fear of loneliness in old age, although she recognises that the largest Dutch-Jewish postwar group—composed of those in the middle levels of achievement—is functioning reasonably well and is expected to enter (pre-)retirement age without needing to appeal for outside help. See Wanya F. Kruyer, "De schaduwzijde van de babyboomers [The dark side of the babyboomers]," *JONAG Bulletin* 2 (Summer 2009): 6–11. Also available on http://sites.google.com/site/schaduwzijdenl/Home.

23   Gaby R. Glassman, "The Impact of Intergenerational Protection on the Second Generation's Other Relationships," in *Beyond Camps and Forced Labour: Current International Research on Survivors of Nazi Persecution*, ed. Johannes-Dieter Steinert and Inge Weber-Newth. Proceedings of the first international multidisci-

plinary conference, Imperial War Museum, London, January 2003 (Osnabrueck: Secolo, 2005).

24 Perhaps significantly, one of my workshops at a second-generation conference entitled "And, can I say no?" achieved record attendance.

25 All the names in this chapter are fictitious.

26 Maria Yassa, "Nicolas Abraham and Maria Torok—The Inner Crypt," *The Scandinavian Psychoanalytic Review* 2 (2002): 1–14.

27 Yassa, "Nicolas Abraham and Maria Torok," 2.

28 Ibid., 3.

29 See also Art Spiegelman, *Maus II* (New York: Pantheon Books, 1991), 15, where Art refers to his older brother, Richieu, whom he never knew and who died during the Holocaust. Richieu is Art's "ghost brother."

30 Kuhn, "Phantoms in the Family History," 12.

31 This process is described in a fascinating and compelling novel *The Language of Silence* by Merilyn Moos (London: Cressida Press, 2010). In it the narrator, Anna, sets out to uncover the hidden lives of her German-Jewish refugee parents, former Communists, who had to leave Germany in 1933 and came to Britain as political exiles. During her research she finds, in a released MI5 file on her mother, shocking details about her past involvement in some of the greatest ideologies and upheavals of the twentieth century. The novel draws on the author's own experiences.

32 Arietta Slade, "Parental Reflective Functioning: An Introduction," *Attachment & Human Development* 3 (2005): 269–81.

33 Slade, "Parental Reflective Functioning." The Parent Development Interview (PDI) is a semi-structured clinical interview containing forty-five questions that takes approximately ninety minutes to administer.

11

Talking to Ruth Klüger

BRITTA FREDE-WENGER

A scene on a train somewhere in Germany. An elderly lady enters the compartment and takes the seat opposite me. While I am reading, she is watching:

> *Why are you reading this book?*
> *I beg your pardon.*
> *Why are you reading this book?*
> *Well, it's a long train ride, and it's so awkward to read a newspaper on the train.*
> *No, why are you reading this book?*

I am confused. What does she want from me? Who is she?

> *Actually, a friend of mine recommended it to me. Have you read it?*
> *I wrote it.*

This scene never took place. I have never met Ruth Klüger. Still, this scene came to my mind when I read her *weiter leben*.[1] I find Klüger's book unique in at least one respect. Somehow, it watches me, Britta Frede-Wenger, reading it. And since her recollections give a personal account, why not answer with remarks just as subjective and non-academic? So I choose this imaginary scene for an imaginary (non)dialogue between Ruth Klüger and me, two women whose only commonality apart from being female is probably that our mothers taught us German as a first language. We come from different backgrounds, belong to different generations, and have different stories.

Among my mother's earliest childhood recollections as a three year old is the burning synagogue in Nuremberg, where she lived as the daughter of a German engineer who worked in a *kriegswichtiger Betrieb*[2] and was drafted in late 1944. My father applied for access to his father's Wehrmacht files three years ago, forty-three years after my grandfather's death. I doubt that either of them really knows what their fathers saw during the war. I do not remember a conversation about Nazi times and the war when my grandmothers were there; both of them died before I could ask them. (Would I have had the courage to ask?) This leaves me with a gap in memory.

Ruth Klüger was born in Vienna in 1931 and survived Theresienstadt, Auschwitz-Birkenau, Christianstadt, and a dangerous flight back to Germany, from where she emigrated to the United States in the late forties. A professor of German, she wrote her biography after spending time as a visiting scholar at the University of Göttingen. The book was originally written and published as *weiter leben* (Living on) in German in 1992, and the dedication says: "To the Göttingen friends—a German book." An English-language edition came out in 2001 entitled *Still Alive*, and the dedication reads: "In memory of my mother Alma Hirschel: 1903–2000." These changes indicate two things: what seems to be a translation is a second version that takes into account both that time has passed and that its readership is different. Moreover, the book can be read in different ways. It is a survivor's story and a reflection on today's Germans, but it is also a painful story about a daughter and a mother. To keep this painful story from her mother, Klüger did not publish an English edition, which her mother could have easily picked up in a bookstore in the United States, and rewrote it after her mother's death.[3]

Erin McGlothlin calls the two books "equally valid autobiographical expressions" written in different situations, with different impetuses and with different readerships in mind.[4] For these reasons, the books are similar, but not identical. My reading is based almost exclusively on *weiter leben*, a book that, strange as this may sound, I feel was written with me in mind.[5] More than that: it was written in order to trigger my response, since Klüger writes:

> You don't have to identify with me, I'd rather you don't. . . . But let me at least provoke you, don't hide yourselves, don't claim from the outset that

it's none of your business or that it's only your business within a fixed framework that has a priori been laid out with compass and straight-edge or that you have already seen and born the photographs of piles of corpses and completed your share of guilt and sympathy. Engage in arguments, be ready to join discussions![6]

Be an active reader! Respond![7] So here I am in my imaginary train compartment, a setting that is both intimate and distant. With extremely little space and no opportunity to hide, people who do not know each other and will probably never meet again are destined to spend time together. My initial reaction to the story of Ruth Klüger's survival is this: she is angry. Not only does she recall the events of the thirties and forties, she also goes back and forth in time and tells me how various people—many of them in Germany—have reacted to her person and her story. I feel compelled to do the same.

It is almost immediately apparent that Ruth Klüger is angry at various typical reactions to the Nazi past. She takes up readers' responses and comments on them, while continuing her own train of thought. There are modes of *Vergangenheitsbewältigung* that she finds insufficient, that make her angry. *Vergangenheitsbewältigung*—what a strange term. It translates as "coming to terms with the past." But the verb "bewältigen" means much more: it means "to cope with," "to handle," and even "to master." A possible antonym of these last meanings could be "to lose control over" and, consequently, to risk being overwhelmed. Maybe this is it: whenever she comes across people who have "mastered the past" in this sense, her anger breaks through. The question that the book continuously presents to its reader is this: "What is the way you do *Vergangenheitsbewältigung*?"

First, I stumble over the "whitewashers."[8] Klüger uses this term for two young former volunteers at the Auschwitz memorial site. Their job was to help preserve the site; they literally "whitewashed the fences," in her eyes an absurd, futile, and even ridiculous enterprise. Without judging these two volunteers, she exposes them. Why?

Britta: What's so absurd and ridiculous about trying to keep up the memorial sites? Don't they give us a place to learn, to remember, and to mourn? "Never again!" is probably the sentence most often written into the guest books of any memorial site. I'm sure that these volunteers did their work with the best intentions.

Ruth: "Do we expect that our unsolved questions will be answered if we hang on to what's left: the place, the stones, the ashes? We don't honor the dead with these unattractive remnants of past crimes; we collect and keep them for the satisfaction of our own necrophilic desires. Violated taboos, such as child murder and mass murder, turn their victims into spirits, to whom we offer a kind of home that they may haunt at will. Perhaps we are afraid they may leave the camps, and so we insist that their deaths were unique and must not be compared to any other losses or atrocities. Never again shall there be such a crime."⁹

Britta: So, are you saying that keeping the site and memorializing the event in a museum, unintentionally and maybe unconsciously serves the purpose of giving a "home" to the crime and the shadow it casts? Do we put "the ghosts" inside, so we can safely live outside? Do we really build museums because we need them to keep control? Do we need the museums so that we stay in control of the Holocaust ghosts and aren't overwhelmed by them?

For Ruth Klüger, museums and memorial sites seem to serve one main purpose. They help their visitors. Does she imply that the fences, which mark "inside" and "outside," also mark the space in which the Nazi crimes are remembered? Does she imply that a lot of visitors are shocked and touched there, but leave unchanged? Do museums really offer a place that you can visit and—what's more important—that you can leave behind?

There is a second dimension. The volunteers think they have found answers. They seem to have a very clear and unshakable picture of "victim" and "perpetrator," of "good" and "evil." "Good" and "evil," "in" and "out," "victim" and "perpetrator." These dualistic terms help to give answers that Klüger finds dangerously simplistic because history is complex. So what bothers her about the "white-washers" is not only the kind of work they did; it is a form of *Vergangenheitsbewältigung* that seems to have "understood," and in this sense "mastered" the past and, more than that, even assumes a moral lesson from Auschwitz.

Ruth (recalling a discussion with two PhD candidates in Göttingen): One of the students reports how in "Jerusalem he made the acquaintance of an old Hungarian Jew who was a survivor of Auschwitz, and yet this man cursed the Arabs and held them all in contempt. 'How can someone who comes from Auschwitz talk like that?' the German asks. I get into the act and argue, perhaps more hotly than need be. What did he expect? Auschwitz was no instructional institution . . . You learned nothing there, and least of all humanity and tolerance."10

Britta: I have to admit that I both agree and disagree with you here. Of course, you are right. It is fundamentally wrong to conclude that somebody who has experienced hate and violence must walk away as a good person. But, on the other hand, what you're saying goes against something that my generation has heard over and over again: You have to learn the "lesson of Auschwitz!" I have never been prompted to question the assumption that there is such a "lesson." Neither has your student. His logic, however, includes the assumption that those who witnessed the event must also be the ones who learned this "lesson" first-hand. This logic might be naive and even false— still it is understandable. And it should make us both discuss two things: What is it that somebody is supposed to learn from or have learnt from Auschwitz? And who is to learn from or have learnt from Auschwitz? And: is this a universal lesson or are there acceptable exceptions?

I have already said that the book confronts the reader: What is your way of "dealing" with the past? Are you a "white-washer?" Is remembrance something that takes place in a neatly designed space that you can easily walk away from, or does it influence the way you think and act? Or are you a dualist: Do you think you have understood? Do you remember in terms of "good" and "evil?" These are questions that should not be answered— but that we should expose ourselves to self-critically. They are like fingers pointing at sore spots of *Vergangenheitsbewältigung.*

This last question already points to another type of *Vergangenheitsbe-wältiger.* While I do not think Ruth Klüger uses this term, adherents of this type might be called *Besserwisser,* "know-it-alls." In her book, they come in different guises and trigger a no less angry response than the "white-wash-ers" do. While some of the "white-washers" are described as "caught up in a kind of chamber of horrors cum melodrama," in a state of emotional tur-moil in the face of "evil," a "fog" in which "you can't make out any details, so why try?" "know-it-alls" categorize the crime with different results.[11]

Gisela, for example, the wife of a Princeton colleague, "informs" Ruth Klüger that, after all, Theresienstadt "wasn't all that bad."[12] Ruth Klüger does not accuse the "know-it-alls" of intentionally relativizing or playing down the events. However, they follow a strategy of categorizing. Gisela "was determined to reduce the past until it fit into the box of a clean German conscience that won't cause her countrymen to lose any sleep." Categorizing does not imply trying to make good. It might, however, be a form of oversimplification and insensitivity. As I said, the "know-it-alls" are not necessarily deniers. The danger that I see Ruth Klüger point to is that they think they "know." Again, history is too complex for simple answers. Is this way of categorizing another way of "giving a home" to the ghosts, of controlling the uncontrollable?

Britta: Before, I asked you about the "lesson of Auschwitz." Now, I am reminded of a visit in the Holocaust Memorial Museum in Washington. In the museum shop you can buy mugs that say: "Think about what you saw!" Isn't that a clear plea to learn and to study? I wonder whether and how it is possible to learn without applying categories, dangerous as it may be. Or are you just pointing out that we should continue to watch ourselves in the work we do and, at the least, watch our use of language critically so that we don't lose the wider picture?

Ruth: ———

Britta: Ruth, the more I read, the more ambivalent I am. On the one hand, you often display very little respect for the people you have met; on the other hand, you almost seem to be jealous of them at times. Why? Furthermore, did you notice that when you reflected on the "white-washers" strategy, you used the inclusive "we" form?

There are many more people and events that she recollects, people who print her poems but do not talk to her, people who lean towards Holocaust-kitsch, people (often men) whose blatantly voyeuristic questions lead her to the accusation that "[t]here is a thriving cottage industry of pornography based on the camps," and Germans whose "philosemitism" makes them blind to the fact that the use of Yiddish that is so in vogue in Germany mostly comprises negative terms.[13]

Britta: What you say about the use of Yiddish surprises me. "Chutzpah" has made its way into modern German, and—you're right—mostly with negative connotations. Any others? But what interests me more: why did you delete this paragraph in your English version of the text? Because you didn't think the American readership would be able to relate or because you didn't want this readership to get an image of these Germans that you didn't intend?

Ruth: ———

I feel irritated and provoked by her writing. And I still haven't heard an answer:

Britta: Why do all these people make you angry?

I am reading about her life in the United States and about times when the Holocaust and her story were not openly denied but simply ignored.

Ruth: "Part of this is that people didn't like to see my number. A symbol of humiliation, people say, have it removed. A symbol of the ability to live and survive, say I, because when I wasn't forced to hide myself and my name any more it was part of the liberation not to have to cover the Auschwitz number. . . . 'Who gives you the right to walk around like a memorial?' an elderly Jew once said to me. Ditha [Ruth's adopted sister, called Susie in Still Alive*] has also heard people say that she wants this number to make others feel guilty. Shouldn't these people reflect on why seeing such a number makes them so aggressive? (And what are we supposed to think when—without being asked—you swear never to forget?)"*[14]

Britta: Is this where your anger comes from? The absurd experience of being accused of being who you are, for having this unique and painful story, for not fitting and not wanting to fit into people's neatly designed "boxes" and categories of Vergangenheitsbewältigung?

Ruth: "You talk about my life but you talk over my head. You pretend to mean me, but you don't mean anything but your own emotion."[15]

Touché. That really hurts. She feels used. Many people think they feel empathy, but she accuses them of mixing up empathy with sentimentality. While empathy is genuinely directed to the Other, sentimentality can circle around the self. As a result, there are people who think they remember, but really only prove their own sensitivity to themselves. Klüger feels used and deprived: I am a witness and yet you do not want to be confronted with my story any more. My story might not fit your theories, but still I expect you to respect it! Klüger's book can be read as an appeal for an ongoing dialogue with the individual story: "In reality, this reality, too, was different for each of us."[16]

Vergangenheitsbewältigung—I read between Klüger's lines—can have quite an egotistic side. That's a blow that renders me speechless and I get defensive. However, I don't have to find the right words. Another reader has found them for me:

Ruth: "One of my friends reads this, shakes his head and says: 'You complain that no one asked questions. But you also complain about the questions they did ask. You are hard to satisfy.'"[17]

Britta: Among all the readers' remarks that you have decided to put into your book this strikes me most because you leave it uncommented. Why?

Ruth:————

An answer can be found in the English version of the book. Here Ruth Klüger comments: "Damn right, I *am* hard to satisfy."[18]

I am three-quarters through *weiter leben* when I come across these lines, and I realize that I have missed something in my search for the origin of Ruth Klüger's anger. Now I suddenly remember many passages in which she has not really been any gentler with herself than she has been with others: "These pages hardly deal with the Nazis. I didn't know any Nazis, but I knew the difficult, neurotic people whom they oppressed, families who hadn't had ideal lives anymore than their Christian neighbors had."[19] While exposing others, Ruth Klüger is far from pretending to "know it all" herself—not then and not now. On the contrary, she quotes the verses that she wrote as a child, knowing that, while she "boasted" about her experience, they were really just rhymes of a child that made adults smile benevolently.[20] She talks about her feelings of dislike for her mother while, at the same time, she admits that her mother often made the right, courageous decision and that she had her own traumas. In *weiter leben*, I find instances in which she claims that she is "oversimplifying," that she is even feeling "self-pity."[21] She even shows the reader how she changes her mind while writing the book. During their flight west, a pastor provided her, her mother, and her sister with false names. Once again *weiter leben* differs from *Still Alive* here. In *weiter leben*, Ruth Klüger first makes the point that names are not important and may be left behind, and then picks up the phone to call her mother and find out her own false name.[22] Does she prove herself wrong? I don't think so. The author, who watches her reader, allows herself to be watched in return, and she admits that she is caught in the situation, as well.

In *Still Alive* she characterizes her friend, the German writer Martin Walser, as the person who epitomizes "what attracts and repels me about his country."[23] Attraction and disgust, love and hate—her relationship to Germany, to Germans and to her mother seems to move between these two poles.

But the book does not end on a tragic note. Klüger stretches out an imaginary hand to the defensive reader. Later in life, she has three close girlfriends. One of them, Anneliese (in *Still Alive*, her name is Lieselotte), spent years of her childhood forced into bed by an undefined illness.

Ruth: "[Lieselotte] and I had similar backgrounds in that we each had an unorthodox childhood that strained the imagination. Sickness as a kind of prison—I should have been able to imagine that, but I could not imagine how one grows up lying in bed. I asked her for details and didn't listen to the answers or didn't keep them in mind, so that I had to ask again. Not to get up for years, then to get up, then to have to do it all over again, and spend more time in bed. Lieselotte says, 'An unnatural situation becomes natural if it is the norm, whatever it happens to be.' That's how it was in the camps, too, and still I was frustrated trying to imagine immobility. I tried to empathize honestly, then perhaps not so honestly, because it was bothersome and unpleasant. I reacted as others react to survivors of the camps, and thus assumed an attitude which I criticize in others."[24]

I try to read the face of the elderly lady who has been so relentless in her critique of others. And I see no demeaning look in her face. She has just admitted that she finds it tiring and impossible to really relate. Here is an experience that we might share: the knowledge that it is incredibly difficult to empathize honestly.

Britta: Can I get it right and understand you? Is there a way out?

Ruth: "[I] learned slowly what you learn in friendships: to unburden your-self and inspect the bundle that you've had to carry, to find some tools that will serve to grasp and come to grips with what others have on their backs, instead of running in circles within an idiosyncratic enclosure of barbed wire."[25]

Britta: Let me put this into my own words to make sure I don't get you wrong. We will continue to run around in circles sentimentally; we will not even start to understand each other unless we think about ourselves. There is a saying in my German dialect: Jeder hat sein Päckle zu tragen. (Every-body has to carry his or her own bundle), and it means that everybody has to face and come to terms with the challenges of one's own life—different as they may be. So the way to empathy (let us not talk about friendship or understanding) between you and me requires the ability to reflect on my own situation and then abstract from it. And I am well aware that bundles are not equally heavy.

Throughout the book, Ruth Klüger has struck me as terribly, at times pain-fully authentic. Does she want to provoke this kind of authenticity in her reader, too? I am reminded of the episode with the two PhD candidates referred to earlier. The slightly enlarged English version of this scene ends with the following paragraph:

Ruth: "Absolutely nothing good came out of the concentration camps, I hear myself saying, with my voice rising, and he [the student] expects catharsis, purgation, the sort of thing you go to the theater for? They were the most use-less, pointless establishments imaginable. That is the one thing to remember about them if you know nothing else. No one agrees, and no one contradicts me. Who wants to get into an argument with the old bag who's got that num-ber on her arm? Germany's young intellectuals bow their heads over their soup plates and eat what's in front of them. Now I have silenced them, and that wasn't my intention. There is always a wall between the generations, but here the wall is barbed wire. Old, rusty barbed wire."[26]

Ruth Klüger has not only watched me, she has also watched herself; in these lines, she confesses what it means to her to spend time with young Germans: "The way you deal with my story hurts me . . . And yet, it is not my intention to silence you . . . It pains me to see you bow your heads and finish your soup . . . but there is rusty barbed wire between your world and mine." In just two or three sentences, she has revealed a central message to "Germany's young intellectuals" and I understand why—whatever else it may be—*weiter leben* is "a German book."

It pains Klüger to see that her anger might have hurt me. But there is something else. She sees young Germans look down and "finish the soup." Although this scene does take place in a cafeteria, I cannot help but think about the double meaning of this phrase. If somebody has left you in a real dilemma, you can say that you have to "finish the soup" that somebody else has "handed to you."

I clearly remember what I felt after a visit to the memorial site in Majdanek. I was the only German in a group of North Americans. I was not sad, I was furious, I was genuinely angry. I felt that I had to "finish a soup" that I had not asked for. However, I did not feel that it was appropriate to show or even tell anyone about this anger. I held it back. It seemed more appropriate to keep silent, and I even felt an unvoiced expectation to be more emotional than I really was. So what did I do? I "bowed my head," ready to finish the soup.

Britta: Ruth Klüger, having read your book, I wonder whether you would have come up to me and asked me, "Doesn't this make you angry?" and whether this would have been the opening to a heated, authentic argument. This is the one appeal that I read in your book: "Be authentic!"

Be authentic! First and foremost, this implies the necessity to add a prefix to the Holocaust Memorial Museum's "Think about what you saw!": "Think about who you are!" And bring yourself, your genuine questions, problems, shortcomings, and emotions into the part of the challenge of remembrance that says: "Think about what you saw!" And when thinking about what you saw, be aware that *Vergangenheitsbewältigung* has nothing to do with "mastering" for good. It can only mean finding a way of living on, of *weiter leben.*

Britta: Some time ago, I saw a movie called And Along Come Tourists.[27] *It tells the story of Sven, a fictional German volunteer at the Auschwitz memorial site—a potential "whitewasher." Sven tries to understand, to find his own way of dealing authentically with the complexity of the place and its ghosts, the characters that live and work there. And he fails. At the end of the movie, he packs his suitcase saying: "This is far too complicated for me." And yet in the final scene, Sven returns with a class of school children and their "know-it-all" history teacher—knowing that he cannot not do this work, either. Back then in Majdanek, I bowed my head and didn't show what I really felt. Today, I am a teacher myself and, like Sven in the movie, my students, the fourth generation after the Holocaust, would probably not just bow their heads. If they were asked to, some of them might walk away just like Sven. There are people here who complain that too few young people attend Holocaust Memorial Services. Is this due to what has come to be called Holocaust fatigue? Or do these young people really consider Germany's history none of their business? Maybe. But having read your book, there might be another possible explanation. What if you are right when you are angry about sentimentality in Holocaust remembrance? What if at least some of these people do not attend because they are authentic! Norbert Reck, a theologian who has worked at the Dachau Memorial Site for years, observes: "Today 'remembering' is hardly a public display of feelings of guilt (this has been banned to the private realm); much more, it is a celebration of one's own utter sadness about the stories of horror. This has nothing to do with truly dealing with the history of one's own national and family history."*[28] *Reck is far from denying or ridiculing genuine emotions among those forever wounded by the history of the Holocaust. However, he points his finger at those who display too much sentimentality and too little authentic empathy. In* Am Ende kommen Touristen, *Sven returns. What if at least some young Germans unconsciously understand that it is time for more authenticity? Would this make it possible to open a new chapter in Holocaust remembrance? Possibly there is a readiness among the new generation of Germans to honestly think about who they are, to explore and face the individual stories of failure, indifference, of guilt and occasional bravery in their families and their communities. It is about time! It is about time for me to look at my paternal grandfather's Wehrmacht files, and to find out what exactly was so* kriegswichtig *about my maternal grandfather's job in Nuremberg.*

NOTES

1 Ruth Klüger, *weiter leben: Eine Jugend* (Living on: A youth) (München: dtv, 1994, 2007). Wherever possible, I quote from the English edition: Ruth Klüger, *Still Alive: A Holocaust Girlhood Remembered* (New York: The Feminist Press at the City University of New York, 2001). Passages that are not included in the English version are quoted according to the German text. They were translated by me.

2 Industry that was of imminent importance to the war effort.

3 Compare to *Still Alive*, 210, and Erin McGlothlin, "Autobiographical Re-vision: Ruth Klüger's *weiter leben* and *Still Alive*," *Gegenwartsliteratur* 3 (2004): 46–70, 52f.

4 McGlothin, "Autobiographical Re-vision," 47.

5 In both *weiter leben* and *Still Alive*, Klüger reflects on her audience at one point. In *weiter leben*, she writes: "Who am I writing this for in the first place? Well, I'm certainly not writing this for Jews, because I wouldn't do this in a language that was spoken, read, and loved by so many Jews back then when I was a child that it was regarded as the Jewish language by many, the language, however, that only very few Jews know well today. So am I writing for those who cannot or don't want to feel with either the perpetrators or with the victims, and for those who don't think it is psychologically healthy to read and hear too much about human atrocities? Am I writing for those to whom I radiate an unsurmountable foreignness? Let me put it differently, I am writing for Germans. But are you really like this? Do you want to be like this?" (142) Since Klüger herself is so outspoken about both her intended audience and her own impetus for writing, i.e., triggering a response in her reader, I do not agree with Erin McGlothlin when she claims that the reader should "engage in a dialogical process of reading whereby they move from one text to the other and back again" (47). While this dialogical process is valuable as an analytical tool, an interpretation that takes the form of a personal response to the challenge posed by Klüger in both texts independently seems to be a possible form of reading, too.

6 Klüger, *weiter leben*, 142. Drawing on P. R. Bos's findings, McGlothlin writes: "Klüger attempts to bring her German readers into her reconstruction and reinterpretation of the past by provoking them with her polemical rumination of the past on both the global and the intensely personal points of Holocaust memory." "Autobiographical Re-vision," 56.

7 Compare McGlothin, "Autobiographical Re-vision," 57: "Klüger designates her audience in terms that are less common to traditional autobiographical projects. Rather than defining her audience as merely passive (and potentially shamed) recipients of her life narrative, she invites and incites them to become, in a sense, co-producers of a narrative that in her view is still in the making."

8 Compare Klüger, *Still Alive*, 64: "those who whitewash fences." In *Still Alive*, Klüger refers to them as the "Tom Sawyers," an expression that will be easily understandable for an American readership but not necessarily for a German one.

9 Klüger, *Still Alive*, 64.

10 Ibid., 65.

11 Ibid., 73.

12 Ibid.

13 Ibid., 184.

14 Klüger, *weiter leben*, 237.

15 Ibid., 201.

16 Ibid., 83. Compare McGlothlin, 64: "While generalization is useful for helping to create a common discursive sphere, the critical faculty of differentiation must next come into play if we are to try to understand the ways in which a roughly similar event can be experienced in myriad ways by diverse individuals."

17 Klüger, *Still Alive*, 184.

18 Ibid.

19 Ibid., 52.

20 Ibid., 154.

21 Klüger, *weiter leben*, 215, 279.

22 Ibid., 181.

23 Ibid., 169. She uses the pseudonym "Christoph" for Walser in *weiter leben* to avoid name-dropping. (Renata Schmidtkunz, *Im Gespräch. Ruth Klüger* [An interview with Ruth Klüger]. Wien: Mandelbaum, 2008, 55.)

24 Klüger, *Still Alive*, 194f.

25 Ibid., 195.

26 Ibid., 65.

27 Original title: *Am Ende kommen Touristen*. DVD. Directed by Robert Thalheim. 2007; Hamburg: Warner Home Video, 2008.

28 Norbert Reck, "Kitsch oder Kritik: Von den verborgenen Tagesordnungen der Erinnerung [Kitsch or critique: The hidden agendas of remembrance]," *Dachauer Hefte* 25 (2009): 161–73.

Selected Bibliography

Allen, Ann Taylor. "The Holocaust and the Modernization of Gender: A Historio-graphical Essay." *Central European History* 30, no. 3 (1997): 349–64.

Aly, Götz. *"Final Solution": Nazi Population Policy and the Murder of the European Jews.* Translated by Belinda Cooper and Allison Brown. London: Arnold, 1999.

———. *Into the Tunnel: The Brief Life of Marion Samuel, 1931–1943.* Translated by Ann Millin. New York: Metropolitan Books in association with the United States Holocaust Memorial Museum, 2007.

Améry, Jean. "How Much Home Does a Person Need?" In Améry, *At the Mind's Limits.* Bloomington: Indiana University Press, 1980.

Amesberger, Helga, and Brigitte Halbmyr. "Nazi Differentiations Mattered: Ideological Intersections of Sexualized Violence during National Socialist Persecution." In *Life, Death, and Sacrifice: Women and Family in the Holocaust,* edited by Esther Herzog, 181–96. Lynbrook, NY: Gefen Books, 2008.

Annual National Affiliate Show. Soho 20 Chelsea, New York City, 2010, 2006, and 2005.

Antelme, Robert. *L'Espèce humaine.* Paris: Gallimard, 1947. Translated as *The Human Race* by Jeffrey Haight and Anne Mahler. Evanston, IL: Northwestern University Press, 2003.

Aolain, Fionnuala Ni. "Sex-Based Violence and the Holocaust: A Reevaluation of Harms and Rights in International Law." *Yale Journal of Law and Feminism* 12, no. 1 (2000). http://www.law-lib.utoronto.ca/diana/fulltext/aola1.html.

Apel, Dora. *Memory Effects: The Holocaust and the Art of Secondary Witnessing.* New Brunswick, NJ: Rutgers University Press, 2002.

Apenszlak, Jaco, ed. *The Black Book of Polish Jewry: An Account of the Martyrdom of Polish Jewry under the Nazi Occupation.* American Federation for Polish Jews, 1943. Reprint, Westport, CT: Brohan Press, 1999.

Arad, Yitzhak, Shmuel Krakowski, and Shmuel Specto, eds. *The Einsatzgruppen*

Reports: Selections from the Dispatches of the Nazi Death Squads' Campaigns against the Jews in Occupied Territories of the Soviet Union July 1941-January 1943. New York: Holocaust Library, 1989.

Arendt, Hannah. *The Origins of Totalitarianism.* New York: Meridian Books, Inc., 1958.

———. *Eichmann in Jerusalem.* New York: Viking, 1963.

———. *Men in Dark Times.* San Diego, CA: Harcourt Brace Jovanovich Publishers, 1968.

———. *The Life of the Mind.* New York: Harcourt Brace Jovanovich, 1978.

———. *Rahel Varnhagen: The Life of a Jewess.* Translated by Richard and Clara Winston. Baltimore, MD: Johns Hopkins University Press, 1997.

———. *The Human Condition.* Chicago: University of Chicago Press, 1998.

Aroneanu, Eugene, comp. *Inside the Concentration Camps: Eyewitness Accounts of Life in Hitler's Death Camps.* Translated by Thomas Whissen. Westport, CT: Praeger, 1996.

Baer, Elizabeth R. "Rereading Women's Holocaust Memoirs: Liana Millu's *Smoke Over Birkenau.*" In *Lessons and Legacies VIII: From Generation to Generation*, edited by Doris L. Bergen, 157–174. Evanston, IL: Northwestern University Press, 2008.

Baer, Elizabeth R., and Myrna Goldenberg, eds. *Experience and Expression: Women, the Nazis, and the Holocaust.* Detroit, MI: Wayne State University Press, 2003.

Barnett, Ruth. "The Other Side of the Abyss: A Psychodynamic Approach to Working with Groups of People Who Came to England as Children on the Kindertransport." *British Journal of Psychotherapy* 12 (1995): 175–94.

Bartov, Omer. "Kitsch and Sadism in Ka-Tzetnik's Other Planet: Israeli Youth Imagine the Holocaust." *Jewish Social Studies* 3, no. 2 (1997): 42–76.

———. "Interethnic Relations in the Holocaust as Seen through Postwar Testimonies: Buczacz, East Galicia, 1941–1944." In *Lessons and Legacies VIII: From Generation to Generation*, edited by Doris L. Bergen, 101–24. Evanston, IL: Northwestern University Press, 2008.

Bauman, Zygmunt. *Modernity and the Holocaust.* Ithaca, NY: Cornell University Press, 2000.

Bell, Richard H. *Simone Weil: The Way of Justice and Compassion.* Lanham, MD: Rowman and Littlefield, 1998.

Benhabib, Seyla. "Hannah Arendt and the Redemptive Power of the Narrative." In *Hanna Arendt: Critical Essays*, edited by Lewis P. Hinchman and Sandra K. Hinchman, 111–37. Albany, NY: SUNY Press, 1994.

———. *The Reluctant Modernism of Hannah Arendt.* Lanham, MD: Rowman and Littlefield, 2003.

Benz, Ute. "Traumatization through Separation: Loss of Family and Home as Childhood Catastrophes." *Shofar: An Interdisciplinary Journal of Jewish Studies* 23, no. 1 (2004): 85–95.

Benz, Wolfgang. "Emigration as Rescue and Trauma: The Historical Context of the Kindertransport." *Shofar: An Interdisciplinary Journal of Jewish Studies* 23, no. 1 (2004).

Berg, Mary. *The Diary of Mary Berg: Growing Up in the Warsaw Ghetto.* 1945. Reprint, Oxford: Oneworld Publications Limited, 2007.

Bergen, Doris L. *Twisted Cross: The German Christian Movement in the Third Reich.* Chapel Hill: University of North Carolina Press, 1996.

———. "Sex, Blood, and Vulnerability: Women Outsiders in German-Occupied Europe." In *Social Outsiders in Nazi Germany,* edited by Robert Gellately and Nathan Stoltzfus, 273–93. Princeton, NJ: Princeton University Press, 2001.

———. *War and Genocide: A Concise History of the Holocaust.* Lanham, MD: Rowman and Littlefield, 2003.

———. "Sexual Violence in the Holocaust: Unique and Typical?" *Lessons and Legacies VII: The Holocaust in International Perspective,* edited by Dagmar Herzog, 179-200. Evanston, IL: Northwestern University Press, 2006.

Berman-Fischer, Gottfried. *Bedroht-Bewahrt: Weg eines Verlegers.* Frankfurt: Fischer, 1971.

Bethge, Werner. *Entfaltung jeder Form des Massenwiederstandes: Die Bedeutung der illegalen Funktionarstagung der Meinungen.* Heidelberg: GNN Verlag, 2001.

Biro, Matthew. "Representation and Event: Anselm Kiefer, Joseph Beuys, and the Memory of the Holocaust." *The Yale Journal of Criticism* 16, no. 1 (2003): 113–46.

Blanchot, Maurice. *The Writing of the Disaster.* Translated by Ann Smock. Lincoln: University of Nebraska Press, 1995.

———. *The Infinite Conversation.* Translated by Susan Hanson. Minneapolis: University of Minnesota Press, 1992.

Blend, Martha. *A Child Alone.* London: Vallentine Mitchell, 1995.

Bock, Gisela. *Zwangssterilisation im Nationalsozialismus. Studien zur Rassenpolitik und Frauenpolitik.* Opladen, Germany: Westdeutscher Verlag, 1986.

Bock, Gisela, ed. *Genozid und Geschlecht. Jüdische Frauen im nationalsozialistischen Lagersystem.* Frankfurt: Campus, 2005.

book bodies. Indy Art Museum, Indiana, 2007.

Bookish. Indianapolis, IN: Harrison Center for the Arts, 2009.

Borowski, Tadeusz. *This Way to the Gas, Ladies and Gentlemen.* Translated by Barbara Vedder. 1947; reprint, New York: Penguin, 1967.

Bos, Pascale. "Women and the Holocaust: Analyzing Gender Difference." In *Experience and Expression: Women, the Nazis, and the Holocaust,* edited by Elizabeth R. Baer and Myrna Goldenberg, 23–52. Detroit: Wayne State University Press, 2003.

Braiterman, Zachary. *(God) After Auschwitz.* Princeton, NJ: Princeton University Press, 1998.

Brenner, Rachel Feldhay. *Writing as Resistance: Four Women Confronting the Holocaust.* University Park: Pennsylvania State University Press, 1997.

Bridenthal, Renate, Atina Grossman, and Marion Kaplan, eds. *When Biology Became Destiny: Women in Weimar and Nazi Germany.* New York: Monthly Review Press, 1984.

Browning, Christopher R. *Ordinary Men: Reserve Police Battalion 101 and the Final Solution in Poland.* New York: HarperCollins, 1992.

———. *The Origins of the Final Solution: The Evolution of Nazi Jewish Policy, Septem-*

ber 1939–March 1942. Lincoln: University of Nebraska Press, 2004.

Browning, Christopher R., Richard S. Hollander, and Nehama Tec, eds. *Every Day Lasts a Year: A Jewish Family's Correspondence from Poland.* Cambridge, UK: Cambridge University Press, 2007.

Brownmiller, Susan. *Against Our Will: Men, Women, and Rape.* New York: Bantam, 1967.

Bryant, Chad. *Prague in Black: Nazi Rule and Czech Nationalism.* Cambridge, MA: Harvard University Press, 2007.

Bunting, Aimee. "Representing Rescue: The National Committee for Rescue from Nazi Terror, the British and the Rescue of Jews from Nazism." *The Journal of Holocaust Education* 9, no. 1 (2000): 65–84.

Burleigh, Michael. *The Racial State.* Cambridge, UK: Cambridge University Press, 1991.

Butler, Judith. *Gender Trouble: Feminism and the Subversion of Identity.* New York: Routledge, 1990.

Cassuto, U. *A Commentary on the Book of Genesis, Part Two: From Noah to Abraham.* Translated by Israel Abrahams. Jerusalem: Magnes Press, Hebrew University, 1964.

Cernyak-Spatz, Susan. *Protective Custody: Prisoner 34042.* Cortland, NY: N and S Publishers, 2005.

Cesarani, David. "Introduction." In *Into the Arms of Strangers: Stories of the Kindertransport,* edited by M. Harris and D. Oppenheimer, 1–19. New York: MJF Books, 2000.

Chanter, Tina. "Eating Words: Antigone as Kofman's Proper Name." In *Enigmas: Essays on Sarah Kofman,* edited by Penelope Deutscher and Kelly Oliver, 189–202. Ithaca, NY: Cornell University Press, 1999.

Chatwood, Kirsty. "Schillinger and the Dancer." In *Sexual Violence against Jewish Women during the Holocaust,* edited by Sonja M. Hedgepeth and Rochelle G. Saidel, 61–74. Waltham, MA: Brandeis University Press, 2010.

Clark, Elizabeth, and Herbert Richardson, eds. *Women and Religion: A Feminist Sourcebook of Christian Thought.* New York: HarperCollins, 1977.

Cohen, Elie A. *Human Behavior in the Concentration Camp.* New York: Grosset and Dunlap / The Universal Library, 1953.

Cohen, Judy, moderator. www.womenandtheHolocaust.com.

Coles, Robert. *Simone Weil: A Modern Pilgrimage.* Radcliffe Biography Series. Reading, MA: Addison-Wesley Publishing, 1989.

Cooke, Miriam, and Angela Woolacott, eds. *Gendering War Talk.* Princeton, NJ: Princeton University Press, 1993.

Copelon, Rhonda. "Surfacing Gender: Reconceptualizing Crimes against Women in Time of War." In *Mass Rape: The War against Women in Bosnia-Herzegovina,* edited by Alexandra Stiglmayer, 187–218. Lincoln: University of Nebraska Press, 1994.

Crane, Cynthia. *Divided Lives: The Untold Stories of Jewish Christian Women in Nazi Germany.* New York: Palgrave / Macmillan, 2000.

Crnkovic, Gordana P. "Interview with Agnieszka Holland." *Film Quarterly* 5, no. 2 (Winter 1998–99): 2–9. http://links.jstor.org/sici=0015-1386%28199824%2F199924@2952%3A2%3C2%3AIWAH%3E2.0.CO%3B2-R.

———. "Inscribed Bodies, Invited Dialogues and Cosmopolitan Cinema." *Kinoeye* http://www.kinoeye.org/04/05/crnkovic05_n02.php. November 2004, vol. 4, issue 5.

Curio, Claudia. "'Invisible' Children: The Selection and Integration Strategies of Relief Organizations." *Shofar: An Interdisciplinary Journal of Jewish Studies* 23, no. 1 (2004): 41–56.

Danieli, Yael. "Differing Adaptational Styles in Families of Survivors of the Nazi Holocaust: Some Implications for Treatment." *Children Today* (September–October 1981): 6–36.

———. "Psychotherapists' Participation in the Conspiracy of Silence about the Holocaust." *Psychoanalytic Psychology* 1 (1984): 23–42.

———. "Treating Survivors and Children of Survivors of the Nazi Holocaust." In *Posttraumatic Therapy and Victims of Violence,* edited by F. Ochberg, 278–94. New York: Brunner / Mazel, 1988.

Davidson, Shamai. "Psychological Aspects of Holocaust Trauma in the Life Cycle of Survivor-Refugees and Their Families." In *The Psychosocial Problems of Refugees: Collected Papers from the International Conference on the Psychosocial Problems,* edited by Ron Baker, 21–31. Keffolds, UK, August 1981. London: European Consultation on Refugees and Exiles / British Refugee Council, 1983.

de Beauvoir, Simone. *The Second Sex.* Translated and edited by H. M. Parshley. New York: Alfred A. Knopf, 1953.

de Lauretis, Teresa. *Technologies of Gender: Essays on Theory, Film, and Fiction.* Bloomington: Indiana University Press, 1987.

Derrida, Jacques. "Sarah Kofman (1934–1994)." In Derrida, *The Work of Mourning.* Chicago: University of Chicago Press, 2001.

De Sica, Vittorio. *Garden of the Finzi Contini.* Film; Italian with English subtitles. Original title *Il Giardino dei Finzi Contini,* 1971.

Desbois, Fr. Patrick. *The Holocaust by Bullets: A Priest's Journey to Uncover the Truth behind the Murder of 1.5 Million Jews.* Translated by Catherine Spencer. New York: Palgrave / Macmillan, 2008.

Des Pres, Terence. *The Survivor: Anatomy of Life in the Death Camps.* New York: Oxford University Press, 1976.

Deutscher, Penelope. "'Imperfect Discretion': Interventions into the History of Philosophy by Twentieth-Century French Women Philosophers." *Hypatia* 15, no. 2 (2000): 163.

Deutscher, Penelope, and Kelly Oliver, eds. *Enigmas: Essays on Sarah Kofman.* Ithaca, NY: Cornell University Press, 1999.

Dietz, Mary G. "Hannah Arendt and Feminist Politics." In *Hannah Arendt: Critical Essays,* edited by Lewis P. Hinchamn and Sandra K. Hinchamn, 231–58. Albany, NY: SUNY Press, 1995.

———. *Turning Operations: Feminism, Arendt, and Politics.* New York: Routledge, 2002.

Distel, Barbara, ed. *Frauen im Holocaust.* Gerlingen: Bleicher, 2001.

Doneson, Judith. *The Holocaust in American Film*. Syracuse, NY: Syracuse University Press, 2002.

Dribben, Judith. *A Girl Named Judith Strick*. New York: Cowles Book Company, 1970.

Drucker, Olga. *Kindertransport*. New York: Henry Holt, 1992.

Dubrovsky, Gertrude W. *Six from Leipzig*. London: Valentine Mitchell, 2004.

Ehrenburg, Ilya, and Vasily Grossman, eds. *The Black Book: The Ruthless Murder of Jews by German-Fascist Invaders throughout the Temporarily-Occupied Regions of the Soviet Union and in the Death Camps of Poland during the War of 1941–1945*. Translated by John Glad and James S. Levine. New York: Holocaust Library, 1980.

Ehrenburg, Ilya, and Vasily Grossman, eds. *The Complete Black Book of Russian Jewry*. Translated by David Patterson. New Brunswick, NJ: Transaction, 2002.

Eichengreen, Lucille. *From Ashes to Life: My Memories of the Holocaust*. San Francisco: Mercury House, 1994.

———. *Haunted Memories: Portraits of Women during the Holocaust*. Exeter, NH: Publishing Works, 2011.

Eisenbruch, Maurice. "The Mental Health of Refugee Children and Their Cultural Development." *International Migration Review* 22, no. 2 (1988): 292–300.

Epstein, Helen. *Children of the Holocaust*. New York: Bantam Books, 1981.

Eschebach, Insa, Sigrid Jacobeit, and Silke Wenk, eds., *Gedächtnis und Geschlecht. Deutungsmuster in Darstellungen des nationalsozialistischen Genozids*. Frankfurt am Main: Campus, 2002.

Fackenheim, Emil L. *Jewish Return into History*. New York: Schocken Books, 1978.

———. "The Holocaust and Philosophy." *The Journal of Philosophy* 82, no. 10 (October 1985): 505–14.

———. *The Jewish Bible after the Holocaust*. Bloomington: Indiana University Press, 1990.

Falk, Richard A., et al. *Crimes of War*. New York: Random House, 1971.

Feinstein, Margarete Myers. *Holocaust Survivors in Postwar Germany, 1945–57*. New York: Cambridge University Press, 2010.

Feinstein, Stephen, ed. and curator. *Absence/Presence: The Artistic Memory of the Holocaust and Genocide*. Exhibition catalogue, Katherina E. Nash Gallery, University of Minnesota, 1999.

Fetterley, Judith. "Reading about Reading." In *Gender and Reading: Essays on Readers, Texts, and Contexts*, edited by E. A. Flynn and P. P. Schweikart. Baltimore, MD: Johns Hopkins University Press, 1986.

Finkelstein, Norman G. *The Holocaust Industry: Reflections on the Exploitation of Jewish Suffering*. London: Verso, 2000.

Finnan, Carmel. "Gendered Memory? Cordelia Edvardson's *Gebranntes Kind sucht der Feuer* and Ruth Klüger's *weiter leben*." In *Autobiography by Women in German*, edited by M. P. Cavies, B. Linklater, and G. Shaw. Oxford: Oxford University Press, 2000.

Fischer, Brigitte B. *Sie schrieben mir, oder was aus meinem Poesiealbum wurde*. München: dtv, 1981.

Florida Center for Instructional Technology. *A Teacher's Guide to the Holocaust*.

College of Education, University of South Florida, 2005.

Flynn, E. A., and P. P. Schweickart, eds. *Gender and Reading: Essays on Readers, Texts, and Contexts.* Baltimore, MD: Johns Hopkins University Press, 1986.

Friedländer, Saul. *Nazi Germany and the Jews.* Vol. 1, *The Years of Persecution, 1933–1939.* New York: HarperCollins, 1997; vol. 2, *The Years of Extermination 1919–1945.* New York: HarperCollins, 2007.

Friedman, Henry. *I'm No Hero: Journeys of a Holocaust Survivor.* Seattle: University of Washington Press, 1999.

Freud, Anna. *Research at the Hampstead Child Therapy Clinic and Other Papers.* London: International Universities Press, 1970.

Freud, Anna, and Dorothy Burlingham. *War and Children.* London: Medical War Books, 1943.

Fulop, Walter. Contribution to *I Came Alone: The Stories of the Kindertransports,* edited by Bertha Leverton and Sarah Lowensohn. Sussex, Eng.Harper: Book Guild, 1990.

Gallant, Mary. *Coming of Age in the Holocaust: The Last Survivors Remember.* Lanham, MD: University Press of America, 2002.

Gamman, Lorraine, and Margaret Marshment, eds. *The Female Gaze: Women as Viewers of Popular Culture.* Seattle, WA: Real Comet Press, 1991.

Gastfriend, Edward. *My Father's Testament: Memoir of a Jewish Teenager, 1938-194.* Edited by Björn Krondorfer. Philadelphia, PA: Temple University Press, 2000.

Gershon, Karen. *We Came as Children: A Collective Autobiography of Refugees.* 1966; reprint, New York: Harcourt, Brace, and World, 1989.

Gertjejanssen, Wendy Jo. "Victims, Heroes, Survivors: Sexual Violence on the Eastern Front During World War II." PhD diss., University of Minnesota, 2004.

Geve, Thomas. *Youth in Chains.* Jerusalem: Rubin Mass, 1981.

Geyer, Michael. "Virtue in Despair: A Family History from the Days of the Kindertransport." *History and Memory: Studies in the Representations of the Past* 17, nos. 1–2 (2005): 323–65.

Gikatilla, Joseph. *Sha'are Orah: Gates of Light.* Translated by Avi Weinstein. San Francisco: HarperCollins, 1994.

Gilbert, Martin. *The Holocaust: A Record of the Destruction of Jewish Life in Europe during the Dark Years of Nazi Rule.* London: Board of Deputies of British Jews, 1978.

———. *Jewish History Atlas.* 1969; reprint, London: George Weidenfeld and Nicholson, 1985.

———. *Kristallnacht: Prelude to Destruction.* New York: HarperCollins, 2006.

Giles, Geoffrey J. "The Denial of Homosexuality and Same-Sex Incidents in Himmler's SS and Police." In *Sexuality and German Fascism,* edited by Dagmar Herzog, 256–90. New York: Berghahn, 2005. Originally published in *Journal of the History of Sexuality* 11, nos. 1–2 (January/April 2002).

Gillespie, Veronica. "Working with the Kindertransport." In *This Working Day World: Women's Lives and the Culture(s) in Britain, 1914-1945,* edited by Sybil Oldfield. London: Taylor and Francis, 1994, 1998.

Ginaite-Rubinson, Sara. *Resistance and Survival: The Jewish Community in Kaunas, 1941–1944*. Oakville, Ont.: Mosaic Press and the Holocaust Centre of Toronto, 2005.

Ginsburgh, Yitzchak. *The Alef-Beit*. Northvale, NJ: Jason Aronson, 1991.

Gissing, Vera. *Pearls of Childhood: The Poignant True Wartime Story of a Young Girl Growing Up in an Adopted Land*. New York: Pan Books, 1990.

Glassman, Gaby R. "The Impact of Intergenerational Protection on the Second Generation's Other Relationships." In *Beyond Camps and Forced Labor. Current International Research on Suvivors of Nazi Persecution*. Proceedings of the First International Multidisciplinary Conference, Imperial War Museum, London, January 2003. Osnabrueck, Germany: Secolo, 2005.

Glowacka, Dorota. *Disappearing Traces: Holocaust Testimonials, Ethics, Aesthetics*. Seattle: University of Washington Press, 2012.

Gopfert, Robekka, and Andrea Hammel. "Kindertransport: History and Memory." *Shofar: An Interdisciplinary Journal of Jewish Studies* 23, no. 1 (2004).

Goldenberg, Myrna. "Different Horrors, Same Hell: Women Remembering the Holocaust." In *Thinking the Unthinkable: Meanings of the Holocaust*, edited by Roger Gottlieb, 150–66. New York: Paulist Press, 1990.

———. "Lessons Learned from Gentle Heroism: Women's Holocaust Narratives." *Annals of the American Academy of Political and Social Science* 548, no. 1 (1996): 78–93.

———. "'From a World Beyond': Women in the Holocaust." *Feminist Studies* 22, no. 3 (Fall 1996): 667–87.

———. "Women's Voices in Holocaust Literary Memoirs." *Shofar: An Interdisciplinary Journal of Jewish Studies* 16, no. 4 (Summer 1998): 75–89.

———. "Memoirs of Auschwitz Survivors: The Burden of Gender." In *Women and the Holocaust*, edited by Dalia Ofer and Lenore J. Weitzman. 327–39. New Haven, CT: Yale University Press, 1999.

Goldhagen, Daniel Jonah. *Hitler's Willing Executioners*. New York: Knopf, 1996.

Gotfryd, Bernard. *Anton the Dove Fancier and Other Tales of the Holocaust*. New York: Washington Square Press, 1990.

Gottlieb, Amy Zahl. *Men of Vision: Anglo-Jewry's Aid to Victims of the Nazi Regime, 1933–1945*. London: Weidenfeld and Nicholson, 1998.

Gottschall, Jonathan. "Explaining Wartime Rape." *Journal of Sex Research* 41, no. 2 (May 2004): 129–36.

Grant, George. "In Defence of Simone Weil." *Idler* 15 (January–February 1988): 36–40.

Grau, Günter, ed. *Hidden Holocaust? Gay and Lesbian Persecution in Germany, 1933–1945*. Translated by Patrick Camiller. London: Cassell, 1995.

Gray, Francis du Plessix. *Simone Weil*. New York: Viking / Penguin, 2001.

Gross, Jan. *Neighbors: The Destruction of the Jewish Community in Jedwabne, Poland*. Princeton, NJ: Princeton University Press, 2001.

Gubar, Susan. *Poetry After Auschwitz: Remembering What One Never Knows*. Bloomington: Indiana University Press, 2003.

Grunfeld, Judith. *Shefford: The Story of Jewish School Community in Evacuation, 1939-1945*. London: Soncino Press, 1980.

Gurewitsch, Brana, ed. *Mothers, Sisters, Resisters: Oral Histories of Women Who Survived the Holocaust*. Tuscaloosa: University of Alabama Press, 1998.

Gyöngyössy, Imre, and Barna Kabay. *The Revolt of Job*. Film, 1983. Original title *Jób lázadása*.

Haas, Aaron. *In the Shadow of the Holocaust: The Second Generation*. Ithaca, NY: Cornell University Press, 1990.

Hammel, Andrea. "Representatives of Family in Autobiographical Texts of Child Refugees." *Shofar: An Interdisciplinary Journal of Jewish Studies* 23, no. 1 (2004): 121-30.

Hannam, Charles. *A Boy in That Situation: An Autobiography*. New York: Harper and Row, 1977.

Hart, Kitty. *Return to Auschwitz*. New York: Atheneum, 1984.

Harvey, Elizabeth. *Women and the Nazi East*. New Haven, CT: Yale University Press, 2003.

Heger, Heinz. *The Men with the Pink Triangle*. Translated by David Fernbach. Boston: Alyson Publications, 1980.

Heimler, Eugene. *Night of the Mist*. Translated by André Ungar. New York: Vanguard, 1959.

Heineman, Elizabeth. "Sexuality and Nazism: The Doubly Unspeakable." *Journal of the History of Sexuality* 11, no. 1/2 (January–April 2002): 22–66.

Heinemann, Isabel. *"Rasse, Siedlung, deutsches Blut": Das Rasse- und Siedlungshauptamt der SS und die rassenpolitische Neuordnung Europas*. Göttingen: Wallstein, 2003.

Heinemann, Marlene E. *Gender and Destiny: Women Writers of the Holocaust*. New York: Greenwood Press, 1986.

Herman, Judith L. *Trauma and Recovery: The Aftermath of Violence from Domestic Abuse to Political Terror*. New York: Basic Books, 1992.

Hertzog, Esther, ed. *Life, Death, and Sacrifice: Women and Family in the Holocaust*. Jerusalem: Gefen Publishing House, Ltd., 2008.

Herzog, Dagmar. *Sex After Fascism: Memory and Morality in Twentieth-Century Germany*. Princeton, NJ: Princeton University Press, 2005.

Heschel, Susannah. "Does Atrocity Have a Gender? Feminist Interpretations of Women in the SS." In *Lessons and Legacies VI: New Currents in Holocaust Research*, edited by Jeffrey Diefendorf, 300–321. Evanston, IL: Northwestern University Press, 2004.

Hilberg, Raul. *The Destruction of European Jews*. New York: Holmes and Meier, 1985.

Hilberg, Raul. *Perpetrators, Victims, Bystanders: The Jewish Catastrophe, 1933-1945*. New York: HarperCollins, 1992.

Hirsch, Marianne. *The Mother/Daughter Plot: Narrative, Psychoanalysis, Feminism*. Bloomington: Indiana University Press, 1989.

———. *Family Frames: Photography, Narrative, and Postmemory*. Cambridge, MA: Harvard University Press, 1997.

———. "Marked by Memory: Feminist Reflections on Trauma and Transmission." In *Extremities: Trauma, Testimony, Community*, edited by Nancy K. Miller and Jason Tougaw, 71–91. Urbana: University of Illinois Press, 2002.

———. "Nazi Photographs in Post-Holocaust Art: Gender as an Idiom of Memorialization." In *Crimes of War: Guilt and Denial in the Twentieth Century*, edited by Omer Bartov, Atina Grossmann, and Mary Nolan. New York: The New Press, 2002.

———. "The Generation of Postmemory." *Poetics Today* 29, no. 1 (2008): 103–28.

Hirsch, Marianne, and Leo Spitzer. "Gendered Translations: Claude Lanzmann's *Shoah*." In *Claude Lanzmann's* Shoah: *Key Essays*, edited by Stuart Liebman. New York: Oxford University Press, 2007.

Hirschberger, Hermann, MBE. www.ajr.org.uk/kindersurvey. Survey for the Association of Jewish Refugees. 2008.

Hitchcock, William I. *The Bitter Road to Freedom*. New York: The Free Press, 2008.

Hochstadt, Steve. *Sources of the Holocaust*. New York: Palgrave / Macmillan, 2004.

Hoffman, Eva. *Lost in Translation: A Life in a New Language*. New York: Dutton, 1989.

———. *After Such Knowledge*. London: Vintage, 2005.

Homeland / Heimaten. DAI. Heidelberg, Germany, 2004.

hooks, bell. *Talking Back: Thinking Feminist, Thinking Black*. Boston, MA: South End Press, 1989.

Holland, Agnieszka. *Angry Harvest*. Film, 1985. Original title *Bittere Ernte*.

Horowitz, Sara [R.]. *Voicing the Void: Muteness and Memory in Holocaust Fiction*. New York: SUNY Press, 1997.

———. "Gender, Genocide, and Jewish Memory." *Prooftexts* 20, nos. 1 and 2 (Winter/Spring 2000): 158–90.

———. "Gender in Holocaust Representation." *Teaching the Representation of the Holocaust*, edited by Marianne Hirsch and Irene Kacandes, 111–12. New York: MLA, 2004.

———. "The Gender of Good and Evil: Women and Holocaust Memory." In *Gray Zones: Ambiguity and Compromise in the Holocaust and Its Aftermath*, edited by Jonathan Petropoulos and John K. Roth, 165–78. New York: Berghahn, 2005.

Insdorf, Annette. *Indelible Shadows: Film and the Holocaust*. Cambridge, UK: Cambridge University Press, 2002.

Isaacson, Judith Magyar. *Seed of Sarah: Memoirs of a Survivor*. Urbana: University of Illinois Press, 1990.

Jewish Black Book Committee. *The Black Book: The Nazi Crime against the Jewish People*. New York: Duell, Sloan, and Pearce, 1946.

Kaplan, E. Ann. *Feminism and Film*. Oxford: Oxford University Press, 2000.

Kaplan, Marion A. *Between Dignity and Despair: Jewish Life in Nazi German*. New York: Oxford University Press, 1999.

Kaplan, Thomas Pegelow. *The Language of Nazi Genocide: Linguistic Violence and the Struggle of Germans of Jewish Ancestry*. New York: Cambridge University Press, 2009.

Karay, Felicja. "Women in Forced Labor Camps." In *Women and the Holocaust,* edited by Dalia Ofer and Lenore Weitzman, 285–309. New Haven, CT: Yale University Press, 1998.

Kater, Michael H. *Doctors under Hitler.* Chapel Hill: University of North Carolina Press, 1989.

Katz, Esther, and Joan Ringelheim, eds. *Proceedings of the Conference, Women Surviving: The Holocaust.* New York: Institute for Research in History, 1983.

Ka-tzetnik 135633. *Shivitti: A Vision.* Translated by Eliyah De-Nur and Lisa Herman. New York: Harper & Row, 1989.

Keneally, Thomas. *Schindler's List.* New York: Touchstone, 1982.

Klee, Ernst, Willi Dressen, and Volker Reiss, eds. *The Good Old Days: The Holocaust as Seen by Its Perpetrators and Bystanders.* Translated by Deborah Burnstone. New York: Simon and Schuster, 1991.

Karpf, Anne. *The War After.* London: Heinemann, 1996.

Kleinman, Susan, and Ghana Moshenko. "Class as a Factor in the Social Adaption of the Kindertransport Kinder." *Shofar: An Interdisciplinary Journal of Jewish Studies* 23, no. 1 (2004): 28–40.

Klimov, Elem, dir. *Come and See.* Film, 1986. Original title *Idi i smotri,* 1985.

Klüger, Ruth. *weiter leben: Eine Jugend.* Munchen: dtv, 1994.

———. *Still Alive: A Holocaust Girlhood Remembered.* New York: The Feminist Press at the City University of New York, 2001.

Kochan, Miriam. "Women's Experience of Interment." In *The Internment of Aliens in Twentieth Century Britain,* edited by David Cesarani and Anthony Kushner, 147–66. New York: Routledge, 1993.

Kofman, Amy, and Kirby Dick, dirs. *Derrida: The Movie.* New York: Zeitgeist Films, 2002.

Kofman, Sarah. "Rousseau's Phallocratic Ends." Translated by Mara Dukats. *Hypatia* 3, no. 3 (Fall 1988): 123–36.

———. *Rue Ordener, Rue Labat.* Translated by Ann Smock. Lincoln: University of Nebraska Press, 1996.

———. *Smothered Words.* Translated by Madelaine Dobie. Evanston, IL: Northwestern University Press, 1998.

———. *Selected Writings.* Stanford, CA: Stanford University Press, 2007.

Kohl, Christiane. *The Maiden and the Jew: The Story of a Fatal Friendship in Nazi Germany.* Translated by John S. Barrett. Hanover, NH: Steerforth Press, 1997.

Koonz, Claudia. *Mothers in the Fatherland: Women, the Family, and Nazi Politics.* New York: St. Martin's, 1987.

———. "A Tributary and a Mainstream: Gender, Public Memory, and the Historiography of Nazi Germany." In *Gendering Modern German History,* edited by Karen Hagemann and Jean H. Quataer, 147–68. New York: Berghahn, 2007.

Korte, Mona. "Bracelet, Hand Towel, Pocket Watch: Objects of the Last Moment in Memory and Narration." *Shofar: An Interdisciplinary Journal of Jewish Studies* 23, no. 1 (2004).

Kovály, Heda Margolius. *Under a Cruel Star: A Life in Prague, 1941–1968.* Translated by

Helen Epstein and Franci Epstein. New York: Holmes & Meier, 1997.

Kramarae, Cheris. "Proprietors of Language." In *Women and Language in Literature and Society*, edited by Sally McConnell-Ginet, Ruth Borker, and Nelly Furman. New York: Praeger, 1980.

Kremer, S. Lillian. *Women's Holocaust Writing: Memory and Imagination*. Lincoln: University of Nebraska Press, 1999.

Kristeva, Julia. *Hannah Arendt: Life Is a Narrative*. Translated by Frank Collins. Toronto: University of Toronto Press, 2001.

Kroger, Marianne. "Child Exiles: A New Research Area?" *Shofar: An Interdisciplinary Journal of Jewish Studies* 23, no. 1 (2004).

Krondorfer, Björn. *Remembrance and Reconciliation: Encounters Between Young Jews and Germans*. New Haven, CT: Yale University Press, 1995.

———. "Ratner's Kosher Restaurant." In *Second Generation Voices: Reflections by Children of Holocaust Survivors and Perpetrators*, edited by Alan and Naomi Berger, 258–69. Syracuse, NY: Syracuse University Press, 2001.

———. "Is Forgetting Reprehensible? Holocaust Remembrance and the Task of Oblivion." *Journal of Religious Ethics* 36, no. 2 (June 2008): 233–67.

Krondorfer, Björn, ed. *Men's Bodies, Men's Gods: Male Identities in a (Post-)Christian Culture*. New York: New York University Press, 1996.

Kruk, Herman. "Diary of the Vilna Ghetto." Translated by Shlomo Noble. *YIVO Annual of Jewish Social Science* 13 (1965): 20.

———. *The Last Days of the Jerusalem of Lithuania: Chronicles from the Vilna Ghetto and the Camps, 1939–1944*. Edited by Benjamin Harshav; translated by Barbara Harshav. New Haven, CT: Yale University Press, 2002.

Kruyer, Wanya F. "De schaduwzijde van de babyboomers." *JONAG Bulletin* 2 (Summer 2009/5769): 6–11.

Kuhn, E. *Women's Pictures: Feminism and Cinema*. London: Routledge & Kegan Paul, 1982.

Kuhn, Phillip. "Phantoms in the Family History (Part 1)." *Second Generation Voices. Newsletter of the Second Generation Network* No. 8 (May 1998).

Kushner, Anthony, and Katherine Knox. *Refugees in an Age of Genocide: Global, National and Local Perspectives during the Twentieth Century*. London: Frank Cass, 1999.

Kuttner, Paul. *Endless Struggle: Reminiscences and Reflections*. New York: Vantage Press, 2009.

Kuwalek, Robert. "Izbica Lubelska." In *Encyclopedia of Camps and Ghettos*. Vol. 2, *German Run Ghettos*. Edited by Martin Dean; translated by Steven Seegel. Bloomington: Indiana University Press, 2011.

Langer, Lawrence. *Versions of Survival: The Holocaust and the Human Spirit*. Albany, NY: SUNY Press, 1982.

Lanzmann, Claude. *Shoah*. Film, 566 minutes. DVD edition, American zone: New Yorker Video, #51003. 1985.

———. *Shoah: An Oral History of the Holocaust*. New York: Pantheon, 1985.

———. *Shoah: The Complete Text of the Acclaimed Holocaust Film*. New York: Da Capo, 1995.

Laquer, Walter. *The Holocaust Encyclopedia*. New Haven, CT: Yale University Press, 2001.

Laska, Vera. *Women in the Resistance and in the Holocaust: The Voices of Eyewitnesses*. Westport, CT: Greenwood, 1983.

Lassner, Phyllis. *Anglo-Jewish Women Writing the Holocaust: Displaced Witnesses*. New York: Palgrave / Macmillan, 2008.

Leitner, Isabella, with Irving Leitner. *Fragments of Isabella*. New York: Thomas Crowell, 1978.

Lengel-Krizman, Narcisa. "A Contribution to the Study of Terror in the So-Called Independent State of Croatia: Concentration Camps for Women in 1941–1942." *Yad Vashem Studies* 20 (1990).

Lengyel, Olga. *Five Chimneys,* 1959; reprint, London: Granada Publishing, 1972.

Levenkron, Nomi. "Death and the Maidens: 'Prostitution,' Rape and Sexual Slavery during World War II." In *Sexual Violence against Jewish Women during the Holocaust,* edited by Sonya Hedgepeth and Rochelle Saidel, 13–28. Waltham, MA: Brandeis University Press, 2010.

Leverton, Bertha, and Sarah Lowenstein. eds. *I Came Alone: The Stories of the Kindertransports*. Sussex, UK: The Book Guild, Ltd., 1990.

Levi, Primo. *The Drowned and the Saved*. Translated by Raymond Rosenthal. New York: Summit, 1988.

———. *Survival in Auschwitz*. Translated by Stuart Woolf. New York: Touchstone, 1996.

Levin, Nora. *The Holocaust Years: The Destruction of European Jewry, 1933–1945.* 1973; reprint, Malabar, FL: Krieger Publishing Company, Inc., 1990.

Littell, Jonathan. *The Kindly Ones*. Translated by Charlotte Mandell. New York: Harper, 2008. Originally published as *Les Bienveillantes,* 2006.

Loeve, Yehuda. *Nesivos Olam: Nesiv Hatorah*. Translated by Eliakim Willne. Brooklyn, NY: Mesorah, 1994.

London, Louise. *Whitehall and the Jews, 1933–1948: British Immigration Policy and the Holocaust*. Cambridge, UK: Cambridge University Press, 2000.

Loshitzky, Yosefa, ed. *Spielberg's Holocaust: Critical Perspectives on* Schindler's List. Bloomington: Indiana University Press, 1997.

MacKinnon, Catharine A. "Turning Rape into Pornography: Postmodern Genocide." In *Mass Rape: The War against Women in Bosnia-Herzegovina,* edited by Alexandra Stiglmayer, 73–81. Lincoln: University of Nebraska Press, 1994.

———. "Rape, Genocide, and Women's Human Rights." In *Mass Rape: The War against Women in Bosnia-Herzegovina,* edited by Alexandra Stiglmayer, 183–96. Lincoln: University of Nebraska Press, 1994.

Malle, Louis. *Au Revoir, Les Enfants*. Film, 1987.

Manoschek, Walter, *"Es gibt nur eines für das Judentum: Vernichtung." Das Judenbild in deutschen Soldatenbriefen, 1939–194*. Hamburg: HIS Verlag, 1995.

Marcus, Paul, and Alan Rosenberg, eds. *Healing Their Wounds*. New York: Praeger, 1981.

Marrus, Michael. *The Unwanted: European Refugees in the Twentieth Century*. New York: Oxford University Press, 1985.

Martin, Elaine, ed. *Gender, Patriarchy, and Fascism in the Third Reich: The Response of Women Writers.* Detroit: Wayne State University Press, 1993.

Maurel, Micheline. *An Ordinary Camp.* New York: Simon and Schuster, 1958.

McGlothlin, Erin. "Autobiographical Re-vision: Ruth Klüger's *weiter leben* and *Still Alive.*" *Gegenwartsliteratur* 3 (2004): 46–70.

Melson, Robert. *False Papers: Deception and Survival in the Holocaust.* Urbana: University of Illinois Press, 2000.

Meyer, Beate. *Jüdische Mischlinge: Rassenpolitik und Verfolgungserfahrung.* Hamburg: Dölling and Galitz, 1999.

Mihaileanu, Radu. *Train of Life.* Film, 1999. Original title *Train de Vie.*

Milchman, Alan, and Alan Rosenberg. "The Need for Philosophy to Confront the Holocaust as a Transformational Event." *Dialogue and Universalism,* nos. 3–4 (2003): 65–80.

Millu, Liana. *Smoke over Birkenau.* Translated by Lynne Sharon Schwartz. Evanston, IL: Northwestern University Press, 1991.

Milton, Edith. *Tiger in the Attic.* Chicago: University of Chicago Press, 2005.

Minnich, Elizabeth Kamarck. "Liberal Learning and the Arts of Connection for the New Academy." Washington, DC: Association of American Colleges and Universities, 1995.

———. *Transforming Knowledge.* 2nd edition. Philadelphia: Temple University Press, 2005.

Mohanty, Chandra Talpade. "Under Western Eyes: Feminist Scholarship and Colonial Discourses." In *Third World Women and the Politics of Feminism,* edited by C. T. Mohanty, A. Russo, and L. Torres. Bloomington: Indiana University Press, 1991.

Monologues/Dialogues. Arthur M. Glick Jewish Community Center Gallery, Indianapolis, IN, 2004.

Moos, Merilyn. *The Language of Silence.* London: Cressida Press, 2010.

Moraga, Cherríe, and Gloria Anzaldúa, eds. *This Bridge Called My Back: Writings by Radical Women of Color.* New York: Kitchen Table Women of Color Press, 1983.

Morris, Leslie. "Berlin Elegies: Absence, Postmemory, and Art after Auschwitz." In *Image and Remembrance: Representation and the Holocaust,* edited by Shelly Hornstein and Florence Jacobowitz, 288–303. Bloomington: Indiana University Press, 2003.

Morrison, Jack G. *Ravensbrück: Everyday Life in a Women's Concentration Camp, 1939–45.* Princeton, NJ: Markus Wiener, 2000.

Mühlhäuser, Regina. "Rasse, Blut und Männlichkeit: Politiken sexueller Regulierung in die besetzten Gebieten der Sowjetunion (1941–1945)." *Feministische Studien: Zeitschrift für Interdisziplinäre Frauen- und Geschlechterforschung* 25, no. 1 (2007): 55–69.

Mulvey, Laura. "Visual Pleasure and Narrative Cinema." *Screen* 16, no. 3 (Autumn 1975): 6–18.

Nancy, Jean-Luc. "Foreword: Run, Sarah, Run!" In *Enigmas: Essays on Sarah Kof-*

man, edited by Penelope Deutscher and Kelly Oliver, viii–xvi. Ithaca, NY: Cornell University Press, 1999.

Nathorff, Hertha. *Das Tagebuch der Hertha Nathorff, Berlin-New York, Augzeichnungen, 1933–1945*. Frankfurt am Main: Fischer Taschenbuch, 1988. The title translates into English as *Diary of Hertha Nathorff: Berlin-New York Recordings, 1933 to 1945*.

Narayan, Uma. "Contesting Cultures: 'Westernization,' Respect for Cultures, and Third-World Feminists." In *Dislocating Cultures: Identities, Traditions, and Third World Feminisms*. New York: Routledge, 1997.

Nevins, Thomas R. *Simone Weil: Portrait of a Self-Exiled Jew*. Chapel Hill: University of North Carolina Press, 1991.

Niewyk, Donald, ed. *Fresh Wounds: Early Narratives of Holocaust Survival*. Chapel Hill: University of North Carolina Press, 1998.

Nomberg-Przytyk, Sara. *Auschwitz: True Tales from a Grotesque Land*. Translated by Roslyn Hirsch. Chapel Hill: University of North Carolina Press, 1985.

Ofer, Dalia, and Lenore J. Weitzman, eds. *Women in the Holocaust*. New Haven, CT: Yale University Press, 1998.

Oldfield, Sybil, "It Is Usually She: The Role of British Women in the Rescue and Care of the Kindertransport Kinder." *Shofar: An Interdisciplinary Journal in Jewish Studies* 23, no. 1 (2004): 57–70.

Oliver, Kelly. "Sarah Kofman's Queasy Stomach and the Riddle of the Paternal Law." In *Enigmas: Essays on Sarah Kofman*, edited by Penelope Deutscher and Kelly Oliver, 174–88. Ithaca, NY: Cornell University Press, 1999.

Orth, Karin. "The Concentration Camp SS as a Functional Elite." In *National Socialist Extermination Policies: Contemporary German Perspectives and Controversies*, edited by Ulrich Herbert, 306–34. New York: Berghahn, 2000.

Ortner, Sherry B. "Is Female to Male as Nature Is to Culture?" In *Woman, Culture, and Society*, edited by Michelle Zimbalist Rosaldo and Louise Lamphere. Stanford, CA: Stanford University Press, 1974.

Pagels, Elaine. *Adam, Eve, and the Serpent*. New York: Vintage House, 1989.

Paul, Christa. *Zwangsprostitution: Staatlich errichtete Bordelle im Nationalsozialismus*. Berlin: Edition Hentrich, 1994.

Pawelczynska, Anna. *Values and Violence: A Sociological Analysis*. Berkeley: University of California Press, 1980.

Perl, Gisela. *I Was a Doctor in Auschwitz*. 1948; reprint, Salem, NH: Ayer Company, 2005.

Perrin, M. J., and G. Thibon. *Simone Weil as We Knew Her*. New York: Routledge, 2003.

Petropoulos, Jonathan, and John K. Roth, eds. *Gray Zones: Ambiguity and Compromise in the Holocaust and Its Aftermath*. New York: Berghahn Books, 2005.

pushmepullyou at Mathers Museum, Indiana University, Bloomington, 2008.

Przyrembel, Alexandra. "Transfixed by an Image: Ilse Koch, the 'Kommandeuse' of Buchenwald." Translated by Pamela Selwyn. *German History* 19, no. 3 (2001): 369–99.

Radok, Alfréd, dir. *Distant Journey*. Film, 1950. Original title *Daleka Cesta*.

Reck, Norbert. "Kitsch oder Kritik: Von den verborgenen Tagesordnungen der Erinnerung." *Dachauer Hefte* 25 (2009): 161–73.

Reagin, Nancy R. *Sweeping the German Nation: Domesticity and National Identity in Germany, 1870–1945.* New York: Cambridge University Press, 2007.

Resnais, Alain. *Night and Fog.* Film, 1955. Original title *Nuit et Brouillard.*

Rigg, Bryan Mark. *Hitler's Jewish Soldiers.* Lawrence: University Press of Kansas, 2002.

Ringelblum, Emmanuel. *Notes from the Warsaw Ghetto: The Journal of Emmanuel Ringelblum.* Edited and translated by Jacob Sloan. New York: Schocken Books, 1958.

Ringelheim, Joan. "The Unethical and the Unspeakable: Women and the Holocaust." *Simon Wiesenthal Center Annual* 1 (1984): 69–87.

———. "Women and the Holocaust: A Reconsideration of Research." *Signs* 10, no. 4 (1985): 741–61.

———. "Women and the Holocaust: A Reconsideration of Research." In *Different Voices: Women and the Holocaust,* edited by Carol Rittner and John K. Roth, 373–418. St. Paul, MN: Paragon House, 1993.

Rittner, Carol, and John Roth, eds. *Different Voices: Women and the Holocaust.* St. Paul, MN: Paragon House, 1993.

Rittner, Carol, and Sondra Myers, eds. *The Courage to Care: Rescuers of Jews during the Holocaust.* New York: New York University Press, 1986.

Roth, John K. "Equality, Neutrality, Particularity: Perspectives on Women and the Holocaust." In *Experience and Expression: Women, the Nazis, and the Holocaust,* edited by Elizabeth R. Baer and Myrna Goldenberg, 5–22. Detroit: Wayne State University Press, 2003.

Rosenberg, Alan, and Paul Marcus. "The Holocaust as a Test of Philosophy." In *Echoes from the Holocaust: Philosophical Reflections on a Dark Time,* edited by Alan Rosenberg and Gerald E. Myers. Philadelphia, PA: Temple University Press, 1988.

Rosenberg, Alfred. *Race and Race History and Other Essays.* Edited by Robert Pais. New York: Harper & Row, 1974.

Rosenblatt, Roger. *Children of War.* Garden City, NY: Anchor Press/Doubleday, 1983.

Rousset, David. *A World Apart.* London: Secker and Warburg, 1951.

Rubin, Gayle. "The Traffic in Women: Notes on the Political Economy of Sex." In *Toward an Anthropology of Women,* edited by Rayna R. Reiter. New York: Monthly Review Press, 1975.

Rubenstein, William, and Hilary L. Rubenstein. *Philosemitism: Admiration and Support in the English-Speaking World for Jews, 1840–1939.* New York: St. Martin's Press, 1999.

Russell, Axel, Donna Plotkin, and Nelson Heapy. "Adaptive Abilities in Nonclinical Second-Generation Holocaust Survivors and Controls: A Comparison." *American Journal of Psychotherapy* 31, no. 4 (October 1985): 564–79.

Sacks, Sir Jonathan, Chief Rabbi of the United Hebrew Congregations of the Commonwealth. "Only by bringing the past alive can we be sure to keep our future free." Monthly Credo Column, *The Times,* 22 April 1995, 9.

Saidel, Rochelle. *The Jewish Women of Ravensbrück Concentration Camp.* Madison: University of Wisconsin Press, 2006.

Sagi-Schwartz, Abraham, Nina Koren-Karie, and Tirtsa Joels. "Failed Mourning in the Adult Attachment Interview: The Case of Holocaust Child Survivors." *Attachment and Human Development.* Special Issue: *Extreme Life Events and Catastrophic Experiences and the Development of Attachment across the Life Span* 5, no. 4 (December 2003): 398-408.

Saltzman, Lisa. *Anselm Kiefer and Art after Auschwitz.* New York: Cambridge, 1999.

———. *Making Memory Matter: Strategies of Remembrance in Contemporary Art.* Chicago: Chicago University Press, 2006.

Schikorra, Christa. "Forced Prostitution in the Nazi Concentration Camps." In *Lessons and Legacies VII: The Holocaust in International Perspective*, edited by Dagmar Herzog, 169-78. Evanston, IL: Northwestern University Press, 2006.

Schlink, Bernhard. *Heimat als Utopie.* Frankfurt: Suhrkamp, 2000.

Schmetterling, Astrid. "Archival Obsessions: Arnold Dreyblatt's *Memory Work.*" *art journal* (Winter 2007): 71-83.

Schmidtkunz, Renata. *Im Gesprach: Ruth Klüger.* Vienna: Mandelbaum, 2008.

Schneider, Gertrud, ed. *Journey into Terror: Story of the Riga Ghetto.* 1979; reprint, Westport, CT: Praeger, 2001.

———. *Muted Voices: Jewish Survivors of Latvia Remember.* New York: Philosophical Library, 1987.

———. *The Unfinished Road: Jewish Survivors of Latvia Look Back.* Westport, CT: Praeger, 1991.

———. *Exile and Destruction: The Fate of Austrian Jews, 1938-1945.* Westport, CT: Praeger, 1995.

———. *Mordechai Gebirtig: His Poetic and Musical Legacy.* Westport, CT: Praeger, 2000.

Schoenfeld, Gabriel. "Auschwitz and the Professors." *Commentary* (June 1998): 42-46.

———. "Controversy: Feminist Approaches to the Holocaust." *Prooftexts: A Journal of Jewish Literary History* 21, no. 2 (Spring 2001): 277-79.

Schulz, Christa. "Weibliche Häftlinge aus Ravensbrück in Bordellen der Männerkonzentrationslager." In *Frauen in Konzentrationslagern Bergen-Belsen, Ravensbrück,* edited by Claus Füllberg-Stolberg et al. Bremen: Edition Temmen, 1994.

Schwarz, Gudrun. *Eine Frau an seiner Seite: Die Ehefrauen in der 'SS-Sippengemeinschaft.'* Berlin: Aufbau, 2000.

Schweickart, Patrocinio P. "Reading Ourselves: Toward a Feminist Theory of Reading." In *Gender and Reading: Essays on Readers, Texts, and Contexts,* edited by E. A. Flynn and P. P. Schweikart. Baltimore, MD: Johns Hopkins University Press, 1986.

Schwertfeger, Ruth. *Women of Theresienstadt: Voices from a Concentration Camp.* New York: Berg, 1988.

Scott, Joan Wallach "Gender: A Useful Category of Analysis." In *Feminism and History,* edited by Joan Wallach Scott. Oxford Readings in Feminism. New York: Oxford University Press, 1996.

Selo, Laura. *Three Lives in Transit.* New York: Excalibur Press, 1992.

Seifert, Ruth. "War and Rape: A Preliminary Analysis." In *Mass Rape: The War against Women in Bosnia-Herzegovina,* edited by Alexandra Stiglmayer, 54–72. Lincoln: University of Nebraska Press, 1994.

Sereny, Gitta. *Into That Darkness: An Examination of Conscience.* New York: Vintage, 1984.

Sharples, Caroline. "Kindertransport." *History Today* 54, no. 1 (2004): 23–35.

Shelley, Lore. *Auschwitz: The Nazi Civilization. Studies in the Shoah,* vol 1. Lanham, MD: University Press of America, 1992.

Shik, Na'ama. "Infinite Loneliness: Some Aspects of the Lives of Jewish Women in the Auschwitz Camps according to Testimonies and Autobiographies from 1945–1948." In *Lessons and Legacies VIII,* edited by Doris L. Bergen, 125–56. Evanston, IL: Northwestern University Press, 2008.

Shirer, William. *The Rise and Fall of the Third Reich.* New York: Simon & Schuster, 1959.

Simon-Nahum, Perrine. "Hannah Arendt: Repères chronologiques." *Le Magazine Littéraire* 445 (September 2005): 36–38.

Singer, Flora. *Flora: I Was But a Child.* Jerusalem: Yad Vashem, 2007.

Slade, Arietta. "Parental Reflective Functioning: An Introduction." *Attachment and Human Development* 3 (2005): 269–81.

Smith, Joan. "Holocaust Girls." In *Misogynies: Reflections on Myth and Malice,* edited by Joan Smith, 125–38. New York: Fawcett Columbine, 1991.

Smith, Leonard. "Thank God for the Kindertransport (A Letter)." *History Today* 54, no. 5 (2004).

Spiegelman, Art. *Maus I* and *Maus II.* New York: Pantheon Books, Inc., 1986, 1991.

Steinbacher, Sybille. *'Musterstadt' Auschwitz. Germanisierungspolitik und Judenmord in Ostoberschlesien.* Munich: K. G. Saur, 2000.

———. *Auschwitz: A History.* Translated by Shaun Whiteside. London: Penguin, 2005.

Steinberg, Jules. *Hannah Arendt on the Holocaust: A Study of Suppression of Truth.* Lewiston, ME: The Edwin Mellen Press, 2000.

Stoltzfus, Nathan. *Resistance of the Heart: Intermarriage and the Rosenstrasse Protest in Nazi Germany.* New York: W. W. Norton and Company, 1996.

Szobar, Patricia. "Telling Sexual Stories in the Nazi Courts of Law: Race Defilement in Germany, 1933–1945. *Journal of the History of Sexuality* 11, no. 1/2 (2002): 131–63.

Sündenbock. Meshulash Exhibit, Neue Synagoge, Berlin, 2007.

Tec, Nehama. *Resilience and Courage: Women, Men, and the Holocaust.* New Haven, CT: Yale University Press, 2003.

Theresienstadter Gedenkbuch: Die Opfer der Judtransporte aus Deutschland nach Theresienstadt. 1945. Institut Theresienstadter Initiative Academia, 2000.

Theweleit, Klaus. *Male Fantasies.* 2 vols. Translated by Stephen Conway. Minneapolis: University of Minnesota Press, 1987.

Tillion, Germaine. *Ravensbrück.* Translated by Gerald Satterwhite. New York: Doubleday, 1975.

Tory, Avraham. *Surviving the Holocaust: The Kovno Ghetto Diary.* Translated by

Jerzy Michalowicz. Cambridge, MA: Harvard University Press, 1990.

Tracy, David. "Simone Weil: The Impossible." In *The Christian Platonism of Simone Weil*, edited by E. Jane Doering and Eric O. Springsted. Notre Dame, IN: University of Notre Dame, 2004.

Trifold. Williamsburg Art and Historical Center, Brooklyn, NY, 2010.

Turner, Barry. *. . . And the Policeman Smiled.* London: Bloomsbury, 1990.

Tydor, Judith Baumel. *Double Jeopardy: Gender and the Holocaust.* London: Vallentine-Mitchell, 1998.

Valent, Paul, ed. *Child Survivors of the Holocaust.* New York: Brunner-Routledge, 2002.

Van Ijezendoorn, Marinus H., Marian J. Bakermans-Kranenburg, and Abraham Sagi-Schwartz. "Are Children of Holocaust Survivors Less Well-Adapted? A Meta-Analytic Investigation of Secondary Traumatization." *Journal of Traumatic Stress* 16 (2003): 5, 459–69.

Verhoeven, Michael. *The Nasty Girl.* Film, 1990. Original title *Das schreckliche Mädchen.*

———. *My Mother's Courage.* Film, 1995. Original title *Mutters Courage.*

Vinocur, Ana. *A Book without a Title.* Translated by Valentine Isaac and Ricardo Iglesia. New York: Vantage, 1976.

Vuletic, Aleksandar-Saša. *Christen jüdischer Herkunft im Dritten Reich. Verfolgung und Selbsthilfe, 1933–1939.* Mainz: P. von Zabern, 1999.

Wagner, Richard. "Jewry in Music." In *The Jew in the Modern World: A Documentary History*, edited by Paul Mendes-Flor and Jehuda Reinharz. New York: Oxford University Press, 1995.

Walk, Joseph. *Das Sonderrecht für die Juden im NS-Staat: Eine Sammlung der gesetzlichen Massnahmen und Richtlinien—Inhalt und Bedeutung.* 2nd ed. Heidelberg: CF Muller Verlag, 1996.

Wardi, Dina. *Memorial Candles: Children of the Holocaust.* New York: Routledge, 1992.

Waxman, Zoë Vania. *Writing the Holocaust: Identity, Testimony, Representation.* Oxford: Oxford University Press, 2006.

Weil, Simone. *Intimations of Christianity among the Ancient Greeks.* Translated by Elizabeth Chase Geissbuhler. Boston, MA: Beacon Press, 1959.

———. *Seventy Letters.* Translated by Richard Rees. London: Oxford University Press, 1968.

———. *Notebooks.* Translated by Arthur Wills. London: Oxford University Press, 1972.

———. *Gravity and Grace.* Translated by Emma Craufurd. London: Routledge and Kegan Paul, 1972.

———. *Oppression and Liberty.* Translated by Arthur Wills and John Petrie. Amherst: University of Massachusetts Press, 1973.

———. *Waiting on God.* Translated by Emma Craufurd. London: Fontana, 1974.

Weinreich, Max. *Hitler's Professors: The Part of Scholarship in Germany's Crimes against the Jewish People,* New Haven, CT: Yale University Press, 1999.

Wells, Leon. *The Death Brigade.* New York: Holocaust Library, 1978.

Wingfield, Nancy, and Maria Bucur, eds. *Gender and War in Twentieth-Century Europe.* Bloomington: Indiana University Press, 2006.

Witnesses. Center for Book Arts, New York, 2008.

Wolin, Richard. *Heidegger's Children.* Princeton, NJ: Princeton University Press, 2001.

Yassa, Maria. "Nicolas Abraham and Maria Torok—The Inner Crypt." *The Scandinavian Psychoanalytic Review* 2 (2002): 1–14.

Young-Bruehl, Elisabeth. *Hannah Arendt: For Love of the World.* New Haven, CT: Yale University Press, 1982.

Zahra, Tara. *Kidnapped Souls: National Indifference and the Battle for Children in the Bohemian Lands, 1900–1948.* Ithaca, NY: Cornell University Press, 2008.

Zalman, Schneur. *Likutei Amarim Tanya.* Translated by Nissan Mindel. New York: Kehot, 1981.

Zipfel, Gaby, with Regina Mühlhäuser et al. *"Meine Not ist nicht einzig." Sexuelle Gewalt in kriegerischen Konflikten: Ein Werkstattgespräch. Mittelweg* 38, no. 18 (2009): 3–25.

Zyskind, Sara. *Stolen Years.* Translated by Margarit Inbar. Minneapolis, MN: Lerner, 1981.

ARCHIVAL SOURCES

Correspondence among members of the Gittler and Müller families is found in the Lieselotte Müller Letters and Documents, Conesus, NY, in the custody of Müller's niece, Karen Andolora, Conesus, NY.

Gittler Family Correspondence, #2009. Archives, United States Holocaust Memorial Museum.

International Tracing Service Digital Collection, United States Holocaust Memorial Museum.

University of Southern California Shoah Foundation Institute for Visual History and Education, accessed 22 February 2010 at the United States Holocaust Memorial Museum.

Contributors

KAREN BALDNER is a visual artist based in the book arts and printmaking. She grew up in Germany in a Jewish family who had been persecuted by the Nazi regime. Her work is inspired by the dynamics of life's paradoxes and takes this interest to the cathartic aspects of collaborative projects. Karen's work has been supported by Fulbright and NEA Grants as well as state grants from Arkansas and Indiana. She shows extensively throughout the United States and Europe and teaches at Herron School of Art & Design at IUPUI, Indianapolis, Indiana.

DORIS L. BERGEN is the Chancellor Rose and Ray Wolfe Professor of Holocaust Studies in the Department of History at the University of Toronto. Her publications include *Twisted Cross: The German Christian Movement in the Third Reich* (1996), *War and Genocide: A Concise History of the Holocaust* (2003 and 2008), *The Sword of the Lord: Military Chaplains from the First to the Twenty-First Centuries* (edited, 2003), *Lessons and Legacies VIII* (edited, 2009), and numerous articles and essays on gender, religion, and ethnicity in Nazi Germany, World War II, and the Holocaust, and comparatively in other cases of genocide and extreme violence. She is a member of the Academic Advisory Committee of the Center for Advanced Holocaust Studies at the United States Holocaust Memorial Museum.

SUZANNE BROWN-FLEMING is Director of Visiting Scholar Programs at the United States Holocaust Memorial Museum's Center for Advanced Holocaust Studies (CAHS). Her book *The Holocaust and Catholic Conscience: Cardinal Aloisius Muench and the Guilt Question in Germany*

(University of Notre Dame Press) was among the 2006 University Press Books Selected for Public and Secondary School Libraries by the American Association of University Presses (category of religion). Her book chapters, essays, and articles have appeared in the *New Catholic Encyclopedia,* the *Lessons and Legacies* volumes, H-German daily internet forum, and the scholarly journals *Religion in Eastern Europe, Holocaust and Genocide Studies,* and *Kirchliche Zeitgeschichte* (Contemporary Church History). Her current research project, "Eugenio Pacelli and the German Catholic Bishops, 1933–1939," is a study of the Vatican nunciature in Munich and Berlin during the Weimar Republic and the period of Eugenio Pacelli's tenure as Secretary of State.

BRITTA FREDE-WENGER received her PhD in Catholic theology at the University of Tübingen, Germany, in 2004 with a dissertation on the post-Holocaust Jewish thought of Emil L. Fackenheim. This work, the first German-language monograph on Fackenheim's thought, was awarded the Promotionspreis "Religion und Ethik" (2. Preis), issued by the Interdisciplinary Forum on Religion at the University of Erfurt, Germany. From 1999–2001, Dr. Frede-Wenger worked as an academic assistant to the Catholic theological faculty in Tübingen. Since she completed her teacher training in 2007, she has worked at the Studienkolleg Obermarchtal, a Catholic high school in Southern Germany, where she teaches English and Catholic Religion to upper level students. Frede-Wenger's recent publications include an essay on "Dimensions of Responsibility: A German Voice on the Palestinian-Israeli Conflict in the Post-Shoah Era" in *Anguished Hope: Holocaust Scholars Confront the Palestinian-Israeli Conflict,* eds. L. Grob and J.K. Roth (2008).

MARY J. GALLANT is associate professor and chair of the Department of Sociology and Anthropology at Rowan University. As research faculty she specializes in theory and inaugurated a course entitled Sociology of the Holocaust. She counts among her most treasured publications a monograph based on primary research with Holocaust survivors, *Coming of Age in the Holocaust: the Last Survivors Remember* (2002). Her methodology in this work honors the memory of Gregory Prentice Stone, co-founder of the symbolic interactionist paradigm in sociology. With Harriet Hartman, President of SSSJ, she co-authored, "Holocaust Education for the New Millennium: Assessing Our Progress," in *The Journal of Holocaust Educa-*

tion 10(2): 1–28. Her recent work on collective memory and the Holocaust focuses on Israel and Germany as part of her research focus on institutional processes after genocide, atrocity, and war.

GABY R. GLASSMAN is a psychologist and psychotherapist in private practice in London. The daughter of Holocaust survivors, her particular interest is in the transgenerational transmission of trauma. She has facilitated second-generation groups for nearly twenty-five years, working also with groups of child survivors, second and third generation in Prague, Berlin, and Brussels. She is a patron of the Prague-based Rafael Institute, the first trauma training and treatment institute in Central and Eastern Europe. Her publications include "The Impact of Intergenerational Protection on the Second Generation's Other Relationships," in *Beyond Camps and Forced Labour. Current International Research on Survivors of Nazi Persecution*, eds Johannes-Dieter Steinert & Inge Weber-Newth , Osnabrück, 2005; and "Irene Bloomfield's Work on Intergenerational Communication within Families Affected by Nazi Persecution" in *Group Analysis, The Journal of Group Analytic Psychotherapy* 36, no. 1 (2003).

DOROTA GLOWACKA teaches critical theory and Holocaust studies in the Contemporary Studies Programme at the University of King's College in Halifax, Canada. She is the author of *Disappearing Traces: Holocaust Testimonials, Ethics, Aesthetics* (University of Washington Press, 2012), and is a co-editor of *Between Ethics and Aesthetics* (SUNY Press, 2002) and *Imaginary Neighbors: Mediating Polish-Jewish Relations after the Holocaust* (Nebraska UP, 2007).

MYRNA GOLDENBERG has taught Holocaust studies at Montgomery College, the University of Maryland, and The Johns Hopkins Graduate School of Arts and Sciences, and has lectured widely on women and the Holocaust both here and abroad. In 2005–2006, she was the Ida E. King Distinguished Visiting Scholar of Holocaust Studies at The Richard Stockton College of New Jersey. She has published formative articles on women's Holocaust memoirs, the crime of *Rassenshande*, starvation as a weapon of war, and co-edited, with Elizabeth Baer, *Experience and Expression: Women, the Nazis, and the Holocaust* (2003), and with Rochelle L. Millen, *Testimony, Tensions, and Tikkun: Teaching the Holocaust in Colleges and Universities* (2007). Her current research focuses on American Jewish women's poetry on the Holocaust. She also founded an NEH-supported Humanities Center at Montgomery College, MD and published numerous reviews and articles on curriculum transformation and American Jewish women's literature and history in journals including *Potomac Review: A Journal of Arts and Humanities, Women Today, Belles Lettres,* and the *Community College Humanities Review.* Dr. Goldenberg was recognized by the Association of Community College Trustees and the Community College Humanities Association for outstanding teaching and by various groups for her work on human rights and community activism.

BJÖRN KRONDORFER is professor of religious studies at St. Mary's College of Maryland. His field of expertise is religion and culture, with an emphasis on gender studies, cultural studies, and Holocaust studies. His publications include, among others, *Male Confessions: Intimate Revelations and the Religious Imagination* (2010), *Men and Masculinities in Christianity and Judaism* (2009), *Mit Blick auf die Täter* [Facing perpetrators: on German theology after 1945] (2006), *Remembrance and Reconciliation: Encounters Between Young Jews and Germans* (1995), *Men's Bodies, Men's Gods* (1996), and *Body and Bible: Interpreting and Experiencing Biblical Narratives* (1992). He serves on the editorial boards of several academic journals and facilitates intercultural dialogues nationally and internationally. He has collaborated with artist Karen Baldner since 2001.

ROCHELLE L. MILLEN is professor of Religion at Wittenberg University. Recipient of many grants and awards, Dr. Millen has authored numerous book chapters and essays. She is editor of *New Perspectives on the Holocaust: A Guide for Teachers and Scholars* (1996), author of *Women, Birth, and Death in Jewish Law and Practice* (2004), and co-editor of *Testimony, Tensions and Tikkun: Reflections on Teaching the Holocaust in Colleges and Universities* (2007). She is co-founder and for seven years served as co-chair of the Religion, Holocaust, and Genocide Group of the American Academy of Religion. Millen serves on the Academic Advisory Board of the Hadassah-Brandeis Institute, the Board of the Ohio Council on Holocaust Education, and the Church Advisory Committee of the United States Holocaust Memorial Museum. In 1995, she received the prestigious Samuel Belkin Memorial Award for Professional Achievement from Stern College for Women of Yeshiva University.

DAVID PATTERSON holds the Hillel Feinberg Chair in Holocaust Studies at the University of Texas at Dallas. A winner the National Jewish Book Award and the Koret Jewish Book Award, Professor Patterson has published more than thirty books and more than 140 articles and book chapters on philosophy, literature, Judaism, and the Holocaust. His writings have been anthologized in several collections, and his books include *Genocide in Jewish Thought*; *A Genealogy of Evil: Antisemitism from Nazism to Islamic Jihad*; *Emil L. Fackenheim: A Jewish Philosopher's Response to the Holocaust*; *Jewish-Christian Dialogue: Drawing Honey from the Rock* (co-authored with Alan L. Berger); *Open Wounds: The Crisis of Jewish Thought in the Aftermath of Auschwitz*; and *Wrestling with the Angel: Toward a Jewish Understanding of the Nazi Assault on the Name*.

AMY H. SHAPIRO is professor of Philosophy and Humanities at Alverno College in Milwaukee, Wisconsin. She has published articles and presented papers on gender and pedagogy, pedagogy and the Holocaust, and critical thinking and critical thinking and the Holocaust. From 1999–2005 she was Director of the Holocaust Education and Resource Center at the Milwaukee Coalition for Jewish Learning where she expanded Holocaust education to reach a broad and diverse audience in the greater Milwaukee Community. Recently she led the team that developed the Women and Gender Studies program at Alverno College and is co-chair of the program. Her most recent work, *Philosophically Becoming*, is a philosophical memoir about becoming a language philosopher.

All the contributors to this book, with the exception of Karen Baldner, are participants in the Stephen S. Weinstein Holocaust Symposium at Wroxton College. Doris Bergen participated in the Symposium in 2008.

Index

family placements in, 204, 205, 206,
207; funds for, 202, 203; and Gittler
family, 183; lessons from, 209–10; and
long-term care, 200; and long-term
mass rescue, 202–3; numbers rescued
by, 200; organizers of, 200–220; and
post-war reunions, 211; and rates of
mental illness, 208; and social class,
201, 203, 208, 210

Kleinman, Susan, 210

Klimov, Elem, 23

Klüger, Ruth, 6, 130, 239–50; anger of, 241,
245, 246, 249; and audience, 240–41,
243, 245, 246, 247, 248, 251n5, 251n7;
and Auschwitz, 240, 241–43, 245; on
authenticity, 248, 249; and *Besserwisser*, 243–44; and camps, 240, 247,
248; childhood of, 240; on empathy,
245, 247–48; on friendships, 248;
and Germans, 247, 248–49, 251n5;
girlfriends of, 247; and history, 242,
244; and individual story, 246; and
memory, 241, 242, 243, 245, 248,
250; and mothers, 240, 246, 247; on
museums and memorial sites, 241–42;
and names, 247; and past, 131, 241, 242,
243, 244, 251n6; on philosemitism,
244; on pornography based on camps,
244; readers of, 248, 251n5; rewriting
by, 240; on sentimentality, 250; sister
of, 245, 247; *Still Alive*, 36–37n59;
weiter leben, 131, 239, 240; *weiter leben*
(English version), 246; on whitewashers, 241, 251n8

Knight, Henry, 7

knowledge, 80, 90, 91, 93, 94, 95

Knox, Katherine, *Refugees in an Age of
Genocide*, 199, 213–14n5, 214n7

Kochan, Miriam, "Women's Experience of
Internment," 216n21

Kofman, Berek, 46, 47–48, 49, 50, 57n50

Kofman, Sarah, 13, 28, 39–41, 45–50, 52–54;
on Arendt, 54n5; and biography,
45–46, 47, 49, 50, 52; "Damned Food,"

57n46; and the feminine, 41, 48, 50,
53, 54; and feminism, 40; and history,
49–50, 53; and Holocaust, 46, 50, 53,
54; and Jews, 49–50, 53, 54; and Judaism, 46–47, 49; and memory, 46, 47, 50,
52; *Le mepris des Juifs*, 53; and mothers, 28, 47–48, 49–50; "'My Life' and
Psychoanalysis," 46; and philosophy,
40, 41, 47, 48–50, 52, 53; reputation
of, 40; *Le respect des femmes*, 48; *Rue
Ordener, Rue Labat*, 46–48, 49, 50, 52,
57n50, 57n59; "*Shoah* (or Dis-grace),"
38; *Smothered Words*, 46, 47, 53; and
women, 48–49, 50, 53, 54

Kohelet Rabbah, 165

Kohl, Christiane, *The Maiden and the Jew*,
124n19

Konig, Fineza, 46, 47–48, 49–50

Koonz, Claudia, *Mothers in the Fatherland*, 12, 18

Korte, Mona, 208

Kovaly, Heda, *Under a Cruel Star*, 22

Kovno Ghetto, 171

Krasny Ghetto, 107

Krasnystaw, 178

Kristallnacht (November pogroms),
102, 125n27, 214n6; and Baldner, 147;
emigration after, 183; and *Kindertransport*, 199, 200, 201; punitive tax after,
193–94n41; rape during, 105

Kristeva, Julia, 40; *Hannah Arendt*, 55n18

Krondorfer, Björn, 132–61; and art, 135–36,
137–38; *Blechhammer, 1943-44* (2007),
150; family and background of, 134–35,
136, 149–51; "From Pulp to Palimpsest," 130; *Ghosts* (2010), 137; "Heimat"
(2005), 139–40, 159–60; *Male Confessions*, 146; *Men and Masculinities in
Christianity and Judaism*, 146; *Men's
Bodies, Men's Gods*, 145, 146;
Obituaries/Nachrufe (2005), 152, 153;
pushmepullyou (2007), 136, 150; *Tik-
kun/Mending* (2006), 134;